The Political Economy of Democracy and Tyranny

by
Norman Schofield

Oldenbourg Verlag München

Bibliografische Information der Deutschen Nationalbibliothek

Die Deutsche Nationalbibliothek verzeichnet diese Publikation in der Deutschen Nationalbibliografie; detaillierte bibliografische Daten sind im Internet über <http://dnb.d-nb.de> abrufbar.

© 2009 Oldenbourg Wissenschaftsverlag GmbH
Rosenheimer Straße 145, D-81671 München
Telefon: (089) 4 50 51-0
oldenbourg.de

Lektorat: Wirtschafts- und Sozialwissenschaften, wiso@oldenbourg.de
Herstellung: Dr. Rolf Jäger
Coverentwurf: Kochan & Partner, München
Gedruckt auf säure- und chlorfreiem Papier
Gesamtherstellung: Books on Demand GmbH, Norderstedt

ISBN 978-3-486-58826-2

Contents

Foreword

The social and natural sciences are, in many respects, based on the work of Thomas Hobbes, in his *Leviathan* of 1651, and of Isaac Newton in his *Philosophiae naturalis principia mathematica* of 1687 and the *Optiks* (1704). Newton's underlying philosophy of science was transmitted throughout Europe by Voltaire's book on the *Elements of Newton's Philosophy* (published in 1738).

The human sciences, and especially political economy and moral philosophy, were developed further in France by Etienne Condillac's *Essay on the Origin of Human Knowledge* (1746) and Turgot's *Reflections on the Formation and Distribution of Wealth* (1766), and in Scotland by David Hume's *Essays Moral and Political* (1742) and *A Treatise of Human Nature* (1752), culminating in Adam Smith's *The Theory of Moral Sentiments* (1759) and *Wealth of Nations* (1776). Finally in 1785, the Marquis de Condorcet published his *Essai sur l'application de l'analyse à la probabilitié des voix* (*Essay on the Application of Analysis to the Probability of Decisions*).

In August 1784, after the success of the revolutionary war against Great Britain, Thomas Jefferson had arrived in Paris as Minister Plenipotentiary, to take over from Benjamin Franklin. Condorcet had been appointed the Permanent Secretary of the Academy of Science, in August 1776 and had close contact with Franklin in that context. After his arrival in Paris, Jefferson was introduced by Franklin to Condorcet at the salon of the comtesse d'Houdetot. From then on, Jefferson also frequented the salon of Sophie de Grouchy, Condorcet's wife. Sophie was later to translate Adam Smith's *Theory of Moral Sentiments,* adding a number of her essays on Sentiment to the translated volume. Jefferson's later writings on debt and the benefit of free trade indicate that he was much influenced by the ideas of Turgot, Smith and Condorcet.[1]

During his time in Paris, Jefferson communicated regularly with James Madison, particularly over the discussions in the Constitutional Convention. Moreover, in 1787, Jefferson sent Condorcet's *Essai to* Madison, together with a copy of a book by Jefferson's friend, Mazzei. Condorcet's *Essai* included what is now called the *Jury Theorem.* This provides a formal reason why a committee or polity, using majority rule, will make a better choice than a single, average member. There is indirect evidence, discussed in Chapter 1 of this book, that Madison had this result in mind when he formulated the argument, in *Federalist X,* that the choice of a Chief Magistrate in the extended Republic will lead to the *probability of a fit choice.*

The immense debt that France had accumulated, partly as a result of the aid provided to the thirteen Colonies, obliged Louis XVI to call the Estates General, and eventually this led to the Revolution in France. In June 1789 Jefferson contributed to

---

[1] See McLean (2004, 2006a,b) and Schofield (2006a) for further explorations of the connections between the French and Scottish Enlightenments and the creation of the American Republic.

the drafting by Lafayette of the *Déclaration des Droits de l'Homme et du Citoyen.* In the midst of the Revolution, Jefferson and Condorcet had a farewell dinner on September 17, 1789. In 1791, after Jefferson had returned to the United States, Condorcet was elected to the National Assembly, and then became its Secretary. The Girondists, including Condorcet, lost the contest for a constitutional monarchy, and after the execution of Louis XVI on 21 January 1793, the Jacobins took power. In October, Condorcet was declared a traitor and forced to flee. In the next few months he wrote *Esquisse d'un tableau historique des progrès de l'esprit humain* (*Sketch for a Historical Picture of the Human Mind*), and after his death in March, 1794, Sophie de Grouchy had it published in 1795.

The *Esquisse* was used by Thomas Malthus as the point of departure for his pessimistic book, the *Essay on the Principle of Population* (1798), where he argued against what he saw as Condorcet's excessively optimistic, "Smithian," viewpoint.

In one sense, this present work is an attempt to extend the Condorcetian logic, as expressed in the formal apparatus of the *Essai,* in an effort to judge whether the optimism of the *Esquisse* is justified in a world where a large proportion of humanity lives in what has been termed the Malthusian trap of growing population, poverty and tyranny.

The formal apparatus of economic theory has developed apace since the time of Adam Smith's *Wealth of Nations,* in the work of Ricardo, Pareto, Walras and Marshall, culminating in the mathematical existence theorems for a competitive equilibrium. (von Neumann, 1932; Arrow and Debreu, 1954; McKenzie, 1959). In contrast to the theoretical efforts on the *economic* side of political economy, almost no work on formalizing Condorcet's insights, in his *Essai* on the *political* side of political economy, was attempted until the late 1940's, when Duncan Black and Kenneth Arrow published seminal papers on this topic. In 1948, Black published his paper "On the Rationale of Group Decision Making," and specifically addressed to the question of existence of a voting equilibrium. He followed this in 1958 with his monograph on *The Theory of Committees and Elections.* The monograph emphasized the importance of Condorcet's work in voting theory, but paid much less attention to the Condorcet Jury Theorem. In contrast, recent research has suggested that this latter theorem gives a justification for majority rule as a "truth seeking" device.

Arrow's paper, "A Difficulty in the Concept of Social Welfare" (1950) derives from quite a different tradition of formal political economy, namely the work in welfare economics of von Mises (1935), Bergson (1938), Lange (1938), Schumpeter (1942), von Hayek (1944) and Popper (1945). Arrow shows essentially that any social welfare function (that maps families of individual preferences to a weak social preference) is either imposed or dictatorial. To obtain what Arrow termed this "possibility theorem," he assumed that the social welfare function had universal domain and satisfied a property of positive association of preferences.

As Arrow commented in his paper, the negative result of the "possibility theorem" was "strongly reminiscent of the intransitivity of the concept of domination in the theory of multiperson games" as presented in von Neumann and Morgenstern (1944). Arrow also emphasized that he viewed the theorem as relevant to a situation where individuals make value judgements, rather than to the more typical economic context where agents make choices based on their tastes. Since all political choices are based, to some degree or other, on the aggregation of values, I infer that the "possibility theorem" addresses not just the traditional questions of welfare economics, but the larger issue of the interaction between the political and economic realms. In other words, the relevance of the theorem is not simply to do with the question of voting cycles, or intransitivies, but concerns the larger questions of political economy that were discussed in the work in the 1930' and 1940's.

The formal exercise of proof of existence of an economic equilibrium (obtained between 1932 and 1959) leaves unanswered many questions. For example, can the existence proof be extended from the domain of private commodities to include public goods? More particularly, can democratic procedures be devised to ensure that preference information be aggregated in an "efficient" fashion so that social choice is welfare maximizing? Arrow's possibility theorem suggests that democracy itself may be flawed: indeed it suggests that democratic institutions may (as Madison foresaw in *Federalist X*) be mutable or turbulent.

Thus, difficult questions of institutional design need to be addressed. These questions come back in one sense or another to an interpretation of Arrow's Theorem. In this volume I shall attempt to outline my sense of the current state of the debate.

Chapter 1 first sketches one way of interpreting Arrow's theorem. Since the theorem refers to the aggregation of *preferences,* I argue that any society or legislature can potentially fall into disorder. However, if social decisions also depend on the aggregation of beliefs, then it is possible, as Madison argued in *Federalist X,* that voters will base their judgement of political leaders on the perception of the leaders' inherent or intrinsic quality. This suggests analyzing elections using the formal idea of *valence.* This electoral model is presented as a heuristic device to examine what are called *social contracts*, instituted at times of social quandary. Chapter 2 provides an extensive examination of such a social quandary – the lead up to the election of Lincoln in 1860 and the Civil War. Chapter 3 presents the formal stochastic electoral model to examine the current social quandary in the United States, involving activist groups supportive of the Republican and Democratic Party agendas. Chapter 4 uses this model to compute so-called *Nash equilibria* of party positions in elections in Israel, Turkey and Canada, and provides a brief outline of elections in Britain and the Netherlands. Chapter 5 addresses the question of the relationship between the macro economy and government, in the context of current global economic problems and the possibility of climate change. The social choice model involving activists is extended in Chapter 6 to examine how authoritarian regimes in Argentina, Francoist Spain and the Soviet Union came to power, and were able to retain it for long periods. Chapter 7 continues the discussion of the Soviet Union, and examines the question of regime stability in China and North Korea. The chapter also includes sections on authoritarian regimes in Cuba, Venezuela and Iran. Chapter 8 extends the electoral model to consider a recent election in Russia and the nature of presidential competition in the United States. Chapter 9 gives a number of short essays on themes in political economy, while Chapter 10 presents a summing up, comparing Arrovian theories of preference aggregration with Condorcetian models of belief aggregation. The last chapter concludes with some remarks on the likely consequences of climate change.

I thank Cambridge University Press for permission to include material from Schofield (2006a), Schofield and Sened (2006), and Miller and Schofield (2008), Sage Publications for permission to reprint material from Schofield and Levinson (2008), Blackwell for permission to use material from Schofield (2007), and Schofield and Miller (2007), Accedo Verlag for permission to reprint material from Dixon and Schofield (2001), and Schofield (2008a), and Routledge for permission to reprint material from Schofield (2008b). I thank Maria Gallego, Bernard Gauthier, Manfred Holler and Hannu Nurmi for their helpful comments. The manuscript was typed by Cherie Moore, and many of the diagrams were drawn by Ugur Ozdemir. I am grateful to Guido Cataife, Eric Linhart, Suumu Shikano and Alexei Zakharov for permission to make use of their work. I thank my coauthors Kim Dixon, Micah Levinson, Gary Miller, Ugur Ozdemir, Evan Schnidman and Itai Sened for their collaboration, and my students Paul Bender, Martha King, Mindy Krischer, Sofia Medina, Zharna Shah, and Lexi Shankster for their contributions in Chapters 7, 8 and 9. Versions of Chapters 3 and 4 were presented at the Workshop on Simulation and Electoral Systems, University of Western Piemonte, Alessandria, Italy, June 2007, at the Conference on the Political Economy of Bargaining, Waterloo, April 2008, and at the conference on the Political Economy of Democracy, Barcelona, June 2008.

This work was supported by National Science Foundation grant SES 0715929 and by a research grant from the Weidenbaum Center at Washington University in Saint Louis. The first draft of the manuscript was written during tenure of the Leitner visiting Professorship at the Macmillan Center, Yale University, and completed at ICER, Turin. I thank Ian Shapiro for his hospitality during the visit to Yale.

Norman Schofield
Washington University
Saint Louis, Missouri
July 29, 2008

Chapter 1

Modelling Political Economy

The idea behind this chapter is to provide an extended interpretation of Madison's argument in *Federalist X* (1999 [1787]), and to use ideas from social choice theory and from the work of Douglass North, Mancur Olson and William Riker, in an attempt to develop a "rational choice" approach to the evolution of society. This research program can be regarded as continuing the work of Madison's contemporaries, the Marquis de Condorcet and Pierre-Simon Laplace. In the later sections of the chapter, recent work on modelling elections is also discussed in an attempt to evaluate Madison's contention about the "probability of a fit choice" in the Republic.

I shall attempt to construct the beginnings of a theory of democratic choice that I believe can be used as a heuristic device able to tie together these differing historical accounts. The basic underlying framework is adapted from social choice theory, as I understand it, on which I graft a "stochastic" model of elections. This model is an attempt to extend the Condorcetian theme of electoral judgement. I shall argue that its logic was the formal principle underlying Madison's justification for the Republican scheme of representation that he made in *Federalist* X. While this logic does not imply a general will in the sense of Rousseau, it does suggest that Riker in *Liberalism Against Populism* (Riker, 1982) was overly pessimistic about the nature of democracy. On the other hand, the social choice framework suggests that democracy, indeed any polity, must face difficult choices over what I call chaos and autocracy. These difficult choices are *constitutional quandaries*. The historical choices that I discuss often involve a leader or theorist, *an architect of change,* either in the realm of politics or economics, who interprets or frames the quandary troubling the society in a way that leads to its resolution.

1.1 The Madisonian Scheme of Government

In order to provide a motif for the topics discussed in this chapter, it is worth quoting Madison's argument in *Federalist X.*

> [I]t may be concluded that a pure democracy, by which I mean a society, con-
> sisting of a small number of citizens, who assemble and administer the govern-

ment in person, can admit of no cure for the mischiefs of faction A common
passion or interest will ... be felt by a majority of the whole ... and there is
nothing to check the inducements to sacrifice the weaker party... Hence it is
that such democracies have ever been spectacles of turbulence and contention;
have ever been found incompatible with personal security, or the rights of property; and have in general been as short in their lives, as they have been violent
in their deaths.
A republic, by which I mean a government in which the scheme of representation
takes place, opens a different prospect ...
     The two great points of difference between a democracy and republic, are
first, the delegation of the government, in the latter, to a small number of citizens elected by the rest; secondly, the greater number of citizens and the greater
sphere of country, over which the latter may be extended.
[I]t may well happen that the public voice pronounced by the representatives of
the people, will be more consonant to the public good, than if pronounced by the
people themselves ... .
[I]f the proportion of fit characters be not less in the large than in the small
republic, the former will present a greater option, and consequently a greater
probability of a fit choice.
[A]s each representative will be chosen by a greater number of citizens in the
large than in the small republic, the suffrages of the people will be more likely
to centre on men who possess the most attractive merit.
The other point of difference is, the greater number of citizens and extent of
territory which may be brought within the compass of republican, than of democratic government; and it is this ... which renders factious combinations less to
be dreaded in the former, than in the latter. Extend the sphere, and you take in a
greater variety of parties and interests; you make it less probable that a majority
of the whole will have a common motive to invade the rights of other citizens ...
Hence it clearly appears, that the same advantage, which a republic has over a
democracy ... is enjoyed by a large over a small republic—is enjoyed by the
union over the states composing it.[2]

I shall try to relate Madison's justification for the Republican scheme of representation that he made in *Federalist X* to the social choice theory presented in Schofield
(2008b) and the empirical work on elections by Schofield and Sened (2006) discussed
below.
     The key to my understanding of a general theory of social choice is that any polity
must, on occasion, face difficult choices over what I call *constitutional quandaries*. Simply put, a quandary is a choice situation where all possible options appear extremely unpleasant, and laden with risk and uncertainty.[3] The constitutional feature of the quandary
refers to the likelihood that opinion as regards the correct choice will typically be highly
heterogenous. The actual choice will depend on the political mechanisms used by the

---

[2]James Madison, *Federalist X* (1787) in Rakove (1999).
[3]The choice situation as regards Iraq in late 2007 is such a constitutional quandary.

society, and thus on the constitutional rules that govern political choice.

The results from social choice theory indicate that when preferences, or opinions, are sufficiently heterogenous, then disorder or *chaos* can ensue. The process of social decision-making is denoted by correspondence, Q, so $Q(x)$ is the set of outcomes that can come about from a point x (in the space of alternatives, X) as determined by whatever social rule or political process is used by the society. The idea of *social chaos* is that there are conditions under which, starting from almost any x, it is possible to reach almost *any* possible outcome $y \in Q^t(x)$ by reiterating the social rule. In contrast we can identify the *core* or *social equilibrium*, y, to be some stationary outcome such that $Q(y)$ is empty. An even stronger equilibrium notion is that of an *attractor* of Q : that is a single outcome y with $y = Q^t(x)$, which results from any x, after a sufficient number of iterations of the rule. For any voting procedure, Q, without a dictator, oligarchy or collegium, able to control or restrain social choice, then as the dimension of X increases then so does the likelihood of voting chaos.[4]

While these results focused on voting rules, it seems just as likely that chaos can ensue in a society where war is the method of decision making. When war, or intense and unrestrained conflict dominates, then we can expect chaos, or the unpredictability of outcomes.[5] Indeed, it is possible that any society can fall into chaos, unless some institutional device, such as a collegial veto (or "negative") is constructed to prevent such a situation.[6] For example, Madison argued that

> for the harmony of that [British] Empire, it is evident I think that without the royal negative or some equivalent controul [*sic*] the unity of the system would be destroyed. The want of some such provision seems to have been mortal to the antient[*sic*] Confederacies.[7]

Federalist X suggests that Madison certainly viewed direct democracy as subject to chaos. Since a legislative assembly can be understood as a direct democracy, social choice theory provides a formal basis for Madison's argument about direct democracy and about what he called "mutability" of the legislature.

This first method of mitigating chaos is to impose the concentration of power implied by the existence of a dictator, oligarchy, or collegium. Because a dictator can control

---

[4]As shown in Schofield (2008b), a voting rule is characterized by a family of winning coalitions, $\mathbb{D}$. A *dictator* is a single agent who belongs to every winning coalition and is also winning. An *oligarchy* is a group that belongs to every winning coalition and is itself winning, while a *collegium* is a group of voters that belongs to every winning coalition in $\mathbb{D}$, but need not be winning. Social choice theory suggests chaos is possible when there is no collegium, but only if the dimensionality of the policy space is high. So the closer the political game is to being zero-sum (as in Iraq today) then the more likely is chaos.

[5]Bates *et al.* (2003) estimate that there have been over 400 cases of political instability in the period 1955 to 2002, including 39 cases of genocide, 62 revolutionary wars, 72 ethnic wars and 106 cases of "adverse" regime change such as coup d'etat. The chaos in Zimbabwe after the election in March 2008 is but an example.

[6]The classic example of a fall into chaos is France, from the first meeting of the Estates General in May 1789, through the execution of King Louis XVI in January 1793, followed by the Terror and the deaths of Condorcet in March 1794 and Robespierre in July 1794. The political instability was ended by Naploean's coup d'état in November 1799. See Winik (2007) for example.

[7]Letter to Jefferson, 24 October 1787, in Smith (1995: 498).

every choice, it is very unlikely that such a degree of concentration of power can occur. However, we can use the term *autocrat* for one who controls the levers of power of the polity, without being constrained by some strong form of political veto.[8]

Schofield (2006a) argues that an autocrat is likely to be an extreme risk-taker.[9] The same argument suggests that an autocrat will tend to be more risk-taking than an oligarchy which in turn will tend to be more risk-taking than a collegium. The further discussion in Schofield (2008b) of current U.S.politics strongly suggests that the U.S. president, together with his cabinet, is a collegium in the current situation where the Republican members of the Senate are able to block legislation that is contrary to the policy preferences of the President.[10]

However, because Congress may be factionalized, it can, as Madison expected, exhibit what he called "mutability"—a degree of disorder or incoherence in the laws that are passed. My understanding of the U.S. Constitution is that the Presidential veto was designed to overcome Congressional mutability. Madison, of course, was concerned that the President would gain autocratic power, and to avoid this, the Congressional super-majority counter-veto was devised. However, even with the counter-veto, the President does have some autocratic power, and I shall use the term *weak autocrat* to characterize his power. It is evident that there is a tendency for U.S. presidents to display the degree of risk preference that characterizes autocrats.

I judge that Congress will generally be risk-averse, which is why, I believe, power to declare war resides in Congress. From this perspective, the weak autocracy that I ascribe to the president is an important feature of the U.S. constitution because risk taking is an essential component of presidential power.[11] Moreover, Congressional risk-avoidance has the effect of delaying the resolution of fundamental constitutional quandaries. Typically, a *quandary* can only be faced if there is a risk-taking leader capable of forcing resolution. Schofield (2008b) discusses examples of presidential risk-taking by Eisenhower in 1957 and Johnson in 1964, both of which entailed conflict over civil rights be-

---

[8] It has been suggested that the *Codex Justintianus,* prepared by order of Justinian the Great in Constantinople in 533 CE, while setting out a system of Roman Law that was the basis for the Civil Law of Europe, also gave legitimacy to the imperial or kingly autocrat. See Rosen (2007). Currently, many states seem to be stable autocracies or to be falling into autocracy, witness Chavez's Venezuela, and Mahmoud Ahmadinejad's Iran. On the other hand, the assassination of Benazir Bhutto, in Pakistan on 27 December, 2007, led the way to the defeat of Musharraf's party in the election on February 18, 2008, and the coalition government of the Pakistan Peoples Party and the Pakistan Muslim League. On 24 February, 2008, Raúl Castro took over as president of Cuba from his brother, Fidel, after Fidel had been in power 49 years. In Russia, Putin's protege, Dmitri Medvedev, gained 69% of the vote for the presidency on March 2, 2008, soundly beating the Communist Party candidate, Gennadi Zyuganov and the nationalist, Vladimir Zhirinovsky, thus maintaining the system of oligarchic democracy. On May 8, Putin was confirmed as Prime Minister by a vote of 392 out of 450 in the Duma. See Nemtsov and Milov (2008) on the extent of Putin's power.

[9] No formal reason is given, but there are many examples in support of the hypothesis: Ghenghis Khan, Attila, Philip II of Spain, Napoleon. The historical examples of imperial-risk taking given in Kennedy (1987) give credibility to the hypothesis. See also Kershaw (2007) on risk taking by the Axis leaders in World War II.

[10] A minority of 41 Republican senators can block cloture and so prevent the vote on a bill.

[11] Many writers since Schlesinger (1973) have used the term "imperial presidency" for the weak autocracy of the president.

C=Chaos
Kosova, Lebanon,
Iraq, etc

"Chaos"

Stability axis

D=Democratic
stability
Weak Autocrat

"Stability"   Risk axis

B=Blocking veto   Single veto group   Oligarchy   A=Autocracy
"extreme risk avoidance"   or collegium   "extreme risk taking"
The European Union   The Praesidium   N.Korea

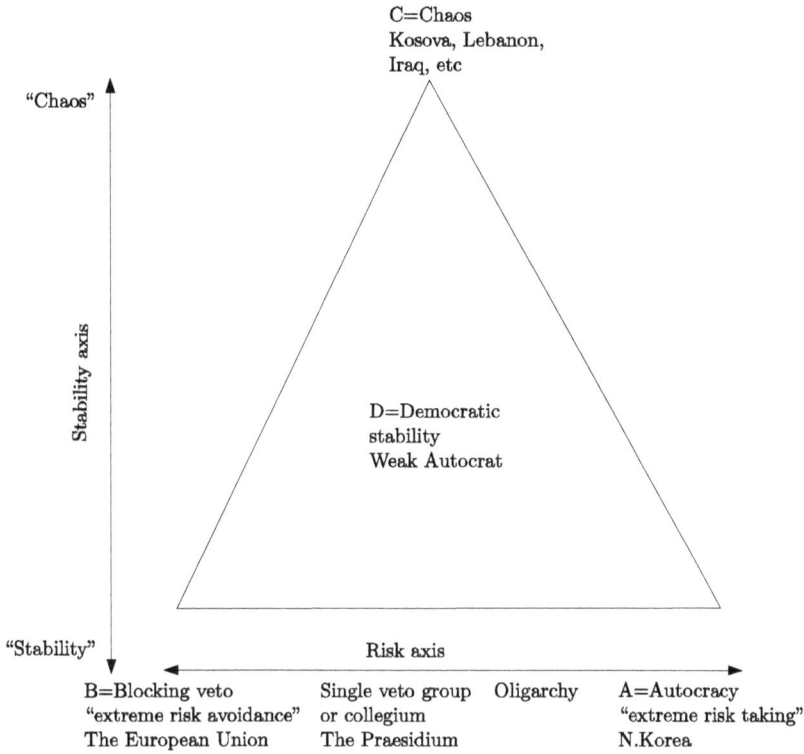

Figure 1.1: Chaos and Risk

tween the president and Congress. At the same time, the purpose of the Congressional
veto, aside from restraining any tendency to full autocracy, is to cause the president to
temper his risk-preference with caution.[12]

Figure 1.1, taken from Schofield (2006a) is a schematic representation of the balance
between chaos and risk. Notice, however, that this figure is not intended to imply that
a risk-taking autocrat is a sufficient method to avoid chaos. While Mugabe is clearly
a risk-taking autocrat in Zimbabwe, his attempts to retain power in the early part of
2008 plunged the country into disorder. The figure is intended to suggest that some
concentration of power is necessary to avoid chaos, but that the extent of autocracy
must be balanced by electoral or social judgement, rather than preference.

As Madison argues in *Federalist X,* the choice of leader should be for those who

---

[12]A good example of this is the caution displayed by Franklin D. Roosevelt in late 1941 as he moved the
country to a war-footing, paying attention to public opinion and the concerns of Congress (Kersaw, 2007).

"possess the most attractive merit." It is important for the constitutional balance between president and Congress that the president be elected by a method that gives what
Madison called "a probability of a fit choice." Since presidential choices will be made
in the context of uncertainty and risk, it is vital that the electorate use their judgement
in making a fit choice for president. Madison clearly hoped that the selection of the
President would be founded on judgement, rather than preference, and that this selection would not exhibit the disorder that he believed attended pure democracy, and could
render the legislature ineffective.

It can be argued that Madison developed his argument in *Federalist* X, on the basis
of his reading of Condorcet's *Essai* of 1785.[13] In constrained situations where we may
assume that judgements predominate, and voters evaluate the options in a clear-sighted
fashion, then their choice of Chief Magistrate may indeed be well formed in the way
that both Condorcet and Madison thought possible.[14]

Madison hoped that, because the election of the Chief Magistrate involved the selection of a person, rather than an option (as in the passage of a law), then judgement
rather than preference or interest would predominate. In Section 3 of this chapter I
shall consider a more general model where judgement and preference are both incorporated. It is of course entirely possible that beliefs or judgements in the electorate can be
transformed in a chaotic fashion. Nonetheless, it is possible that electoral belief can be
associated with what may be called a *core belief.* Since a *core,* in social choice theory,
is an unbeaten alternative, we can, by analogy, use the notion of a *core belief* to refer to
belief that has general acceptance in the society.[15]

The next section presents an institutional narrative making use of the idea of a core
belief to interpret and formalize the ideas of North, Olson and Riker.

1.2   An Institutional Narrative

North's early work with Thomas (North and Thomas, 1973, 1977) attempted an economic explanation of the transition from hunter/gatherer societies to agriculture. Later,
he proposed a "neoclassical theory of the state," wherein "Leviathan" contracts to set
up a system of property rights and taxes (North, 1981). His later work has focused

---

[13]Condorcet's Jury theorem in the *Essai* refers to the probability that a jury makes a correct choice on the
basis of majority rule. Schofield (2006a) argues that Madison received work by Condorcet from Jefferson in
Paris, and acknowledged receipt on 6 September 1787. This suggests that Madison adapted Condorcet's idea
during the Fall of 1787, while writing *Federalist X* for publication on 22 November 1787. See also Schofield
(1972).

[14]On September 4, 1787, the Constitutional Convention had agreed that the President be selected by a
majority of an Electoral College, where the weight of each state was given by the sum of its members of the
Senate plus the sum of its members of the House of Representatives. The Convention had rejected choice by
Congress, by the legislatures of the states and by direct election by the people.

[15]Of course, a core belief can change rapidly. A core belief in the U.S. electorate circa 2003 was that there
existed a close connection between al-Qaeda and Saddam Hussein, and this belief provided the justification
for the invasion of Iraq. This belief has turned out to be false. By late 2007 a core belief was forming that the
U.S. should leave Iraq.

on institutions, and how they change as a result of incentives, knowledge and beliefs (North, 1990, 1994, 2005). One of his most persuasive pieces is his work with Weingast (North and Weingast, 1989) on the Glorious Revolution in 1688 in Britain, and how this transformed Britain's ability to manage debt, fight wars (particularly with France), and develop an empire. More recently, North has concentrated on the conditions that may enhance social stability (North, Wallis, and Weingast, 2008).

Much of Olson's work has attempted to grapple with understanding how some societies are successful and others much less so. In his early book, Olson (1965) argued that cooperation may fail, as individuals pursue their selfish ends (by strikes, revolutions, etc.) and indirectly constrain economic growth. (Olson's argument was interpreted by Schofield,1975, in terms of the prisoner's dilemma. See Chapter 4 for a discussion). Later, Olson (1982) used this argument to provide a "declinist" explanation of why stable democracies such as Britain and the U.S. appeared less vital (in the 1980's) than the newer democracies of the post World War II era (such as France, Germany, Japan, etc.).

I shall also make use of Riker's work on American Federalism, particularly the logic underlying the need for Union in 1787 (Riker, 1953, 1964, 1987) and the stability of parties as coalitions (Riker, 1962). After working for a number of years on rational choice theory (Riker and Ordeshook, 1973), Riker returned to American political history, to interpret key events in terms of "heresthetic" (1984, 1986, 1996). Riker coined the word heresthetic from the greek $\alpha\iota\rho\epsilon\tau\iota\kappa o\varsigma$, meaning "able to choose." His book on *Liberalism Against Populism* (1982) argued that the chaos results of social choice theory implied that populism, in the sense of existence of a "general will" was vacuous. At best, all one could hope from democracy was the liberal capacity to remove autocrats.[16]

In this section I shall consider aspects of the work of North, Olson and Riker, and shall briefly sketch the narrative scheme that I shall use, based loosely on the notion of factor coalitions forming in the policy space. Rogowski (1989) earlier made use of the assumption, from economic theory, that there can be assumed to be three factors of production: land, labor and capital. External and internal features may grant advantages to particular coalitions of these factor "interests." For example, the U.S. in the late 1700's could be characterized as abundant in land, with both labor and capital relatively scarce. Principal imports were manufactures, intensive in capital and skilled labor. Thus protection in the form of tariffs would necessarily benefit capital and "industrial labor." In contrast, since land was abundant, this economic interest, together with "agricultural labor," would benefit from free trade. Consequentially, the political conflict between the commercial Federalist Party and the agrarian Jeffersonian Republicans, at the election of 1800, can be interpreted in factor terms. However, some of the elements of the controversy of that time can only be understood with respect to earlier factor conflicts in Britain, in the period from 1688.

North and Weingast (1989) had argued that the creation of the Bank of England in 1693 provided a method of imposing credible commitment on Parliament.This would

---

[16]Whether Riker's argument has any validity is still the subject of much discussion. See Mackie (2003); McGann (2006); McLean (2008).

have the effect of reducing the price of public debt. [17] The dilemma facing any government of that time was that war had become more expensive than government revenue could cover. Consequently, governments, or monarchs, became increasingly indebted. Risk-preferring, or war-loving, monarchs, such as Philip II of Spain or Louis XIV of France, were obliged to borrow. As their debt increased, they were forced into repudiation, thus making it more difficult in the future to borrow. Since the Bank of England "managed" the debt in Britain after 1693, there was an incentive for Parliament to accept the necessary taxation, and also to avoid repudiation. However, it was clear after 1688 that William III would pursue the war with France with great vigor and cost. Contrary to the argument of North and Weingast, this escalating debt could, in fact, force Parliament to repudiation. Until 1720, it was not obvious how Parliament could be obliged to commit to fiscal responsibility. How this was done was through the brilliant strategy of Robert Walpole, first "prime" minister.

The fundamental problem was that the majority of members of both Commons and Lords were of the landed interest. The obvious method of funding government debt (which had risen to 36 million pounds sterling by 1713) was by a land tax. Indeed the land tax raised approximately 50 percent of revenue. War weariness had brought in a Tory government in 1710, and the obvious disinclination of the Tory landed gentry to pay increasing land taxes forced up the interest rate on long term government debt from 6 percent to 10 percent (Stasavage, 2002). In some desperation the government created the South Sea Company in 1711. After Queen Anne died in 1714, and the Hanoverian, George I, became sovereign, increasing speculation in South Sea Company stock and then the collapse of the "bubble" in September 1720, almost bankrupted the government. Walpole stabilized confidence in the Company by a swap arrangement with the Bank of England. In April 1721, Walpole, became Chancellor of the Exchequer and First Lord of the Treasury, and began his scheme to stabilize government debt by instituting a complex system of customs and excise. By restricting imports, mostly foodstuffs and land intensive commodities, this system had the effect of supporting the price of the scarce commodity, land. From 1721 to 1810, these excise taxes and customs raised an increasing share of government revenue.[18] O'Brien (1988: 16). comments that these historical data provide

> some statistical support for suggestions that the burden of taxation on the aristocracy declined during the eighteenth century. Not until they confronted Napolean did the upper classes once again undertake the kind of sacrifices for the defence of property that they had made under William III. [W]ith the repeal of the Pitt's income tax in 1816 the situation reverted to the *status quo ante bellum*.

As Brewer (1988) has described, the system required a sophisticated and skilled

---

[17]Quinn (2001) suggests that there was a crowding out, in the sense that while the cost of public debt fell, the cost of private debt rose, at least in the short run until 1705.

[18]Tax receipts as a percentage of national income rose from 10.8% in 1720 to 18.2% in 1810. The share of customs and excise in government income was about 73% in 1720 and 82% in 1800 (O'Brien, 1988: 15).

bureaucracy. The Walpole device had many effects. Firstly, it ushered in a long period of Whig dominance.[19] The Walpole "bargain" of 1721 essentially created a compact between the "commercial" Whig interests and both Whig and Tory "landed" interests, securing their Parliamentary support for continued war with France. By supporting land prices, the bargain led to increased investment in agriculture.[20] Although agricultural output increased in Britain (by 76% between 1740 and 1860) the population grew even more rapidly (increasing from about 6 million in 1740 to 21 million in 1860. Britain became increasingly dependant on food imports, particularly from the U.S. However, the combination of protection of land and population growth led to an increase of the cost of living of 43% between 1740 and 1800, and a decline of the real wage. It is estimated that 80% of subsistence farmers were forced off the land between 1780 and 1810 (Aron ,2007). The fall of real wages until the end of the Napoleonic Wars, coupled with a rise in GDP/capita suggests that income inequality increased in this period. The model of political economy of Acemoglu and Robinson (2005) would suggest that the compact could only be maintained by a severe restriction of the franchise. Real wages started to rise after the end of the Napoleonic Wars, but it was not until 1867 that the franchise was extended to any great degree, while protection of land was maintained until the repeal of the Corn Laws in 1846.[21]

In brief, the Walpole compact

- helped maintain the Whig elite in power,

- transformed agriculture, forcing people off the land and into the cities,

- facilitated rapid population growth, because of the availability of agricultural imports from the United States,

- led to the creation of efficient capital markets, eventually facilitating the expansion of manufacturing,

---

[19]From 1721 to 1783 eleven out of thirteen prime ministers were Whig, while the Earl of Bute (1762-1763) and Lord North (1770-1782) were Tory. In contrast, from the time of the Tory, William Pitt the Younger (prime minister during 1783-1801 and 1804-1806), until Benjamin Disraeli (1868, 1874-1880) there were fourteen Tory or Conservative prime ministers out of eighteen.

[20]Allen (1988) estimates that the rental on land rose from about 0.5 pounds per acre in 1725 to 1.5 pounds per acre in 1825.

[21]The connection between population growth, food production and the real wage has been extensively analyzed by Clark (2005, 2007a, b). On population growth in particular, see Clark (2007a: 36). Clark (2007b) refers to the tendency of population to rise to match food production as the "Malthusian Trap" after Thomas Malthus ([1798], [1830], 1970). Malthus wrote his essay to contradict the more optimistic views of Condorcet's *Esquisse* (1795). On Condorcet's *Esquisse* see Baker (2004) and Rothschild (2001). Clark (2007a) also estimates an increase of agricultural imports into Britain from zero in 1730 to 22% of GDP in 1860, while Clark (2005: 1325) estimates the real wage in the decade 1800-1809 to be about 10% below that of 1730. However, he estimates that there was an increase of 66% by 1860. See also Floud and McClosky (1994).

- which paid for food imports, thus indirectly providing the population resources to extend the empire,

- allowed the Whig government to borrow the capital required for Britain to finance the long war against France,

- caused the impoverishment of a considerable proportion of the population until 1815, inducing a large immigrant flow, first to the thirteen colonies and then, after 1783, to the greatly expanded United States

This last effect necessitated the maintenance of a restricted franchise, since extending the franchise could have led to Parliamentary disorder, destroying the compact, and with it, the Whig dominance.

It was also crucial for this dynamic path of Britain's economic development that there be a plentiful and cheap supply of (land intensive) agricultural goods from the United States.This was facilitated by the availability of land and the growth of the American population.

A key aspect of the origin of the synergetic relationship between Britain and America was the success of the thirteen colonies in their revolution against Britain. The principal factor in this was the success of Britain in the Seven Years War against France (1758-1763). This gave Britain the entire area east of the Mississippi, including Quebec, while France ceded New France (Louisiana) to Spain. After Pontiac's Rebellion at the end of the war, Britain tried to prevent settler encroachments into the Ohio Valley first by the Proclamation Act (1763) and then the Quebec Act (1774). It has been suggested that Adam Smith had the idea of the Quebec Act. Whatever the motivation of the British Government, the Quebec Act infuriated both the elite and the people. The arrival of a fleet of 130 transport ships in New York, under General Howe, was intended to intimidate the Colonies. Word arrived from France that Louis XVI had been persuaded by the Foreign Minister, Vergennes to provide resources[22] to the Colonies, and I argue that this information was crucial in the decision by the Continental Congress to declare Independence. French aid was decisive for the American success. In September 1781, French fleet blockaded the British army under Cornwallis at Yorktown , and a French army of 6,500 men helped Washington force the surrender of the British.

The population of the thirteen colonies had increased from about two hundred thousand in 1700 to nearly nine hundred thousand in 1750 to 2.8 million by 1790 and 5.3 million by 1800. A contribution to this population growth was the emigration of 80,000 from England and Wales, 115,000 from Ireland, and 75,000 from Scotland (including 15,000 highlanders) between 1700 and 1780 (Harper, 2003).

The rapid expansion of this food-producing agrarian empire can, in large degree, be attributed to the election of Thomas Jefferson in 1800. By the 1790's, Jefferson was well aware of the implications of the Walpole compact in terms of impoverishment and concentration of power. His reading of the works of Henry St. John, Viscount Bolingbroke, led him to believe that the land-capital bargain led to corruption, as well as

---

[22] 10 million livres eventually.

the filling of Parliament by placement. In fact, Bolingbroke's arguments against Walpole were, to some degree, invalid, since the compact did make it possible for Britain to manage its debt, fight its wars and create an empire. Bolingbroke's logic was, however, valid for the U.S. Hamilton's attempt in 1793 to recreate Walpole's system would have necessitated both a land tax and tariff protection. Since U.S. imports were primarily manufactures, a tariff would protect the scarce factor, capital, associated with these imports. In Jefferson's view, this would have disadvantaged the landed interest. By creating an agrarian coalition, essentially of the Southern slave-owning landed interest, and western free farmers, Jefferson created a long-lasting compact under which the U.S. became the food supplier for Britain.

The Jeffersonian-Jacksonian agrarian coalition survived until 1860, and it was the expansion of the U.S. agrarian empire through the Louisiana Purchase of 1803/4 and the Treaty of Guadalupe Hidalgo after the war with Mexico that provided the agricultural basis for Britain's expansion. However, the gain of Mexican territory led to the southern slave owner's demand for expansion of the slave interest to the Pacific, and this ultimately destroyed the Jeffersonian-Jacksonian Democracy in the Civil War.

The aftermath of the Civil War created a new coalition, of commercial interests and industrial labor, as represented by the presidential victory of the Republican, McKinley, over the populist Democrat, William Jennings Bryan in 1896. From this perspective, U.S. politics in the period 1896-1956 can be interpreted in terms of a single factor dimension, *capital*, since we can regard the interest of land to be generally in opposition to capital. Thus, for the period from 1896 until the 1930's, the inclination of Republicans for the preservation of a hard money or gold standard rule was in opposition to the need for available credit in the agricultural sector.

In the 1960's, agitation for greater civil rights brought the labor axis into prominence. L. B. Johnson's positioning on this axis contributed to his great electoral victory in 1964, but also opened the way for the Republican Party to adopt an increasingly conservative position on the social dimension and gain political control in the southern states (Miller and Schofield, 2003).

Returning to Britain in the nineteenth century, Figure 1.2 compares British and French import protection, and clearly indicates the degree to which British imports were protected in the early part of the century.

This figure suggests that the Walpole compact was still based on protection of land and restriction of the franchise, at least until the Repeal of the Corn Laws in 1846. As McLean describes,this first decrease in protection was effected by Robert Peel, leader of the Tories (or Conservatives), together with Wellington in the Lords, against the interests of the majority of their party. Famine in Ireland made it obvious to Peel and Wellington that unless food prices were lowered then social unrest could lead to civil strife.[23] By the 1860's, Britain's economic lead allowed for further reduction in the protection of land, in the form of Gladstone's budget of 1861, which reduced the duty on wine and repealed

---

[23] 2 million people emmigrated from Ireland in the period 1846-1856, while the U.S. population jumped in this decade from 23 million to about 32 million. The population of England had grown, but only to about 20 million.

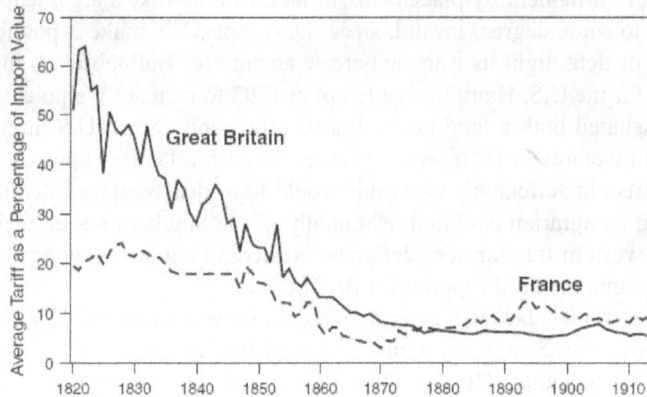

Figure 1.2: Tariff revenue as a fraction of all imports (Nye, 2007), with permission of Princeton University Press.

the paper tax (Aldous, 2006). McLean (2001) also discusses the astonishing ability of Disraeli to push through the Reform Bill in 1867, with the support of the Radicals in the House of Commons, thereby doubling the enfranchised population.

Figure 1.3 presents a schematic figure showing the opposition between the Liberals, led by Gladstone, and the Tories, led by Disraeli. The figure is meant to suggest that Disraeli understood that the hold on the Tories by the landed interest had to be broken, in order to oppose the Whigs, or Liberals, dominated by capital. Disraeli's maneuver essentially changed the "partisan cleavage line," separating the Whigs and the Conservative, from its position in 1850 to a new position in 1867, as illustrated in the figure. (The catenary in this figure is defined in Chapter 3 below).[24] It is possible that Disraeli's maneuver. depended on beliefs about Empire. For industrial labor, "Empire" meant the opportunities for emigration and a better life in the Dominions of, Canada and South Africa. By using the rhetoric of "Empire," the Conservatives could hope to appeal to working class voters.[25]

It has been a long standing controversy whether political economy is best described by the concepts of "equilibrium" or "chaos." In his later work, after 1980, Riker saw chaos as fundamental property, and focused on key "contingent" events in U.S. political history, like the Ratification of the U.S. Constitution in 1787-88, or the onset of the Civil War in 1860-61.

The brief description of British and U.S. political history offered here suggests that

---

[25]Later, in 1876, Disraeli as Prime Minister effected the Royal Titles bill, proclaiming Victoria *Regina et Imperatrix*. Disraeli's maneuver probably allowed the Conservatives to compete electorally with the Liberals until the First World War.

Extend Franchise/   SOCIAL
Empire   DIMENSION

Radicals

Disraeli

Partisan cleavage
line. 1867

Conservatives   Partisan cleavage
                                           line. 1850

Whigs

ECONOMIC
DIMENSION   W

Land   Capital

                                                                    Liberal catenary
                                           Gladstone

                                                             G'

                                           Free Traders

                                                                                            Liberals

Free Trade

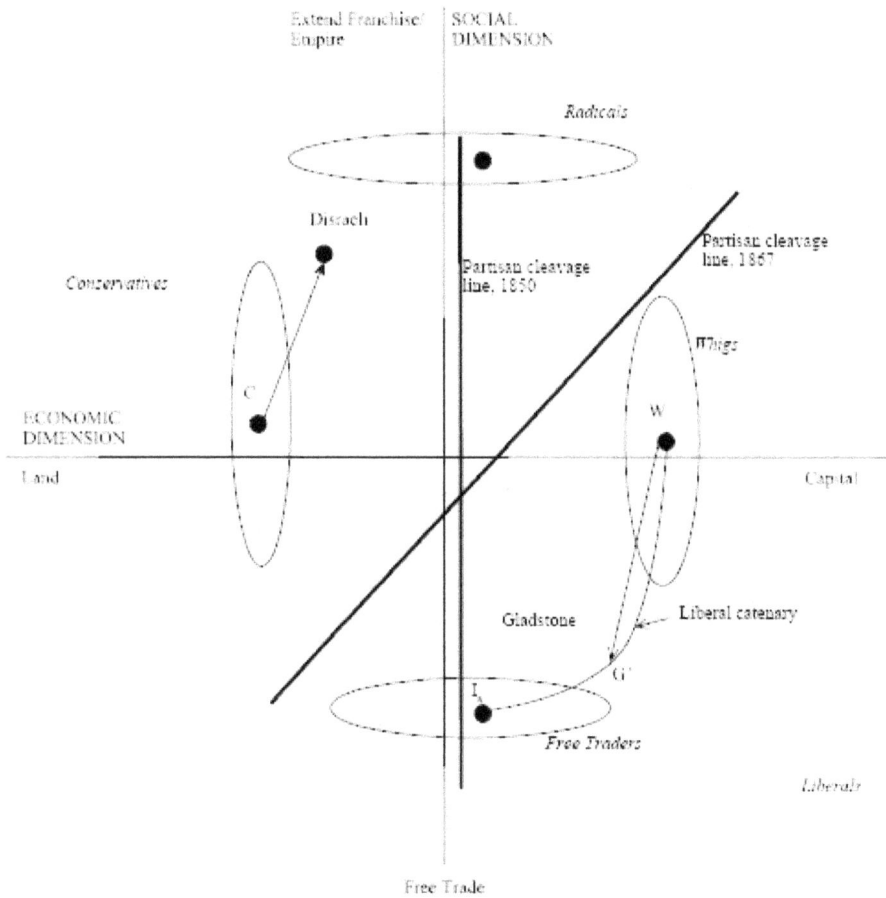

Figure 1.3: Tories and Liberals in Britain in 1867

neither equilibrium nor chaos are accurate descriptions of social choice. Instead, there can be long periods during which the political economic equilibrium is quite stable. However, equilibria can be destroyed and dramatically transformed at key historical periods, as briefly described above.

The thrust of the argument in Schofield (2006a) is that *architects of political change* may respond to constitutional quandaries by creating new political economic equilibria. We can enumerate some of these transformations:

- the glorious revolution of 1688, and the later creation of the Walpole compact that created the foundation of the British empire, but required limited franchise in Britain and Ireland,

- the slow dissolution of this compact, first by Peel and Welligton in 1846 and more completely by Disraeli in 1867, leading to an enlarged franchise, free trade and British hegemony,

- the break between the American Colonies and Britain in 1776-1783, caused by the conflict over the land of the Ohio Valley, and the creation of a new compact in the form of the Declaration of Independence,

- the constitutional compact of 1787/8 based on the 3/5 representation rule for the non-free people, giving southern states greater representation, but combined with the Northwest ordinance, restricting slavery from Federal Territories,

- the Jeffersonian compact of 1800 leading to the American agrarian empire, that allowed for the rapid expansion of the US population, as well as the maintenance of slavery,

- the dissolution of this compact by Lincoln after 1860, again due to conflict over land, between the slave owning southern elite and southern industrial interests over control of the west,

- conflict between eastern capital interests and western populism in 1896 in the contest between William McKinley and William Jennings Bryan,

- The New Deal compact to protect labor, founded during the presidency of F. D. Roosevelt from 1932 on,

- conflict over the extension of the franchise and the creation of the Great Society compact by the Civil Rights and Voting Acts of 1964 and 1965 during the presidency of Johnson,

- the response by the Republican party leading to the capture of the southern states during the presidencies of Nixon and Reagan,

- the destruction of the Great Society compact by George W. Bush using the fear generated by 9/11/2001, taking on autocratic power and attempting to make the United States the global hegemon,

- the increasing dependency of the United States on the autocracies of Saudi Arabia, Pakistan, China and Russia,

- the creation of a fractured world, with numerous failed states in the Middle East and Africa.

This narrative suggests that preferences, or interests, on economic factors, or dimensions, play an important role in political decisions. However, the manner in which these interests are transformed into beliefs is, to a considerable degree, still a matter of conjecture. Indeed, how these beliefs take political expression seemingly depends on the perception and strategies of political leaders such as Walpole, Peel, Disraeli or Gladstone in Britain, and Franklin, Washington, Madison, Jefferson, Lincoln Johnson, Reagan and G.W. Bush in the United States.

The general argument is that the theoretical accounts, posing chaos against centrist equilibrium, miss the underlying feature of dynamic stability, in the U.S. in particular. For example, the transformations in the United States, listed above, led Miller and Schofield (2003) to suggest that political parties in the U.S. slowly cycle in the two-dimensional policy space, created in the period just prior to the Civil War. In certain periods (such as 1896-1920) the principal axis is one of land/capital. However, in the more general situation, which has held from 1964 to the present, a second dimension, *the social axis* (a reflection of the free labor/slave axis) is also necessary for understanding political change.

While the transformations that have occurred in the United States can often be attributed to risk-taking leaders, it is also the case that the Madisonian constitutional balance requires that the risk-taking of a president can, at least in principle, be balanced by the risk-aversion of Congress.

The narrative presented in this section suggests that when beliefs rather than simply preferences or interests are relevant, then polities based on majority rule can maintain a kind of structural stability, balanced between chaos and the rigidity of permanent equilibrium.

I now attempt to formulate a Madisonian model of election, that is in principle applicable to any democratic polity.

1.3   Preferences and Judgements

We assume that individuals have preferences that are can be represented in terms of utility functions on some "policy" space X. This space characterizes both voter interests, and possible eventualities. The space X embodies preferences over economic factors—labor, capital and land—with an additional political axis involving civil rights or religion.

The interests or beliefs of the population or "electorate," N (of size n) are described by a set $\{x_i\}$ of "ideal points," one for each "voter," $i = 1, \ldots, n$. An individual's ideal point in the space, X, is used to describe or represent that voter's interests. In

the empirical models discussed in Schofield and Sened (2006), the ideal point can be
obtained from a survey.

The set of options, P, of size p, is a set $\{z_j\}$, each one being a point in X. In
the situation of an election, each element of N is a declaration of intended or proposed
policy. There is one for each candidate, j. While it is usual to conceive of each z_j as
simply a point, we can easily allow z_j to involve various possibilities, associated with
differing probabilities of occurrence.

The "latent utility," u_{ij} of voter i for candidate j has the form

$$u_{ij}(x_i, z_j) = \mu_{ij}(x_i, z_j) - A_{ij}(x_i, z_j) + \theta_j^{\mathrm{T}} \eta_i + \varepsilon_{ij}. \tag{1.1}$$

Here $\theta_j^{\mathrm{T}} \eta_i$ models the effect of the sociodemographic characteristics, η_i, of voter i
in making a political choice. That is, θ_j is a k-vector specifying how the various sociodemographic variables appear to influence the choice for option j, so $\theta_j^{\mathrm{T}} \eta_i$ is simply a
number indicating the influence of i's sociodemographic characteristics on the propen-
sity to choose j.

The term $A_{ij}(x_i, z_j)$ is a way of representing the "preference disagreement" between the interests of voter i and the jth option. The function $A_{ij}(x_i, z_j)$ is determined
by the distance between x_i, the preferred position (or ideal point) of voter i and z_j, the
declared policy of candidate j.

The model is stochastic because $\{\varepsilon_{ij}\}$ is a set of possibly correlated *disturbances*.
The term $\mu_{ij}(x_i, z_j)$ is the perception by a voter, i, with ideal point, x_i, of the "valence"
of the option presented by the candidate j. This valence is a way of modelling the non
policy *judgement* by voter i of the quality of candidate j.[26]

In the general model, the probability, ρ_{ij}, that voter i chooses option j is

$$\rho_{ij} = \mathrm{Pr}[u_{ij}(x_i, z_j) > u_{ij}(x_i, z_k) \text{ for all } k \neq j]. \tag{1.2}$$

We can apply this model in various ways.

First, consider the pure preference based "non-stochastic" or deterministic case
where all $\varepsilon_{ij} = 0$, the valence is zero and $A_{ij}(x_i, z_j) = \beta||x_i - z_j||^2$, where $|| - ||$ is
the Euclidean norm and $\beta > 0$ is the spatial parameter.

The results on social choice theory imply that if decision making is binary (pitting
one option against another), and based on majority rule, or more generally on a non-
collegial voting mechanism, then disorder (in terms of the non-existence of a core or
social choice) can ensue as long as the dimension of W is sufficiently large.

In the stochastic model, we assume, on the contrary, that $\{\varepsilon_{ij}\} \neq 0$, with $\{\varepsilon_{ij}\} =
\{\varepsilon_j\}$ independent of i, and also pairwise independent and identically distributed.[27] This
model can be interpreted as focusing on the "beliefs" or judgements of the participants.
In particular, if the spatial coefficient, β is identically 0, then this is a situation of pure

---

[26]Chapter 3 discusses the nature of valence more fully.
[27]More complex models allow for correlation between these disturbances.

"belief aggregation." Individuals will choose among the various options with probability determined by the valence judgement that they have made. I suggest that the final decision is often the consequence of what I call a *belief cascade*. As more individuals decide that option z_s, say, is superior, then other voters will in turn, be swayed to form a judgement in favor of z_s. By analogy with the social choice notion of a core, a *core belief* is one held by a majority of the society. Condorcet (1785) in his *Essai* argued essentially that a core belief would tend to be a correct belief. Roughly speaking, *Condorcet's Jury Theorem* asserts that, in a binary choice situation, the probability that a majority selects the true outcome will be greater than the probability that a typical individual will select the truth. Rae (1969) and Schofield (1972a, b) used a version of the theorem to argue that majority rule would be "rationally" chosen by an uncertain society as a constitutional rule, since this rule would maximize the probability of a fit choice.

Since judgement will vary in a society, we can model the variation in beliefs in the society by supposing that the valence terms $\{\mu_{ij}(x_i, z_j)\} = 0$ but that judgement is determined solely by the sociodemographic characteristic, η_i, of the individual. While this would induce some variation in judgements, voting models based on this assumption perform poorly in predicting voter choice. Moreover, the jury theorem depends on the condition of voter (pairwise) "statistical independence" which is a very strong assumption. Indeed, this assumption would not be satisfied in the case that voter judgements were based solely on sociodemographic characteristics.[28]

This suggests considering a more general case when $\beta \neq 0$, so both interests and judgements are involved. As discussed Schofield (2008b), such a model requires considering how the various candidates respond to the pattern of electoral preferences and beliefs. The simplest case is of *exogenous or intrinsic valence*, where $\mu_{ij}(x_i, z_j) = \lambda_j$, for all i. The model showed that only in the case that the differences between the candidate valences $\{\lambda_j\}$ are "low" (in comparison to the product of β and the electoral variance) can we expect "convergence" to the electoral mean.[29] Convergence implies that the mean electoral preferred point corresponds to a core belief about social policy. Indeed, when all parties converge to the electoral mean, then we can view this point as the "social attractor." However, the empirical examples of elections in Israel and Turkey in Chapter 5 show that when the valence differences are sufficiently high, then parties will adopt different policy positions on a principal electoral axis. Parties with the highest electoral valence will position themselves closer to the electoral center, and depending on the electoral regime, will either gain an electoral majority, or will be at the legislative core. While there will be a core, it will not be an attractor, since there can exist groups with divergent political beliefs in the society. Thus existence of a core belief depends in a delicate way on the distribution of the intrinsic valences or judgements of the electorate, and the response of political agents to these beliefs.

The empirical examples suggest that it is necessary to extend the electoral model

---

[28]For example, individual preferences in Iraq are very probably determined by such sociodemographic characteristics, and there is little likelihood of the Jury Theorem being valid in this context.

[29]The necessary condition is given in terms of a bound on the convergence coefficient, c. See the definition of this coefficient in the next section .

by assuming $\mu_{ij}(x_i, z_j) = \lambda_j + \mu_j(z_j)$, for all i. This additional component of belief, $\mu_j(z_j)$, called *activist valence,* is a function of the behavior of activists, but is again independent of i. This model assumes that a party's valence is directly influenced by the contributions of activists, and these contributions are indirectly determined by the policy position adopted by the candidate or party leader. Note that as $\mu_j(z_j)$ increases, then the probability that a voter chooses option j also increases. The model implies that parties balance the centrifugal tendency associated with activist support against the centripetal attraction of the electoral center.[30]

However, when the electoral rule is PR, then even small parties can gain representation in the legislature. This suggests that activist groups with diverse preferences may support parties that are far from the electoral center. Indeed, the logic of the model suggests that activist groups have little incentive to coalesce under PR. Thus, these diverse activist groups will support a diverse set of parties. The data presented in Schofield (2008b) indicate that PR results in a fragmented legislatures.

It is obviously possible to extend this model, by allowing an individual's beliefs to be function of the ideal point. In some sense, incorporating sociodemographic characteristics does allow for this kind of variation in beliefs.

One of the long standing puzzles arising from the study of U.S. politics is why precisely the plurality or majoritarian feature of the U.S. electoral system generates a two party structure rather than the fragmented political configurations that appear to hold under PR.[31] The discussion below leads to the conjecture that the plurality system of the US gives greater power to activists. Activist groups seem to face increasing to size, because of the nature of the electoral system, and this forces coalescence.[32] If this hypothesis is valid, then it would provide a reason why political competition under plurality leads to the two-party system.

Because there generally will exist two dimensions of policy, the various activist groups will tend to coalesce into at most four separate and opposed groups. Even in the United States, the two party system can break down, and it is probable that conflict within such activist groups at times of constitutional quandary generates the realignment of the political system.

Although the changes wrought by such reconfiguration are the result of transformations in the beliefs of the electorate, the hope that Madison had over the "probability of a fit choice" will depend on the ability of the electorate to ascertain the quality of candidates through their accurate judgement of the worth of past decisions.

The next section of the chapter presents some further details of the stochastic model set out in the above to address the political transformations discussed in the historical narrative.

---

[30]Formal results for this model are presented in Schofield (2006b) and below in Chapter 3.

[31]Riker, 1953, 1964, 1987; Duverger, 1954; Filippov, Ordeshook and Shvetsova, 2004.

[32]Once the groups have formed, they may face decreasing returns from the support they provide.

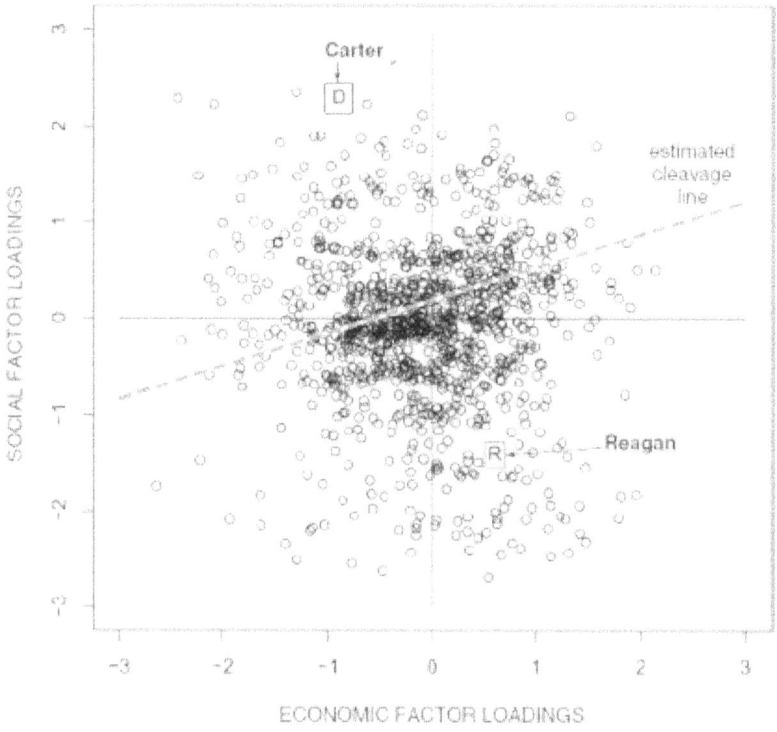

Figure 1.4: U.S.Voter Distribution in 1980

1.4   The Stochastic Model of Elections

A standard result in the class of stochastic electoral models is *the mean voter theorem*—that all candidates converge to the electoral mean when they are motivated to maximize vote share (McKelvey and Patty, 2006). An illustration of non-convergence of presidential candidate positions is provided in Figure 1.4.[33] This presents an analysis of the distribution of voter preferred points, obtained from the national election survey for the Presidential election of 1980, together with estimated positions of the candidates, Carter and Reagan. It can be seen in the figure that the "estimated cleavage line" slightly misses the origin, indicating an asymmetry of some kind between the two candidates

Empirical research on elections in a number of countries including the United States and Britain[34], and Turkey[35] has constructed multinomial conditional probit (MNP) and logit (MNL) models and shown that the addition of *candidate or party valence* (Stokes, 1992) adds to the statistical significance of the estimations. As discussed in section 3 of this chapter, exogenous valence, λ_j, is the electoral perception of the "quality" of a candidate or party leader of party, j. In empirical models this valence is assumed to be independent of the position of the party or candidate, and simply reflects the overall degree to which the party is perceived to have shown itself able to govern effectively in the past, or is likely to be able to govern well in the future (Penn, 2009). These models are discussed further in Chapters 3 and 4.

Since it is usual to assume in empirical models that the stochastic component of the model is associated with errors or disturbances that have the "Type I extreme value distribution," this assumption is imposed on the formal model (see Dow and Endersby (2004). Schofield (2007) obtains the necessary and sufficient conditions for *the mean voter theorem* to be valid when the candidates have differing valences. These conditions are expressed in terms of a convergence coefficient, c, that can be computed from the parameters of the empirical model, namely the spatial coefficient, β, the valence differences and the electoral variance, v^2, of the electoral distribution. First let ρ_1 be the probability that a voter chooses the party with lowest valence, λ_1, where the other candidate valences are $\{\lambda_2, \lambda_3, \ldots, \lambda_p\}$, and all candidates are at the same position at the electoral origin. Then

$$\rho_1 \;=\; \left[1 + \sum_{k \neq 1} \exp\left[\lambda_k - \lambda_1 \right] \right]^{-1} \tag{1.3}$$

$$\text{and } c \;=\; 2\beta[1 - 2\rho_1]v^2. \tag{1.4}$$

The sufficient condition for convergence is that $c < 1$, while the necessary condition is that $c < w$, where w is the dimension of the space.

---

[33] This figure is taken from Schofield, Miller and Martin (2003).

[34] Schofield (2005); Schofield and Sened (2006); Schofield, Miller and Martin (2003); Miller and Schofield (2003, 2008); Schofield and Miller (2007).

[35] Schofield, Ozdemir and Schnidman (2008).

When the sufficient condition is satisfied, then all candidates will adopt vote maximizing positions at the electoral mean. When the necessary condition fails, then no candidate will adopt such a position, and the candidate with the lowest valence will chose the most radical policy position.

The formal model has been extended recently to take account of the influence of activists on party and candidate positioning. The key idea of this work is that of a contract curve between different activist groups. As Chapter 3 shows, these contract curves will influence the optimal positions of political leaders.[36]

Figure 1.5 presents a schematic representation of the influence of activists in Britain in 1997-2005. The importance of the "empire," mentioned earlier, was reflected in Thatcher's electoral success in 1979 and the 1980's. Indeed, a recent empirical analysis of electoral beliefs in Britain (Schofield, 2005) make it clear that in addition to the usual economic (or "capital") axis, it is necessary to employ a second "social" axis. This axis incorporates "civil rights," but is also characterized by attitudes to European Union. Conservative MP's responses to a questionnaire on this topic suggest that they are strongly opposed to the incorporation of Britain within the European Union. In other words, political beliefs, that were founded on an economic rationale dating back over a hundred years, are still relevant, in a somewhat different form, today.

Figure 1.6 gives a similar representation of the influence of activist groups in pulling U.S.presidential candidates such as Johnson and Goldwater away from the electoral origin.[37] Miller and Schofield (2008) suggest that U.S. politics is subject to continuously realigning forces induced by these activist coalitions. These act in a clockwise direction in the two-dimensional policy space, following the arcs designated as contract curves between the activist groups as shown in Figure 1.6. It is possible that similar realignments occur in Britain, as suggested above by the discussion of the political decisions made in 1867 and those in 1997.

Miller and Schofield also argue that U.S. politics has become increasingly dominated by the contributions from socially conservative activists at C in Figure 1.6. The alliance between socially conservative activists at C and big business, located at R, has led to Repulican manipulation of electoral opinion, calling into question the validity of Madison's belief in the probability of a "fit choice."[38]

However, the model suggests that at a time of constitutional quandary, the influence of activist groups may become less intense, and the importance of electoral valence could lead to elections that center on those who "possess the most attractive merit and the most diffusive and established characters,"as suggested by Madison. Figure 1.6 indicates there has been a rotation in the position of the major parties in the United States. Miller and Schofield (2003) have inferred from this that there has been a continual rotation from the time of the election of Lincoln in 1860 to the present. Figure 1.7 gives a schematic representation of the election of 1860, where the horizontal axis is the usual

---

[36]This model is discussed further in Chapter 3.
[37]See Miller and Schofield (2003) and Chapter 3.
[38]See also Gore (2007).

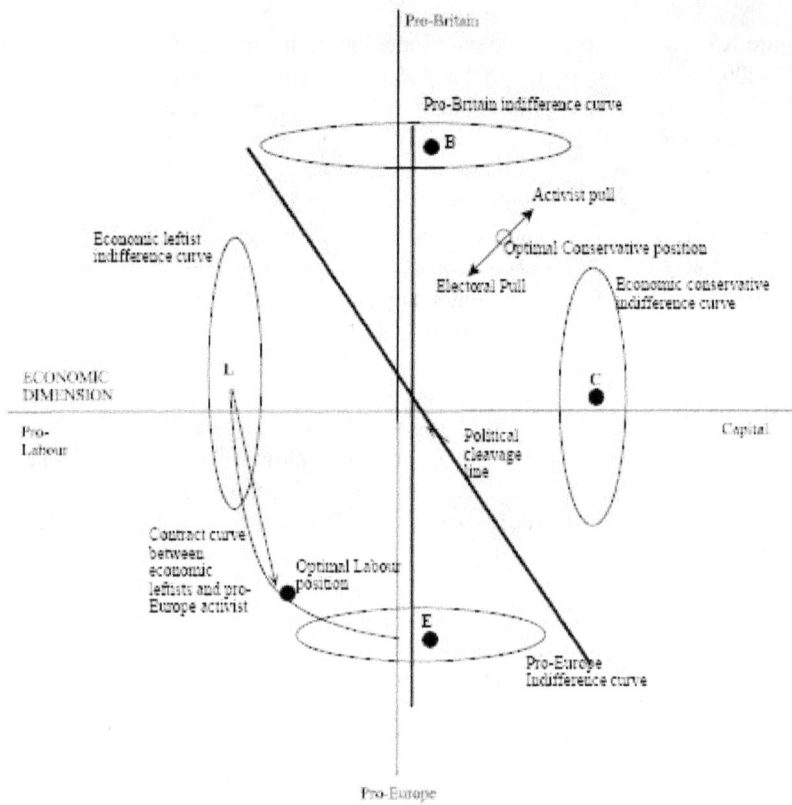

Figure 1.5: Activists in Britain in 1997

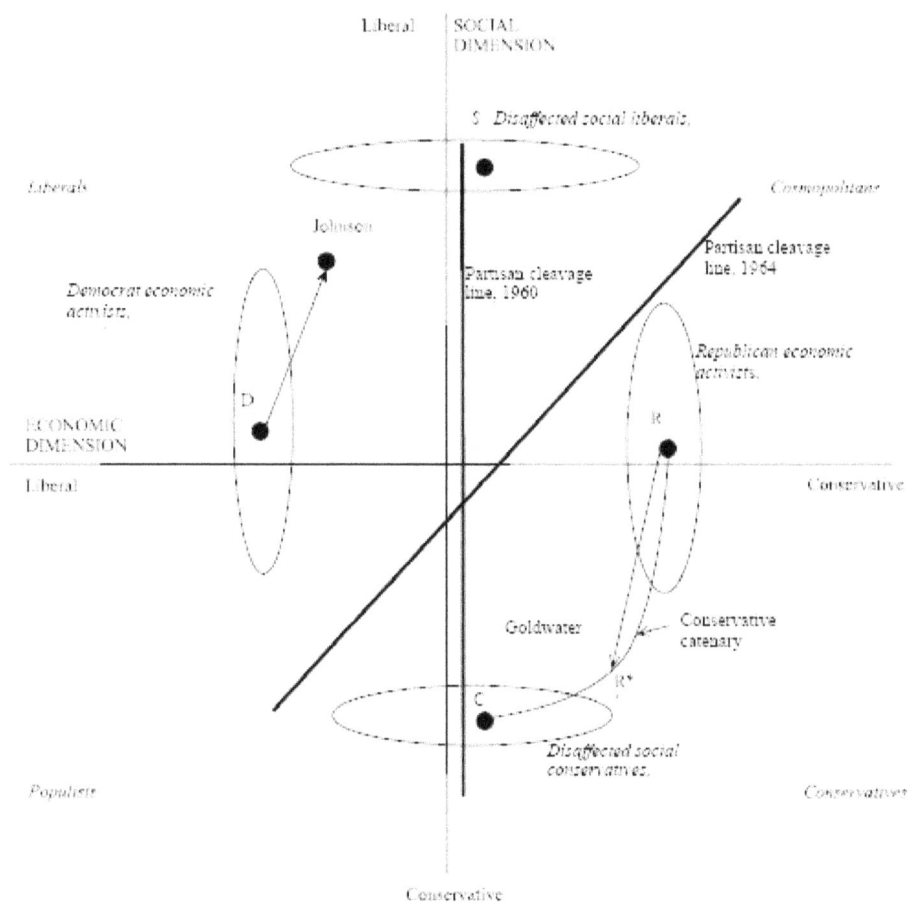

Figure 1.6: Activist catenaries in the United States

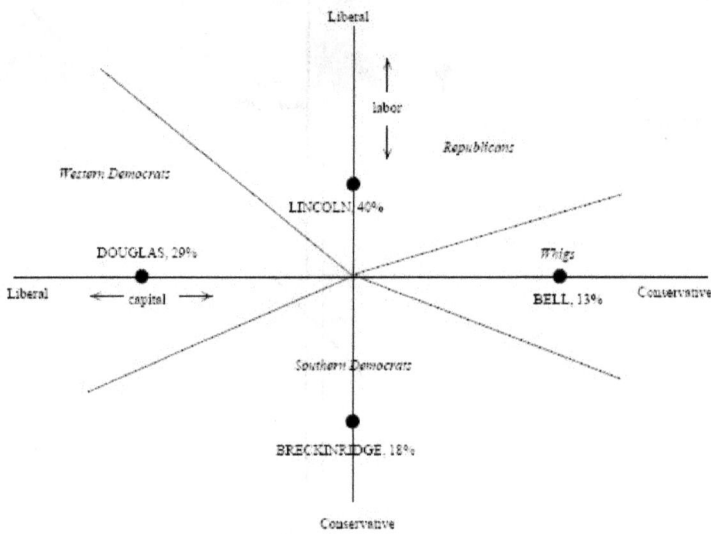

Figure 1.7:   The election of 1860

economic dimension, while the vertical axis represents the social axis. The election of Lincoln is discussed at length in the next chapter. Chapter 3 develops the model for U.S. elections and suggests that by 1896, the Republican candidate, William McKinley, had adopted a position very much more pro-capital, or conservative position on the economic axis, while his Democrat opponent, William Jennings Bryan, had adopted a populist stance. Comparing Figure 1.4 with Figure 1.7 suggests that the Republican and Democrat parties have "switched positions" over this period of 120 years, as a result of the continuing realignment of the parties.

1.5 Concluding Remarks

The stochastic spatial model is a potentially powerful tool for studying the interaction between activists, political candidates and the electorate in a representative democracy.[39] Chapter 3 will discuss some of this current research on the relationship between electorally induced preferences and voting behavior in the United States. Chapter 4 gives a detailed analysis of elections in Israel, Turkey, Canada, and brief accounts of elections in Britain and the Netherlands. The model will also be used in Chapter 6 to examine the conditions under which authoritarian regimes remain stable.

The results of Chapter 3 and 4 allow us to draw some inferences about the differences in party behavior between polities with electoral systems based on plurality rule in contrast to those based on proportional representation, as in many European countries.

The analysis suggests the following set of hypotheses:

1. The pure spatial model of *direct democracy,* based on *preferences* alone indicates that the occurrence of a core, or unbeaten alternative, is very unlikely in a direct democracy using majority rule, when the dimension of the policy is at least two (Schofield, 1985; McKelvey and Schofield, 1987; Saari, 1997). However, a social choice concept known as the heart, a generalization of the core, will exist, and converges to the core when the core is non-empty. (Schofield 1999).

2. A legislative body, made up of democratically elected representatives, can be modeled in social choice terms. Because party strengths will be disparate, a large, centrally located party may be located at a core position. Such a party, in a situation with no majority party, may be able to form a minority government. A more typical situation is one with no core party. In such a case, the legislative heart can give an indication of the nature of bargaining between parties as they attempt to form a winning coalition government.

3. This theory of legislative behavior takes as given the position and strengths of the parties. Because a centrally located party may dominate coalitional bargaining, and because such a party should be able to garner a large share of the vote, there would appear to be a strong *centripetal* tendency in all electoral systems.

---

[39]See also Acemoglu and Robinson (2005).

4. However, estimates of party positions suggest that parties adopt quite heterogenous positions.[40] This suggests that there is a countervailing or *centrifugal* force that affects all parties. While core parties can be observed in a number of polities with electoral systems based on proportional rule, the dominance of such central parties can be destroyed, particularly if there is a tendency to political fragmentation and social conflict.

5. It is very unlikely that the heterogenous positions of the parties can be accounted for in terms of a stochastic model of elections based on *exogenous* valence alone. This stochastic model gives a good prediction of party location in elections for the Knesset in Israel. However, it has been shown to give a poor account of party positioning in divergence in Britain (Schofield, 2005). This suggests that party location can be better modeled, as a balancing act between the *centripetal electoral* pull, and the *activist centrifugal pull*.

6. Under *proportional electoral methods*, there need be no strong tendency forcing activist groups to coalesce, in order to concentrate their influence. If activist groups respond to this impulse, then activist fragmentation will result in party fragmentation. As the example from Israel illustrate, parties tend to be scattered throughout the policy space. Activist groups, linked to small parties, may aspire to political office. This is indicated by the observation that the bargaining domain in the legislature (the heart) often includes small, low valence parties.

7. Under *plurality rule*, small parties face the possibility of extinction. Unlike the situation in a polity based on proportional rule, an activist group linked to a small party in a plurality polity has little expectation of influencing government policy. Thus activist groups face increasing returns to size. The activist model of elections presented in Chapter 3 suggests that when there are two dimensions of policy, then there will tend to be a small number of activist groups. When the electoral system is highly majoritarian as in the United States,there will be a tendency for these various groups to coalesce into at two opposed party coalition.

8. Athough the two party configuration. In the United States may be in equilibrium at any time, the tension within the activist coalitions induces a slow rotation, and thus *slow* political realignment. Presidential candidates must balance the centripetal electoral effect against the centrifugal valence effect.

9. On occasion in the United States, the conflict within activist groups is so pronounced that the two party system breaks down. Such a collapse of the activist cohesion may herald a major realignment, induced by the creation of a new policy dimension, such as civil rights. Schofield (2008b) and Miller and Schofield (2008) discuss this at length.

10. The effect of the difference between plurality rule and proportional representation

---

[40] See the expert estimates of party positioning given in Benoit and Laver (2006) and the spatial maps using these data presented in Schofield (2008b).

can be seen in the U.S. primary races of 2008. The Republican party tends to use a first pass the post (or plurality system) and this gave McCain a dominant lead by February, 2008. In contrast,the Democrat party has a much more proportional det of rule. As a consequence, there was no dominant Democrat candidate, and Clinton and Obama were neck and neck in the early part of the race. Eventually, Obama was able to pull ahead through his very high valence.

11. The well known relationship between proportional representation and a degree of political fragmentation (hypothesized by Riker, 1953, and Duverger, 1954) may be accounted for indirectly as a consequence of the logic forced on activist groups rather than parties themselves.

12. Since an authoritarian regime must also maintain support, whether from military or capitalist elite, or even from the population, the activist model can be adapted to the non-democratic situation. Whether or not pro-regime or ant-regime activist will coalesce, as under plurality democratic rule, or fragment, as under proportional democratic rule, will depend on whether the technology of power exhibits increasing or decreasing returns to scale.

13. In a polity such a present-day Iraq, neither fully democratic nor autocratic, it would seem that power does not exhibit increasing returns to scale. The interest groups in the polity do not coalesce, and chaos ensues.

1.6   Appendix: The Constitution of the United States

We the People of the United States, in Order to form a more perfect Union, establish Justice, insure domestic Tranquility, provide for the common defence, promote the general Welfare, and secure the Blessings of Liberty to ourselves and our Posterity, do ordain and establish this Constitution for the United States of America.

Article. I. - The Legislative Branch

Section 1 - The Legislature

All legislative Powers herein granted shall be vested in a Congress of the United States, which shall consist of a Senate and House of Representatives.

Section 2 - The House

The House of Representatives shall be composed of Members chosen every second Year by the People of the several States, and the Electors in each State shall have the Qualifications requisite for Electors of the most numerous Branch of the State Legislature.

No Person shall be a Representative who shall not have attained to the Age of twenty five Years, and been seven Years a Citizen of the United States, and who shall not, when elected, be an Inhabitant of that State in which he shall be chosen.

(Representatives and direct Taxes shall be apportioned among the several States which may be included within this Union, according to their respective Numbers, which shall be determined by adding to the whole Number of free Persons, including those

bound to Service for a Term of Years, and excluding Indians not taxed, three fifths of
all other Persons.) (The previous sentence in parentheses was modified by the 14th
Amendment, section 2.) The actual Enumeration shall be made within three Years after the first Meeting of the Congress of the United States, and within every subsequent
Term of ten Years, in such Manner as they shall by Law direct. The Number of Representatives shall not exceed one for every thirty Thousand, but each State shall have at
Least one Representative; and until such enumeration shall be made, the State of New
Hampshire shall be entitled to chuse three, Massachusetts eight, Rhode Island and Prov-
idence Plantations one, Connecticut five, New York six, New Jersey four, Pennsylvania
eight, Delaware one, Maryland six, Virginia ten, North Carolina five, South Carolina
five and Georgia three.

When vacancies happen in the Representation from any State, the Executive Authority thereof shall issue Writs of Election to fill such Vacancies.

The House of Representatives shall chuse their Speaker and other Officers; and shall
have the sole Power of Impeachment.

Section 3 - The Senate

The Senate of the United States shall be composed of two Senators from each State,
(chosen by the Legislature thereof,) (The preceding words in parentheses superseded by
17th Amendment, section 1.) for six Years; and each Senator shall have one Vote.

Immediately after they shall be assembled in Consequence of the first Election, they
shall be divided as equally as may be into three Classes. The Seats of the Senators
of the first Class shall be vacated at the Expiration of the second Year, of the second
Class at the Expiration of the fourth Year, and of the third Class at the Expiration of
the sixth Year, so that one third may be chosen every second Year; (and if Vacancies
happen by Resignation, or otherwise, during the Recess of the Legislature of any State,
the Executive thereof may make temporary Appointments until the next Meeting of the
Legislature, which shall then fill such Vacancies.) (The preceding words in parentheses
were superseded by the 17th Amendment, section 2.)

No person shall be a Senator who shall not have attained to the Age of thirty Years,
and been nine Years a Citizen of the United States, and who shall not, when elected, be
an Inhabitant of that State for which he shall be chosen.

The Vice President of the United States shall be President of the Senate, but shall
have no Vote, unless they be equally divided.

The Senate shall chuse their other Officers, and also a President pro tempore, in the
absence of the Vice President, or when he shall exercise the Office of President of the
United States.

The Senate shall have the sole Power to try all Impeachments. When sitting for that
Purpose, they shall be on Oath or Affirmation. When the President of the United States
is tried, the Chief Justice shall preside: And no Person shall be convicted without the
Concurrence of two thirds of the Members present.

Judgment in Cases of Impeachment shall not extend further than to removal from
Office, and disqualification to hold and enjoy any Office of honor, Trust or Profit under
the United States: but the Party convicted shall nevertheless be liable and subject to

Indictment, Trial, Judgment and Punishment, according to Law.

Section 4 - Elections, Meetings

The Times, Places and Manner of holding Elections for Senators and Representatives, shall be prescribed in each State by the Legislature thereof; but the Congress may at any time by Law make or alter such Regulations, except as to the Place of Chusing Senators.

The Congress shall assemble at least once in every Year, and such Meeting shall (be on the first Monday in December,) (The preceding words in parentheses were superseded by the 20th Amendment, section 2.) unless they shall by Law appoint a different Day.

Section 5 - Membership, Rules, Journals, Adjournment

Each House shall be the Judge of the Elections, Returns and Qualifications of its own Members, and a Majority of each shall constitute a Quorum to do Business; but a smaller number may adjourn from day to day, and may be authorized to compel the Attendance of absent Members, in such Manner, and under such Penalties as each House may provide.

Each House may determine the Rules of its Proceedings, punish its Members for disorderly Behavior, and, with the Concurrence of two-thirds, expel a Member.

Each House shall keep a Journal of its Proceedings, and from time to time publish the same, excepting such Parts as may in their Judgment require Secrecy; and the Yeas and Nays of the Members of either House on any question shall, at the Desire of one fifth of those Present, be entered on the Journal.

Neither House, during the Session of Congress, shall, without the Consent of the other, adjourn for more than three days, nor to any other Place than that in which the two Houses shall be sitting.

Section 6 - Compensation

(The Senators and Representatives shall receive a Compensation for their Services, to be ascertained by Law, and paid out of the Treasury of the United States.) (The preceding words in parentheses were modified by the 27th Amendment.) They shall in all Cases, except Treason, Felony and Breach of the Peace, be privileged from Arrest during their Attendance at the Session of their respective Houses, and in going to and returning from the same; and for any Speech or Debate in either House, they shall not be questioned in any other Place.

No Senator or Representative shall, during the Time for which he was elected, be appointed to any civil Office under the Authority of the United States which shall have been created, or the Emoluments whereof shall have been increased during such time; and no Person holding any Office under the United States, shall be a Member of either House during his Continuance in Office.

Section 7 - Revenue Bills, Legislative Process, Presidential Veto

All bills for raising Revenue shall originate in the House of Representatives; but the Senate may propose or concur with Amendments as on other Bills.

Every Bill which shall have passed the House of Representatives and the Senate, shall, before it become a Law, be presented to the President of the United States; If he approve he shall sign it, but if not he shall return it, with his Objections to that House in which it shall have originated, who shall enter the Objections at large on their Journal, and proceed to reconsider it. If after such Reconsideration two thirds of that House shall agree to pass the Bill, it shall be sent, together with the Objections, to the other House, by which it shall likewise be reconsidered, and if approved by two thirds of that House, it shall become a Law. But in all such Cases the Votes of both Houses shall be determined by Yeas and Nays, and the Names of the Persons voting for and against the Bill shall be entered on the Journal of each House respectively. If any Bill shall not be returned by the President within ten Days (Sundays excepted) after it shall have been presented to him, the Same shall be a Law, in like Manner as if he had signed it, unless the Congress by their Adjournment prevent its Return, in which Case it shall not be a Law.

Every Order, Resolution, or Vote to which the Concurrence of the Senate and House of Representatives may be necessary (except on a question of Adjournment) shall be presented to the President of the United States; and before the Same shall take Effect, shall be approved by him, or being disapproved by him, shall be repassed by two thirds of the Senate and House of Representatives, according to the Rules and Limitations prescribed in the Case of a Bill.

Section 8 - Powers of Congress

The Congress shall have Power To lay and collect Taxes, Duties, Imposts and Excises, to pay the Debts and provide for the common Defence and general Welfare of the United States; but all Duties, Imposts and Excises shall be uniform throughout the United States;

To borrow money on the credit of the United States;

To regulate Commerce with foreign Nations, and among the several States, and with the Indian Tribes;

To establish an uniform Rule of Naturalization, and uniform Laws on the subject of Bankruptcies throughout the United States;

To coin Money, regulate the Value thereof, and of foreign Coin, and fix the Standard of Weights and Measures;

To provide for the Punishment of counterfeiting the Securities and current Coin of the United States;

To establish Post Offices and Post Roads;

To promote the Progress of Science and useful Arts, by securing for limited Times to Authors and Inventors the exclusive Right to their respective Writings and Discoveries;

To constitute Tribunals inferior to the supreme Court;

To define and punish Piracies and Felonies committed on the high Seas, and Offenses against the Law of Nations;

To declare War, grant Letters of Marque and Reprisal, and make Rules concerning Captures on Land and Water;

To raise and support Armies, but no Appropriation of Money to that Use shall be for a longer Term than two Years;

To provide and maintain a Navy;

To make Rules for the Government and Regulation of the land and naval Forces;

To provide for calling forth the Militia to execute the Laws of the Union, suppress Insurrections and repel Invasions;

To provide for organizing, arming, and disciplining the Militia, and for governing such Part of them as may be employed in the Service of the United States, reserving to the States respectively, the Appointment of the Officers, and the Authority of training the Militia according to the discipline prescribed by Congress;

To exercise exclusive Legislation in all Cases whatsoever, over such District (not exceeding ten Miles square) as may, by Cession of particular States, and the acceptance of Congress, become the Seat of the Government of the United States, and to exercise like Authority over all Places purchased by the Consent of the Legislature of the State in which the Same shall be, for the Erection of Forts, Magazines, Arsenals, dock-Yards, and other needful Buildings; And

To make all Laws which shall be necessary and proper for carrying into Execution the foregoing Powers, and all other Powers vested by this Constitution in the Government of the United States, or in any Department or Officer thereof.

Section 9 - Limits on Congress

The Migration or Importation of such Persons as any of the States now existing shall think proper to admit, shall not be prohibited by the Congress prior to the Year one thousand eight hundred and eight, but a tax or duty may be imposed on such Importation, not exceeding ten dollars for each Person.

The privilege of the Writ of Habeas Corpus shall not be suspended, unless when in Cases of Rebellion or Invasion the public Safety may require it.

No Bill of Attainder or ex post facto Law shall be passed.

(No capitation, or other direct, Tax shall be laid, unless in Proportion to the Census or Enumeration herein before directed to be taken.) (Section in parentheses clarified by the 16th Amendment.)

No Tax or Duty shall be laid on Articles exported from any State.

No Preference shall be given by any Regulation of Commerce or Revenue to the Ports of one State over those of another: nor shall Vessels bound to, or from, one State, be obliged to enter, clear, or pay Duties in another.

No Money shall be drawn from the Treasury, but in Consequence of Appropriations made by Law; and a regular Statement and Account of the Receipts and Expenditures of all public Money shall be published from time to time.

No Title of Nobility shall be granted by the United States: And no Person holding any Office of Profit or Trust under them, shall, without the Consent of the Congress, accept of any present, Emolument, Office, or Title, of any kind whatever, from any King, Prince or foreign State.

Section 10 - Powers prohibited of States

No State shall enter into any Treaty, Alliance, or Confederation; grant Letters of Marque and Reprisal; coin Money; emit Bills of Credit; make any Thing but gold and silver Coin a Tender in Payment of Debts; pass any Bill of Attainder, ex post facto Law, or Law impairing the Obligation of Contracts, or grant any Title of Nobility.

No State shall, without the Consent of the Congress, lay any Imposts or Duties on Imports or Exports, except what may be absolutely necessary for executing it's inspection Laws: and the net Produce of all Duties and Imposts, laid by any State on Imports or Exports, shall be for the Use of the Treasury of the United States; and all such Laws shall be subject to the Revision and Controul of the Congress.

No State shall, without the Consent of Congress, lay any duty of Tonnage, keep Troops, or Ships of War in time of Peace, enter into any Agreement or Compact with another State, or with a foreign Power, or engage in War, unless actually invaded, or in such imminent Danger as will not admit of delay.

Article. II. - The Executive Branch

Section 1 - The President

The executive Power shall be vested in a President of the United States of America. He shall hold his Office during the Term of four Years, and, together with the Vice-President chosen for the same Term, be elected, as follows:

Each State shall appoint, in such Manner as the Legislature thereof may direct, a Number of Electors, equal to the whole Number of Senators and Representatives to which the State may be entitled in the Congress: but no Senator or Representative, or Person holding an Office of Trust or Profit under the United States, shall be appointed an Elector.

(The Electors shall meet in their respective States, and vote by Ballot for two persons, of whom one at least shall not lie an Inhabitant of the same State with themselves. And they shall make a List of all the Persons voted for, and of the Number of Votes for each; which List they shall sign and certify, and transmit sealed to the Seat of the Government of the United States, directed to the President of the Senate. The President of the Senate shall, in the Presence of the Senate and House of Representatives, open all the Certificates, and the Votes shall then be counted. The Person having the greatest Number of Votes shall be the President, if such Number be a Majority of the whole Number of Electors appointed; and if there be more than one who have such Majority, and have an equal Number of Votes, then the House of Representatives shall immediately chuse by Ballot one of them for President; and if no Person have a Majority, then from the five highest on the List the said House shall in like Manner chuse the President. But in chusing the President, the Votes shall be taken by States, the Representation from each State having one Vote; a quorum for this Purpose shall consist of a Member or Members from two-thirds of the States, and a Majority of all the States shall be necessary to a Choice. In every Case, after the Choice of the President, the Person having the greatest Number of Votes of the Electors shall be the Vice President. But if there should remain two or more who have equal Votes, the Senate shall chuse from them by Ballot the Vice-President.) (This clause in parentheses was superseded by the 12th Amendment.)

The Congress may determine the Time of chusing the Electors, and the Day on which they shall give their Votes; which Day shall be the same throughout the United States.

No person except a natural born Citizen, or a Citizen of the United States, at the time of the Adoption of this Constitution, shall be eligible to the Office of President; neither shall any Person be eligible to that Office who shall not have attained to the Age of thirty-five Years, and been fourteen Years a Resident within the United States.

(In Case of the Removal of the President from Office, or of his Death, Resignation, or Inability to discharge the Powers and Duties of the said Office, the same shall devolve on the Vice President, and the Congress may by Law provide for the Case of Removal, Death, Resignation or Inability, both of the President and Vice President, declaring what Officer shall then act as President, and such Officer shall act accordingly, until the Disability be removed, or a President shall be elected.) (This clause in parentheses has been modified by the 20th and 25th Amendments.)

The President shall, at stated Times, receive for his Services, a Compensation, which shall neither be increased nor diminished during the Period for which he shall have been elected, and he shall not receive within that Period any other Emolument from the United States, or any of them.

Before he enter on the Execution of his Office, he shall take the following Oath or Affirmation:

"I do solemnly swear (or affirm) that I will faithfully execute the Office of President of the United States, and will to the best of my Ability, preserve, protect and defend the Constitution of the United States."

Section 2 - Civilian Power over Military, Cabinet, Pardon Power, Appointments

The President shall be Commander in Chief of the Army and Navy of the United States, and of the Militia of the several States, when called into the actual Service of the United States; he may require the Opinion, in writing, of the principal Officer in each of the executive Departments, upon any subject relating to the Duties of their respective Offices, and he shall have Power to Grant Reprieves and Pardons for Offenses against the United States, except in Cases of Impeachment.

He shall have Power, by and with the Advice and Consent of the Senate, to make Treaties, provided two thirds of the Senators present concur; and he shall nominate, and by and with the Advice and Consent of the Senate, shall appoint Ambassadors, other public Ministers and Consuls, Judges of the supreme Court, and all other Officers of the United States, whose Appointments are not herein otherwise provided for, and which shall be established by Law: but the Congress may by Law vest the Appointment of such inferior Officers, as they think proper, in the President alone, in the Courts of Law, or in the Heads of Departments.

The President shall have Power to fill up all Vacancies that may happen during the Recess of the Senate, by granting Commissions which shall expire at the End of their next Session.

Section 3 - State of the Union, Convening Congress

He shall from time to time give to the Congress Information of the State of the Union, and recommend to their Consideration such Measures as he shall judge necessary and expedient; he may, on extraordinary Occasions, convene both Houses, or either of them, and in Case of Disagreement between them, with Respect to the Time of Adjournment, he may adjourn them to such Time as he shall think proper; he shall receive

Ambassadors and other public Ministers; he shall take Care that the Laws be faithfully executed, and shall Commission all the Officers of the United States.

Section 4 - Disqualification

The President, Vice President and all civil Officers of the United States, shall be removed from Office on Impeachment for, and Conviction of, Treason, Bribery, or other high Crimes and Misdemeanors.

Article III. - The Judicial Branch

Section 1 - Judicial powers

The judicial Power of the United States, shall be vested in one supreme Court, and in such inferior Courts as the Congress may from time to time ordain and establish. The Judges, both of the supreme and inferior Courts, shall hold their Offices during good Behavior, and shall, at stated Times, receive for their Services a Compensation which shall not be diminished during their Continuance in Office.

Section 2 - Trial by Jury, Original Jurisdiction, Jury Trials

(The judicial Power shall extend to all Cases, in Law and Equity, arising under this Constitution, the Laws of the United States, and Treaties made, or which shall be made, under their Authority; to all Cases affecting Ambassadors, other public Ministers and Consuls; to all Cases of admiralty and maritime Jurisdiction; to Controversies to which the United States shall be a Party; to Controversies between two or more States; between a State and Citizens of another State; between Citizens of different States; between Citizens of the same State claiming Lands under Grants of different States, and between a State, or the Citizens thereof, and foreign States, Citizens or Subjects.) (This section in parentheses is modified by the 11th Amendment.)

In all Cases affecting Ambassadors, other public Ministers and Consuls, and those in which a State shall be Party, the supreme Court shall have original Jurisdiction. In all the other Cases before mentioned, the supreme Court shall have appellate Jurisdiction, both as to Law and Fact, with such Exceptions, and under such Regulations as the Congress shall make.

The Trial of all Crimes, except in Cases of Impeachment, shall be by Jury; and such Trial shall be held in the State where the said Crimes shall have been committed; but when not committed within any State, the Trial shall be at such Place or Places as the Congress may by Law have directed.

Section 3 - Treason

Treason against the United States, shall consist only in levying War against them, or in adhering to their Enemies, giving them Aid and Comfort. No Person shall be convicted of Treason unless on the Testimony of two Witnesses to the same overt Act, or on Confession in open Court.

The Congress shall have power to declare the Punishment of Treason, but no Attainder of Treason shall work Corruption of Blood, or Forfeiture except during the Life of the Person attainted.

Article. IV. - The States

Section 1 - Each State to Honor all others

Full Faith and Credit shall be given in each State to the public Acts, Records, and judicial Proceedings of every other State. And the Congress may by general Laws prescribe the Manner in which such Acts, Records and Proceedings shall be proved, and the Effect thereof.

Section 2 - State citizens, Extradition

The Citizens of each State shall be entitled to all Privileges and Immunities of Citizens in the several States.

A Person charged in any State with Treason, Felony, or other Crime, who shall flee from Justice, and be found in another State, shall on demand of the executive Authority of the State from which he fled, be delivered up, to be removed to the State having Jurisdiction of the Crime.

(No Person held to Service or Labour in one State, under the Laws thereof, escaping into another, shall, in Consequence of any Law or Regulation therein, be discharged from such Service or Labour, But shall be delivered up on Claim of the Party to whom such Service or Labour may be due.) (This clause in parentheses is superseded by the 13th Amendment.)

Section 3 - New States

New States may be admitted by the Congress into this Union; but no new States shall be formed or erected within the Jurisdiction of any other State; nor any State be formed by the Junction of two or more States, or parts of States, without the Consent of the Legislatures of the States concerned as well as of the Congress.

The Congress shall have Power to dispose of and make all needful Rules and Regulations respecting the Territory or other Property belonging to the United States; and nothing in this Constitution shall be so construed as to Prejudice any Claims of the United States, or of any particular State.

Section 4 - Republican government

The United States shall guarantee to every State in this Union a Republican Form of Government, and shall protect each of them against Invasion; and on Application of the Legislature, or of the Executive (when the Legislature cannot be convened) against domestic Violence.

Article. V. - Amendment

The Congress, whenever two thirds of both Houses shall deem it necessary, shall propose Amendments to this Constitution, or, on the Application of the Legislatures of two thirds of the several States, shall call a Convention for proposing Amendments, which, in either Case, shall be valid to all Intents and Purposes, as part of this Constitution, when ratified by the Legislatures of three fourths of the several States, or by Conventions in three fourths thereof, as the one or the other Mode of Ratification may be proposed by the Congress; Provided that no Amendment which may be made prior to the Year One thousand eight hundred and eight shall in any Manner affect the first and fourth Clauses in the Ninth Section of the first Article; and that no State, without its Consent, shall be deprived of its equal Suffrage in the Senate.

Article. VI. - Debts, Supremacy, Oaths

All Debts contracted and Engagements entered into, before the Adoption of this Constitution, shall be as valid against the United States under this Constitution, as under the Confederation.

This Constitution, and the Laws of the United States which shall be made in Pursuance thereof; and all Treaties made, or which shall be made, under the Authority of the United States, shall be the supreme Law of the Land; and the Judges in every State shall be bound thereby, any Thing in the Constitution or Laws of any State to the Contrary notwithstanding.

The Senators and Representatives before mentioned, and the Members of the several State Legislatures, and all executive and judicial Officers, both of the United States and of the several States, shall be bound by Oath or Affirmation, to support this Constitution; but no religious Test shall ever be required as a Qualification to any Office or public Trust under the United States.

Article. VII. - Ratification Documents

The Ratification of the Conventions of nine States, shall be sufficient for the Establishment of this Constitution between the States so ratifying the Same.

Done in Convention by the Unanimous Consent of the States present the Seventeenth Day of September in the Year of our Lord one thousand seven hundred and Eighty seven and of the Independence of the United States of America the Twelfth. In Witness whereof We have hereunto subscribed our Names.

Go Washington - President and deputy from Virginia

New Hampshire - John Langdon, Nicholas Gilman

Massachusetts - Nathaniel Gorham, Rufus King

Connecticut - Wm Saml Johnson, Roger Sherman

New York - Alexander Hamilton

New Jersey - Wil Livingston, David Brearley, Wm Paterson, Jona. Dayton

Pensylvania - B Franklin, Thomas Mifflin, Robt Morris, Geo. Clymer, Thos FitzSimons, Jared Ingersoll, James Wilson, Gouv Morris

Delaware - Geo. Read, Gunning Bedford jun, John Dickinson, Richard Bassett, Jaco. Broom

Maryland - James McHenry, Dan of St Tho Jenifer, Danl Carroll

Virginia - John Blair, James Madison Jr.

North Carolina - Wm Blount, Richd Dobbs Spaight, Hu Williamson

South Carolina - J. Rutledge, Charles Cotesworth Pinckney, Charles Pinckney, Pierce Butler

Georgia - William Few, Abr Baldwin

Attest: William Jackson, Secretary

Chapter 2

Dred Scott and the Election of Lincoln

Note.[41]

It is a commonplace in positive political theory to suppose that policy disagreements between parties can be expressed in terms of a single "ideological dimension." Vote maximization by parties (under plurality rule), theoretically leads inexorably to convergence at the voter median, or mean. In fact, however, there seems little evidence of such convergence. One possibility is that policy outcomes reside in a higher dimensional space. In economic theory, it is natural to emphasize the utilization of at least *three* economic factors, capital, labor and land . Political coalitions may form in an attempt to modify the *institutional* equilibrium in the three dimensional economic factor space. Whether or not such coalitions can form may depend on the stability of earlier compromises, so we would not in general expect all three economic factors to be relevant at all times.

Schofield (2006a) explores the possibility that a factor dimension can become prominent when sections of the population feel under threat because of an attempt to modify the political equilibrium associated with that dimension. For example, a primary cause of the American Revolution of 1776-1783 was the attempt by the British, under the Quebec Act of 1774, to close the Ohio Valley to settlement. The colonists' understanding that the political equilibrium gave them access to the Ohio Valley was denied by the British. Instead, the British perceived a need to change this institutional equilibrium because they, in turn, had to face the demands (in the form of a rebellion) of the Indian tribes of the Ohio Valley. Since the cost to the colonists of acquiescence to Britain was high, they were willing to fight a "Revolutionary War" to arrest the change of equilibrium.

Similarly, in 1787 the Spanish posed a threat to the new United States, in their effort to close the Mississippi. Hamilton, Jay and Madison all argued in the *Federalist Papers* that it was necessary to create a stronger federal structure to counter this threat. Riker (1964) in his discussion of federalism argues that Beard (1913) was incorrect to see only economic motives behind the move to federalism in 1787. In fact,

---

[41] This chapter was co-authored by Norman Schofield and Kim Dixon.

Riker and Beard are both justified in their differing interpretations. The Spanish threat clearly brought the political issue of federation into prominence. Once the threat was perceived, however, the question of institutional change became important (Schofield, 2001a). As Beard observed "merchants, money lenders, security holders, manufacturers, shippers, capitalists and financiers" all preferred a dollar backed by a credible commitment to a "hard-money principle." In contrast, "non-slaveholding farmers and debtors" would prefer a "soft money principle."[42] The external threat forced, in a sense, an agreement over federation that initially favored this "hard money principle." Once the threat faded, however, political disagreements over what was essentially a policy on the economic dimension became increasingly salient. Over time, conflict between Federalists and Jeffersonian Republicans became more pronounced on this dimension of capital, and came to be re-interpreted in political terms about the nature of states' rights.

The equilibrium on this capital dimension was always affected by the compromise or outcome on the two other dimensions of land and labor. In attaining the federal solution of 1787, slavery had been accepted (for a period of at least twenty years). Clearly this had profound effects on the economic factor dimension of labor. Expansion of the U.S. into Florida, then the Louisiana Purchase and finally the acquisition of the western territories, after war with Mexico, not only changed the factor availability of land, but modified the need for credit, and affected the labor equilibrium.

The question that this chapter attempts to address is the manner by which the labor "equilibrium," or slavery compromise, became profoundly important in the period from 1840 on, eventually leading to the "disequilibrium" of the 1860 election and the Civil War. In line with the earlier analyses of 1776 and 1787, we shall argue that the labor dimension became even more salient for the northern electorate after the *Dred Scott* decision of March 1857. This decision by the Supreme Court essentially denied that slaves had any rights under the Constitution. Lincoln was able to persuade a significant proportion of the electorate that this decision provided a signal that the South did indeed constitute a threat to the North, because of the probable intention to extend slavery to the free northern states.

The argument we shall give owes something to the earlier analysis by Riker (1982) of the slavery issue from 1830. Riker's general point was that, until 1856 or so, the Whig and Democrat intersectional coalitions were opposed in a political space that essentially comprised a single dimension. We may view this dimension as economic, with Whigs representing an eastern hard money principle, while Democrats emphasized expansion, and easy credit. Typically, presidential elections were relatively closely fought. Martin Van Buren, for example, won the 1836 presidential election with about 57% of the popular vote. Given the plurality nature of the electoral college, this translated into 170 electoral college votes, out of 294, with 124 distributed between his three Whig challengers. Van Buren's electoral victory depended both on the North (101 electoral college votes out of 130) and the South (57 out of 94).

Congress passed the gag-rule in January 1840, to prevent discussion of the ques-

---

[42]Beard (1913: 17).

tion of slavery (possibly as a consequence of the agitation over the *Amistad* affair: see Schofield, 1999a, for discussion). Van Buren, in turn, lost the 1840 presidential election to the Whig, William Harrison, because the northern Democrat support was seriously weakened. Harrison won over half the southern electoral college votes, and almost all the northern electoral college. In 1844, Van Buren expected to be nominated as the Democrat presidential candidate, but southern Democrats imposed a $\frac{2}{3}$ majority rule in the nominating convention. After eight ballots, the southerner, James Polk, of Tennessee, won the nomination. As Thomas Hart Benton said in his memoirs, "here ends the history of this long intrigue-one of the most elaborate, complex and daring ever practised in an intelligent country."[43] Polk won the presidential election, taking 77 out of 112 northern electoral college votes, and 60 out of 84 of the southern electoral college . However, the election was very close indeed. The Whig, Clay, took just over 48% of the popular vote, to Polk's almost 50% . As Riker noted, the Liberty candidate, James Birney, had 10,000 votes in New York. Had Clay won these voters, he would also have won New York, and thus the presidential election. Riker suggests this was the "beginning of the end for both Whig and Democratic intersectional alliances."[44]

Indeed, these intersectional alliances almost collapsed immediately. In December 1844, 55 northern Democrats in the House voted with 53 Whigs to rescind the gag-rule. Presumably these northern Democrats were angered (as was Thomas Hart Benton) at the betrayal by their southern Democrat allies. Nonetheless the intersectional alliances did not completely collapse. In 1848, the Democrat, Cass, gained 127 electoral college seats in the North (out of 290) and 48 (out of 91) in the South. Van Buren had his revenge on southern Democrats in this election. As a Free Soil candidate he took 10% of the popular vote and weakened Democrat support in the North, sufficient to give the Whig, Zachary Taylor, the presidency. In the election of 1852, the free-soil candidate, John Hale, took only 5% of the popular vote. This had an insignificant effect on the presidential election, since the Democrat, Franklin Pierce, won with about 51% of the popular vote, winning 92 (out of 110) of the northern electoral college and 76 (out of 88) of the southern electoral college.

By 1856, John Fremont, the candidate for the new Republican party, was able to win 33% of the popular vote, two-thirds of the electoral college vote in the North and over one half in the West (in the relatively new states of California, Iowa, Oregon and Wisconsin). It has been suggested that until 1850 (with the admission of California as a state), a convention had been maintained to preserve a balance rule of free and slave states in the Senate. What is obvious, however, is that the creation of new states in the West would have an impact on the availability of land, and on the natural economic consequences over the labor and capital equilibria. Such an expansion would naturally lead to an "undersupply" of labor with respect to the availability of land.

However, the interests of land, labor and capital may diverge in interesting ways. The western Democrat, Stephen Douglas clearly had a preference for ready credit (and increase in the availability of land). The position of the Whig, or Conservative Unionist,

---

[43] Benton (1856: 595).
[44] Riker 1982: 223).

John Bell represents conservative or protectionist interests, on the capital dimension. Bell's position could appeal to holders of capital and also industrial labor. The southern Democrat, John Breckinridge, represents slave owning, land holders. His policy would be to hold down the price of labor, by maintaining the slavery institution. Lincoln represents a policy of free mobility in labor.

There are some implicit conflicts both between Douglas and Breckinridge, and between Douglas and Lincoln. Douglas attempted to appeal to labor, seeing great opportunities in the new states of the West. However, his political position involved the attempt to form a coalition with southern Democrat land owners (implicitly incorporating the notion of states' rights). Although he hoped this would appeal to free labor, it is clear that labor could potentially be threatened by slavery itself. It was this threat that Lincoln articulated.

In the election of 1860, Lincoln took over 1.8 million voters (out of about 4.7 million) or 40%, and won 180 electoral college seats (out of 303, or nearly 60%). Douglas with nearly 1.4 million votes (or 30%) only won 12 electoral college seats. Breckinridge, with 850,000 votes (or 18%) concentrated in the South, took 72 electors, while Bell (with 600,000, or 12%) only won 39 electors (27 in the South, and 12 in the Border states).

Riker (1982:230) offered this election as an example of the potential disequilibrium of politics. He suggests that in binary choice, a majority of the voters in 1860 would have preferred Douglas to Lincoln, a majority preferred Lincoln to Bell, a majority preferred Bell to Douglas, with Breckinridge least preferred. The cycle between Douglas, Lincoln, and Bell them implies that agenda manipulation could lead to any outcome. This may well be, but Riker's argument is only valid in a committee, where the three alternatives (Douglas, Lincoln, Bell) are static outcomes, and voting is interpreted using some agenda process. In fact, the election was governed by plurality rule in the electoral college. As such, Lincoln won easily.

What is less clear is why Lincoln won this plurality election. One argument is offered, in a sense, by Mackie (2003). He suggests that there was in fact no pairwise voting cycle. Instead simple majorities preferred Douglas to Lincoln to Bell to Breckinridge.

Indeed he suggests the election can be interpreted in terms of a single dimension, where "latitude is attitude." Thus the "upper North" voted for Lincoln, the "lower North" voted Douglas, the "upper South" voted Bell, and the "lower South," Breckinridge. By this reasoning, Riker's inference of a cycle (based on the assumption that most Lincoln voters preferred Bell to Douglas) is implausible. However, by Mackie's logic, the poor showing by Douglas in the electoral college must be due to his supporters being concentrated in States where Lincoln supporters were more numerous. Moreover, on a one dimensional policy space it is unlikely that an extreme candidate (on that dimension), such as Lincoln, could win a plurality. I contend that understanding the election requires consideration of at least two dimensions of policy.

It was important for Riker's interpretation of this election that the second dimension (labor) was part of the electoral calculus. In his book on *Manipulation*, Riker (1986) contended that Lincoln trapped Douglas by a "heresthetic" question at Freeport, on

August 27, 1858, during their campaign for Illinois Senator. However, Lincoln asked Douglas if the people of a U.S. territory could exclude slavery prior to the formation of a State Constitution. Douglas answered that they could, and Riker infers that this helped Douglas win the Senate seat. However, by the same answer, Douglas alienated southern Democrats. Inevitably, this led to the split in the Democrat nomination convention in May 1860, and to the opposition of Douglas and Breckinridge. Riker argues that "Lincoln won the Republican nomination, in no small part because of the heresthetic ability displayed in the campaign of 1858, and was elected president by a plurality. [Lincoln's] question ... should be interpreted as the capstone of the Republican strategy of splitting the Democratic majority."[45].

We quibble with Riker's interpretations of this maneuver. Firstly, slavery interests in the South were already disenchanted with Douglas before August, 27, 1858. The *Chicago Press and Tribune*, quoted, on August 22, 1858, from an article in the influential *Mobile Register*, that Douglas was "in a position to offer the Democrat Party the alternative of a probable success in the next presidential campaign if [the South] accepted the modified platform he has prepared for them or of certain defeat and permanent destruction as a party if they do not. There is ruin to them as a national party in either horn of the dilemma ... but there is demoralization as well as disaster in one."

Thus, even before Douglas had a chance to respond at Freeport, he must have known that his chance of winning overwhelming southern support was slim.

Prior to the 1860 election, the Democratic National Convention met in Charleston, on April 23 but adjourned, without selecting a candidate. The reason for the impasse was the $\frac{2}{3}$ rule, mentioned earlier. A majority of the delegates had, however, expressed support for Douglas. This may have had an effect on the choice of Lincoln by the Republican convention, meeting in late May in 1860. Although the abolitionist, Seward, had an initial plurality (but not a majority) Lincoln was eventually chosen after other candidates dropped out. It is possible that Seward lost not because of the split in the Democrats, but because Bell and Everett (of Massachusetts) had been chosen in early May as the presidential and vice presidential candidates for the Conservative National Union Party (the remnant of the Whigs). Seward would not have done well against Bell and Everett in the East.

Finally, Riker considers that the split between Douglas and Breckinridge was crucial for Lincoln's victory. This is not plausible. Had Douglas and Breckinridge contested on a combined Democrat platform, Lincoln would still have won. In every state that Lincoln beat Douglas, he would also have won over a combined Douglas-Breckinridge slate. In the East, Lincoln's principal challenger was Bell, not Douglas.

Riker's account is designed to offer an "heresthetic" explanation why Lincoln was able to win 40% of the popular vote (and approximately 60% of the northern vote), while the Republican Fremont, in 1856, could only gain 33%. Clearly the labor axis and the slavery issue were relevant in 1856, but some change in perception or electoral preference occurred between the two elections.

---

[45]Riker (1986: 5).

Had the popular vote for the Conservative National Union Party been 21% in 1860 (as it was in 1856 for the Whigs), then Bell would have received over a million votes. This suggests that over 400,000 voters in the North switched allegiance to the Republican party, and it was this that gave Lincoln the election. What provoked this electoral switch was the credibility of Lincoln's argument about the consequence and meaning of the *Dred Scott* decision.

Although the Supreme Court Decision was only made in March 1857, Lincoln had studied the decision and was ready to argue against it by June 1857. In the Illinois State House in Springfield, on June 26, 1857, Lincoln made his case. Firstly, if the decision had been made

> in accordance with legal public expectation, and ... on historical facts," then it would be "factious, nay, even revolutionary, to not acquiesce in it as a precedent.[46]

But

> The *Dred Scott* decision was, in part, based on assumed historical facts which were not really true ... Chief Justice Taney, in delivering the opinion of the majority of the court insists at great length that negroes were no part of the people who made, or for whom was made, the Declaration of Independence, or the Constitution of the United States ... [But] Judge Curtis in his dissenting opinion, shows that in five of the then thirteen states ... free negroes were voters.[47]

Moreover,

> [i]f resistance to the decisions of the Supreme Court in [the matter of] the *Dred Scott* case ... be forced upon the country as a political issue, it will become a distinct and naked issue between the friends and the enemies of the Constitution – the friends and enemies of the supremacy of the laws [48].

In his speech of acceptance as Republican candidate for Senator from Illinois on June 16, 1858, Lincoln said

> I believe this government cannot endure permanently half *slave* and half *free*. I do not expect the Union to be *dissolved* — I do not expect the house to *fall* — but I *do* expect it will cease to be divided. It will become *all* one thing, or *all* the other. Either the opponents of slavery, will arrest the further threat of it ... or its *advocates* will push it forward, till it shall become alike lawful in *all* the States, *old* as well as *new* – *North* as well as *South* [49].

Finally, as argued in Schofield (2006a), it was not Lincoln's second question to

---

[46]Fehrenbacher (1989a: 393).
[47]Ibid., p. 395.
[48]Ibid., p. 393.
[49]Ibid. p. 426.

Figure 2.1: Dred Scott and his wife, Harriet, photographed by Fitzgibbon and published in *Frank Leslie's Illustrated Newspaper*, New York, 27 June, 1857

Douglas at Freeport on August 27, 1858, that was important. Lincoln's third question was:

> If the Supreme Court of the United States shall decree that states cannot exclude slavery from their limits, are you in favor of acquiescing in adopting, and following such a rule of political action?[50]

Lincoln obviously implied by this question that, while the *Dred Scott* decision only extended slavery to the Territories, the next step would be to extend it to the States. Clearly Lincoln believed that the *Dred Scott* decision signaled a profound threat to free labor in the North. To see why this belief was credible, the next sections of the chapter will discuss in detail why this case came before the Supreme Court and will attempt to make clear what it signified.

2.1 Background to the Dred Scott Decision

Dred Scott was born in Virginia about 1800. He became the property of Peter Blow, although when and how is unknown. Peter Blow was born in 1771 in southeastern Virginia and married Elizabeth Taylor in 1800. They eventually had 11 children. In 1818, the Blow family moved to Alabama, living in two different areas before eventually

---

[50]Fehrenbacher (1989a: 542).

moving to St. Louis in 1830. With them was their slave, Dred Scott.

The need for a slave was much more limited in the thriving and bustling urban setting of St. Louis, already being referred to in 1830 as the "gateway to the West." It was not clear in what capacity Dred Scott was working for the Blows, as they had opened up a boarding house called the Jefferson Hotel. He could have been hired out, with his income helping to support family members.[51] Scott did not stay with the family long in St. Louis. Elizabeth Blow died in the summer of 1831 from a lingering disease, with Peter Blow following shortly after on June 23, 1832. While there is much debate on when precisely Dred Scott was sold by the Blow family, either before or after Peter Blow's death, there is no question that as of December 1, 1833, he was owned by Dr. John Emerson.[52]

Emerson had been appointed assistant surgeon in the Army of the United States, to take effect December 1, 1833, the same day he reported for duty at Fort Armstrong in the State of Illinois. He was accompanied by his slave, Dred Scott. After about two and one-half apparently miserable years, Emerson was transferred to Fort Snelling, which was located in the newly created Wisconsin Territory. While at Fort Snelling in 1836, Dred Scott met and married in 1836 a young girl, Harriet Robinson, the slave of Major Lawrence Taliaferro.

The marriage is of significance because there was an actual civil ceremony, "an event not often accorded to unfortunates held in bondage," which was, in fact, officiated over by Taliaferro acting as justice of the peace. At the time, slave states did not recognize slave marriages, because it would have undermined the property interests of the owner, because no American states allowed slaves to make contracts, such as a civil marriage contract, and because recognition of slave marriages might have caused slaves to claim other rights.[53]

There are different theories as to how Harriet left Taliaferro and went to marry Dred Scott. It was possible that Taliaferro gave Harriet her freedom, as he wrote in 1864 biography that he *gave* her to him, and in a newspaper interview around the same time he referred to his "marrying the two and *giving the girl her freedom*."[54] However, it was also claimed that Emerson bought Harriet from Taliaferro and gave the couple permission to marry.[55] While the lawyers for Dred Scott may have later argued that his marriage before a justice of the peace was proof that both Emerson and Taliaferro thought the slaves were free persons, the lawyers' arguments were invalidated by the fact that Emerson continued to treat Dred Scott and his wife as slaves, often hiring them out to others.[56]

Emerson was to again be transferred, this time to Fort Jesup, Louisiana, where he reported on November 22, 1837. He initially did not take the Scotts with him, leaving them at Fort Snelling where he rented them to other people. While at Fort Jesup, Emer-

---

[51] Ehrlich (1979: 11).
[52] Ehrlich (1979: 11-15), Fehrenbacher (1981: 121-3), Hopkins (1951: 3-5).
[53] Finkelman (1997: 16).
[54] Ehrlich (1979: 21).
[55] Hopkins (1951: 5).
[56] Finkelman (1997: 16).

son met, courted, and married Eliza Irene Sanford on February 6, 1838. Shortly after his marriage to Mrs. Emerson, who was known as Irene, he sent for Dred and Harriet Scott, who joined him in April 1838. After only five months, Emerson was transferred back to Fort Snelling, making the trip upriver in September 1838 with his wife and two slaves. Along the way, Harriet gave birth to a daughter, Eliza, while the steamboat *Gipsey* was north of the state of Missouri along the Mississippi River.

Less than two years later, Emerson was transferred to Florida to the zone of military operations of the Seminole War. He traveled downriver with his wife, Dred, Harriet and Eliza Scott, leaving them in St. Louis while he continued on to Florida. Mrs. Emerson lived with her father, Alexander Sanford, in St. Louis, while it appears that Dred and Harriet Scott may have spent the time either working for Sanford or hired out to different people. Emerson returned to St. Louis in 1842 upon his discharge from the Army. Apparently discouraged from beginning a private practice in St. Louis, he moved, with his wife, to Davenport, Iowa in the spring of 1843. It is thought they did not take Dred and Harriet Scott with them, instead leaving them in St. Louis to continue to be hired out.

On December 29 of that year, Emerson died in Davenport. Apparently sensing death was imminent, he had prepared a will only a few hours earlier. He bequeathed most of his property to his wife for the term of her natural life, with the proviso that she could sell all or part for support and maintenance, with the remainder to go to his month-old daughter, Henrietta. The will named John F. A. Sanford (Mrs. Emerson's brother) and George L. Davenport (friend) executors of the estate in Iowa. Iowa law required the nominees to appear before the probate court within 20 days after the will had been probated. Davenport appeared and was duly appointed. Sanford never appeared and was never appointed as executor.

Since legal action also was required in Missouri, the court named Alexander Sanford (Mrs. Emerson's father) administrator of the estate in Missouri. Alexander Sanford "dawdled over his responsibilities in Missouri and had not yet filed a final report when he died in 1848," leaving Mrs. Emerson full control of her husband's property. There is no evidence John Sanford (brother) ever participated in the process of executing his brother-in-law's will.

Mrs. Emerson returned to St. Louis after her husband's death. At some point until 1846, Dred and Harriet Scott were loaned to Captain Henry Bainbridge, Mrs. Emerson's brother-in-law, who had transferred to St. Louis in 1843. One account states that Dred Scott tried to buy his and his family's freedom from Mrs. Emerson in February 1846.[57] She refused. In March of 1846, Mrs. Emerson hired out the Scotts to Samuel Russell. One month later, in April 1846, Dred and Harriet Scott sued for their freedom.

---

[57]Ibid. p. 10.

2.2   The Compact over Slavery

The thirteen states in existence as the U.S. Constitution was signed in 1776 was only a beginning for the United States. It had only just begun to grow. And with that growth came the question of what to do about slaves. By the early 1800's, the several states had declared their intentions regarding slaveholding status within its boundaries.[58] As new territories and states were added to the Union, the slaveholding status of those new territories and states were considered. Thus, political action was taken as property increased the size of the United States.

In July 1787, a plan of government for the new West won approval in Congress. This measure explicitly applied only to "the territory of the United States North West of the river Ohio."[59] The sixth article, which was introduced by the only state, Massachusetts, which had at the time abolished slavery, read:

> There shall be neither slavery nor involuntary Servitude in the said territory otherwise than in the punishment of crimes, whereof the party shall have been duly convicted; provided always that any person escaping into the same, from whom labor or services is lawfully claimed in any one of the original States, such fugitive may be lawfully reclaimed and conveyed to the person claiming his or her labor or service as aforesaid.[60]

This ordinance won approval by a unanimous vote of the eight states present, even though only three were northern. This seemed to be an indication the slave holding south was not yet concerned with its political strength.

At about the same time, the Constitutional Convention was meeting in Philadelphia where it addressed congressional power over new territories. It eventually encompassed that power in the phrase: "The Legislature shall have power to dispose of and make all needful rules and regulations respecting the territory or other property belonging to the United States."[61] This vague phrase would later be interpreted by the U.S. Supreme Court in the *Dred Scott Case*. It was thought this expansion of congressional power took into account the five-week old Northwest Ordinance of 1787.[62]

The Northwest Ordinance, which was renewed by the new United States government under the Constitution in 1789, was important to Dred Scott because the state of Illinois was carved out of the Northwest Territory. When it was admitted into the Union in 1818, its constitution prohibited slavery. That prohibition was still in effect when Dred Scott lived there from 1833 to 1836.

The Louisiana Purchase in 1803 again brought the issue of slaveholding in the territories to the forefront. Although there were several measures offered or introduced

---

[58]The states abolished slavery in the following years: Vermont, 1777; Massachusetts (including Maine), 1780; New Hampshire, 1783. Gradual abolition was won in Pennsylvania, 1780; Rhode Island and Connecticut, 1784; New York, 1799, and New Jersey, 1804. See Filler (1986: 26).

[59]North and Rutten (1987).

[60]Fehrenbacher (1981: 42).

[61]Ibid. p. 42).

[62]North and Rutten (1987)

into Congress, both for and against slaveholding in the area, the final legislation con-
verting the district of Louisiana into a full-fledged territory neither authorized nor prohibited slavery. Presumably, then, slaveholding was still legal under previous French or
Spanish law. In 1812, having admitted the Orleans Territory as the state of Louisiana,
Congress changed the name of the remaining Louisiana Territory to Missouri Territory,
again with no reference to the Northwest Ordinance or its anti-slavery article "Missouri
remained slaveholding territory by virtue of congressional default."[63]

This "non-intervention" policy held for several years, until sometime after the War
of 1812, when some northern members of Congress opposed the admission of Missouri as a slaveholding state.[64] This protest in 1819 was an attempt to recover some
ground which had been passively yielded by the northern members during the preceding 15 years.[65] The House passed Missouri enabling legislation with an amendment
prohibiting the further introduction of slavery to Missouri and freeing slave children
born after the date of the state's admission. The Senate refused to accept the House bill
unless the amendment was deleted. In 1820, the state of Maine applied for admission
to the Union. Its enabling legislation became tied up with the still languishing Missouri enabling legislation, with neither bill being passed through both the House and
the Senate. The House had passed the Maine bill and sent it to the Senate, however,
the Senate amended it by adding a Missouri enabling act with no restrictions on slavery. Eventually, the Senate added an amendment to the package that "declared slavery
to be 'forever prohibited' in the remainder of the Louisiana cession lying north of 36
(degrees) 30 (minutes)."[66] The House initially refused to accept the Senate's package,
but eventually approved what would become known as the Missouri Compromise.

The territory where Fort Snelling was formed would be governed by the Missouri
Compromise. The Fort, established in 1819 as Fort St. Anthony, was located on the
north bank of the now Minnesota River, where it flowed eastward into the Mississippi
River. Part of the newly created Wisconsin Territory, the Fort was located on the west
bank of the Mississippi River, "in that portion of the Louisiana Purchase territory where
slavery had been prohibited by the Missouri Compromise of 1820."[67] Dred Scott once
again lived in free territory during his two years at Fort Snelling.

"Throughout the colonial period and after the American Revolution, slavery was
accepted by most Americans as a normal and inevitable aspect of their affairs."[68] The
Revolutionary War did aid the cause of some slaves whose owners saw fit to manumit
them as a reward for serving in the Revolution.[69] However, the invention of the cotton

---

[63] Fehrenbacher (1981: 48).

[64] While all other territories at the time were expressly assimilated to the Northwest Ordinance, either
affirming or excluding the anti-slavery clause found in the Ordinance, the acts that created the Louisiana-
Missouri Territory omitted all reference to it. Fehrenbacher describes the effect it created as establishing the
purest form of a "non-intervention" policy.

[65] Feherenbacher (1981: 49).

[66] Ibid., p. 52.

[67] Ehrlich (1979: 19).

[68] Filler (1986: 16).

[69] In 1782, Virginia repealed a law restraining manumissions, and within nine years 10,000 slaves had been

gin by Eli Whitney in 1793 made the use of slaves in the cultivation of cotton a more profitable venture; "thereafter, the southern leadership became more assertive in defense of its rights."[70] The Industrial North did not have as strong a financial interest in slave labor as did the South.

As time went on, though, people's sentiments became less about economics and more about personal philosophies, with less of a sectional division. "By 1825, North and South were clearly distinguishable in their attitude toward slavery, but not in the attitude toward the Negro."[71] When the Marquis de Lafayette visited the country in that year, he was "dismayed by the amount of anti-Negro prejudice he observed everywhere, and recalled that during the Revolution, "black and white soldiers messed together without hesitation."[72]

Even if support for slavery in the South came mostly from an economic perspective, the South's poor whites and non-slaveholders, who would have had no vested interest in the perpetuation of slavery, "chose to despise the Negro and adopt in exaggerated form the view point of the patricians."[73] As abolitionists grew in power, Southerners came together and adopted "a stern uniformity in outlook and a program of repressing liberal thought."[74]

While Northern states were the first to abolish slavery, this did not necessarily mark the beginning of an abolitionist movement. The first group to take a stand on the abolition of slavery was the Quakers, perhaps with the publication of Ralph Sandiford's *A Brief Examination of the Practice of the Times* in 1729. There were several free, and wealthy, black Americans who contributed to the abolition movement, but for the most part, "(a)ntislavery forces North and South failed signally to utilize the free Negro, despite the fact that his own efforts in behalf of slaves probably exceeded those of all others."[75] John Rankin developed the best-known "underground railroad" station in Ripley, Ohio.[76]

One movement that received much support, including a $100,000 federal appropriation, was The American Society for Colonizing the Free People of Colour of the United States developed in the early 1800's, a Society whose goal was to obtain a territory on the coast of Africa, or somewhere not the United States, to receive free or emancipated blacks. The support this movement garnered gave great strength to the idea that "the presence of free Negroes troubled white people North as well as South."[77]

Abolition efforts seemed to be coming to the forefront as the 1820's wore on.

Numerous events contributed to the growth of a crisis psychology in both the North and the South. There was the Andrew Jackson 'revolution' of 1828, his

---

freed. Jay (1835: 27-28, as cited in Filler (1986: 18, note 6)).

[70] Ibid., p. 18.
[71] Ibid., p. 20
[72] Ibid. , p. 20.
[73] Filler, p. 23.
[74] Ibid., p. 23.
[75] Ibid., p. 32.
[76] Ibid., p. 31.
[77] Ibid., p. 37.

election to the Presidency, which overturned established political alliances. The year 1829 teemed with incidents, including the official ending of slavery in Mexico, which caused the Yankee settlers of Texas to be concerned for their slave property. That same year saw a cruel riot against the free Negroes of Cincinnati which caused many of them to flee the city and state, clouded as it was by a Black Code. In 1829, too, there was a debate on the slave trade in the District of Columbia, which resulted in resolutions condemning the trade and even looking to the gradual abolition of slavery.[78]

In August 1831, Nat Turner, a slave and religious fanatic, led a revolt of about 70 slaves in southeast Virginia. In one day, 57 men, women and children were killed by the revolting slaves. In turn, many of the slaves were massacred, without trial, by white troops and militia. "This latest of major slave plots evoked memories, North and South, of the gruesome violence which had been reported during the struggles in Santo Domingo several decades before."[79] It alerted Virginians to the dangers among which they lived, and to their need for guarantees against further insurrections."[80]

Despite any personal feelings of the individual white Americans toward free or enslaved blacks, a legal question arose regarding what to do about slaves who were moved from a slaveholding to a non-slaveholding state or territory, in violation of the law. Even more difficult to answer was what happened to a slave who was moved back to a slaveholding state, after residing in a free area.

To the substantive question there were three basic answers:
(1) The law of slavery remained attached to a slave when he entered a free state; his status did not change.
(2) The slave taken by his master into a free state became a free man and remained so permanently, wherever he might go thereafter.
(3) The slave taken into a free state became free in the sense that his master lost the power to control him, but upon his returning to a slaveholding state, the status of slave was reattached to him.[81]

Early on, there was some tacit agreement to this question. Based on *Somerset v. Stewart* (1772), an English case which stood for the idea that without positive law legalizing slavery, any slave brought into England became free, early abolitionists argued "slavery was contrary to natural law and without legal status beyond the boundaries of the jurisdiction establishing it by positive law."[82] Both southerners and northerners were willing to accept the doctrine, with the southerners agreeing it applied to slaves domiciled by their masters on free soil and with the northerners generally agreeing it should not apply to instances of transit, sojourn, or temporary residence.[83] Many courts, in-

---

[78] Ibid., p. 71.
[79] Feherenbacher (1981: 25).
[80] Filler (1986: 72).
[81] Fehrenbacher (1981: 27).
[82] Ibid., p. 28.
[83] Ibid., p. 29.

cluding southern courts, consistently ruled that a slave taken to a free state to live by his masters was freed. The Missouri Supreme Court, in fact, in 1824 in *Winney v. White-sides*,[84] freed a slave who had been taken to Illinois. Over the next 13 years, the Missouri court heard another 10 cases, "always deciding that slaves gained their freedom by either working in a free jurisdiction[85] or living there long enough to be considered a resident,"[86] even if the slave afterwards returned to Missouri.[87]

One of the most liberal states on this question, but not alone, Missouri was joined by Kentucky, Louisiana, and Mississippi as slave states whose courts upheld the freedom of slaves who lived in a free state or territory. As late as 1837, the Missouri Supreme Court reaffirmed this principle and it had made no further decisions on this principle before Dred Scott brought his suit in 1846.[88]

2.3   The Dred Scott Case

The Missouri Courts: *Dred Scott v. Irene Emerson.*

What is commonly thought of as "The Dred Scott Case" was actually the culmination in the U.S. Supreme Court of several trials and appellate hearings held over the course of 11 years. Why Dred Scott brought the case in 1846, or at all, after it had been more than six years since their residency in a free state, has been a matter of much speculation. "How did an illiterate slave who could not even sign his name know that he had a legal basis for freedom?"[89]

One thought was that it was only in 1846 that Dred Scott discovered he had a strong legal claim to freedom.[90] He may have learned this from his former masters, the Blows, after returning from service with Captain Bainbridge. He apparently renewed his acquaintance with the Blows, who then provided him financial support for his litigation. While their motive is unknown, it is considered without a political agenda as it is thought the Blow's benevolence, particularly that of the son Taylor Blow, had "sprung wholly from a personal affection extending back to his boyhood."[91]

Another possible way Dred Scott learned of his right to freedom was through his wife Harriet. She joined Rev. John R. Anderson's Second African Baptist Church in the

---

[84] 1 Missouri Reports 476 (1824).

[85] As held in *John Merry v. Tiffin and Menard* 1 Missouri Reports 725 (1827), this included slaves living in any territory where slavery was prohibited by the Ordinance of 1787. *See also Franocois La Grange v. Pierre Chouteau, Jun* 2 Missouri Reports 20 (1828) and *Theoteste alias Catiche v. Pierre Courteau* 2 Missouri Reprorts 145 (1829). See Ehrlich (1979: 41).

[86] Finkelman (1997: 20).

[87] As held in *Philip Tramel v. Adam* 2 Missouri Reports 157 (1829). *See also Vincent v. James Duncan* 2 Missouri Reports 214 (1830), *Ralph v. Coleman Duncan* 3 Missouri Reports 195 (1833), and *Julia v. Samuel McKinney* 3 Missouri Reports 275 (1833). See Ehrlich (1979: 41).

[88] *Daniel Wilson v. Edmund* 4 Missouri Reports 597 (1837). See Ehrlich (1979: 42).

[89] Ehrlich (1979: 35).

[90] Finkelman (1997: 19).

[91] Feherenbacher (1981: 122).

early 1840's. Anderson had been a former slave who worked as a typesetter for Elijah P. Lovejoy, an antislavery editor in Alton, Illinois.[92] It was possible Anderson or someone else in the church told Harriet the Scotts were entitled to their freedom.

There was another "friend" who appeared early in the Dred Scott case, a mysterious friend who was not only a benefactor to Dred Scott, but who may have had something to do with the initiation of the case. Attorney Francis B. Murdoch filed the initial documents charging Mrs. Emerson and also signed a bond accepting responsibility for the costs that might accrue in the case.[93] The mystery surrounding Murdoch has to do with his motive for stepping into Dred Scott's life. He had previously practiced law and was elected prosecuting attorney in Alton, Ill., the location where Alton abolitionist minister and pamphleteer Elijah P. Lovejoy was killed. "As Alton's city attorney, Murdoch prosecuted both antislavery and proslavery zealots charged with capital offenses tied to slavery, however his sympathies were with those opposed to slavery."[94] After the Lovejoy killing, Murdoch moved to St. Louis, where he may or may not have known Harriet Scott's pastor, Reverend Anderson.

Contemporary writers of Dred Scott's time suggested the case originated as a test case, initiated by one or the other of proslavery or antislavery supporters, in order to substantiate their point of view.[95] In 1907, one lawyer argued the theory that the reason for the case was financial; that a freedom suit would pave the way for a second suit for back wages once the court found the Scotts had been held illegally. These theories were dismissed by one researcher who located missing court documents which indicated the points of law and arguments raised by the counsel. Ehrlich details his search for the missing court records of the *Dred Scott* case. Around 1900, the original records were removed from the Circuit Court in St. Louis by George W. Taussig, a St. Louis lawyer and one of Henry Blow's close friends. He died before writing anything about the case. His nephew had been storing his dead uncle's papers, and went to burn them. As he was throwing papers into the furnace, one bundle got caught on the lip of the furnace, with the words "Dred Scott, a man of color, vs. Irene Emerson." He pulled the papers from the furnace and returned them to the Circuit Court. It is unknown, though, how many documents were lost to the furnace before he pulled them from the fire. There were also copies of some of the original documents filed with the Missouri Supreme Court. Ehrlich went to the Court in 1947 and located copies of the documents, only to be told by the clerk of the court that the files had been missing for decades. Ehrlich volunteered to search for the records himself, feeling the integrity of his doctoral dissertation was at stake. Five years later in 1956, after a file-by-file and drawer-by-drawer search, he found the papers a "scant few feet from where they should have been in the first place."[96] These documents seem to indicate the only issue at hand for Dred Scott and his family

---

[92] Finkelman (1997: 19).

[93] Before a slave could sue for freedom, the slave had to represent "security to the clerk for all costs that may be adjudged against him or her." In the *Dred Scott Case*, the attorneys representing the Scotts typically posted this security throughout the course of the litigation.

[94] Ehrlich (1979: 37).

[95] Ibid., p. 33.

[96] Ibid., p.188.

was to gain their freedom from slavery.

"At no time were the politics of slavery, the morality of slavery, the views of any political or civic leader, financial considerations, or any other issues raised. The case purely and simply involved a Negro slave who sued for one thing and one thing only — to obtain his freedom."[97] This was not even an unusual suit. "Besides, the central question raised in the suit — whether extended residence on free soil liberated a slave — was not an issue in American politics and had been tested many times in the Missouri courts, with consistent results."[98] There was no reason to think this case would be decided otherwise.

The case began on April 6, 1846, when Dred and Harriet Scott filed petitions in the Missouri Circuit Court in St. Louis requesting permission to bring suit against Irene Emerson to establish their right to freedom based on their residence on free soil. Before a slave could actually sue for freedom, he first had to petition the circuit court of Missouri, or its judge, for permission to sue. The judge, if he believed the grounds for suit set forth in the petition, set four conditions for that permission. First, the slave had to present security (*see* note 56); second, that he have liberty to attend his counsel and the court; third, that he not be subject to severity on account of his application; and fourth, that he not be removed out of the jurisdiction of the court.[99] The judge granted their petitions, and on the same day, the Scotts initiated actions of trespass for assault and false imprisonment against Mrs. Emerson, complaining that she had "beat, bruised and ill-treated him" and then imprisoned him.[100] The action also averred that Dred was a "free person" held in slavery and claimed damages of ten dollars. A suit for freedom took the conventional form of a suit for damages in which it was understood that the alleged acts of the defendant were lawful chastisement of a slave by his master, but constituted assault and false imprisonment if the plaintiff were indeed a free person.

Although the suit was brought in April 1846, the case was not tried until June 30, 1847, with Samuel Bay now representing Dred Scott. The witnesses for Dred Scott testified Dr. Emerson had held him as a slave in Missouri and in free territory, with Samuel Russell testifying he had hired Scott from Mrs. Emerson and paid for the hire to her and her father. This was to establish Mrs. Emerson still claimed Scott as her slave in Missouri. However, under cross-examination, Russell testified his wife had done the actual hiring and he actually did not know if the money for the hire went to Mrs. Emerson. The defense thus argued "the technicality that Dred Scott had not legally proved that it was specifically Mrs. Emerson who was holding him as a slave in Missouri."[101]

Agreeing with the defense, the judge instructed the jury that Russell's testimony was not legal evidence to prove what the law required. Thus instructed, the jury returned a verdict in favor of Mrs. Emerson. Dred Scott had not gained his freedom that day.

---

[97] Ibid., p. 34.
[98] Fehrenbacher (1981: 129).
[99] Ehrlich (1979: 42)
[100] Fehrenbacher (1981: 129).
[101] Ehrlich (1979: 46).

Immediately after the verdict, attorney Bay moved for a new trial, contending this technicality could be resolved by calling Mrs. Russell. Judge Hamilton did not render a decision until December 2, 1847, when he did order a new trial. Meanwhile, on July 1, 1847, Alexander P. Field and David N. Hall initiated a new case on behalf of Dred Scott, naming John Sanford, Irene Emerson, and Samuel Russell defendants. It was not precisely known why this suit was instituted, unless it was to ensure at least one master would be found guilty of the offenses alleged.[102] When the court noted on July 31 there were two cases charging Mrs. Emerson with the same offense, it ordered one be dropped. The attorneys dropped the new case, continuing with the original one.

After Judge Hamilton ordered the new trial, the attorney for Mrs. Sanford filed a bill of exceptions for an appeal to the Supreme Court of Missouri. Before the court convened, Mrs. Emerson relinquished direct control over Dred Scott. On March 17, 1848, the sheriff of St. Louis County assumed direct custody of Dred Scott with the order to hire him out "to the best advantage during the pendency of this suit,"[103] with all payments made to the sheriff, who would account for the wages to the party that won the suit at the termination of the litigation.

The Supreme Court of Missouri convened on March 20, 1848, with Dred Scott's case being heard April 3, 1848. The issue was the decision by the lower court to grant a new trial, not whether or not Dred Scott was entitled to his freedom. Exactly one year after the first trial, June 30, 1848, the Missouri Supreme Court handed down its decision dismissing the writ of error. Dred Scott would receive his new trial.

It is noteworthy to mention that Dred Scott's case had yet to stir up any particular interest or public reaction. The only notice it did receive was a routine listing in the newspapers recounting Missouri Supreme Court cases.[104] This tends to support the theory that the case was not initially brought to support any political agenda but merely to gain the freedom of a slave and his family.

The case was not called until January 12, 1850, about a year and a half after the Missouri Supreme Court upheld Dred Scott's right to a new trial. An overloaded court docket, influential St. Louisans persuading the court to take up other litigations, a fire that ravaged a large part of the city, and cholera all contributed to the delay.[105] The faces of the attorneys had changed, but the issues were the same as from the first trial. This time, a deposition from Mrs. Russell was read into the record which stated she had hired out the Scotts from Mrs. Emerson. This time, the jury returned a verdict stating "the defendant is guilty of manner and form as in the plaintiff's declaration alleged."[106] Judge Hamilton ordered Dred Scott recover his freedom against the defendant. He was a free man, and in the law of Missouri he had been since 1833 when he first went to Fort Armstrong, as was his wife and their two daughters. And this freedom had yet to cause a stir outside of the Scott household. "So unimportant and insignificant was this case that

---

[102] Ibid., p. 48
[103] Ibid., p. 49
[104] Ibid, p. 50.
[105] Ibid., p. 51.
[106] Ibid., p. 53.

when its title was inadvertently omitted from routine newspaper listings of St. Louis court proceedings no one thought it worth the trouble even to print a correction.[107]

From all indications, it seems the *Dred Scott Case* should have ended there. It was, for the time period, a routine case of a slave seeking freedom from his owner. The owner had even ceased to have an interest in the slave, as Dred Scott had been working for hire under the sheriff's supervision since 1848 and Mrs. Emerson had even moved from St. Louis sometime in 1849 or 1850. It is surprising that her attorneys (called Hugh A. Garland and Lyman D. Norris) would first move for a new trial, and then file a bill of exceptions, thus setting the appeal procedure to the Missouri Supreme Court in motion

It is possible that Mrs. Emerson's brother, John F. A. Sanford, who had been looking after the affairs of her deceased husband's estate, was a "shrewd and prosperous" businessman who was not going to lose property and money[108] when there was a chance to retain it.[109] The attorneys could also have noted the composition of the Missouri Supreme Court had changed, with two pro-slavery justices on the bench.[110] It should be noted, though, the briefs of the lawyers still did not argue the politics of slavery, even though the issue of slavery had found its way into Missouri politics.

There was an attempt by the Missouri legislature to unseat U.S. Senator Thomas Hart Benton, a free-soil democrat who opposed proslavery resolutions introduced in the U.S. Senate by John C. Calhoun on February 19, 1847. The Missouri Legislature passed the "Jackson Resolutions" on March 6, 1849, which reaffirmed Calhoun's proslavery principles and instructed Missouri senators conform with them. On May 26, 1849, Benton declared his position for the electorate of Missouri, appealing to the people of Missouri to stand by him to maintain the Union. As noted above, two of the three Missouri Supreme Court justices were bitter political, and personal, enemies of Benton.[111]

The briefs were filed on March 8, 1850, for the regular March term of the Supreme Court. Due to an unusually heavy docket, the court was unable to take up the case during that term, however it had reached a decision by the time it convened its next term in October 1850. "Napton and Birch, both resolute anti-Benton Democrats, favored a proslavery decision overturning the previous decisions upholding the validity of the Ordinance of 1787; Ryland, on the other hand, wanted to retain the old precedents as they existed, and he was prepared to write a dissenting opinion expressing this view."[112] Despite this view, Ryland changed his mind after the court convened and agreed to concur so a unanimous decision could be delivered.

Napton was to write the decision, but he was never to do so. He sent away for Lord Stowell's *Slave Grace* case opinion, but it had not arrived when he lost his seat in

---

[107] Ibid., p. 54.

[108] All the income earned by Dred Scott since he had been in the care of the sheriff would be turned over to the winner of the case. It would be a fairly substantial sum..

[109] Ehrlich (1979: 56).

[110] William B. Napton and James H. Birch were political enemies of Senator Thomas Hart Benton, and thus held proslavery views, while John R. Fyland was pro-Benton. See Ehrlich (1979: 55).

[111] Ehrlich (1979: 58-59).

[112] Ibid., p. 60.

the August, 1851 election of judges for Missouri courts. The newly-elected Missouri
Supreme Court, again with two members committed to overthrowing precedents based
on the Ordinance of 1787, finally considered the *Dred Scott Case* November 29, 1851,
on the original written briefs resubmitted by Dred Scott's attorney. But, before the
court's opinion was prepared, Mrs. Emerson's counsel obtained permission to file a
new brief. This is significant because in his revised brief, attorney Norris raised doubts
for the first time about the applicability of the Ordinance of 1787 and the Missouri
Compromise. He also introduced racial overtones in the *Dred Scott Case*.

> Neither sound policy nor enlightened philanthropy should encourage in a Slave-
> holding State, the multiplication of a race whose condition could be neither that
> of freemen or slave [and] whose existence [and] increase in this anomalous char-
> acter, without promoting their individual comforts [and] happiness[,] tends only
> to dissatisfy and corrupt those of their own race [and] color remaining in a State
> of Servitude.[113]

With Norris' new brief added to the record, the Missouri Supreme court considered
the briefs and announced its decision March 22, 1852. In a two-to-one decision, the
Missouri Supreme Court overturned all precedents by deciding the courts of Missouri
were under no obligation to recognize the laws of any other state if they conflicted with
the laws of Missouri. While the court did not deny a slave could obtain freedom by
going into free territory, but once he returned to Missouri, he reverted to slavery under
Missouri law. The opinion of the court also seemed to succumb to the racial overtones
found in Norris' brief.

> Times now are not as they were, when the former decisions on the subject were
> made. Since then not only individuals but States have been possessed with a
> dark and fell spirit in relation to slavery, whose gratification is sought in the
> pursuit of measures whose inevitable consequence must be the overthrow and
> destruction of our government. Under such circumstances, it does not behoove
> the State of Missouri, to show the least countenance to any measure which might
> gratify this spirit. She is willing to assume her full responsibility for the existence
> of slavery within her limits, nor does she seek to share or divide it with others.
> Although we may for our own sake regret that the avarice and hardheartedness of
> the progenitors of those who are now so sensitive on the subject, ever introduced
> the institution among us, yet we will not go to them to learn law, morality or
> religion on the subject.[114]

Thus, the court declared the judgement of the lower court be reversed and the case be
remanded for a new judgment, consistent with the proceedings. While the decision was
recognized as important by some newspapers in Missouri,[115] others made no mention

---

[113] Ibid., p. 63.
[114] *Scott v. Emerson* 15 Missouri Reports 582, 586-587 (1852).
[115] Among them the St. Louis *Daily Missouri Republican*.

of it whatsoever. A Washington, D. C. paper[116] noted the decision giving bare details of the decision, but made no editorial comment regarding the case. The case had yet to become a rallying point in the controversy over slavery.

Back in St. Louis, the Circuit Court of St. Louis County received the Supreme Court decision April 10, 1852. A routine motion to turn over the proceeds of the Scotts' hire since 1848 surprisingly was overruled, on June 29 of that year. The records are silent as to why the motion was overruled until January 25, 1854, when the case was "(c)ontinued by consent, awaiting decision of the Supreme Court of the United States."[117] A new case had been instituted in the U.S. Federal courts November 2, 1853. The sheriff kept the money and the Scotts remained slaves.

The Federal Courts: *Dred Scott v. John F. A. Sanford*

Another of the Dred Scott mysteries is how and why the case was transferred to a federal action, with no one questioning John Sanford's right to act on behalf of Mrs. Emerson. While he may have acted in good faith, it appears he was never legally authorized to act on behalf of Dr. Emerson's estate. However, Sanford had moved to New York and could be brought into federal court in a diversity suit. It does appear Dred Scott's new lawyer, Roswell M. Field, had been mistakenly informed that Scott and his family had been sold to Sanford, with an agreed statement of facts averring that "shortly before the commencement of the suit Scott and his family had been 'sold [and] conveyed' to Sanford."

> But this statement was inaccurate and erroneous. The evidence is unmistakable. In the first place, the agreed statement asserted that it was Dr. Emerson who had 'sold [and] conveyed Scott to Sanford; yet Emerson had died some ten years earlier. Even more conclusive are the circumstances surrounding Scott's eventual emancipation. On May 26, 1857, two and one-half months after the Supreme Court declared him still a slave, Scott was granted his freedom by Taylor Blow, to whom the slave in the meantime had been sold — not by Sanford, but by Dr. and Mrs. Chafee. Sanford had died in New York only three weeks earlier, on May 5, 1857; but probate records of his estate in both New York and St. Louis indicate that Scott never was a part of that estate.[118]

The person who did the informing was Charles Edmund La Beaume, a brother-in-law of the Blows, and a benefactor of Dred Scott's from the beginning of the litigation in 1846. It is speculated that he perhaps declared this falsity either in an altruistic effort to gain a new trial for Dred Scott, as the state courts had already disappointed him, or in an attempt to test certain slavery principles, with Dred Scott merely being on hand to benefit possibly from the trial. The answer is not known.

Even more interesting, though, is why Sanford admitted to ownership when he could

---

[116] *Daily National Intelligencer*
[117] Ehrlich (1970: 70).
[118] Ibid., p. 75.

have terminated the litigation at its inception by showing he did not own the slave as alleged. It is suggested his failure to do so "almost *prima facie* suggests collusion."[119] Even if he allowed the case to continue to support the political interests of proslavery Democrats, of whose party he was actively involved, there was never any proof who did the "importuning" or the "badgering."[120] Thus, the case went forward.

The circuit court convened in St. Louis on April 3, 1854. In response to the charges filed against him, Sanford filed a plea in abatement denying the jurisdiction of the court. He argued Scott was not a citizen of Missouri, on account of his being a black of African descent whose ancestors were brought into the country and sold as slaves, thus there was not true diversity as the case did not involve legitimate citizens of different states. This was the first time the right of a black person to be a citizen of the United States was questioned in the *Dred Scott* case. These legal issues had to be argued before the case could proceed to a trial on the facts.

The decision by the court on April 25 recognized that while slave states disagreed with the policy of giving a free black the right to sue, it also meant that neither could he *be* sued, and thus obtained "a very substantial privilege and immunity that free white citizens did not possess." Thus, the Court held "every person born in the United States and capable of holding property was a citizen having the right to sue in the United States courts.' If Scott was free, he had the right to sue."[121] The trial had to go forward on the facts to determine if Scott were free or slave, based on his residence in free territory.

If Sanford and his attorney truly meant for the *Dred Scott* case to be a test case on the merits of the Ordinance of 1787, they would not have attempted to have the case thrown out of court for a different reason, the citizenship question. This argument "has every semblance of a genuine attempt by the defendant to avoid being sued."[122]

The case was heard on May 15, 1854, interestingly enough, *not* in the Old Court-house, as is in St. Louis. It was instead held in a private building, the Papin building, down the street because state courts had occupied all the courtrooms. Scott's lawyer, Field, requested the court to instruct the jury Scott was free by virtue of the Ordinance of 1787, the Constitution of Illinois and the Missouri Compromise. The judge refused to give such instructions, instead instructing the jury that "the law covering the facts of the case did not operate to grant the slave his freedom."[123] The judge explained to the jury that removal of the slave into Illinois only suspended slavery temporarily, and upon their returning to Missouri, the master's right to the slave was revived. He also explained the provisions in the Illinois Constitution that emancipated slaves were penal in nature against slaveholders and therefore other states, such as Missouri, did not have to enforce them. Essentially, as a U.S. court, he was following the State courts' interpretation of their own law, since the above were the reasons given by the majority in the Missouri Supreme Court.

---

[119] Ibid., p. 77.
[120] Ibid., p. 77.
[121] Ibid., p. 84.
[122] Ibid., p. 85.
[123] Ibid., p. 86.

On the basis of these instructions, the jury found in favor of defendant Sanford. After losing a motion to set aside the verdict and grant a new trail, Scott's attorney began an appeal to the Supreme Court of the United States. And still, the case merited no more mention than a brief summary in the antislavery *St. Louis Daily Morning Herald.*

The U.S. Supreme Court: First Arguments

Even while Dred Scott's case was not garnering much media attention, the opposing viewpoints on the slavery issue seemed to be growing in voice. Two weeks after the *Dred Scott* decision in St. Louis, President Franklin Pierce signed the Kansas-Nebraska Act into law, thereby repealing the slavery prohibition of the Missouri Compromise. "The sleeping tiger of sectionalism was now awake and seething with fury. The press, the pulpit, and the public forum, both North and South, raged with denunciation and defiance."[124]

The case was filed December 30, 1854, but was not heard until February of 1856 due to a crowded docket. Montgomery Blair, attorney for Dred Scott, filed a brief arguing Scott was free because Missouri precedent had previously upheld a slave's freedom based upon his residence in a free state and that the Missouri court injected then-current political views into its decision. He also addressed the jurisdictional question of whether a Negro of African descent could be a citizen of the U.S., noting the numerous suits that had been brought in federal court by and against free blacks with their status as citizens having the right to sue not being questioned. The written brief by Missouri Senator Henry S. Geyer, attorney for John Sanford, was filed, no copy is currently in existence, therefore its contents are unknown. There was also a second brief, filed by Johnson, the second attorney for Sanford.

The oral arguments, with the attorneys allotted three hours each instead of the usual two, as per the request of Johnson, began February 11, 1856. There is also no detailed record of the oral arguments, but it is assumed Blair argued the points he raised in his brief. Again, not much was written about the arguments of Geyer and Johnson, but "*(f)or the first time the* Dred Scott *case was referred to as involving the constitutionality of the Missouri Compromise,*"[125] with the attorneys arguing Dred Scott had *never* been free because Congress did not have that authority. They did acknowledge Scott's residence in the state of Illinois, arguing he could have been free in Illinois, but his slave status resumed when he returned voluntarily to Missouri.

Even with the introduction of this new argument, there was still little attention paid to the case in the Supreme Court. Major Washington papers briefly described the attorneys' arguments, with assorted papers in other states, including New York, Baltimore, and Boston, being the first newspapers outside Washington to mention the case. "All these reports were very short, mentioning only that a litigation was before the Supreme Court involving the constitutionality of the Missouri Compromise, the citizenship of blacks, and the rights of slaveholders to take their slaves into free states. There were

---

[124] Ibid., p. 89.
[125] Ibid., p. 95.

neither details nor editorial comment."[126]

The Court consulted on the case for the first time on February 22. This was the first of several consultations over the next three months, until the Court announced it had ordered the case to be reargued by counsel at the next term. While these consultations were traditionally confidential, the issued discussed seemed to make their way to the press. It appeared the main discussion centered around whether the Court should discuss the plea in abatement raised in the earlier Court. If the plea should have been sustained, the Court would not even have jurisdiction to hear the merits of the case.

There were several reasons raised as to why the Court ordered the case to be reargued. One accusation was that the judgment was being postponed for political reasons until after the 1856 presidential election. It was suggested this was part of a conspiracy to repeal the Missouri Compromise, paving the way for legalization of slavery throughout the country. Another reason, the most widely accepted, is that rearguing the case would prevent Justice McLean from "delivering a dissent that might either propel him into the Republican presidential nomination or at the very least make available authoritative judicial doctrine for the Republican campaign."[127] The final reason for the delay could simply have been a genuine desire on the part of the justices to undertake a more thorough review of the issues. The motion to reargue was approved unanimously. If McLean wished to deliver his opinion before the election, he would not have voted to delay the decision.

The decision to reargue the case still raised very little hubbub. Some newspapers mentioned it briefly in their routine summaries of action taken by the Supreme Court. Even "(the strongly antislavery Washington, D.C., *National Era* printed a small article noting the adjournment of the Supreme Court, but it made no mention of the *Dred Scott* case — and its own editor, Gamaliel Bailey, had assumed financial responsibility for the case while it was in the Supreme court."[128] The curtain had yet to fall on the final act of the *Dred Scott* case, though.)

The U.S. Supreme Court: Second Arguments

Before December 1856, and the rearguing of the *Dred Scott* case, the sectional breach between North and South grew.
On May 21, 1856, a band of proslavery 'border ruffians' virtually destroyed the city of Lawrence, center of the free-state population of Kansas Territory. The next day Representative Preston S. Brooks of South Carolina brutally assaulted Senator Charles Sumner at his seat in the United States Senate shortly after the Massachusetts abolitionist's delivery of a virulent attack on slavery. Two days later came John Brown's blood bath at Pottawotomie Creek.[129]
A presidential election also took place, with the Democrat James Buchanan carrying

---

[126] Ibid., p. 97.
[127] Ibid., p. 104.
[128] Ibid., p. 108.
[129] Ibid., p. 109.

the day. Sectionalism had quieted in the intervening period, but in his last State of the Union address on December 2, President Pierce rekindled the controversy by stating "Congress does not possess constitutional power to impose restrictions of this character [referring to the recent Kansas-Nebraska Act] upon any present or future State of the Union."[130]

On that same day, December 2, Geyer filed his brief on behalf of Sanford, devoting a considerable portion to the citizenship issue. He distinguished a slave's temporary residence in a state from a permanent one, arguing Scott was only in the free state temporarily. Geyer also argued the Missouri Compromise was unconstitutional and Dred Scott was therefore never free in the first place.

Blair, the attorney for Scott, pointed out in his supplementary brief, filed December 15, that citizenship should not even be an issue in this case, because Sanford had not appealed the action taken on the plea in abatement, instead going forward to argue the merits. Most of his brief, though, dealt with the constitutionality of the Missouri Compromise. He listed 13 acts of Congress legislating over slavery in various territories, and referenced 14 judicial decisions which recognized the constitutional right of Congress to legislate over slavery. Blair argued that the defendant's brief challenged the legality of the Missouri Compromise based on the fact that "the 1820 statute conflicted with a *state* law as interpreted by a *state* supreme court, that 'a species of property recognized in the laws of the states cannot be held in the territories'"[131] If this argument prevailed, it would allow state authority to supersede federal authority, subjecting Congress to the state legislatures.

The oral arguments were heard over four days, beginning December 15, 1856. In the end, Blair spent nearly five hours justifying the power in Congress to legislate the abolishment of slavery. He also argued the citizenship issue, stating it was not an issue in the appeal and not properly subject to review by the Court. Turning to the merits, he argued a state could, in fact, prohibit slavery and Dred Scott's residence in Illinois made him free.

George Tickner Curtis, who had joined Blair in arguing for Scott, examined the Constitution, concluding the "clear intent of the framers of the constitution was that Congress should have absolute authority over a territory while it remained in that status."[132] When the territory became a state, the state could then decide upon its local institutions, such as slavery.

Geyer, in his oral argument for Sanford, discussed the citizenship issue, arguing the court must review the plea in abatement in order to determine if it had jurisdiction. On the merits of the case, he argued the state of Illinois could legislate slavery within the state, but it had no effect on someone brought into the state who was already a slave. With regard to the Missouri Compromise, he argued Congress only had the power to institute municipal governments in a territory, preparing it for eventual statehood. There was no express grant of power in the Constitution.

---

[130] Ibid., p. 112.
[131] Ibid., p. 115.
[132] Ibid., p. 121.

Johnson, in his argument for Sanford, noted the Union's Fifth Amendment requirement to protect property rights, even if that property were a man. His argument against
the Missouri Compromise noted that in making rules and regulations for the territories, "Congress could do nothing that was detrimental either to the United States or to
any one state."[133] In legislating on slavery in the territories, it could harm either the interests of the free states or of the slave states, depending on its position; thus, it was
unconstitutional for Congress to legislate at all on this issue.

With the arguments completed, the court consulted. There was a marked difference
in public reaction this time. "In contrast with the sparse publicity before, news of the
oral arguments now was disseminated in the press throughout the country."[134] The case
was taken up by the court on February 14, with several discussions occurring before the
court came to a conclusion. Justice Nelson was to prepare the Opinion of the Court,
working under the instructions that he was "not to touch upon either the citizenship
of Negroes or the constitutionality of the Missouri Compromise, to limit his statement
very carefully to the particular circumstances of Dred Scott, and not to make any gen-
eralizations that might associate the decision with any partisan political doctrines."[135]
That decision was never finished. Three justices, McLean, Curtis and Wayne, have
been accused of causing the majority to change its attitude and discuss citizenship and
the Missouri Compromise. Another thought is that it was Wayne himself, a proslavery
Georgia Democrat, who was responsible for the reverse. There is also evidence of out-
siders exerting influence on the court to invalidate congressional prohibition of slavery
in the territories. The president-elect himself corresponded with several justices, trying to determine the outcome before his inauguration.[136] While there is no definitive
answer as to what happened, what is known is that after Nelson began to write his opinion, *"Wayne proposed that the decision should include the two vital questions Nelson
was omitting."*[137] After a brief discussion, five justices from slave states, "now decided
[they] could peacefully settle the slavery issue by declaring the Missouri Compromise
unconstitutional,"[138] with Chief Justice Taney writing the opinion.

Before the decision of the Court was handed down, James Buchanan was inaugu-
rated as president. As he pointed out in his inaugural address, the principle of popular
sovereignty, the will of the majority, had been the basis for his party's victory and his
election. Then he came to that critical point, the differences between northern and
southern views over the interpretation of that principle:

> A difference of opinion has arisen in regard to the point of time when the peo-
> ple of a Territory shall decide this question for themselves. This is, happily, of
> matter of but little practical importance. Besides, it is a judicial question, which
> legitimately belongs to the Supreme Court of the United States, before whom it

---

[133] Ibid., p. 120.
[134] Ibid., p. 122.
[135] Ibid., p. 127.
[136] Ibid., p. 128-129.
[137] Ibid., p. 129.
[138] Ibid., p. 129.

is now pending, and will, it is understood, be speedily and finally settled. To their decision, in common with all good citizens, I shall cheerfully submit, whatever this may be.[139]

Two days later, March 6, 1857, Chief Justice Taney took his seat on the bench, made a routine announcement, and then began to read the Opinion of the Court in the case of *Dred Scott v. John F. A. Sanford.* Two and one-half hours later, he was done. But did he truly speak for the majority? "Whether Roger Brooke Taney's opinion was in fact the Court's opinion has been for a long time a matter of controversy.... . Undoubtedly a majority concurred in the basic judgment that Dred Scott did not have the right to sue, and in that respect Taney did indeed speak for the court. But beyond that, Taney's colleagues differed markedly in the reasons *why* Scott could not sue, and for none of those reasons was there an indisputable concurring majority."[140]

While the Court could have avoided conflict by staying with the original Nelson opinion, once it chose to decide the matter, the outcome was likely not a great surprise to anyone at the time.[141] The court had a seven to two majority of southerners and moderate northerners. Apparently, abolitionists and the press launched their assaults before the decision was announced, anticipating the outcome. Taney's opinion, despite extensive revisions he is supposed to have made to the original oral opinion read in the Court, was blatantly racist, calling black men "beings of an inferior order" with "no rights which white men were bound to respect."

The Opinion of the Court essentially turned on the question of jurisdiction. Taney found that the African race were not intended to be granted rights and benefits in the Constitution, and thus Dred Scott was not a citizen of Missouri, and not entitled to sue in federal court. Interestingly, though, having declared the Court lacked jurisdiction, Taney proceeded to evaluate the case on its merits. While there is continuing argument over whether this evaluation was *obiter dictum,* in other words not finding on future courts, Taney stated that while the Supreme Court corrected one error of the lower court, there was nothing depriving the appellate court from further reviewing the record and correcting any material errors. Thus, the main body of his opinion dealt with the right of Congress to legislate over slavery, concluding Congress could not prohibit slavery nor pass any law depriving a citizen of the United States of his property. Therefore, Dred Scott was not a citizen both because he was black and a slave and did not have the right to sue in federal courts.

The Supreme Court and the President truly seemed to hope this decision would put a peaceable end to the slavery conflict in the United States. While it is true that sometimes authority putting the proverbial "foot down" on one side of an issue will at least cease the argument, the slow burn of the slavery issue through the years led to an emotionally-charged atmosphere in the United States in 1857 that was not going to be placated with dictates from on-high.

---

[139] Ibid., p. 133.
[140] Ibid., p. 137.
[141] Ibid., p. 140.

Both southerners and Republicans used the opinion for their own ends; the southerners as a campaign document, and the Republicans picked out the less defensible
passages for their use.[142] Though the South received the legal sanction it desired, enforcement was not so easy. It is stated many opposed war and desired compromise, "but
as the free-soil North refused to accept the dictates of the Supreme Court, so the South
would refuse to accept the results of a popular election. Defiance of law was no longer
the trademark of dissidents."[143]

Although not immediately leading to war, the *Dred Scott* decision brought the issue
of slavery to center stage in the election of 1860. One man's search for freedom for his
family became the search for freedom for thousands of men and their families. And in
the end, he lost. The Supreme Court instructed the lower court to rule against jurisdiction, thus denying Dred Scott and his family access to the courts which could set them
free. Why their owner had not set them free ten years before when she appeared to have
no interest in owning slaves is still a mystery. The footnote to the story is that after
the litigation, Taylor Blow, the son of Scott's original owner, obtained ownership of the
Scott family from their owners. He then "appeared before the Circuit Court, and formally entered the emancipation of Dred Scott, his wife, Harriet, and the children, Eliza
and Lizzie."[144] About a year after gaining his freedom, Dred Scott died on 17 September 1858. His headstone at the St. Louis Calvary Cemetery was erected almost one
hundred years later in 1957 by the descendants of Taylor Blow.[145]

2.4   Core Beliefs, Cascades and the Civil War

The publicity surrounding the Lincoln-Douglas debates in 1858 led to Lincoln's invita-
tion to New York and New Haven. In his speeches there, in February and March 1860,
he focused on the nature of the slavery compromise within the Constitution, arguing that
the Founders in 1787 had considered that slavery could be prohibited, certainly from the
Territories, by the Federal government. More importantly, the Founders marked slavery "as an evil not to be extended, but to be tolerated and protected only because of and
so far as its actual presence among us makes that toleration and protection a necessity"
(Lincoln 1989b, p. 120). Lincoln immediately went on to comment on the *Dred Scott*
decision.

Perhaps you will say the Supreme Court has decided the disputed Constitutional
question in your favor. Not quite so.... . The Court have substantially said, it is your
Constitutional right to take slaves into the federal territories, and to hold them there
as property ... . [The decision] was made in a divided Court, by a bare majority of
the Judges, and they not quite agreeing with one another in the reasons for making it

---

[142]Filler (1986: 299).
[143]Filler (1986: 299).
[144]*Frank Leslie's Illustrated Newspaper*, New York, 27 June, 1857.
[145]*Westward*, published by the Jefferson National Expansion Memorial Historical Association (Winter,
1982) Vol. 1, No. 1, p. 10.

(Lincoln, 1989b, p. 126).

In his speech in New Haven a week later, Lincoln drew the logical inference from the *Dred Scott* decision concerning the effect on free labor:

> *I am glad to see that a system of Labor prevails in New England under which laborers CAN strike when they want to* ... *I like* the system which lets a man quit when he wants to, and wish it might prevail everywhere.[146]

It is clear that Lincoln implied by this remark that it could follow on from the *Dred Scott* decision that slaves could be legitimately imported into northern free states as laborers. *Dred Scott* thus potentially threatened free labor in the North. Lincoln's speeches created a *belief cascade* among the northern electorate. It was not so much that a new issue, slavery, was created so that preferences could be manipulated, in some sense, as Riker suggested. Slavery, and the question of abolition, had always been an issue but had never provoked a significant majority in the North. Although the "fundamental" preferences of northern voters presumably may not have changed, we can infer that the beliefs of a significant majority in the North did change, as it became plausible that free labor could be seriously affected by the consequences of the *Dred Scott* decision. Let us call this the *Dred Scott* belief. As a consequence of the prevalence of this belief in the North, Lincoln was nominated by the Republican Party and eventually won a majority of the electoral college votes.

Since an unbeaten outcome (under a voting rule) is usually called a "core," we shall be consistent with this terminology in referring to the Dred Scott belief as a "core belief" in the northern electorate.[147]

We suggest that this core belief came into being rapidly in the northern electorate, through this "belief cascade" triggered by Lincoln's speeches.[148] Lincoln became an "Architect of Political Change," in the sense that, through his acts, the canker of the slavery compromise was eventually eliminated from the way the Constitution was understood.

To oversimplify, to some extent, in the northern electorate there were two beliefs: q (the *Dred Scott* belief that the South intended to extend slavery) and $(1 - q)$ (it did not intend this threat). Obviously these are belief probabilities, and these will vary in the population. Electing Lincoln can be assumed to lead to secession, and Civil War, with some probability (r). The cost of this is enormous (C). With some probability (p), the North will lose, and with probability $(1 - p)$ it will win and prevent the expansion of

---

[146]Fehrenbacher (1989b: 144).

[147]It is appropriate at this point to spell out how game theorists understand the differences between preferences and beliefs. The most abstract approach is presented in Leonard Savage (1954). Fundamental preferences are the primitive parameters. In choosing between lotteries of outcomes an individual reveals beliefs about the world, the subjective probabilities of events. Given these beliefs the individual chooses acts that are rational *vis-à-vis* the fundamental preferences. In most cases, however, the fundamental preferences cannot be deduced from acts, unless there is a technique of also deducing beliefs. If beliefs change, then rational acts change.

[148]The idea of a belief cascade transforming a constitution is developed in Schofield (2006a). These work build on earlier ideas of Bikchandani, *et al.* (1992), Denzau and North (1994) and Lohmann (1994).

slavery. It is clear that only if the probable cost (say S) to the North of the extension of slavery is also enormous, does it make sense to choose Lincoln. It is also obvious that any behavior by the South to increase q or S will increase the probability of war. The same is true if there are reasons to believe that the cost of the war is low, or the probability of winning is high. The obvious point is that a "tipping" can occur so that "aggressive" acts by one side can provoke rational changes in belief by the other, making war more likely. For such an analysis to make sense, however, it is necessary that the beliefs (particularly q) and the estimated costs (C and S) have some "rational" basis in credibility. The arguments by Lincoln in 1860 were clearly designed to justify the *Dred Scott* belief.

One aspect of the formation by November 1860 of this "core belief" is that it is resolved what may be considered to be a "constitutional quandary" — a state of extreme uncertainty, in both northern and southern electorates. The nature of this quandary can be understood by considering again the process of selection of the Democrats and Republican candidates in early 1860.

As mentioned above, the Democrat nominating convention met in April 23, 1860, in Charleston. The first controversy was generated by a letter from the southerner, Jefferson Davis, withdrawing his name from the list of candidates, and advising the Mississippi delegation to withdraw from the Convention if Stephen Douglas were nominated. By April 30, the convention had adopted a platform that included the declaration "that the Democratic Party will abide by the decision of the Supreme Court of the United States over the institution of slavery in the Territories." A resolution "that the rights of citizens in property of persons (namely slaves) must be protected in the Territories by the Federal Authorities" had been rejected. The delegates from eight slave states (controlling 37.5 votes) retired from the Convention in protest. This "southern" convention passed its own pro-slavery resolutions, as well as one favoring the acquisition of Cuba. As the *New York Times* (May 4, 1860) commented, "the contest between the two sections of the Union has at last penetrated the Democratic party and rendered it impossible for the two wings to agree upon a declaration of principles." The remaining delegates resolved that a vote of two-thirds (of the whole original number) should be essential to a nomination. On May 1, the first ballot gave Douglas 145.5 votes out of 252 of the remaining delegates.[149] By the 55th ballot the next day the total for Douglas had increased to 151.5 (a majority of the whole Convention) but not a two-thirds majority. Delegates from states as different as California, Tennessee, Missouri, Virginia, Oregon and Minnesota still refused to vote for Douglas. By 148 to 100 the convention voted to adjourn. The Douglas delegates tried an amendment to meet in Baltimore on 1 June, but this was defeated. As the *New York Times* editorial commented, "The South believes sincerely that the North seeks power in order to crush slavery ... ." but it must instead "make up its mind to lose the sway it has exercised so long."

Just as it was expected that Douglas would win the Democratic nomination, so was William Seward expected to win the Republican nomination in Chicago in May. On

---

[149]Fractional delegate votes were possible then as they are now.

May 17, prior to nomination, the party had adopted a platform of seventeen planks. The second plank argued for the maintenance of the Union, as bound by the principles of the Declaration of Independence and the Federal Constitution. The eighth denied "the authority of Congress, or a Territorial Legislature – to give legal existence to Slavery in any Territory of the United States." The twelfth argued for an increase in the tariff "to encourage the development of the industrial interests of the whole country" and to secure "to the workingman, to mechanics and manufacturers an adequate reward for their skill, labor and enterprise." The thirteenth demand "the passage by Congress of the complete and satisfactory Homestead measure ... ." The sixteenth asserted that "a railroad to the Pacific Ocean is imperatively demanded by the interests of the whole country." In line with Figure 1.7 in Chapter 1, this Republican platform is consistent with a moderate protectionist policy for both labor and capital, while stressing the expansion of free labor to the west.

On May 18, the first ballot gave Seward 173.5 to Lincoln's 102 (out of a total of 465). Nearly 190 delegate votes were split between 10 other candidates. On the second ballot the scattered votes dropped to 100, while Seward and Lincoln took 184.5 and 181 respectively. On the third ballot enough delegates from Massachusetts, Ohio and Oregon switched to Lincoln to give him 230.5 votes. Finally 4 delegates from Massachusetts chose Lincoln, giving him first a majority and, eventually, the unanimous vote.

It is obvious from these brief descriptions that the Republican party was united behind Lincoln, but that the southern radical wing of the Democrats was intent, in all probability, with secession. The election of Bell or Douglas in November 1860 might have moderated the probability of secession but would have left the North open to the threat of the extension of slavery. The consequence of election of Lincoln, while almost certainly resulting in southern secession, depended on Lincoln's response to secession. After Lincoln's speech accepting the Republican nomination on May 19, 1860, he made no public comment, except for a brief remark at a rally in August. Because Lincoln kept his own council, the northern electorate could plausibly infer that Lincoln's election, leading to southern secession, would remove the southern threat. The cost of this would, of course, be economic dislocation. However, with some probability Lincoln would deny the legal justification for southern secession. Whether or not the North would accept Lincoln's argument depended on the moral and political basis for the maintenance of the Union. It is to this that we now turn.

The response of the South to Lincoln's election in November, 1860, was to some degree summed up by James Buchanan, the outgoing Democrat President, in his annual message to Congress on December 3, 1860.

> The long continued and intemperate interference of the northern people with the question of slavery in the southern States has at last produced its natural effects. The different sections of the Union are now arrayed against each other and the

time has arrived . . . when hostile geographical parties have been formed.[150]

Lincoln had well understood this perception by the South. At his speech at the Cooper Institute on February 27, 1860, he had said

> . . . what will satisfy [the South]? We must not only let them alone, but we must, somehow, convince them that we do let them alone . . . . [We must] cease to call slavery *wrong*, and join [the South] in calling it *right* . . . and this must be done in *acts* as well as *words* . . . . We must pull down our Free State . . . constitutions[151]

Shortly after Buchanan's speech the South Carolina state convention on December 20 declared that the state was no longer part of the Union. On January 9, 1861, South Carolina troops fixed on a vessel carrying reinforcements to Fort Sumter.

The Crittendon Resolutions of January 16, 1861, were an attempt by Congress to provide a compromise advantageous to the South. The first resolution proposed the extension of the Missouri Compromise line (36 deg 30′) to the Pacific. In all territories north of this line, slavery was to be prohibited, while to the South, slavery was to be recognized without interference by Congress. The sixth resolution corresponded to one of the planks of the Republican party platform, guaranteeing "that no amendment shall be made to the constitution which shall authorize or give to Congress any power to interfere with slavery in any of the States by whose laws it . . . is allowed."[152]

Lincoln rejected this effort at compromise. In a letter to William Seward on February 1, 1861, Lincoln declared "I am inflexible. I am for no compromise which *assists* or *permits* the extension of the institution [of slavery] on soil owned by the nation" [Lincoln 1989b, 197]. The constitutional quandary that now faced the nation was over the understanding of the nature of Union. The declaration of secession by South Carolina implicitly asserted that the logic of Union depended on Madison's argument in *Federalist 10*. Madison had proposed that the extended republic made the formation of a tyrannical majority unlikely. According to the secessionist argument, the disagreement over slavery had destroyed the heterogeneity of the republic, creating a tyrannical northern majority. The object of the Constitution was to restrain such a majority, and it had failed. Thus could be reasserted "the right of a people to abolish a government when it becomes destructive of the ends for which it was instituted."[153]

In his discussion of the Articles of Confederation in *Federalist 43*, Madison argued "that a breach by either of the parties [to a compact between independent sovereigns or states] absolves the other, and authorizes them if they please, to pronounce the treaty violated and void."[154] However, Madison also noted in *Federalist 43* that "[A]mong the advantages of a confederate republic, . . . an important one is . . . that should a popular

---

[150] Jaffa (2000: 170), quoting from Buchanan (1960)
[151] Fehrenbacher (1989b: 128-9).
[152] Quoted in Jaffa (2000: 244).
[153] Quoted in Jaffa (2000: 231).
[154] Madison in Rakove (1999: 251).

insurrection happen in one of the states, the others are able to quell it."[155]

The South essentially asserted the Calhoun doctrine that the Union was created through the ratification of the Constitution in 1787-8. As such, it was a compact between independent states, and these states had the right to secede when the basis for the compact was destroyed. In Lincoln's inaugural address on March 4, 1861, he denied this logic.

> The Union is much older than the Constitution. It was formed in fact, by the Articles of Association in 1774. It was matured and continued by the Declaration of Independence in 1776. It was further matured and the faith of all the then thirteen States expressly plighted and engaged that it should be perpetual, by the Articles of Confederation of 1778. And finally, in 1787, one of the declared objects for ordaining and establishing the Constitution was *"to form a more perfect union."*[156]

For Lincoln southern secession was nothing more than an insurrection. As Jaffa (2000:193) notes, Lincoln's constitutional argument had a foundation in the agreement made in February 1825 between Madison and Jefferson about the fundamental principles and documents of the Union. As Madison wrote

> [O]n the distinctive principles of the government of our own state, and that of the United States, the best guides are to be found in
>
> 1. The Declaration of Independence as the fundamental act of Union of these States.
> 2. the book known by the title of the "Federalist" [157]

Lincoln closed his inaugural speech with a call for peace.

> We are not enemies, but friends ... . Though passion may have strained, it must not break our bonds of affection.[158]

Nonetheless, the speech was interpreted by the people of the Confederate states to mean that war was inevitable.[159] The secession of the Confederate states justified the formation of a second core belief in the northern states that the southern acts were not constitutional, but insurrectionary. Thus the belief cascade, triggered by the *Dred Scott* decision in 1857, led to two distinct and incompatible beliefs in the North and South over the constitutional basis for the Union.

---

[155] Madison in Rakove (1999: 249).
[156] Fehrenbacher (1989b: 217-8).
[157] Madison in Rakove (1999: 809).
[158] Fehrenbacher (1989b: 224).
[159] Donald, 1995: 284).

Chapter 3

Politics in the United States

3.1 Elections and Realignments

Note[160]

"This referendum has the potential to rip our party apart," said Missouri Republican Kenny Hulshof, speaking of a ballot measure that would constitutionally guarantee the right to conduct stem cell research.[161] The measure is strongly supported by the leading businesses and by their pro-business Republican allies. However, it is even more vehemently opposed by the social conservative wing of the Missouri Republican party, who regard stem cell research as tantamount to abortion.

Is this issue just a flash in the pan, or does it have long-term implications for the evolving identity of both the Republican and Democratic parties? Miller and Schofield (2003, 2008) have argued that the two-dimensional nature of American politics guarantees long-run instability in the U.S. party system. Any given winning coalitional basis for a party must inevitably generate possibilities for the losers, by appealing to pivotal groups on one dimension or another.

Americans have strong feelings about economic ideology—favorable toward business or else favorable toward the use of governmental power to shield consumers and labor from the market risks of monopoly, shoddy consumer products, and environmental degradation. While the particular issues on the agenda may vary, the shared ideological dimension allows for a degree of structure and predictability in policy. Knowing that a voter is a member of a labor union or an executive of a Fortune 500 company allows one to predict that voter's position on a consumer protection bill or a trade treaty. However, it does not necessarily allow one to predict that same voter's feelings about social policies—race, abortion, prayer in schools, or other traditional issues.

The independence of electoral perceptions on the policy dimensions is illustrated by the analysis of Schofield, Miller and Martin (2003) who examined National Election Survey Data for the U.S. elections of 1964 and 1980 and used factor analysis to

---

[160]This chapter is partly based on Miller and Schofield (2003, 2008) and Schofield and Miller (2007).
[161]*New York Times* (12 March 2006).

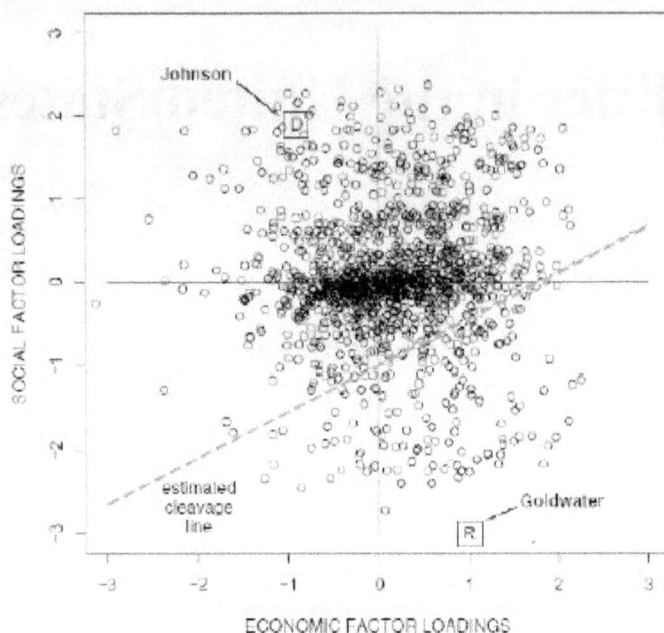

Figure 3.1: The Election of 1964

produce two policy dimensions, one economic and one social.

The points in Figure 3.1 for 1964 represent the ideal or most preferred points of the citizens who undertook the survey, while the candidate positions were obtained by maximum likelihood estimation, given the information from the survey about voter intentions. This analysis merely confirmed the previous results of Poole and Rosenthal (1984) on U.S. Presidential elections. Poole and Rosenthal noted that there was no evidence of convergence to an electoral center, as suggested by the "mean voter theorem."[162] Notice that the voter distribution in Figure 3.1 is essentially normal, with little correlation between the two axes. This implies that these two dimensions of policy are statistically independent. A further finding of Poole and Rosenthal was that the statistical model was enhanced when intercept terms were added to the voter model. Schofield, Miller and Martin argued that these intercept terms be interpreted as *valence*,

---

[162]Hinich (1977).

as proposed by Stokes[163] where the valence of a candidate should be regarded as the non-policy innate attractiveness or *quality* of the candidate, as judged by the average member of the electorate.[164]

A recent formal analysis of the stochastic electoral model has suggested why convergence to an electoral origin will generally not occur. Because voter behavior is probabilistic, Schofield (2007) supposed that candidates adopt policy positions so as to maximize their *expected vote share*. In fact, because a candidate's optimal position will depend on the opponent's position, it is necessary to use the concept of *Nash equilibrium*.[165] When the valence difference between the candidates is significant, then the lowest valence candidate, in equilibrium, must move away from the electoral origin in order to be positioned at an equilibrium, vote maximizing position.[166] In response, the higher valence candidate will adopt a position opposite the lower valence candidate. In Figure 3.1, the *estimated cleavage line* shows the set of voters who are indifferent between Johnson and Goldwater. This line goes through Goldwater's side of the origin, suggesting that Johnson not only had a higher valence than Goldwater, but had captured the center. The figure illustrates the theorem, since it is evident that neither candidate converged to the electoral center.

However, while this formal model provides some theoretical reason why candidates adopt opposed positions, it does not fully specify the equilibrium positions, other than requiring that they belong to a one dimensional domain. While it was once possible to speak one dimensionally, of conservative and liberal candidates, it is now necessary to speak of social liberals, economic liberals, social conservatives and economic conservatives, reflecting the fundamental fact that there are actually four quadrants of the policy space, as in Figure 3.2.

Schofield (2006b) also extended the suggestions of Miller and Schofield by proposing a model that endogenizes that component of valence that is affected by activist support. The model makes use of the fundamental two-dimensionality of the policy space. First, as argued by Miller and Schofield, economic conservatives, at E in Figure 3.2, and social conservatives, at C, both have an incentive to provide resources to a Republican candidate. The *contract curve* between E and C is the set of bargains that economic and social conservative activists may negotiate, over the provision of resources to the Republican candidate. Thus there will be some point on this curve that maximizes the resources available to the Republican candidate, for use in an election effort. These resources enhance that component of valence that the candidate can influence through the

---

[163] Stokes (1963, 1992).

[164] Stokes (1963: 373) used the term *valence issues* to refer to those that "involve the linking of the parties with some condition that is positively or negatively valued by the electorate." Stokes observation is validated by recent empirical work on many polities, as well as a study on the psychology of voting by Westen (2007).

[165] A Nash equilibrium is a set of party positions so that no party may unilaterally change position to gain an advantage.

[166] Schofield (2007) showed that convergence to the electoral center will occur in equilibrium only if a certain convergence coefficient, c, is bounded above by the dimension of the policy space. As discussed in Chapter 1, and later in this chapter, for a large enough valence difference, c will exceed the dimension of the policy space, and then convergence, in equilibrium, *cannot* occur.

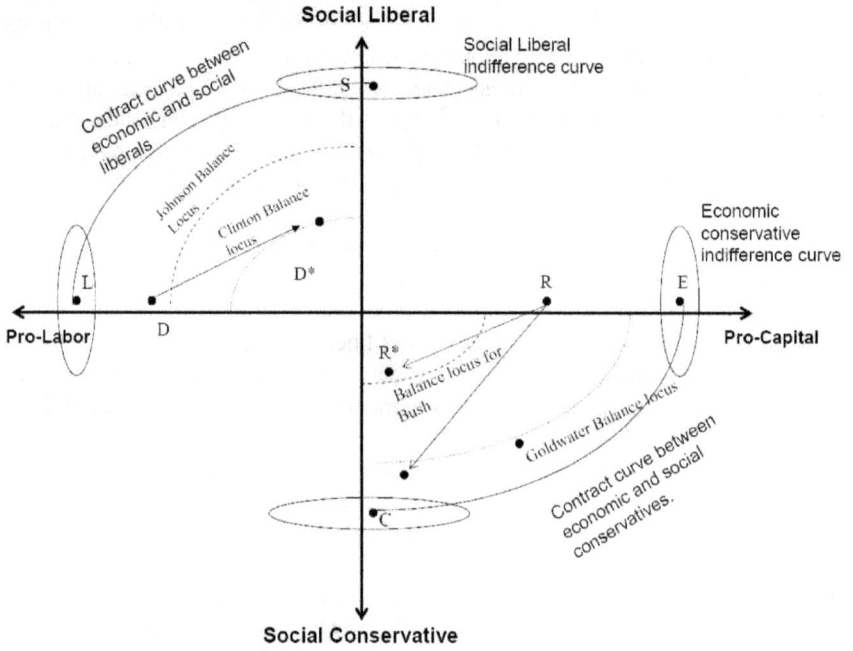

Figure 3.2: Activists in the US

media. This model is based on the presumption that candidates can affect the perceptions of the electorate, by using resources appropriately, either to attack the opponent,
or to appeal to the electorate.[167]

However, the point that maximizes a Republican candidate's resources will not be
the best response to whatever position the Democrat candidate adopts. In general, activists desire policies that are far from the electoral center. Schofield (2006b) obtained
the first order condition for a local Nash equilibrium to this vote-share maximizing
game. This can be expressed as a balance condition for each candidate, where the gradients generated by the various potential activist groups are balanced by an *electoral
pull*. The electoral pull is a gradient that points towards a *weighted electoral mean* for
the candidate. Figure 3.3 presents this balance condition for a Republican candidate
negotiating between two activist groups at R and C. The balance locus is the set of optimal positions of the candidate. The precise equilibrium position, denoted $z_1^*(z_2)$ in
Figure 3.3, will depend on the utility functions of the activist groups, as well as their
resources, and the positions and preferences of the Democrat candidate and supporting
activist groups.[168]

For example, if the innate, or exogenous, valence of a Republican candidate is low
in contrast to an opponent, then the weighted electoral mean of this candidate will be far
from the electoral origin. This implies that the activist effect will be more significant,
and the balance locus for the candidate will be relatively far from the origin. Figure 3.2
uses this idea to suggest that the Goldwater balance locus in the 1964 election was far
from the electoral origin, in contrast to the balance locus of Johnson, with his relatively
high exogenous valence. The intuition behind this idea is that when the intrinsic, or
exogenous, valence of a candidate is high, then the influence and effect of activists will
be low, and vice versa.

The long term consequence of both exogenous and activist valence on U.S. politics
has been to generate a slow realignment of the party positions. As Figure 3.4 suggests,
by 1896, the Republican Party had slowly moved from a Civil War position, similar
to S in Figure 3.2, to a pro-business position, denoted McKinley in Figure 3.4. It can
be argued that Republican candidates adopted a position close to R (in Figure 3.2),
throughout the period from McKinley to Eisenhower. By 1896, the Democrat Party had
moved from its Civil War position at C, to the populist position denoted Bryan (in Figure
3.4). As Figure 3.5 suggests, by the time of the election of F. D. Roosevelt in 1932, the
party had moved to the position marked FDR (in Figure 3.5). The two realignments of
1896 and 1932 were discussed in the classic paper by Key (1955).

In recent elections, Democrat candidates have adopted various positions in the upper left hand quadrant of Figure 3.2, while Republicans have adopted positions in the
lower right hand quadrant. The actual positioning, according to the model, will depend on a circumferential, or centrifugal effect, generated by the activist contributions,
and a radial, or centripetal effect, generated by the electoral pull. Equilibrium positions

---

[167] Schofield (2006b) extended an earlier model of activism originally proposed by Aldridge (1983a,b).

[168] The point denoted $z_1^*(z_2)$ in Figure 3.3 is the local best response by candidate 1 to the position, z_2,
adopted by candidate 2.

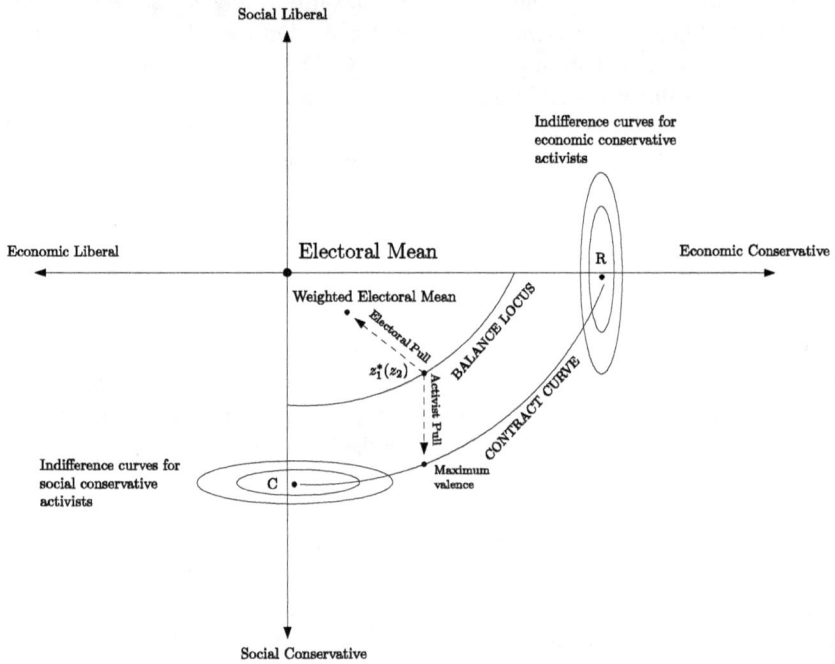

Figure 3.3: The balance locus in the conservative quadrant

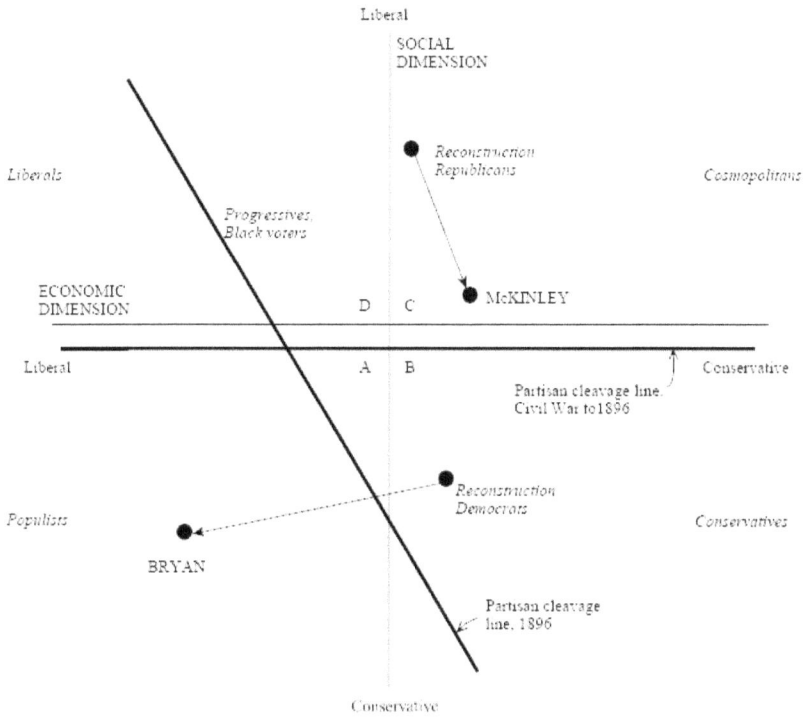

Figure 3.4: Positions of presidential candidates in 1896

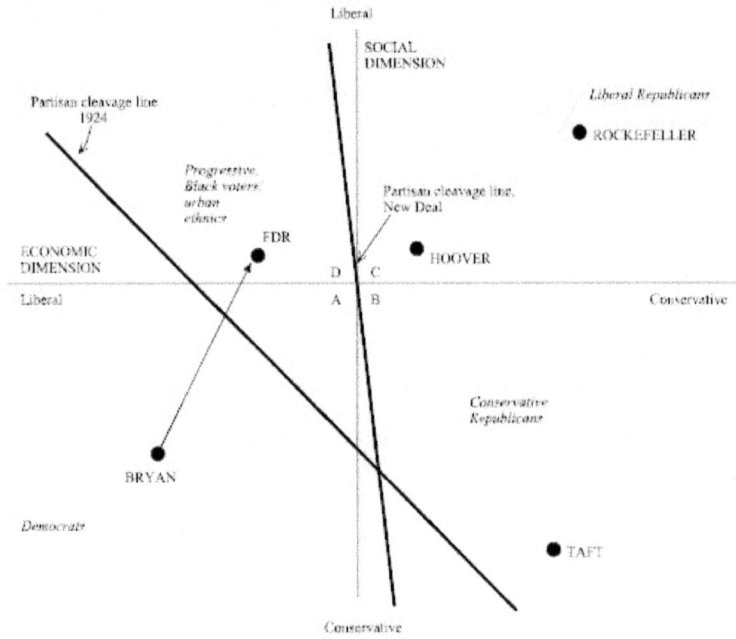

Figure 3.5: Positions of presidential candidates in 1932

will then depend in a complex way on the relative intrinsic valences of the candidates, and the motivations and resources of activists. In Figures 3.2 and 3.3, the activists are represented somewhat simply by points such as S, L, C and E, and by the ratios of saliences (the eccentricity of the "ellipsoidal" utility functions of activists).[169] Saliences can change over time, thus affecting the contract curves.

Table 3.1. (Smith 2005: Tables 11, 12).
Percent Voting for Democratic Congressional Candidates

Low Income Moral Traditionalists		High Income Social Liberals
1972-1980	63%	46%
1982-1990	55%	55%
1992-2000	29%	65%

Definitions
Low-income is defined as 16th percentile or below in annual income.
High-income is defined as 68% percentile or above in annual income
Moral traditionalist opposed abortion under any circumstances.
Social liberals support reproductive rights under any circumstances.

The two factors, social and economic, shown in Figures 3.2 and 3.3 appear to be a robust fact of U.S. politics, and that this has a profound effect on elections. Table 3.1 suggests that "Low Income Moral Traditionalists" (voters with preferred points in the lower left, "populist" quadrant of Figure 3.2) have tended to change their allegiance from Democrat to Republican, while "High Income Social Liberals" (in the upper right "cosmopolitan" quadrant) have switched in the opposite direction. One inference is that this is the result of party re-positioning. Of course, the sub-components that make up these two fundamental factors may slowly change with time, as a result of social events. For example, it is quite obvious that the attitudes with regard to "War against Terror" has become a significant component of the social factor. However, a change in such a sub-component cannot change the factor completely.

A theme of this chapter is that the slow transformation of the component sub-factors has led to a fragmentation of the potential activist groups for both parties. For convenience we can identify some activist groups with key political figures like Hilary Clinton, Edwards, Obama, McCain, Giuliani, Huckabee and Thompson. Figure 3.6 gives a suggestion of the positions of the potential Presidential candidates for 2008, indicating how heterogeneous is the set of their supporting activist coalitions. Note in particular that Huckabee is estimated to have adopted a fairly "populist" policy position, while Giuliani was initially in the "cosmopolitan quadrant."[170]

Obviously there is a link between the campaign expenditures of the candidates and the electoral popularity. This relationship is shown in Figures 3.7 and 3.8.[171]

---

[169] Miller and Schofield (2003) showed that these salience ratios generate the curvature of the contract curves, or *catenaries*, associated with the two candidates.

[170] As observed in the *New York Times* (December 30, 2007). However, Giuliani moved south into the conservative quadrant during the primaries in 2008.

[171] Figures 3.6, 3.7 and 3.8 are based on research by Evan Schnidman.

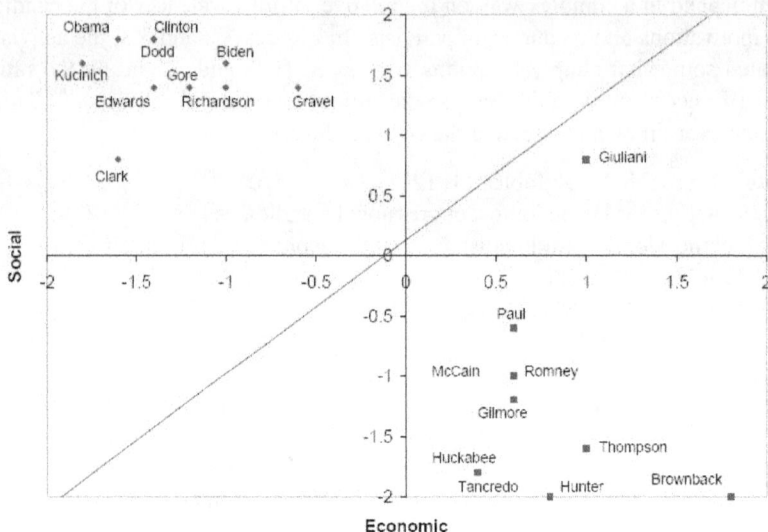

Figure 3.6: Estimated positions of U.S. Presidential candidates for 2008

Estimating the residuals between the linear regression line and the popularity level gives a way of obtaining the intrinsic valences of the various candidates. The figures suggest that Huckabee and McCain (among the Republicans) had relatively high valences, while the contest between Clinton and Obama would depend on their activist contributions.On 3 January, 2007, Huckabee won the Iowa Republican caucus while Obama won the Democrat caucus (with 38% to Clinton's 29%). In the New Hampshire primary a few days later, Clinton was the Democrat winner with 39% to Obama's 36%. After "Super Tuesday" on February 5, and the various contests leading to Pennsylvania on April 22, Clinton and Obama had won 1245 and 1310 delegates, respectively, while McCain dominated with 1162 delegates to Huckabee's 262 and Romney's 142. On May 6, Obama won North Carolina by 56% to 44%, while Clinton only just won Indiana. Although Clinton won Kentucky and North Virginia, Obama's win in Oregon kept him in the lead, so that, by May 22, the delegate totals were 1476 for Obama and 1415 for Clinton. Although Clinton won Puerto Rico on June 1, the counts after Montana and South Dakota on June 3 were 1640 for Clinton and 1764 for Obama, and Obama was declared the Democratic nominee.[172]

---

[172]The Republican Party used a "first past the post" or plurality selection rule for delegates, whereas the Democrat party uses a proportional rule. This accounts for McCain's lead, while neither Clinton nor Obama dominated in the early stages of the delegate race in eterms of delegates. It is plausible that the Republican plurality rule caused activist groups to coalesce round McCain early in the Republican primary race.

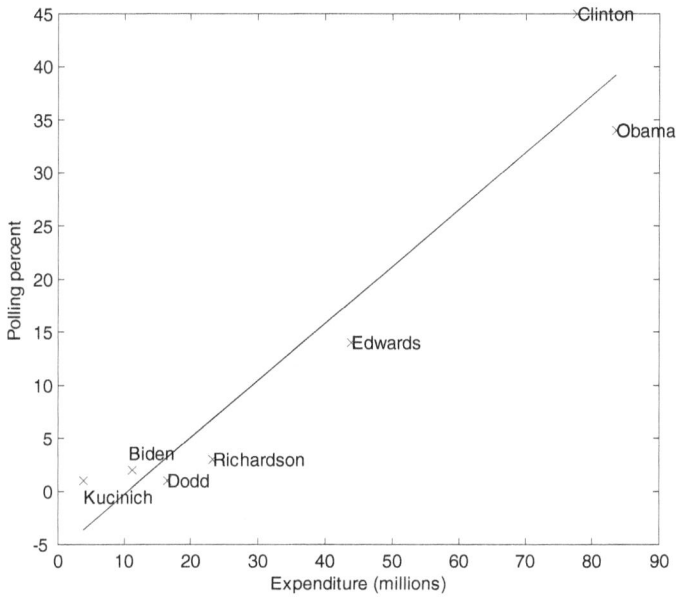

Figure 3.7: Democrat candidate spending and popularity, January 2008

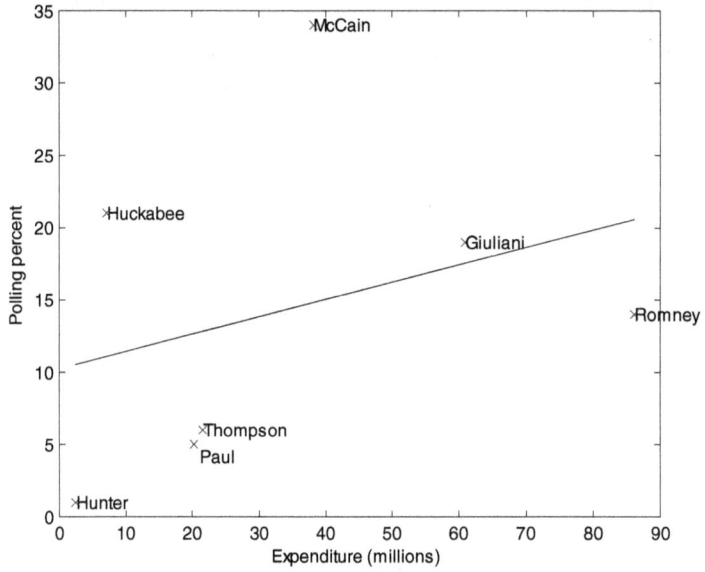

Figure 3.8: Republican candidate spending and popularity, January 2008

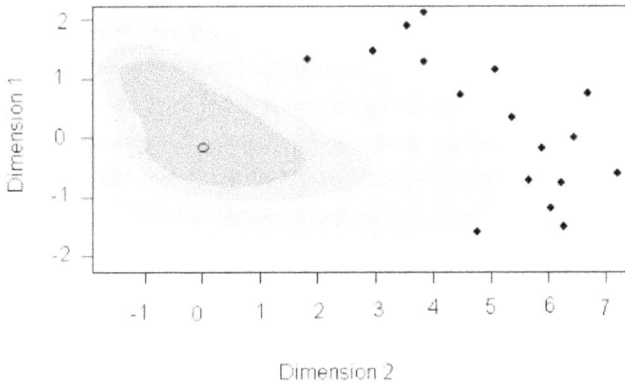

Figure 3.9: The Estimated Voter Distribution in Massachusetts

During the race, Clinton raised about $194 million ($120,000/delegate), Obama $240 million ($140,000/delegate), McCain $66 million ($57,000/delegate) and Huckabee $16 million ($69,000/delegate. Finally Paul gained 5 delegates for $34 million, Giuliani spent $65 million for nothing, and Romney spent $110 million ($612,000/delegate). Both Romney and Giuliani left the race after February 6th, while Huckabee conceded after McCain's successes on March 4. These expenditure/delegate figures give a fairly clear indication of the contenders' intrinsic valences. It was noticeable that Obama was highly successful at raising small contributions through his website.

Secondly, there is the fundamental fact of the federal nature of the United States. The electorate in each state must surely be very different in the way policies are interpreted, and candidates evaluated. Just as an indication, Figures 3.9 and 3.10 show estimates of the sample electoral distribution in Massachusetts and Texas. (For convenience of presentation the figures are rotated, so dimension 1 is the economic axis and dimension 2 is the social axis.) Clearly the distribution in Massachusetts is much more liberal on the social axis, than in Texas, while the distribution on the economic axis appears more conservative in Massachusetts than in Texas.[173]

These various figures are intended as an indication of the complexities of U.S. politics. As Figures 3.1 and 3.2 indicate, to win it is necessary to create a coalition of activists who may very well be enemies in some policy domains, but who may be able to agree to disagree on one dimension in order to prevail on the other. As saliences have diverged within the two classes of activist groups, the groups have become more het-

---

[173]These distributions are obtained from survey samples, based on research by Guido Cataife. The mean of each of the national electoral distributions on each axis is set at 0, but the same scale is used on each axis in the various states. Note the long tail of socially liberal voters in Massachusetts.

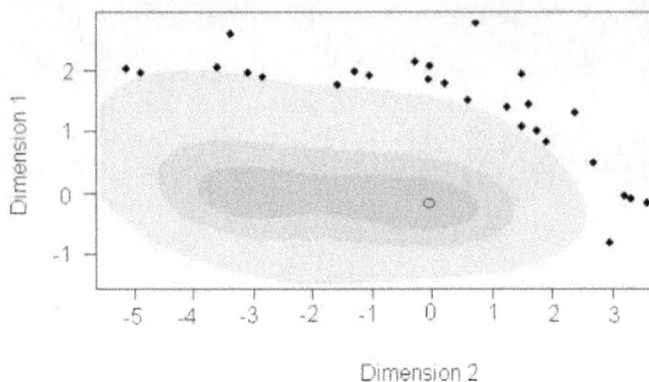

Figure 3.10: The Estimated Voter Distribution in Texas

erogeneous and fragmented. The fact that the electoral distribution has come to vary dramatically in various parts of the country means that activist coalitions, ostensibly in support of one of the parties in one region, may conflict with activist groups for the same party, but in a different region. Indeed, the changing frontiers between the preferred points of activist party coalitions may cause activist groups to change their affiliation. Because of the plurality nature of presidential and Congressional elections, activist coalitions must be aware that fragmentation creates losers. Thus there is a permanent tension between the desire to influence policy, and the winning of elections.

This potential conflict between activist coalitions was recently given expression by John Danforth, a long-standing traditional Republican:

> When government becomes the means of carrying out a religious program, it raises obvious questions under the First Amendment. Take stem cell research. Criminalizing the work of scientists doing such research would give strong support to one religious doctrine, and it would punish people who believe it is their religious duty to use science to heal the sick ... As a senator, I worried every day about the size of the federal deficit. I did not spend a single minute worrying about the effect of gays on the institution of marriage. Today it seems to be the other way around... Our current fixation on a religious agenda has turned us in the wrong direction. It is time for Republicans to rediscover our roots.[174]

This tension provides the energy that drives the constant transformation of politics in the United States. For example, Figure 3.11 suggests that Cosmopolitan states like

---

[174]Danforth (2005)

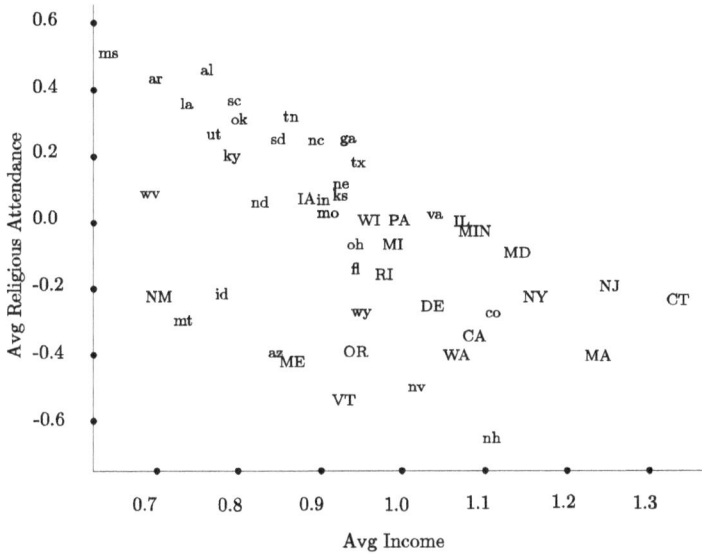

Figure 3.11: Relationship between average income and average religious attendance by state (States that voted Democrat are capitalized, states that voted Republican are lower case)

Connecticut and New Jersey form the base of the Democratic Party while poor, religious states like Mississippi form the base of the Republican Party. These affiliations change with time, as a result of irregular realignments. (See Bartels, 2006, 2008; Merrill, Grofman and Brunell, 2008.)

One major area of policy conflict lies in immigration reform. As Table 3.2 shows, in the Senate on 18 July 2006, 32 Republicans voted against reform, while 23 pro-business Republicans voted yea. Almost all Democraic Senators voted for reform, as a matter of civil rights, but 4 Democrats voted nay, presumably out of fear that immigration would put downward pressure on wages.

Table 3.2. Votes of Democrat and Republican senators on immigration reform

	Democrats		Republicans
Yea	Akaka-HI	Lautenberg NJ	Bennett UT
	Baucus MT	Leahy VT	Brownback KS
	Bayh IN	Levin MI	Chafee RI
	Biden DE	Lieberman CT	Coleman MN
	Bingaman NM	Lincoln AR	Collins ME
	Boxer CA	Menendez NJ	Craig ID
	Cantwell WA	Mikulski MD	DeWine OH
	Carper DE	Murray WA	Domenici NM
	Clinton NY	Nelson FL	Frist TN
	Conrad ND	Obama IL	Graham SC
	Dayton MN	Pryor AR	Gregg NH
	Dodd CT	Reed RI	Hagel NE
	Durbin IL	Reid NV	Lugar IN
	Feingold WI	Sarbanes MD	Martinez FL
	Feinstein CA	Schumer NY	McCain AZ
	Harkin IA	Wyden OR	McConnell KY
	Inouye HI		Murkowski AK
	Jeffords VT		Smith OR
	Johnson SD		Snowe ME
	Kennedy MA		Specter PA
	Kerry MA		Stevens AK
	Kohl WI		Voinovich OH
	Landrieu LA		Warner VA
Total		39	23

	Democrats	Republicans	
Nay	Byrd WV	Alexander TN	Lott MS
	Dorgan ND	Allard CO	Roberts KS
	Stabenow MI	Allen VA	Santorum PA
	Nelson NE	Bond MO	Sessions AL
		Bunning KY	Shelby AL
		Burns MT	Sununu NH
		Burr NC	Talent MO
		Chambliss GA	Thomas WY
		Coburn OK	Thune SD
		Cochran MS	Vitter LA
		Cornyn TX	
		Crapo ID	
		DeMint SC	
		Dole NC	
		Ensign NV	
		Enzi WY	
		Grassley IA	
		Hatch UT	
		Hutchison TX	
		Inhofe OK	
		Isakson GA	
		Kyl AZ	
Total	4	32	

3.2   The Contest between Competing Interests

Many spatial models of elections predict that parties will converge to the center of the electoral distribution.[175] These predictions as regards convergence are at odds with the empirical work presented in Figures 1.4, 3.1, 3.6, as well as the earlier work by Poole and Rosenthal (1984).

The key idea of this chapter is that the convergence result need not hold if there is an asymmetry in the electoral perception of the "quality" of party leaders (Stokes, 1992). The average weight given to the perceived quality of the leader of the jth party is called the party's *valence*. In empirical models, a party's valence is usually assumed to be independent of the party's position, and adds to the statistical significance of the model. In general, valence reflects the overall degree to which the party is perceived to have shown itself able to govern effectively in the past or is likely to be able to govern well in the future (Penn,2009). This chapter offers a general model of elections based on the assumption that there are two kinds of valence. As intimated in Chapter 1, the first kind is a fixed or *exogenous valence*, which for a party. j is denoted λ_j. As in empirical work, we assume that λ_j is held constant at the time of an election, and so is independent of the party's position. The second kind of valence is known as *activist valence*. When party j adopts a policy position z_j, then the activist valence of the party is denoted $\mu_j(z_j)$. Implicitly we adopt a model originally due to Aldrich (1983a,b, 1995) and Aldrich and McGinnis (1989). In this model, activists provide crucial resources of time and money to their chosen party. The party then uses these resources to enhance its image before the electorate, thus affecting its valence. Although activist valence is affected by party position, it does not operate in the usual way by influencing voter choice through the distance between a voter's preferred policy position, say x_i, and the party position. Rather, as party j's activist support, $\mu_j(z_j)$, increases due to increased contributions to the party in contrast to the support $\mu_k(z_k)$ received by party k, then (in the model) all voters become more likely to support party j over party k. The problem for each party is that activists are likely to be more extreme than the typical voter. By choosing a policy position to maximize activist support, the party will lose centrist voters. The party must therefore calculate the optimal marginal condition to maximize vote share. The Theorem presented below gives this as a (first order) *balance condition*.

Moreover, because activist support is denominated in terms of time and money, it is reasonable to suppose that the activist function will exhibit decreasing returns. For example, in an extreme case, a party that has no activist support at all may benefit considerably by a small policy move to favor a particular interest group. On the other hand, when support is very substantial, then a small increase due to a policy move will little effect the electoral outcome. For this reason it is reasonable to assume that the

---

[175]There are many such models: deterministic such as Downs (1957) and many variants; stochastic including Hinich (1977), Enelow and Hinich (1984, 1989), Coughlin (1992), Lin, Enelow and Dorussen (1999), McKelvey and Patty (2006) and Banks and Duggan (2005); mixed strategy including Kramer (1978), McKelvey (1986), Banks, Duggan and LeBreton, (2002, 2006).

activist functions themselves are concave, so their Hessians[176] are everywhere negative-definite. Theorem 3.1 points out that when these functions are sufficiently concave, then the vote maximizing model will exhibit a Nash equilibrium.

Note that a function μ is *concave* if and only if for any real α and positions x, y then

$$\mu(\alpha x + (1 - \alpha)y) \geq \alpha\mu(x) + (1 - \alpha)\mu(y)$$

As the next section of this chapter shows, the first order balance condition for party j is that the equilibrium position z_j^* satisfies the equation

$$\left[\frac{d\mathcal{E}_j^*}{dz_j} - z_j^*\right] + \frac{1}{2\beta}\frac{d\mu_j}{dz_j} = 0. \tag{3.1}$$

Here β is simply a (scalar) weighting factor that specifies the importance of policy difference. The gradient term $\left[\frac{d\mathcal{E}_j^*}{dz_j} - z_j^*\right]$ is the *marginal electoral pull of party j* (at z_j^*). The position, z_j, where $\left[\frac{d\mathcal{E}_j^*}{dz_j} - z_j\right] = 0$ can shown to be given by a specific weighted combination of the voter preferred positions: this position is called the *weighted electoral mean of party j*. In general, if the exogenous valence of party j is increased relative to the valence of the opposition party, then the weighted electoral mean of party j approaches the electoral origin. In other words, everything else equal, the electoral pull on the party is greater the greater is λ_j and the lesser is λ_k. The gradient vector $\frac{d\mu_j}{dz_j}$ is called *the marginal activist pull for party j* (at the position z_j^*) and represents the marginal activist effect on the party's valence. Whether or not a vector of party positions that satisfies this set of balance equation is indeed vote maximizing for all parties depends on a set of second order conditions. These are examined below.

To illustrate the conditions, consider Figure 3.2 again, and suppose that the economic dimension alone is relevant for political policy making. We assume that there is an electoral distribution of voter ideal points, whose mean we take as the electoral origin. If we ignore activism for the moment, then the results of the following section show that there are two very different possibilities, depending on the parameters of the model. There is a *convergence coefficient* (labelled c) defined by the valences, λ_{dem} and λ_{rep}, the variance of the electoral distribution and the coefficient, β. If the valences are sufficiently similar (so this convergence coefficient is bounded above by the dimension of the policy space) then both parties will position themselves at the electoral origin, and both will gain about 50% of the vote. In this case, potential activists are unlikely to be motivated to contribute to the parties. As long as $c \leq 1$, then this convergent situation is stable.

On the other hand, if the valences differ, with $\lambda_{dem} > \lambda_{rep}$, say, and if the electoral variance and β are both sufficiently large, so $c > 1$, then the lower valence party will vacate the origin in order to increase its vote share. This move by the Republican candidate can trigger an activist response. For purposes of exposition, we may suppose that

---

[176]The Hessian is simply a generalized second derivative. See Schofield (2003e).

conservative economic activists have the preferred position E. If the Republican candidate moves away from the origin, to a position similar to R, then conservative activists
would be induced to support this candidate. The asymmetry induced by this support
will cause liberal economic activists at L to support the Democrat. Then the Republican
position will be pulled further towards E, while D will be pulled towards L. Moreover,
if the marginal effect of activists for the Republicans is greater than for the Democrats,
then the optimal Republican candidate position will be further to the right of the origin
than the Democratic position is to the left of the origin. This model implies that once
the convergent equilibrium is destroyed because of some exogenous change in parameters, and activists become motivated to support the appropriate parties,then it can never
be recreated.

The marginal condition given in (Eq.3.1) thus summarizes the conflict between the
attraction of the electoral center and the influence of activists. Note that in terms of the
model, there is no reason why R should be to the right, and L to the left. However,
once the move is made in one direction or the other, then activist support will tend to
reinforce the left-right positioning of the parties.

This simple marginal calculation becomes more interesting when there is a second
"social" dimension of policy. Consider the initial positions, R and D, on either side of,
and approximately equidistant from the origin, as in the figure. Both social conservatives, represented by C and social liberals represented by S would be indifferent between
both parties. A Democratic candidate by moving to position D* will benefit from activist support of the social liberals, but will lose some support from the liberal economic
activists. Note that the figure is based on the supposition that activists are characterized by ellipsoidal indifference contours, reflecting the different saliences they put on
the policy axes. The "contract curve" between the two activist groups, centered at L
and S, is the locus of points given by equating the marginal benefits generated by the
two different activist functions, $\mu_{dem,L}$ and $\mu_{dem,S}$, characterizing the groups centered
at L and S respectively. It can be shown (Miller and Schofield, 2003) that this contract
curve is a *catenary* whose curvature is determined by the eccentricity of the utility functions of the activist groups. We therefore call this contract curve *the Democratic activist
catenary*. It is given by the equation

$$\frac{d\mu_{dem}}{dz_{dem}} = \left[\frac{d\mu_{dem,L}}{dz_{dem}} + \frac{d\mu_{dem,S}}{dz_{dem}}\right] = 0. \qquad (3.2)$$

Adding the marginal electoral pull gives the balance equation for the Democrats:

$$\left[\frac{d\mathcal{E}^*_{dem}}{dz_{dem}} - z^*_{dem}\right] + \frac{1}{2\beta}\left[\frac{d\mu_{dem,L}}{dz_{dem}} + \frac{d\mu_{dem,S}}{dz_{dem}}\right] = 0. \qquad (3.3)$$

The locus of points satisfying this equation is also a catenary, called *the balance locus*
for the Democrat candidate, and is obtained by shifting the Democratic activist catenary
towards the weighted electoral mean of the Democrat Party. In the same way, if there
are two activist groups for the Republicans, generated by functions, $\mu_{rep,E}$ and $\mu_{rep,C}$

, centered at E and C respectively, then we obtain a balance equation.

$$\left[\frac{d\mathcal{E}_{rep}^*}{dz_{rep}} - z_{rep}^*\right] + \frac{1}{2\beta}\left[\frac{d\mu_{rep,C}}{dz_{rep}} + \frac{d\mu_{rep,E}}{dz_{rep}}\right] = 0. \tag{3.4}$$

Again, the locus of points which satisfies this equation is called *the balance locus* for the Republican candidate, and is obtained by shifting the Republican activist catenary to adjust to the electoral pull for the party.

A pair of positions (z_{dem}^*, z_{rep}^*) satisfying these equations is called a *balance solution*. To illustrate, the pair of positions (D*, R*) in Figure 3.2 represent the optimal or equilibrium party positions on the two balance loci. These points are characterized by the negative definiteness of the respective party Hessians of the parties. (The Hessian of the party is just the second derivative of the vote share function). At R* there will be three gradient vectors (the marginal electoral pull, and the two marginal activist pulls) which must sum to zero for the balance condition to be satisfied. The balance loci for the two parties depend on the difference between the exogenous valences λ_{dem} and λ_{rep}. In particular if $\lambda_{dem} - \lambda_{rep}$ is increased for some exogenous reason, then the relative marginal activist effect for the Republicans becomes more important, while for the Democrats it becomes less important.

The positioning of R* in the Conservative electoral quadrant and of D* in the liberal quadrant in Figure 3.2 is meant to suggest the realignment that has occurred since the election of Johnson in 1964. By moving away from a typical Democratic position, L, to a position comparable to D*, Johnson brought about a transformation that eventually lost the south to the Republican party. According to the model just presented, such a move by Johnson can be considered as a rational move to increase voter support. Assuming that the Democratic Party was initially at position L, then the support by the social liberals would be small, but the rate of increase of support (given by the gradient vector $\frac{d\mu_{dem,S}}{dz_{dem}}$ at this position, and associated with a move along the Democratic catenary) would be large in magnitude. Conversely the loss of support, defined by the vector $\frac{d\mu_{dem,L}}{dz_{dem}}$ would be relatively small. A move by Johnson away from L along the catenary would thus lead to a substantial increase in overall activist support. Moreover,because of the empirical evidence that λ_{dem} for Johnson was large in contrast to λ_{rep} for Goldwater, we can infer that Goldwater's dependence on activist support was greater than Johnson's. Thus the magnitude of $\frac{d\mu_{rep,C}}{dz_{rep}}$ provides an explanation why socially conservative activists responded to the new Republican position represented by Goldwater at R*, and dominated the Republican primaries in support of his proposed policies. These characteristics of the balance solution appear to provide an explanation for Johnson's electoral landslide in 1964. This was indicated by the partisan cleavage line for 1964 in Figure 3.1, which separated those voters who were estimated to vote for Johnson, against those estimated to vote for Goldwater (Schofield, Miller and Martin, 2003).

The response by Republican candidates after this election , while taking advantage of the political realignment, has brought about something of a dilemma for both parties.

This can be seen by considering in detail the optimal position on the balance locus. At that point there are two gradients, $\frac{d\mu_{rep,C}}{dz_{rep}}$ and $\frac{d\mu_{rep,E}}{dz_{rep}}$, pointing away from the electoral origin. The marginal contribution, $\frac{d\mu_{rep,E}}{dz_{rep}}$, from economic conservative activists will be negative as the Republican position moves down the balance locus, as in Figure 3.3.

Further movement down the Republican catenary in response to social conservative activism, will induce some economic activists to recalculate the logic of their support. Indeed, members of the business community who can be designated "cosmopolitans," who are economically conservative but relatively liberal in their social values, must wonder about the policy choices of the Republican President.

As the quote by John Danforth in the previous section suggests, there are many potential economic advantages to be gained from medical advances, particularly those resulting from stem cell research. Acquiescence to the policy demands of social conservatives means these gains will be forgone.

In parallel, a Democratic position further along the Democrat catenary, particularly one associated with a Democratic candidate who has exogenous valence higher than the Republican opponent, would bring into being a new gradient vector $\frac{d\mu_{dem,E}}{dz_{dem}}$ associated with activist support from cosmopolitan economic activists. Small moves by such a candidate would induce a significant increase in contributions.

The dynamic logic of this electoral model is that both parties will tend to move in a clockwise direction along their respective catenaries. The model suggests that eventually the Democratic candidate will be located close to S while the Republican candidate will be close to C. From then on populists will dominate the Republican Party and cosmopolitans will dominate the Democrat Party.

3.3   An Outline of the Formal Electoral Model with Activists

The electoral model presented here is an extension of the multiparty stochastic model of McKelvey and Patty (2006), modified by inducing asymmetries in terms of valence. The justification for developing the model in this way is the empirical evidence that valence is a natural way to model the judgements made by voters of party leaders and candidates. There are a number of possible choices for the appropriate model for multiparty competition. The simplest one, which is used here, is that the utility function for the candidate of party j is proportional to the vote share, V_j, of the party in the Presidential election.[177] With this assumption, we can examine the conditions on the parameters of the stochastic model which are necessary for the existence of a pure strategy Nash equilibrium (PNE). Because the vote share functions are differentiable, we use calculus techniques to obtain conditions for positions to be locally optimal. Thus we examine

---

[177] The model could be modified by taking the share of the electoral college votes, or a combination of this and the party vote shares in the elections to Congress. We use this simplifying assumption on vote share in order to present the formal model and obtain a clear set of equilibrium conditions.

what we call *local pure strategy Nash equilibria* (LNE). From the definitions of these equilibria it follows that a PNE must be a LNE, but not conversely. A necessary condition for an LNE is thus a necessary condition for a PNE. A sufficient condition for an LNE is not a sufficient condition for PNE. Indeed, additional conditions of concavity or quasi-concavity are required to guarantee existence of PNE.

The key idea underlying the formal model is that party leaders attempt to estimate the electoral effects of party declarations, or manifestos, and choose their own positions as best responses to other party declarations, in order to maximize their own vote share. The stochastic model essentially assumes that candidates cannot predict vote response precisely, but that they can estimate the effect of policy proposals on the expected vote share. In the model with valence, the stochastic element is associated with the weight given by each voter, i, to the average perceived quality or valence of each candidate.

We first sketch the main results and then provide more formal definitions and proofs in the Appendix.

The data of the spatial model is a distribution, $\{x_i \in X\}_{i \in N}$, of voter ideal points for the members of the electorate, N, of size n. We assume that X is a subset of Euclidean space, of dimension w with w finite. Without loss of generality, we adopt coordinate axes so that $\frac{1}{n}\Sigma x_i = 0$. By assumption $0 \in X$, and this point is termed the *electoral mean*, or alternatively, the *electoral origin*. Each of the parties in the set $P = \{1, \dots, j, \dots, p\}$ chooses a policy, $z_j \in X$, to declare prior to the specific election to be modeled. Let $\mathbf{z} = (z_1, \dots, z_p) \in X^p$ be a typical vector of party policy positions.

Given $\mathbf{z}$, each utility for voter, i, at x_i, given the policy position, z_j of party z_j is the function

$$u_{ij}(x_i, z_j) = \lambda_j + \mu_j(z_j) - \beta\|x_i - z_j\|^2 + \epsilon_j = u_{ij}^*(x_i, z_j) + \epsilon_j.$$

Here $u_{ij}^*(x_i, z_j)$ is the observable component of utility. The constant term, λ_j, is the fixed or *exogenous valence* of party j, The function $\mu_j(z_j)$ is the component of valence generated by activist contributions to agent j. The term β is a positive constant, called the *spatial parameter*, giving the importance of policy difference defined in terms of a metric induced from the Euclidean norm, $\|\cdot\|$, on X. The vector $\epsilon = (\epsilon_1, \dots, \epsilon_j, \dots, \epsilon_p)$ is the stochastic error, whose multivariate cumulative distribution will be denoted by Ψ. The most common assumption in empirical analyses is that Ψ is the *Type I extreme value distribution* (sometimes called Gumbel). The theorems presented in this chapter is based on this assumption. This distribution assumption is the basis for much empirical work based on multinomial logit estimation (Dow and Endersby, 2004).

It is assumed that the exogenous valences are all finite, and the valence vector

$$\lambda = (\lambda_1, \lambda_2, \dots, \lambda_p) \text{ satisfies } \lambda_p \geq \lambda_{p-1} \geq \cdots \geq \lambda_2 \geq \lambda_1.$$

Voter behavior is modeled by a probability vector. The probability that a voter i chooses party j at the vector $\mathbf{z}$ is

$$\rho_{ij}(\mathbf{z}) = \Pr[[u_{ij}(x_i, z_j) > u_{il}(x_i, z_l)], \text{ for all } l \neq j].$$

Here Pr stands for the probability operator generated by the distribution assumption on ϵ.

For any voting model the *likelihood* of a model is

$$\mathbb{L} = \prod_{i \in N, \, j \in P} \rho_{ij}(\mathbf{z}),$$

while the log likelihood of the model is $\log_e(\mathbb{L})$. Clearly as $\mathbb{L}$ approaches 0 then $\log_e(\mathbb{L})$ approaches $-\infty$.

To compare two models, $\mathbb{M}_1$ and $\mathbb{M}_2$, the *Bayes Factor* is $\mathbb{L}(\mathbb{M}_1)/\mathbb{L}(\mathbb{M}_2)$ and the *log Bayes factor* of $\mathbb{M}_1$ against $\mathbb{M}_2$ is $\log_e(\mathbb{L}(\mathbb{M}_1)) - \log_e(\mathbb{L}(\mathbb{M}_2))$. A log Bayes factor over 5.0 for $\mathbb{M}_1$ against $\mathbb{M}_2$ is considered strong support for $\mathbb{M}_1$ (Kass and Raftery, 1995).

The *expected vote share* of agent j is

$$V_j(\mathbf{z}) = \sum_{i \in N} s_{ij} \rho_{ij}(\mathbf{z})$$

Here $\{s_{ij}\}$ are different weights that can be associated with different voters. In the case all weights are equal to $\frac{1}{n}$, we call the model *egalitarian*.

The differentiable function $V : X^p \rightarrow \mathbb{R}^p$ is called the *party profile function*.

In this stochastic electoral model it is assumed that each party j chooses z_j to maximize V_j, conditional on $\mathbf{z}_{-j} = (z_1, \ldots, z_{j-1}, z_{j+1}, \ldots, z_p)$.

A vector $\mathbf{z}^* = (z_1^*, \ldots, z_{j-1}^*, z_j^*, z_{j+1}^*, \ldots, z_p^*)$ is called a *local strict Nash equilibrium* (LSNE) if each z_j locally maximizes V_j,

conditional on $\mathbf{z}_{-j} = (z_1, \ldots, z_{j-1}, z_{j+1}, \ldots, z_p)$.

In the same way the vector $\mathbf{z}^*$ is a *pure strategy Nash equilibrium* or PSNE if each party j chooses z_j to maximize V_j

Now assume that the vector $\mathbf{z}$ is fixed, and let $\rho_{ij}(\mathbf{z}) = \rho_{ij}$ be the probability that i picks j.

Define the p by n matrix array of weights by

$$[\alpha_{ij}] = \left[\frac{s_{ij}[\rho_{ij} - \rho_{ij}^2]}{\sum_{k \in N} s_{kj}[\rho_{kj} - \rho_{kj}^2]} \right]$$

The *balance equation* for z_j^* is given by expression

$$z_j^* = \frac{1}{2\beta} \frac{d\mu_j}{dz_j} + \sum_{i=1}^{n} \alpha_{ij} x_i.$$

The vector $\sum_i \alpha_{ij} x_i$ is a convex combination of the set of voter ideal points and is called the *weighted electoral mean* for party j. Define

$$\frac{d\mathcal{E}_j^*}{dz_j} = \sum_{i=1}^{n} \alpha_{ij} x_i.$$

The balance equation can then be expressed as

$$\left[\frac{d\mathcal{E}_j^*}{dz_j} - z_j^*\right] + \frac{1}{2\beta}\frac{d\mu_j}{dz_j} = 0.$$

The bracketed term on the left of this expression is termed the *marginal electoral pull of party j* and is a vector pointing towards the weighted electoral mean of the party. This weighted electoral mean is that point where the electoral pull is zero. The vector $\frac{d\mu_j}{dz_j}$ is called *the marginal activist pull for party j*.

If $\mathbf{z}^* = (z_1^*, \ldots z_j^*, \ldots z_p^*)$ is such that each z_j^* satisfies the balance equation then call $\mathbf{z}^*$ a *balance solution*.

For the following discussion we note again that by suitable choice of coordinates, the equi-weighted electoral mean $\frac{1}{n}\Sigma x_i = 0$, and is termed the electoral origin.

The following theorem uses the notion of concavity, and is proved in the Appendix.

Theorem 3.1 .

Consider the electoral model $\mathbb{M}(\boldsymbol{\lambda}, \boldsymbol{\mu}, \beta; \Psi)$ based on the Type I extreme value distribution, and including both exogenous and activist valences.

(i) The first order condition for $\mathbf{z}^*$ to be an LSNE is that it is a balance solution.

(ii) If all activist valence functions are highly concave, then a balance solution will be a PNE.

In principle, this activist model can be used to examine the equilibrium position of a political leader, responding to activist demands, and balancing the pull of the electorate, in order to gain resources that can be used to compete with political opponents. Even without activists, convergence to a centrist position, as in the Downsian model, is impossible if the population is sufficiently heterogenous in its beliefs or preferences. In the case that the activist valence functions are identically zero, we write the model as $M(\boldsymbol{\lambda}, \beta; \Psi)$. When all voter weights are identical we call the model egalitarian.

The key consideration for this egalitarian model is whether the electoral origin is a LSNE. Theorem 3.2 shows that when the activist valence functions are identically zero, then for each fixed j, all α_{ij} are identical and equal to $\frac{1}{n}$. Thus, when there is only exogenous valence, the balance solution satisfies $z_j^* = (1/n)\Sigma x_i$, for all j, and we can regard this point $(1/n)\Sigma x_i = 0$. In this case, the marginal electoral pull is zero at the origin and the joint origin $\mathbf{z}_0 = (0, \ldots, 0)$ satisfies the first order condition.

However, when the valence functions $\{\mu_j\}$ are not identically zero, then it is the case that generically $\mathbf{z}_0$ cannot satisfy the first order condition. Instead the vector $\frac{d\mu_j}{dz_j}$ "points towards" the position at which the activist valence is maximized. When this marginal or gradient vector, $\frac{d\mu_j}{dz_j}$, is increased (as activists become more willing to contribute to the party) then the equilibrium position is pulled away from the weighted electoral mean of party j, and we can say the "activist effect" for the party is increased. In the two party case, if the activist valence functions are fixed, but the exogenous valence, λ_j, is increased, or λ_k, (for $k \neq j$) is decreased, then the vector $\frac{d\mathcal{E}_j^*}{dz_j}$ approaches the electoral origin. Thus the local equilibrium of party j is pulled towards the electoral origin. We can say the "electoral effect" is increased.

We now determine the conditions under which the joint origin can be a local equilibrium for the model $M(\boldsymbol{\lambda},\beta; \Psi)$.without activist valence. First let σ^2 be the total electoral variance (this is defined formally in the Appendix). Let ρ_1 be the probability that a voter chooses the lowest valence party, when all parties are at the origin. Define

$$c = c(\boldsymbol{\lambda},\beta; \Psi) = 2\beta[1 - 2\rho_1]\sigma^2$$

to be the *convergence coefficient*.

Theorem 3.2.

(i) The joint origin $\mathbf{z}_0 = (0, \dots, 0)$ satisfies the first order condition to be a LSNE for the model $\mathbb{M}(\boldsymbol{\lambda},\beta; \Psi)$.

(iii) In the case that X is $w$dimensional then the necessary condition for $\mathbf{z}_0$ to be a LNE for the model $\mathbb{M}(\boldsymbol{\lambda},\beta; \Psi)$ is that $c(\boldsymbol{\lambda},\beta; \Psi) \leq w$.

(iv) In the case that X is 2dimensional, a sufficient condition for $\mathbf{z}_0$ to be a LSNE for the model $\mathbb{M}(\boldsymbol{\lambda},\beta; \Psi)$ is that $c(\boldsymbol{\lambda},\beta; \Psi) < 1$.

The proof of Theorem 3.2 is given in the Appendix to this chapter.

Simulation of empirical models with exogenous valence by Schofield and Sened (2006) shows that when $\lambda_p > \lambda_1$, and $c(\boldsymbol{\lambda},\beta; \Psi) > w$, then a non-centrist LSNE exists and satisfies $|z_1^*| > |z_p^*|$. In other words, in equilibrium, the highest valence party will adopt a position closer to the electoral origin.

To provide a test of whether the convergence condition holds in the United States, consider Table 3.4, which presents a one dimensional multinomial logit (MNL) model of the 1992 presidential contest between Clinton, Perot and G.H.W.Bush.[178]

In empirical applications we assume that voter utility has the form

$$u_{ij}(x_i, z_j) = \lambda_j - \beta\|x_i - z_j\|^2 + \theta_j^{\mathrm{T}}\eta_i + \varepsilon_j.$$

Here the k -vector θ_j represents the effect of the k different sociodemographic parameters (class, domicile, education, income, etc.) on voting for the party j while η_i is a k-vector denoting the ith individual's relevant "sociodemographic" characteristics. We use θ_j^{T} to denote the transpose of θ_j so $\theta_j^{\mathrm{T}}\eta_i$ is a scalar. The terms $\{\lambda_j\}$ are the intrinsic valences, and assumed constant at each election, but allowed to vary between elections as the result of unexplained or exogenous shocks. Table 3.4 shows that the low valence candidate, Bush, has $\lambda_{BUSH} = -1.158$, while $\lambda_{CLINTON} = -0.482$ and $\lambda_{PEROT} = 0$.

---

[178]The survey was the American National Election Survey for 1992. The sociodemographic terms in Table 3.4 are defined in Table 3.3.. As in other MNL models in this book, the t-value is the ratio of the estimated coefficient to the standard error and Prob is the probability that the coefficient is insignificant. This US model is normalized with respect to Perot, so all coefficients for Perot are set to zero. The model is based on work by Guido Cataife.

As shown in (3.9) in the Appendix, this implies that

$$\rho_{BUSH} = \frac{e^0}{e^0 + e^{1.158-0.482} + e^{1.158}}$$

$$= \frac{1}{1 + e^{.678} + e^{1.158}} = 0.16.$$

In the same way, $\rho_{CLINTON} = 0.32$.
    The spatial coefficient is $\beta = 0.120$, and the electoral variance is $\sigma^2 = 6.22$.
    Thus the convergence coefficient is

$$c = 2\beta(1 - 2\rho_{BUSH})\sigma^2 = 2(0.120)(0.68)(6.22) = 1.015.$$

Since $w = 1$, the necessary condition fails. As the Appendix shows, we can infer that
the second derivative of Bush's vote share function at the origin is $+ 0.015$, which,
though small, is positive, signifying that the electoral origin is a minimum for the vote
share function of Bush. In the same way, the second derivative of Clinton's vote share
function at the origin is given by

$$C_{CLINTON} = 2\beta(1 - 2\rho_{CLINTON})\sigma^2 - 1$$

$$= 2(0.120)(0.36)(6.22) - 1 = -0.91.$$

Thus the electoral origin is a maximum for Clinton's vote share function. Using the
$[-2.0, +2.0]$ scale of Figure 3.6 the candidate positions were estimated to be

$$(z_{CLINTON}, z_{PEROT}, z_{BUSH}) = (-0.31, +0.57, 1.07).$$

On this economic scale, Clinton is just left of center, Perot moderately right of center,
and G.H.W.Bush fairly far right in comparison with the 2008 Republican candidates illustrated in figure 3.6. Once Bush moves right from the origin to increase vote share,
then Clinton will move left, and Perot will position himself in between. Thus the electorally perceived candidate positions are compatible with the electoral model, and this
provides some justification for its validity.

3.4   Concluding Remarks

The notion of cycles in American history is a venerable tradition. Arthur Schlesinger Sr.
(1939) proposed a sequence of cycles of conservatism versus liberalism: 1787 to 1801
to 1816, then 1816 to 1829 to 1841, 1841 to 1861 to 1869, conservative rule from 1869
to followed by the progressive era, 1901 to 1919, Republican restoration 1918 to 1931,
followed by the New Deal 1931 to Schlesinger's time, but continuing on to 1947. Many
of the books by his son, Arthur Schlesinger Jr (1957, 1958, 1960, 1973) examined
in detail the swing to F. D. Rosevelt in the 1930's and then again to Kennedy in the
1960's. Scholars disagree about the logic of realigning swings (Key, 1955; Nardulli,
1995; Mayhew, 2000, 2002), but the work of Merrill, Grofman and Brunell (2008)

does provide statistical evidence for an electoral cycle of about 26 years. The model presented in this chapter provides some logic to this idea of realignment. It suggests irregular movements by party leaders as each party responds to electoral preferences, activist demands *and* the movement of the opposing party. Figures 3.4 and 3.5 , and related work by Miller and Schofield (2003, 2008) suggest the following transitions:

(i) a move by the Republican Party between 1860 and 1896 to a conservative economic position causing a Democratic Party response to a populist then liberal position

(ii) a degree of dominance by the Republicans causing a liberal Democratic response in the 1930's and the fashioning of the New Deal coalition under Roosevelt

(iii) stasis in the early post war period, with Democrats on the economic left, and Republicans on the economic right. This stasis was changed as a result of Johnson's move on the civil rights axis in the 1960's and the implementaion of the idea of the Great Society

(iv) a Republican response on the civil rights axis that brought many southern states into the Republican coalition, and led to the administrations of Nixon[179], Reagan and G.H.W.Bush

(v) a period from the election of William Clinton in 1992 until 2008 during which time both parties were forced to deal with conflicts between civil rights and economic issues. The incursion into Iraq has created a new component to the civil rights axis. The Republican party may either maintain its conservative economic and social position or move to a more populist economic position in response to the nomination of Barack Obama, with his socially liberal and economically centrist position.[180]

Recent events suggest that a major realignment is in progress.

3.5 Appendix

3.5.1 A Formal Model of Leader Support

Definition 3.1. The Stochastic Model $\mathbb{M}(\lambda, \mu, \beta; \Psi)$ **with Activist Valence.**

Each of the leaders in the set $P = \{1, \ldots, j, \ldots, p\}$ chooses a policy, $z_j \in W$, to declare. Let $\mathbf{z} = (z_1, \ldots, z_p) \in W^p$ be a typical vector of leader positions.

Given $\mathbf{z}$, each citizen, $i \in N = \{1, \ldots, n\}$, is described by a vector

$$\mathbf{u}_i(x_i, \mathbf{z}) = (u_{i1}(x_i, z_1), \ldots, u_{ip}(x_i, z_p))$$

where

$$u_{ij}(x_i, z_j) = \lambda_j + \mu_j(z_j) - \beta||x_i - z_j||^2 + \epsilon_j = u_{ij}^*(x_i, z_j) + \epsilon_j. \quad (3.5)$$

Here $u_{ij}^*(x_i, z_j)$ is the observable component of utility. The term, λ_j, is the fixed or *exogenous valence* of leader j, while the function $\mu_j(z_j)$ is the component of valence

---

[179] See for example Perlstein (2008).
[180] See for example Douthat and Salan (2008).

generated by activist contributions to leader j. The term β is a positive constant, called the *spatial parameter*, giving the importance of policy difference defined in terms of the Euclidean metric, $||a - b||$, on W. The vector $\epsilon = (\epsilon_1, \ldots, \epsilon_j, \ldots, \epsilon_p)$ is the stochastic error, whose multivariate cumulative distribution will be denoted by Ψ.

Citizen behavior is modelled by a probability vector. The probability that a citizen i chooses leader j at the vector $\mathbf{z}$ is

$$\rho_{ij}(\mathbf{z}) = \Pr[[u_{ij}(x_i, z_j) > u_{il}(x_i, z_l)], \text{ for all } l \neq j]. \tag{3.6}$$

$$= \Pr[\epsilon_l - \epsilon_j < u^*_{ij}(x_i, z_j) - u^*_{il}(x_i, z_j), \text{ for all } l \neq j] \tag{3.7}$$

Here Pr stands for the probability operator generated by the distribution assumption on ϵ.

The *expected support* of leader j is

$$V_j(\mathbf{z}) = \frac{\sum_{i \in N} s_{ij} \rho_{ij}(\mathbf{z})}{\sum_{i \in N} s_{ij}} \tag{3.8}$$

The weights $\{s_{ij}\}$ allow for the possibility that individuals belong to different constituencies and have differing political power. Without loss of generality, we normalize and assume for each j that $\sum_{i \in N} s_{ij} = 1$.

In democratic polities based on proportional representation we can assume that each $s_{ij} = \frac{1}{n}$ for all i, j. We call this the *egalitarian* case. In non-democratic polities the weights s_{ij} may differ widely. $\square$

Definition 3.2. The Extreme Value Distribution,Ψ.
The cumulative distribution,Ψ, has the closed form

$$\Psi(x) = \exp\left[-\exp\left[-x\right]\right].$$

The difference between the Gumbel and normal (or Gaussian) distributions is that the latter is perfectly symmetric about zero.

With this distribution assumption, it can be shown (Train, 2003), for each voter i, and leader j, that

$$\rho_{ij}(\mathbf{z}) = \frac{\exp[u^*_{ij}(x_i, z_j)]}{\sum_{k=1}^{p} \exp u^*_{ik}(x_i, z_k)}. \tag{3.9}$$

In this stochastic electoral model it is assumed that each leader j chooses z_j to maximize V_j, conditional on $\mathbf{z}_{-j} = (z_1, \ldots, z_{j-1}, z_{j+1}, \ldots, z_p)$.$\square$

Definition 3.3. Equilibrium Concepts.
(i) A strategy vector $\mathbf{z}^* = (z_1^*, \ldots, z_{j-1}^*, z_j^*, z_{j+1}^*, \ldots, z_p^*) \in W^p$ is a *local strict Nash equilibrium* (LSNE) for the profile function $V : W^p \to \mathbb{R}^p$ iff, for each leader $j \in P$,there exists a neighborhood W_j of z_j^* in W such that

$$V_j(z_1^*, \ldots, z_{j-1}^*, z_j^*, z_{j+1}^*, \ldots, z_p^*) > V_j(z_1^*, \ldots z_{j-1}^*, z_j, z_{j+1}^* \ldots, z_p^*)$$
$$\text{for all } z_j \in W_j - \{z_j^*\}.$$

(ii) A strategy vector $\mathbf{z}^* = (z_1^*, \ldots, z_{j-1}^*, z_j^*, z_{j+1}^*, \ldots, z_p^*)$ is a *local weak Nash equilibrium* (LNE) iff, for each agent j, there exists a neighborhood W_j of z_j^* in W such that

$$V_j(z_1^*, \ldots, z_{j-1}^*, z_j^*, z_{j+1}^*, \ldots, z_p^*) \geq V_j(z_1^*, \ldots z_{j-1}^*, z_j, z_{j+1}^*, \ldots, z_p^*)$$
$$\text{for all } z_j \in W_j.$$

(iii) A strategy vector $\mathbf{z}^* = (z_1^*, \ldots, z_{j-1}^*, z_j^*, z_{j+1}^*, \ldots, z_p^*)$ is a *strict* or *weak, pure strategy Nash equilibrium* (PSNE or PNE) iff W_j can be replaced by W in (i), (ii), above, respectively.

(iv) The strategy z_j^* is termed a "local strict best response," a "local weak best response," a "global weak best response," a "global strict best response," respectively to $\mathbf{z}^*_{-j} = (z_1^*, \ldots, z_{j-1}^*, z_{j+1}^*, \ldots, z_p^*)$. $\square$

Obviously if $\mathbf{z}^*$ is an LSNE or a PNE it must be an LNE, while if it is a PSNE then it must be an LSNE. We use the notion of LSNE to avoid problems with the degenerate situation when there is a zero eigenvalue to the Hessian. The weaker requirement of LNE allows us to obtain a necessary condition for $\mathbf{z}^*$ to be a LNE and thus a PNE, without having to invoke concavity. Of particular interest is the vector

$$x_j^* = \frac{\sum_{i \in P} s_{ij} x_i}{\sum_{i \in N} s_{ij}} = \sum_{i \in N} s_{ij} x_i. \tag{3.10}$$

In the *egalitarian* case, all $s_{ij} = \frac{1}{n}$, and we can transform coordinates so that in the new coordinate system, $x^* = \frac{1}{n} \sum_{i \in N} x_i = 0$. We shall refer to $\mathbf{z}_0 = (0, \ldots, 0)$ as the joint *electorate origin*.

Theorem 3.3 shows that, even in the egalitarian case, the vector $\mathbf{z}_0 = (0, \ldots, 0)$ will generally not satisfy the first order condition for a LSNE, namely that the differential of V_j, with respect to z_j be zero. However, if the activist valence function is identically zero, so that only exogenous valence is relevant, then the first order condition at $\mathbf{z}_0$ will be satisfied.

It follows the definition of the Gumbel distribution, that for voter i, with ideal point, x_i, the probability, $\rho_{ij}(\mathbf{z})$, that i picks j at $\mathbf{z}$ is given by

$$\rho_{ij}(\mathbf{z}) = [1 + \Sigma_{k \neq j}[\exp(f_{jk})]]^{-1} \tag{3.11}$$

where $f_{jk} = \lambda_k + \mu_k(z_k) - \lambda_j - \mu_j(z_j) + \beta ||x_i - z_j||^2 - \beta ||x_i - z_k||^2$. The following section shows that the first order condition for $\mathbf{z}^*$ to be a LSNE is that it be a *balance solution*.

Definition 3.4. The balance solution for the model $\mathbb{M}(\lambda, \mu, \beta; \Psi)$.
Let $[\rho_{ij}(\mathbf{z})] = [\rho_{ij}]$ be the matrix of voter probabilities at the vector $\mathbf{z}$, and let

$$\alpha_{ij} = \frac{s_{ij}[\rho_{ij} - \rho_{ij}^2]}{\sum_{k \in N} s_{kj}[\rho_{kj} - \rho_{kj}^2]}. \tag{3.12}$$

be the matrix of coefficients. The *balance equation* for z_j^* is given by expression

$$z_j^* = \frac{1}{2\beta} \frac{d\mu_j}{dz_j} + \sum_{i=1}^{n} \alpha_{ij} x_i. \tag{3.13}$$

In the previous section we called the vector $\sum_i \alpha_{ij} x_i$ the *weighted electoral mean* for leader j, and wrote it as

$$\sum_{i=1}^{n} \alpha_{ij} x_i = \frac{d\mathcal{E}_j^*}{dz_j}. \tag{3.14}$$

Notice first that the weight α_{ij} shows how the citizen i influence leader j in his choice of policy position. Moreover, the weights for leader j depend on the vector of positions $\{z_{-j}\}$ of leaders other than j. The balance equation can be rewritten as

$$\left[\frac{d\mathcal{E}_j^*}{dz_j} - z_j^* \right] + \frac{1}{2\beta} \frac{d\mu_j}{dz_j} = 0. \tag{3.15}$$

The bracketed term on the left of this expression was called the *marginal electoral pull of leader j*. It is a gradient vector pointing towards this leader's weighted electoral mean. This position is that point where the electoral pull is zero. The vector $\frac{d\mu_j}{dz_j}$ was called *the marginal activist pull for leader j*.

If $\mathbf{z}^* = (z_1^*, \ldots z_j^*, \ldots, z_n^*)$ is such that each z_j^* satisfies the balance equation, then call $\mathbf{z}^*$ the *balance solution*. $\square$

We now give a more formal version of Theorem 3.1.

Theorem 3.3.

Consider the electoral model $\mathbb{M}(\boldsymbol{\lambda}, \boldsymbol{\mu}, \beta; \Psi)$ based on the Type I extreme value distribution, and including both exogenous and activist valences. The first order condition for $\mathbf{z}^*$ to be an LSNE is that it is a balance solution. If all activist valence functions are highly concave, in the sense that their Hessians) or second differentials) have negative eigenvalues of sufficiently great magnitude, then the balance solution will be a PNE.

We emphasize that the *marginal electoral pull of leader j* is a gradient vector pointing towards the weighted electoral mean of the leader, and represents the *centripetal pull* to the center. *The marginal activist pull for leader j* represents the *centrifugal force* generated by the resources made available by activists.

The second order condition for an LSNE at $\mathbf{z}^*$ depends on the negative definiteness of the the Hessian of the activist valence function. If the eigenvalues of these Hessians are negative at a balance solution, and of sufficient magnitude, then this will guarantee that a vector z^* which satisfies the balance condition will be a LSNE. Indeed, this condition can ensure concavity of the vote share functions, and thus of existence of a PNE.

In the case $\mu_j = 0$ for all j, the balance condition becomes

$$z_j = \sum_{i \in N} s_{ij} x_i. \tag{3.16}$$

In the egalitarian case with all weights $\{s_{ij}\}$ identical, then first order balance condition becomes

$$z_j^* = \frac{1}{n} \sum_{i=1}^{n} x_i. \tag{3.17}$$

Again, by a change of coordinates we choose $\frac{1}{n}\Sigma x_i = 0$. In this case, the marginal electoral pull is zero at the origin and the joint origin $z_0 = (0, \ldots, 0)$ satisfies the first order condition. However, since $\mu = 0$, we cannot use the concavity of μ to assert the existence of equilibrium. Schofield (2007) shows that if $\mu = 0$, then there is a coefficient, c, defined in terms of all model parameters and the electoral covariance matrix of the voter preferred points such that $c < w$ is a necessary condition for z_0 to be a LSNE in the egalitarian stochastic vote model.

Definition 3.5. The Electoral Covariance Matrix, ∇.
  Let $W = \mathbb{R}^w$ be endowed with a system of coordinate axes $r = 1, \ldots, w$. For the rth coordinate axis let $\xi_r = (x_{1r}, x_{2r}, \ldots, x_{nr})$ be the vector of the rth coordinates of the set of n voter ideal points. The scalar product of ξ_r and ξ_s is denoted $(\xi_r \cdot \xi_s)$.

(i) The symmetric $w \times w$ *electoral covariance matrix* about the origin is denoted ∇ and is defined by

$$\nabla = \frac{1}{n} [(\xi_r \cdot \xi_s)]_{s=1,\ldots,w}^{r=1,\ldots,w}.$$

(ii) Let $(\sigma_r, \sigma_s) = \frac{1}{n}(\xi_r, \xi_s)$ be the electoral covariance between the rth and s^{th} axes, and $\sigma_s^2 = \frac{1}{n}(\xi_s, \xi_s)$ be the electoral variance on the sth axis, with

$$\sigma^2 = \sum_{s=1}^{w} \sigma_s^2 = \frac{1}{n} \sum_{s=1}^{w} (\xi_s \cdot \xi_s) = trace(\nabla)$$

the total electoral variance. $\square$

We now give a more general version of Theorem 3.2.

Theorem 3.4.
  Consider the electoral model $\mathbb{M}(\lambda, \beta; \Psi)$ based on the Type I extreme value distribution, with only exogenous valence.
  (i) The Hessian of the egalitarian vote share function of party j at z_0 is a positive multiple of the w by w characteristic matrix.

$$C_j = 2\beta(1 - 2\rho_j)\nabla - I \tag{3.18}$$

where I is the w by w identity matrix.

(ii) The necessary and sufficient condition for $\mathbf{z}_0$ to be an LSNE is that all C_j have negative eigenvalues. Since C_1 must also have negative eigenvalues, it follows that a necessary condition for $\mathbf{z}_0$ to be an LNE is that a convergence coefficient, c, defined by

$$c = 2\beta(1 - 2\rho_1)\sigma^2$$

is bounded above by the dimension, w.

(iii) In two dimensions, a sufficient condition is that c is bounded above by 1. In higher dimensions a sufficient condition can be expressed by appropriate bounds on the cofactors of C_1.

While maximization of vote share is an appropriate maximand under proportional egalitarian rule, a more appropriate maximand under plurality rule would be a seat share function

$$S_j(\mathbf{z}) = S_j(V_1(\mathbf{z}), \ldots, V_j(\mathbf{z}), l \ldots, V_n(\mathbf{z}))$$

which might very well be a logistic function of $V_j(\mathbf{z})$. The techniques of the proof of theorems 1 and 2 can be extended to this more general case.$\square$

Proof of Theorem 3.3   Using the extreme value distribution Ψ we have

$$\rho_{ij}(\mathbf{z}) \quad = \quad [1 + \Sigma_{k\neq j}[\exp(f_k)]]^{-1}$$
$$\text{where } f_k \quad = \quad \lambda_k + \mu_k(z_k) - \lambda_j - \mu_j(z_j) + \beta||x_i - z_j||^2 - \beta||x_i - z_k||^2$$

is the comparison function used by i in evaluating party k in contrast to party j. We then obtain

$$\frac{d}{dz_j}[\rho_{ij}] \quad = \quad -\left[2\beta(z_j - x_i) - \frac{d\mu_j}{dz_j}\right][1 + \Sigma_{k\neq j}\exp(f_k)]^{-2}[\Sigma_k \exp(f_k)]$$
$$= \quad \left[2\beta(x_i - z_j) + \frac{d\mu_j}{dz_j}\right][\rho_{ij}][1 - \rho_{ij}].$$

The *expected support* of leader j is.

$$V_j(\mathbf{z}) = \frac{\Sigma_{i\in N} s_{ij}\rho_{ij}(\mathbf{z})}{\Sigma_{i\in N} s_{ij}} \tag{3.19}$$

Without loss of generality we suppose $\Sigma_{i\in N} s_{ij} = 1$. In the egalitarian case, each $s_{ij} = \frac{1}{n}$.

Thus the first order condition for maximizing V_j is:

$$\sum_{i\in N} s_{ij}\frac{d}{dz_j}[\rho_{ij}] = \sum_{i\in N} s_{ij}\left[2\beta(x_i - z_j) + \frac{d\mu_j}{dz_j}\right][\rho_{ij}][1 - \rho_{ij}] = 0. \tag{3.20}$$

Thus $\displaystyle\sum_{i\in N} s_{ij}\left[2\beta z_j - \frac{d\mu_j}{dz_j}\right][\rho_{ij}][1-\rho_{ij}]\ =\ \sum_{i\in N} s_{ij}2\beta x_i[\rho_{ij}][1-\rho_{ij}],$

or $\displaystyle\frac{1}{2\beta}\left[2\beta z_j - \frac{d\mu_j}{dz_j}\right]\ =\ \frac{\sum_{i\in N} s_{ij}x_i[\rho_{ij}][1-\rho_{ij}]}{\sum_{i\in N} s_{ij}[\rho_{ij}][1-\rho_{ij}]},$

or $\displaystyle z_j - \frac{1}{2\beta}\frac{d\mu_j}{dz_j}\ =\ \sum_{i\in N}\alpha_{ij}x_i,$

where $\displaystyle\alpha_{ij} = \frac{s_{ij}[\rho_{ij}-\rho_{ij}^2]}{\sum_{k\in N} s_{kj}[\rho_{kj}-\rho_{kj}^2]}.$ (3.21)

An identical argument holds for each party j giving an equilibrium, satisfying, for all j, the balance equation:

$$\left[\frac{d\mathcal{E}_j^*}{dz_j} - z_j^*\right] + \frac{1}{2\beta}\frac{d\mu_j}{dz_j} = 0,\qquad (3.22)$$

$$\frac{d\mathcal{E}_j^*}{dz_j} = \sum_{i\in N}\alpha_{ij}x_i.\qquad (3.23)$$

This gives the first order condition stated in Theorem 3.1. Let $\mathbf{z}^*$ be a vector satisfying the first order condition.

To examine the second order condition, in the egalitarian case, the Hessian, H_j, of party j is given by

$$\sum_{i\in N} s_{ij}\frac{d^2\rho_{ij}}{dz_j^2}\qquad (3.24)$$

$$= \sum_{i} s_{ij}[\rho_{ij}-\rho_{ij}^2]\left[[1-2\rho_{ij}][\nabla_{ij}] + \left[\frac{d^2\mu_j}{dz_j^2}-2\beta I\right]\right]\qquad (3.25)$$

$$= \left[\frac{d^2\mu_j}{dz_j^2}-2\beta I\right]\sum_{i} s_{ij}[\rho_{ij}-\rho_{ij}^2]\qquad (3.26)$$

$$+ \sum_{i} s_{ij}[\rho_{ij}-\rho_{ij}^2][1-2\rho_{ij}][\nabla_{ij}].\qquad (3.27)$$

Here I is the identity matrix , while

$$[\nabla_{ij}] = \left[2\beta(x_i - z_j)+\frac{d\mu_j}{dz_j}\right]^T\left[2\beta(x_i - z_j)+\frac{d\mu_j}{dz_j}\right]\qquad (3.28)$$

where T denotes the transposed column vector. Since $z_j^*=\frac{1}{2\beta}\frac{d\mu_j}{dz_j} + \frac{d\mathcal{E}_j^*}{dz_j}$,we can regard the symmetric matrix expression involving $[\nabla_{ij}]$ as a measure of electoral variance taken about a weighted electoral mean, $\frac{d\mathcal{E}_j^*}{dz_j}$. Even though the matrix term involving $[\nabla_{ij}]$ may have positive eigenvalues, if the eigenvalues of $\frac{d^2\mu_j}{dz_1^2}$ are negative, and of sufficiently large modulus, then the eigenvalues of $\frac{d^2\mu_j}{dz_j^2} - 2\beta I$ will also be negative, and the Hessian, H_j, will also have negative eigenvalues.

Thus we obtain a sufficient condition for existence of a LSNE at z^*. The same argument holds for existence of a PSNE. $\square$

Proof of Theorem 3.4   Since $\{\mu_j\}$ are all identically zero, then we see that $\rho_{kj} = \rho_j$ is independent of k at $z_0^* = (0, \ldots, 0)$ Thus even in the non-egalitarian case,

$$\alpha_{ij} = \frac{s_{ij}[\rho_{ij} - \rho_{ij}^2]}{\sum_{k \in N} s_{kj}[\rho_{kj} - \rho_{kj}^2]} = s_{ij}.$$

$$\text{and } z_j = \sum_{i \in N} s_{ij} x_i$$

satisfies the first order condition.

In the egalitarian case, $s_{ij} = \frac{1}{n}$, so $z_j = \frac{1}{n}\sum_{i \in N} x_i = 0$, by the coordinate change. This proves $z_0^* = (0, 0, \ldots, 0)$ satisfies the first order condition.

The Hessian H_1, in the egalitarian case is

$$\frac{1}{n}\sum_{i=1}^{n}\frac{d^2\rho_{i1}}{dz_1^2} = [\rho_1 - \rho_1^2]\{[1 - 2\rho_1][\frac{4\beta^2}{n}\sum_{i=1}^{n}\nabla_{i1}(z_1)] - 2\beta I\}.$$

Here $[\nabla_{i1}(z_1)] = [(x_i - z_1)^T(x_i - z_1)$ is the w by w matrix of cross product terms about the point z_1. When $z_1 = 0$ then

$$\frac{1}{n}\sum_{i=1}^{n}\nabla_{i1}(0) = \nabla$$

is the electoral covariance matrix about the origin. The Hessian of V_1 is now given by

$$\frac{1}{n}\sum_{i}\frac{d^2\rho_{i1}}{dz_1^2} = 2\beta[\rho_1 - \rho_1^2]\{2\beta[1 - 2\rho_1]\nabla - I\}.$$

By assumption $1 > \rho_1 \geqslant 0$ so $[\rho_1 - \rho_1^2] \geqslant 0$. Note also that $\rho_1 > 0$. Moreover $\beta > 0$ so the eigenvalues of V_1 can be identified with the eigenvalues of

$$C_1 = [2\beta[1 - 2\rho_1]\nabla - I].$$

A standard result of matrix algebra is that, in the two-dimensional case, C_1 has negative eigenvalues if the determinant

$$\det[2\beta[1 - 2\rho_1]\nabla_0 - I] > 0.\text{and the trace,}$$
$$\text{trace}[2\beta[1 - 2\rho_1]\nabla_0 - I] < 0.$$

Using $\sigma^2 = \text{trace}(\nabla)$, we can then show that the the sufficient condition for negative eigenvalues is given by condition $2\beta[1 - 2\rho_1]\sigma^2 < 1$, or $c(\lambda,\beta;\Psi) < 1$.

The necessary condition for C_1 to have non-positive eigenvalues (and thus for an LNE) is that

$$\text{trace}[2\beta[1 - 2\rho_1]\nabla - I] \leq 0].$$

Thus the necessary condition for C_1 is that $c(\boldsymbol{\lambda},\beta; \Psi) \leq w$. The Hessians for $j = 2, l \ldots, p$, are given by $C_j = [2\beta[1 - 2\rho_j]\nabla - I]$.

$$\begin{aligned}
\text{Now } \lambda_j &\geq \lambda_1 \text{ implies that } \rho_j \geq \rho_1, \\
\text{so } trace(C_1) &\geq trace(C_j) \text{ and} \\
2\beta[1 - 2\rho_1]\sigma^2 &\geq 2\beta[1 - 2\rho_j]\sigma^2, j = 2, \ldots, p.
\end{aligned}$$

Thus if the sufficient condition for C_1 to have negative eigenvalues is satisfied, then it is also satisfied for $C_2, \ldots, C_p$. In addition if the necessary condition for C_1 fails, then it also fails for C_2, etc. Thus the necessary condition for z_0 to be a LNE is that $c(\boldsymbol{\lambda},\beta; \Psi) \leq w$, while the sufficient condition for z_0 to be a LSNE in the two-dimensional case is that $c(\boldsymbol{\lambda},\beta; \Psi) < 1$. $\square$

The sufficient condition for an LSNE in dimension $w > 2$ can be readily obtained, but this will be given by somewhat more complicated conditions on the determinant and cofactors of C_1. $\square$

3.5.2   Model of the 1992 Election

Table 3.3. Explanation of Variables for US model

Variable	Explanation
worsefinan	Whether the voter thinks the national economy got worse.
worseecon	Whether the voter thinks his personal finances got worse.
govjobs	1: The government should see people have jobs. 7: The government should let each person get his own job without intervention.
govhealth	1: The government should provide health plan. 7: Private plans.
govblack	1: The government should help blacks. 7: Blacks should help themselves.
abortion	1: Always be permitted; 4: Never be permitted (2 & 3 intermediate cases)
term	0: Does not favor term limits. 1: Favors.
deficit	The respondent thinks the size of the budget deficit is one of the most important problems facing government
east	Whether the respondent is from East.
south	Whether the respondent is from South.
west	Whether the respondent is from West.
newvoter	Whether the respondent is a new voter.
dem	Whether the respondent is a democrat.
rep	Whether the respondent is a republican.
female	Whether the respondent is female.
educyrs	Years of education.

Table 3.4. MNL model of the 1992 presidential election in the US

	Parameter	Est.	Std. err.	t value	Prob	95% Conf. Interval	
	β coeff.	0.120	0.023	5.340	0.000	0.076	0.164
Bush	λ_{BUSH}	-1.158	1.023	-1.130	0.258	-3.164	0.848
Clinton	$\lambda_{CLINTON}$	-0.483	0.955	-0.510	0.613	-2.355	1.389
Bush	worsefinan	-0.481	0.259	-1.860	0.063	-0.987	0.026
Clinton		0.122	0.230	0.530	0.596	-0.329	0.573
Bush	worseecon	-0.381	0.244	-1.560	0.118	-0.860	0.097
Clinton		0.669	0.270	2.480	0.013	0.140	1.198
Bush	govjobs	0.117	0.086	1.370	0.172	-0.051	0.285
Clinton		0.067	0.075	0.890	0.372	-0.080	0.215
Bush	govhealth	0.220	0.066	3.340	0.001	0.091	0.350
Clinton		0.069	0.067	1.020	0.306	-0.063	0.200
Bush	black	-0.002	0.084	-0.030	0.979	-0.166	0.162
Clinton		-0.210	0.074	-2.850	0.004	-0.354	-0.065
Bush	abortion	-0.451	0.113	-4.010	0.000	-0.672	-0.231
Clinton		-0.021	0.117	-0.180	0.857	-0.250	0.208
Bush	term	0.272	0.321	0.850	0.397	-0.357	0.901
Clinton		0.177	0.270	0.650	0.513	-0.352	0.705
Bush	deficit	-1.003	0.268	-3.740	0.000	-1.528	-0.478
Clinton		-0.418	0.275	-1.520	0.129	-0.958	0.121
Bush	east	-0.277	0.320	-0.860	0.388	-0.905	0.352
Clinton		0.407	0.293	1.390	0.165	-0.168	0.981
Bush	south	0.406	0.302	1.340	0.179	-0.186	0.999
Clinton		0.650	0.300	2.170	0.030	0.062	1.239
Bush	west	-0.307	0.304	-1.010	0.313	-0.904	0.289
Clinton		0.239	0.301	0.790	0.427	-0.350	0.828
Bush	newvoter	0.497	0.325	1.530	0.127	-0.141	1.134
Clinton		-0.283	0.294	-0.960	0.335	-0.858	0.292
Bush	dem	-0.527	0.448	-1.180	0.240	-1.404	0.351
Clinton		1.651	0.319	5.170	0.000	1.025	2.277
Bush	rep	1.366	0.387	3.530	0.000	0.608	2.124
Clinton		-0.830	0.365	-2.280	0.023	-1.545	-0.115
Bush	female	0.563	0.231	2.430	0.015	0.110	1.017
Clinton		0.191	0.220	0.870	0.387	-0.241	0.622
Bush	educyrs	0.101	0.055	1.810	0.070	-0.008	0.209
Clinton		0.032	0.052	0.620	0.534	-0.069	0.134
Bush	age18-29	-1.180	0.390	-3.030	0.002	-1.944	-0.417
Clinton		-0.830	0.377	-2.200	0.028	-1.568	-0.092
Bush	age30-44	-0.731	0.320	-2.280	0.022	-1.358	-0.103
Clinton		-0.729	0.323	-2.260	0.024	-1.362	-0.095
Bush	age45-59	-0.453	0.352	-1.280	0.199	-1.143	0.238
Clinton		-0.140	0.346	-0.410	0.685	-0.818	0.538

Log likelihood = -565
$n = 905$

Chapter 4

Modelling Parliaments

4.1 Legislative Bargaining in Israel

In this chapter the formal model is applied to the examination of politics and elections in Israel, Turkey and Canada, with brief discussion of elections in Britain and the Netherlands.

As in Chapter 3, we assume that each party chooses a preferred position (or *ideal point*) in a *policy space* W. The parties are $P = \{1, \ldots, j, \ldots, p\}$, and the vector of party ideal points is $\mathbf{z} = (z_1, \ldots, z_p)$. After the election we denote the number of seats controlled by party, j, by s_j and let $\mathbf{s} = (s_1, \ldots, s_p)$ be the of the vector of parliamentary seats. We shall suppose that any coalition with more than half the seats is winning, and denote the set of winning coalitions by $\mathbb{D}$. This assumption can be modified without any theoretical difficulty. For each winning coalition M in $\mathbb{D}$ there is a set of points in X such that, for any point outside the set there is some point inside the set that is preferred to the former by all members of the coalition. Furthermore, no point in the set is unanimously preferred by all coalition members to any other point in the set. This set is the Pareto set, $Pareto(M)$, of the coalition. If the conventional assumption is made that the preferences of the actors can be represented in terms of Euclidean distances, then this Pareto set for a coalition is simply the convex hull of the preferred positions of the member parties. (In two dimensions, we can draw this as the area bounded by straight lines joining the ideal points of the parties and including all coalition members.) Since preferences are described by the vector, $\mathbf{z}$, we can denote this as $Pareto(M, \mathbf{z})$. Now consider the intersection of these compromise sets for all winning coalitions. If this intersection is non-empty, then it is a set called the *Core* of $\mathbb{D}$ at $\mathbf{z}$, written $Core(\mathbb{D}, \mathbf{z})$. At a point in $Core(\mathbb{D}, \mathbf{z})$ no coalition can propose an alternative policy point that is unanimously preferred by every member of some winning coalition.

In general, $Core(\mathbb{D}, \mathbf{z})$ will be at the preferred point of one party. The analysis of McKelvey and Schofield (1987) obtained pivotal symmetry conditions that are necessary at a core point. Clearly a necessary and sufficient condition for point x to be in $Core(\mathbb{D}, \mathbf{z})$ is that x is in the Pareto set of every minimal winning coalition. The symmetry conditions depend on certain subgroups called pivot groups. Alternatively, we can determine all median lines given by the pair $(\mathbb{D}, \mathbf{z})$. To illustrate these conditions, consider the configuration of party strengths after the election of 1992 in Israel. (The election results in Israel for the period 1988 to 2003 are given in Table 4.1). The estimates of party positions in Figure 5.1 were obtained from a survey of the electorate carried out by Arian and Shamir (1995), complemented by an analysis of the party manifestos (details can be found in Schofield, Sened and Nixon, 1998; Schofield and Sened, 2006). First we define a median line in the figure to be a line that goes through the positions of two parties, such that a clear majority of the seats can be found on neither side of the line.

Table 4.1. Knesset seats

Party	1988	1992	1996	1999	2003
Labor (LAB)	39	44	34	28	19[a]
Democrat (ADL)	1	2	4	5	2[a]
Meretz (MRZ)	–	12	9	10	6
CRM, MPM, PLP	9	–	–	–	3
Communist (HS)	4	3	5	3	3
Balad	–	–	–	2	3
Left Subtotal	*53*	*61*	*52*	*28*	*36*
Olim	–	–	7	6	2[b]
III Way	–	–	4	–	–
Center	–	–	–	6	–
Shinui (S)	2	–	–	6	15
Center Subtotal	*2*	*–*	*11*	*18*	*17[b]*
Likud (LIK)	40	32	30	19	38[b]
Gesher	–	–	2	–	–
Tzomet (TZ)	2	8	–	–	–
Israel Beiteinu	–	–	–	4	7
Subtotal	*42*	*40*	*32*	*23*	*45*
Shas (SHAS)	6	6	10	17	11
Yahadut (AI, DH)	7	4	4	5	5
Mafdal (NRP)	5	6	9	5	6
Moledet (MO)	2	3	2	4	–
Techiya (TY)	3	–	–	–	–
Right Subtotal	*23*	*19*	*25*	*31*	*22*
Total	120	120	120	120	120

[a] ADL, under Peretz, combined with Labor, to give 21 seats.
[b] Olim joined Likud to give 40 seats, and the right 47 seats.

As Figure 4.1 indicates, all median lines go through the Labor party position, so given the configuration of seats and positions, we can say Labor is the *core party* in

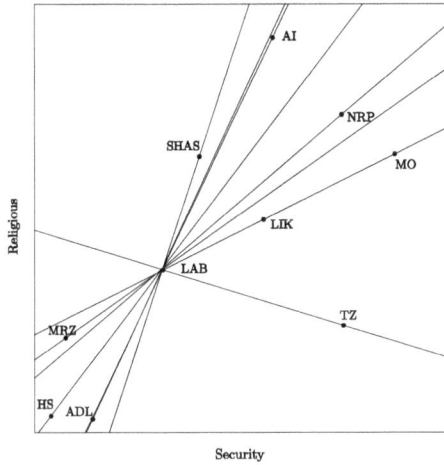

Figure 4.1: The core at the Labor position in the Knesset in 1992

1992. Another way to see that the Labor position, z_{lab}, is at the core is to note that the set of parties above the median line through the Labor-Tsomet positions (but excluding Labor) only control 59 seats out of 120. When the party positions are such that the core does indeed exist, then any government coalition must contain the core party. When the core party is actually at a core position then it is able to influence coalition bargaining in order to control the policy position of the government. Indeed, if we assume that parties are only concerned to control policy, then the party at the core position would be indifferent to the particular coalition that formed. The ability of the core party to control policy implies a tendency for core parties to form minority governments, since they need no other parties in order to fulfill their policy objectives. In fact, in 1992, Rabin first created a coalition government with Shas, and then formed a minority government without Shas.

We have emphasized that in two dimensions the core can be empty. To see the consequences of this, consider the configuration of party positions in Israel after the election of 1988, as presented in Figure 4.2, again using the seat allocations from Table 4.1. In this case there is a median line through the Tzomet, Likud positions, so the coalition of parties above this line is winning. It is evident that the Labor does not belong to the Pareto set of the coalition including Likud, Tzomet and the religious parties. Indeed, it can be shown that the symmetry conditions necessary for the existence of a core are nowhere satisfied. In this case, there are cycles of different coalitions, each preferred by a majority of the legislature to some other coalition policy in the cycle.

The heart, $\mathcal{H}(\mathbb{D}, \mathbf{z})$, given the seat strengths and party positions, is the star-shaped figure, bounded by the five median lines. It is reasonable to conclude, in the absence

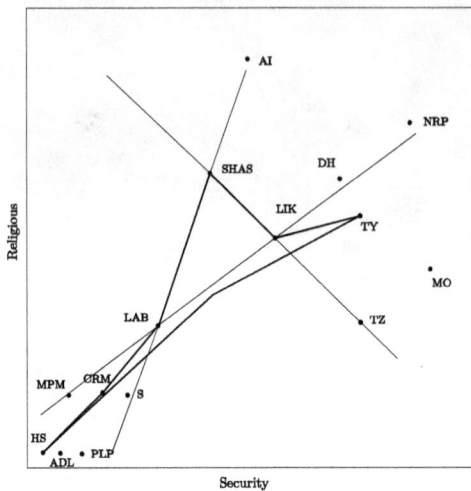

Figure 4.2:   The heart in the Knesset in 1988

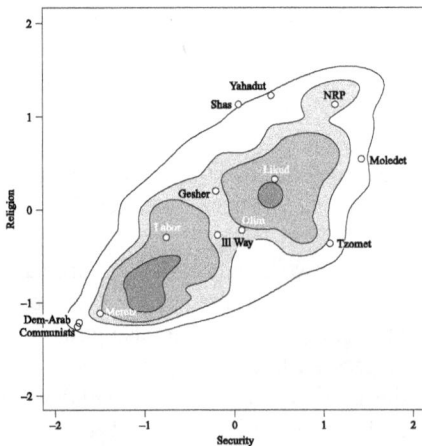

Figure 4.3: Party Positions in Israel 1n 1996, with the estimated voter distribution

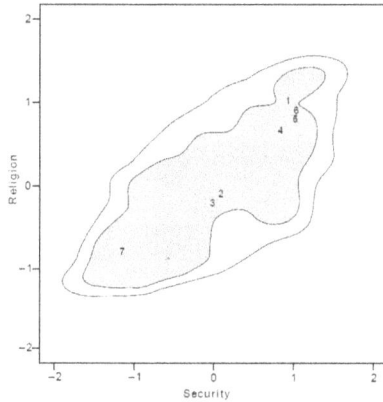

Figure 4.4: Estimated local equilibrium positions in the Knesset in 1996. Key: 1=Shas, 2=Likud, 3=Labor, 4=NRP, 5=Moledet, 6=Third Way, 7= Meretz.

of a core party, that coalition government will be based on a small number of minimal winning coalitions. Notice that this inference provides a good reason to consider using a two dimensional rather than a *one* dimensional model of policy bargaining. In a single dimensional model there will always be a core party (since there will always be a party to which the median legislator belongs). Moreover it can happen that this *median* core party is small in size. For example, in Figure 4.2, if there were only the single security dimension, then the Shas position would be the median, and it could be concluded that Shas could form a minority government. In fact this did not occur. In two dimensions, if a core does exist then it must be at the position of the largest party. We can therefore deduce that in 1992, only Labor could be a core party.

Figure 4.3 shows the positions of the parties after the election of 1996, together with an estimate of the electoral distribution, based on the survey data obtained by Arian and Shamir (1999). Figure 4.4 shows the configuration of one of the local Nash equilibria, estimated using a simulation of the model (Schofield and Sened, 2006). Computation of the eigenvalues of the Hessian of the vote share function of the lowest valence party, the NRP, shows that the joint origin is a saddlepoint of the function. (That is to say, one eigenvalue of the Hessian is positive, so the vote share function has a local minimum along one axis, the principal electoral axis.) Thus vote maximization forces this party away from the origin. Moreover, the convergence coefficient far exceeded 2. We can infer that any LSNE is characterized by all parties adopting positions along the principal electoral axis, oriented at approximately 45 degrees to the security axis. Thus the positions in the figure are compatible with Theorem 3.4 of the previous chapter.

Figure 4.5 gives a schematic representation of the heart, based on party positions af-

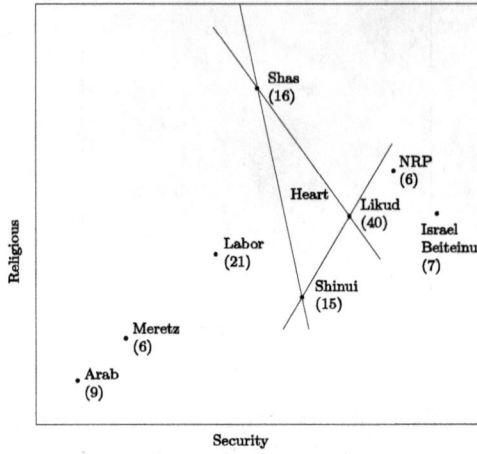

Figure 4.5: The configuration of the Knesset after the election of 2003

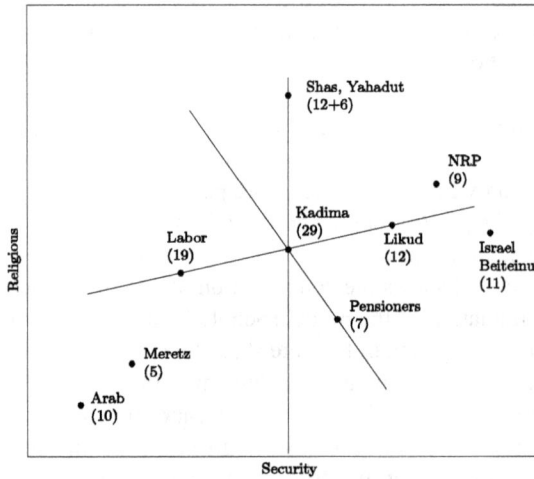

Figure 4.6: The configuration of the Knesset after the election of March 2006

ter 2003. The figure shows Labor with 21 seats, after Am Ehad, with 2 seats, joined Labor in 2003, while Likud has 40 seats after being joined by Olim, with 2 seats. Although Barak, of Labor, became Prime Minister in 1999, he was defeated by Ariel Sharon, of Likud, in the election for prime minister in 2000. The set denoted the heart in this figure represents the coalition possibilities open to Sharon after 2003.

In 2005, Sharon then left the Likud Party and allied with Peres and other senior Labor Party members, to form the new party, *Kadima* ("Forward"). Figure 4.6 gives the estimates of party positions at the March 28, 2006, election to the Knesset. Because of Sharon's stroke in January, 2006, Ehud Olmert had taken over as leader of Kadima, and was able to take 29 seats. Likud only took 12 seats, while the four parties on the upper right of the figure won 38 seats. One surprise of the election was the appearance of a Pensioners' party with 7 seats. As Figure 4.6 indicates, the parties on the right (even with the Pensioners' Party and Likud) do not have the required 61 seats for a majority, so Kadima is located at the core position. Notice, however, that the core position of Kadima is "structurally unstable" in the sense that a small move by Labor on the vertical axis creates the possibility of a counter-Kadima coalition, involving Labor and Likud. As long as Labor is situated at the position given in Figure 4.6, then Kadima will be able to veto any attempt to construct a winning coalition government excluding Kadima.

Because Kadima is at a structurally unstable core, Olmert needed the support of Labor to maintain his coalition. In October 2006, the members of the Kadima-Labor coalition voted to bring Israel Beiteinu into the government. The report, in April 2007, on the failure of the government during the war with Lebanon in Summer 2006 seemed to threaten the Kadima-Labor coalition by bringing about a change in the Labor party leadership. Ehud Barak won the election for the Labor party leader on June 13, 2007, while Shimon Peres became President. On January 15, 2008 Avigdor Lieberman, chairman of Israeli Beiteinu, announced that the party would leave the government because of disagreement over issues such as Jerusalem, the refugees and the contours of a future Palestinian state. On February 3, 2008 Barak agreed to remain in the coalition, thus helping to sustain Kadima in power. However, as of July, 2008, Olmert faces charges of corruption, and has agreed to an election in September for a new party leader. Athough the Kadima government is structurally unstable, in the sense just mentioned, it has opened negotiations with both Syria, over the question of stability in Lebanon, and with Hamas, using Turkey and Egypt as intermediaries. The extreme difficulty of finding a solution to Iran's nuclear capability may destroy the government.

4.2   Elections in Turkey 1999-2007

As in chapter 3, we use sociodemographic variables as proxies for the activist valence functions. Instead of using (Eq.3.5) as the estimator for voter utility, we use the expression

$$u_{ij}(x_i, z_j) = \lambda_j - \beta \|x_i - z_j\|^2 + \theta_j^{\mathrm{T}} \eta_i + \varepsilon_j. \tag{4.1}$$

Here the k -vector θ_j represents the effect of the k different sociodemographic parameters (class, domicile, education, income, etc.) on voting for the party j while η_i is a
k-vector denoting the ith individual's relevant "sociodemographic" characteristics. We
use θ_j^T to denote the transpose of θ_j so $\theta_j^T \eta_i$ is a scalar. The terms $\{\lambda_j\}$ are the intrinsic
valences, and assumed constant at each election, but allowed to vary between elections
as the result of unexplained or exogenous shocks.

When β and $\{\lambda_j\}$ are assumed zero then we call the model pure *sociodemographic*
(SD). When $\theta_j^T \eta_i$ are assumed zero, then the model is called *pure spatial*, and when
all parameters are included then the model is called *joint*. We can use these model to
explain Turkish election results in 1999 and 2002, given in Tables 4.2 and 4.3.

Table 4.2 Turkish election results 1999

Party	.	% Vote	Seats	% Seats
Democratic Left Party	DSP	22.19	136	25
Nationalist Action Party	MHP	17.98	129	23
Virtue Party	FP	15.41	111	20
Motherland Party	ANAP	13.22	86	16
True Path Party	DYP	12.01	85	15
Republican People's Party	CHP	8.71	-	-
People's Democracy Party	HADEP	4.75	-	-
Others	-	4.86	-	-
Independents	-	0.87	3	1

Convergence Coefficient=2.0

Table 4.3. Turkish election results 2002

Party		% Vote	Seats	% Seats
Justice and Development Party	AKP	34.28	363	66
Republican People's Party	CHP	19.39	178	32
True Path Party	DYP	9.54	-	-
Nationalist Action Party	MHP	8.36	-	-
Young Party	GP	7.25	-	-
People's Democracy Party	DEHAP	6.22	-	-
Motherland Party	ANAP	5.13	-	-
Felicity Party	SP	2.49	-	-
Democratic Left Party	DSP	1.22	-	-
Others and Independents	-	6.12	9	2
Total	-		550	

Convergence coefficient = 6.48

Figures 4.7 and 4.9 show the electoral distributions (based on a sample surveys of
sizes 635 and 483, respectively) and estimates of party positions. for 1999 and 2002,

while Figure 4.8 shows the heart in 1999.[181]

Minor differences between these two figures include the disappearance of the Virtue Party (FP) which was banned by the Constitutional Court in 2001, and the change of the name of the Kurdish party from HADEP to DEHAP (though we retain the name HADEP in figure 4.9). In 1999, a DSP minority government formed, supported by ANAP and DYP. This only lasted about 4 months, and was replaced by a DSP-ANAP-MHP coalition. During the period 1999-2002, Turkey experienced two severe economic crises. As Tables 4.2 and 4.3 show, the vote shares of the parties in the governing coalition went from about 53% in 1999 to 15% in 2002. The most important change in 2002 was the appearance of the new Justice and Development Party (AKP) in 2002. This latter party obtained about 35% of the vote and 363 seats out of 550 seats (or 66%) in 2002. In 2007, the AKP increased its vote share to 47%, again taking a majority of 340 (or 63%). Clearly the electoral system had become highly majoritarian, leading to the creation of a core party.

The MNL estimates of the valences of parties such as ANAP fell between 2002 and 1999. In 1999, the estimated λ_{ANAP} was -0.114, whereas in 2002 it was -0.567. The estimated valence, λ_{AKP}, of the new Justice and Development Party (AKP) in 2002 was 1.968, which we might ascribe to the disillusion of most voters with the other parties, and the charisma of Recep Tayyip Erdogan, leader of the AKP.

It is also possible that the change in the nature of the electoral system caused activist groups to coalesce round the AKP. The β coefficient was 0.456 in 1999, and 1.445 in 2002, suggesting that electoral preferences had become more divided.[182]

Table 4.4 Turkish election results 2007

Party		% Vote	Seats	% Seats
Justice and Development Party	AKP	46.6	340	62
Republican People's Party	CHP	20.9	112	20
Nationalist Movement Party	MHP	14.3	71	13
Democrat Party	DP	5.4	-	-
Young Party	GP	3.0	-	-
Felicity Party	SP	2.3	-	-
Independents	-	5.2	27[183]	5
Others	-	2.3	-	-
Total		100	550	100

In the 2007 election, the Kurdish Party (now called the Freedom and Solidarity Party, DTP) contested the election as independents, and thus were not subject to the 10 percent

[181] The estimation is based on a factor analysis of a sample survey conducted by Veri Arastima for TUSES.
[182] Abdullah Gul became Prime Minister after the November 2002 election because Erdogan was banned from holding office. Erdogan took over as Prime Minister after winning a by-election in March 2003.
[183] 24 of these "independents" were in fact supported by the Kurdish DTP -Freedom and Solidarity Party.

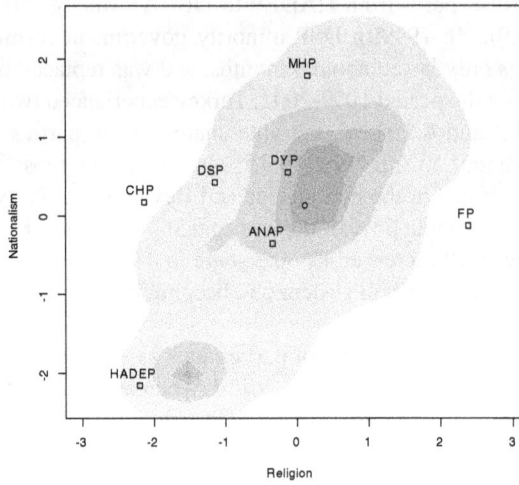

Figure 4.7: Party positions and voter distribution in Turkey in 1999

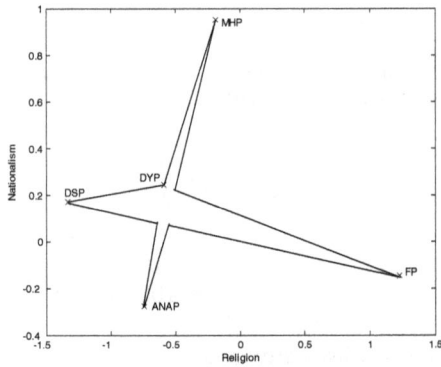

Figure 4.8: The Heart in 1999 in Turkey

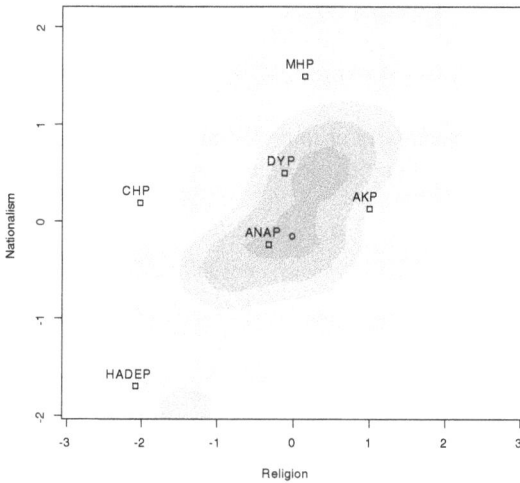

Figure 4.9: Party positions and voter distribution in Turkey in 2002

cut-off. The members of the party were able to win 24 seats. On August 29, 2007, Abdullah Gul, Erdogan's ally in the AKP, was elected president of Turkey. However, on 18 December 2007, the Turkish military authorities arrested Nurettin Demirtas, the leader of the DTP, alleging that he had forged documents to avoid military service. It is more likely because of suspected links between Demirtas and the outlawed Kurdish Workers' Party, the P.K.K.

In the last week of December, 2007, Turkish military forces went into Iraq bombing a number of P.K.K. strongholds. Then in March the Constitutional Court considered whether to shut down the AKP by banning 71 members of the party.

4.2.1   The 1999 Election in Turkey

The electoral variance on the first axis (religion) was found to be 1.20 while on the second axis the electoral variance was 1.14, with the covariance between the two axes equal to 0.78. The electoral variance on the x-axis (religion) is 1.20, while the variance on the y-axis (nationalism) is 1.14. Thus the covariance matrix (defined in the Appendix to Chapter 3) is the 2 by 2 matrix

$$\nabla = \begin{bmatrix} 1.20 & 0.78 \\ 0.78 & 1.14 \end{bmatrix}.$$

For the joint model, the β coefficient is 0.456, while the party with the lowest valence is CHP with $\lambda_{CHP} = -0.673$.[184]

Because we use the Type I distribution, the probability, ρ_{CHP}, that a voter chooses CHP, when all parties are located at the origin, is given by

$$[1 + \exp(0.559) + \exp(1.136) + \exp(1.688) + \exp(0.059) + \exp(3.1]^{-1}$$
$$= 0.028.$$

Equation (3.18) in the Appendix to chapter 3 shows that the Hessian of the vote share function of the CHP (when all parties are at the origin) is

$$C_{CHP} = [2\beta(1 - 2\rho_{CHP})\nabla - I].$$
$$\text{Now } \beta(1 - 2\rho_{CHP}) = 0.4305, \text{ so}$$
$$C_{CHP} = \begin{bmatrix} 0.033 & +0.675 \\ 0.675 & -0.019 \end{bmatrix}.$$

But $trace(\nabla) = 2.34$, so

$$c = 2 \times 0.4305 \times 2.34$$
$$= 2.014.$$

Since $c > 2.0$, we know that at least one eigenvalue of C_{CHP} must be negative. It is easy to show that the eigenvalues of C_{CHP} are $+0.679$ and -0.664. The eigenvector corresponding to the positive eigenvalue is $(+1.04, +1.0)$ while the second minor eigenvector is $(+1.0, -1.04)$.

The first eigenvector corresponds to the *principal electoral component*, or eigenspace, aligned at approximately 45 degrees to the religion axis. On this principal axis, the vote share of the CHP increases as it moves away from the electoral origin. The minor, perpendicular axis is aligned at right angles to the first, and on this axis, the vote share of the CHP decreases as it moves away from the origin. Clearly the origin is a saddlepoint, and we can expect all parties to align themselves close to the principal axis. Many of the parties are so aligned in Figure 4.7. The fact that the some of the parties are located off this axis can be attributed to the influence of activists.

4.2.2   The 2002 Election in Turkey

Again, the empirical model estimates the electoral variance on the first axis (religion) to be 1.18, while on the second axis the variance is 1.15, with the covariance between the two axes equal to 0.74.

Thus

$$\nabla = \begin{bmatrix} 1.18 & 0.74 \\ 0.74 & 1.15 \end{bmatrix}$$

with $trace(\nabla) = 2.33$.

---

[184]See Schofield, Ozdemir and Schnidman (2008) for full details on the joint MNL model. The Bayes factor for the joint model over the pure spatial model was 6.13.

The β coefficient is 1.445, while the party with the lowest valence is ANAP with $\lambda_{ANAP} = -0.567$.

Because we use the Type I distribution, when all parties are located at the origin, the probability, ρ_{ANAP}, that a voter chooses ANAP is given by

$$\begin{aligned} &= [1 + \exp(2.535) + \exp(1.67) + \exp(3.163) + \exp(2.281)]^{-1} \\ &= 0.019. \end{aligned}$$

The Hessian of the vote share function of ANAP (when all parties are at the origin) is

$$\begin{aligned} C_{ANAP} &= [2\beta(1 - 2\rho_{ANAP})\nabla - I] \\ \text{Now } \beta(1 - 2\rho_{ANAP}) &= 1.39, \text{ so} \\ C_{CHP} &= \begin{bmatrix} 2.28 & 2.06 \\ 2.06 & 2.20 \end{bmatrix}. \end{aligned}$$

The convergence coefficient is now given by

$$\begin{aligned} c &= \beta[1 - 2\rho_{ANAP}]trace(\nabla) \\ &= 2 \times 1.39 \times 2.33 = 6.48 \end{aligned}$$

which greatly exceeds the upper bound for convergence to the electoral origin. The major eigenvalue for the ANAP is $+4.30$, with eigenvector $(+1.10, +1.0)$ while the minor eigenvalue is $+0.18$, with orthogonal eigenvector $(-1.0, +1.10)$.

In this case, the electoral origin is a minimum of the vote share function of ANAP. As before, the first eigenvector corresponds to the principal electoral component, or eigenspace, aligned at approximately 45 degrees to the religion axis, while the minor axis is aligned at right angles to the principal axis. The vote share of ANAP increases as it moves away from the electoral origin. Because the major eigenvalue is much larger than the minor, we can expect the parties in equilibrium to adopt positions which will tend to be on the principal electoral axis, though some parties may adopt equilibrium positions lie far from the principal axis. Figure 4.9 is consistent with this inference. It can also be noted that the AKP position in 2002 is closer to the origin that the position of the FP was in 1999. It is possible that the high valence of the AKP not only increased activist support from moderate religious groups, but also induced the party to adopt a more moderate position.

4.3   The 2004 and 2006 Elections in Canada

The Canadian federal election, 2004 (more formally, the 38th General Election), was held on June 28, 2004 to elect members of the Canadian House of Commons of the 38th Parliament of Canada. The Liberal government of Prime Minister Paul Martin lost its majority, but he was able to form a minority government with 135 seats because of the (informal) support of the New Democratic Party until the end of 2005. At that point,

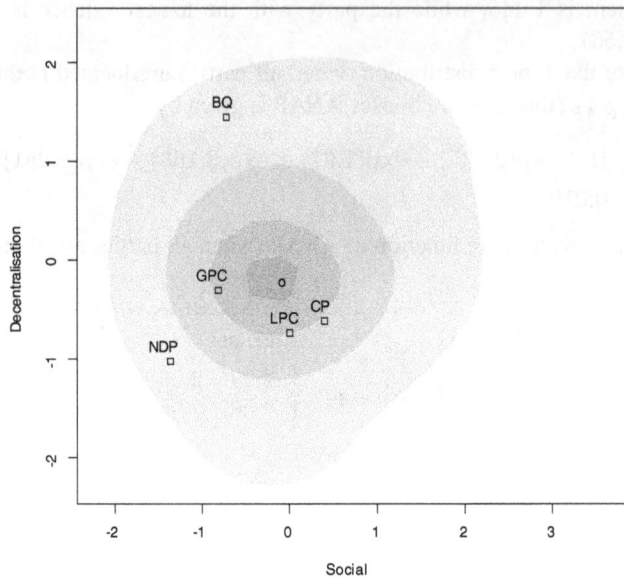

Figure 4.10: The election in Canada in 2004

scandal over corruption and sponsorship forced an election on January 23, 2006. The Conservative Party of Canada won a plurality of seats (40.3%) or 124 out of 308, up from 99 seats in 2004, and 36.3% of the votes, up from 29.6% in the 2004 election (see Tables 4.5 and 4.6). The election resulted in a minority government led by the Conservative Party with Stephen Harper becoming the 22nd Prime Minister of Canada. In the first few months of 2006, the Conservatives received (informal) support from the Bloc Québécois. However, this support proved quite unpopular among their activists in Quebec, so the Bloc began to oppose the Conservatives on issues such as the environmental or policies to do with the military or Afghanistan. Occasionally, when the BQ withdrew their support, the Liberals voted with the Conservatives. Figure 4.10 gives an estimate of the voter distribution and the party positions.[185] The changes between 2004 and 2006 are illustrated by the hearts in Figures 4.11 and 4.12 after these two elections, while Table 4.8 in the Appendix to this Chapter gives details of the logit model, and Tables 4.10 and 4.11 give the coefficients of the factor dimensions. Table 4.9 gives the log Bayes factors, showing that the joint model is superior to both sociodemographic and pure spatial models.

---

[185] Voter ideal points were estimated from survey data available at http://ces-eec.mcgill.ca/surveys.html. See also Blais, et al. (2006).

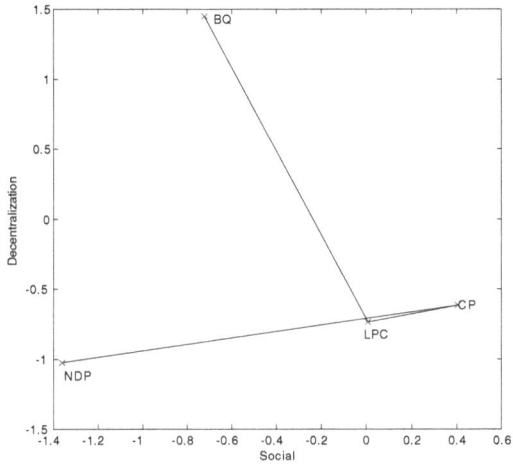

Figure 4.11: The heart in Canada in 2004

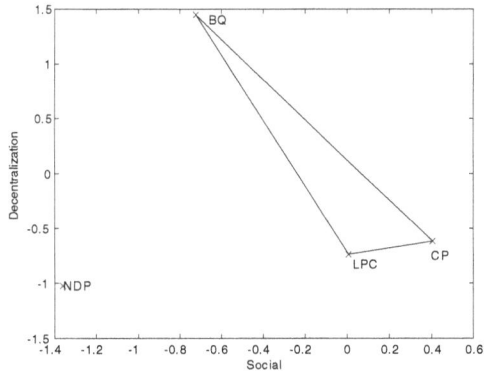

Figure 4.12: The heart in Canada in 2006

Table 4.5 Canadian election, 2004			
Party	Vote share %	Seat	Seat share %
Conservative Party: CP	29.6	99	32
Liberal Party: LPC	36.7	135	44
Bloc Québécois: BQ	12.4	54	18
New Democratic Party: NDP	15.7	19	6
Green Party: GPC	4.3	0	0
Table 4.6. Canadian election, 2006			
Party	Vote share %	Seat	Seat share %
Conservative Party: CP	36.3	124	40.3
Liberal Party: LPC	30.2	103	33.5
Bloc Québécois: BQ	10.5	51	16.5
New Democratic Party: NDP	17.5	29	9.5
Green Party: GPC	4.5	0	0

4.3.1   Computation of the convergence coefficient

Table 4.8 shows that for 2004,

$$(\lambda_{NDP}, \lambda_{CP}, \lambda_{GPC}, \lambda_{LPC}, \lambda_{BQ}) = (+2.296, +1.812, +1.332, 0.0, -7.535),$$

while $\beta = +0.915$ and

$$\nabla = \begin{bmatrix} 1.05 & 0.133 \\ 0.133 & 1.02 \end{bmatrix}.$$

Thus

$$\rho_{BQ} = \frac{1}{1 + e^{1.812+7.535} + e^{2.296+7.535} + e^{1.332+7.535}} = 0.$$

$$2\beta(1 - 2\rho_{BQ}) = 2 \times 0.915 \times 1 = 1.83.$$

$$\text{Hence } C_{BQ} = (1.83) \begin{bmatrix} 1.05 & 0.133 \\ 0.133 & 1.02 \end{bmatrix} - I$$

$$= \begin{bmatrix} +0.92 & +0.24 \\ +0.24 & +0.86 \end{bmatrix},$$

$$\text{so } c = 1.83 \times 2.07) = 3.78$$

The eigenvalues of the characteric matrix of the Bloc Québécois are 1.13 and 0.65 (with eigenvectors $(+1.0, +\frac{7}{8})$ and $(-\frac{7}{8}, +1.0)$, respectively). Since these eigenvalues are both positive, this implies that the electoral origin is a local minimum of the vote share function of the BQ. This further implies that any LNE of the electoral game in 2004 would be one where parties scatter in all directions away from the origin. However, the sociodemographic variable defined by residence in Quebec gives a high coefficient of 10.962 to the BQ. Thus the equilibrium position for the BQ should be north on the

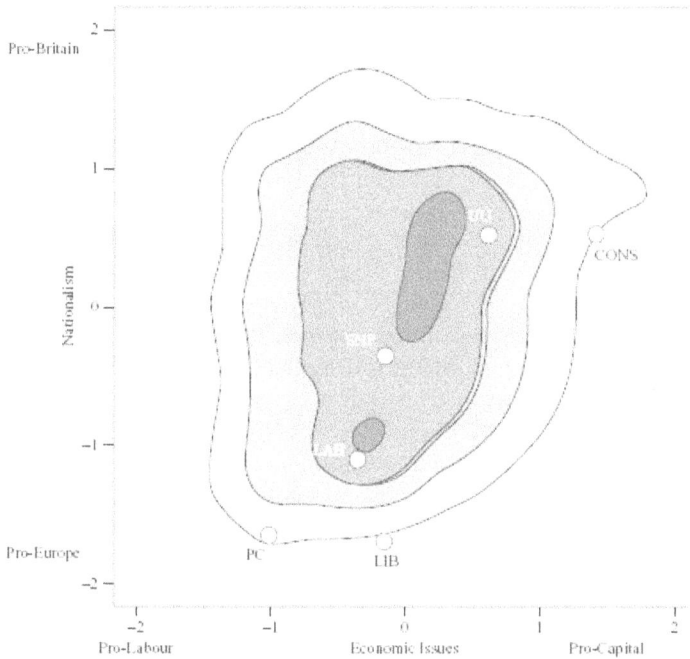

Figure 4.13: Party positions and voter distribution in Britain in 1997

Decentralization axis (as it is in Figure 4.10). Indeed, the BQ estimated position is approximately $(-0.7, +1.4)$, which is close to the second eigenspace. The positions of the other parties in Figure 4.10 may be accounted for by considering the influence of various activist groups.

4.4   Elections in the United Kingdom

Figure 4.13 shows the estimated positions of the parties, based on a survey of Party MPs in 1997 (Schofield, 2005). In addition to the Conservative Party (CONS), Labour Party (LAB) and Liberal Democrat Party (LIB) responses were obtained from Ulster Unionists (UU), Scottish Nationalists (SNP) and Plaid Cymru (PC). The first axis is economic, the second axis concerned attitudes to the European Union (pro-Europe to the "south" of the vertical axis, and pro-Britain to the "north"). The electoral model with exogenous valence was estimated for the election in 1997.

For 1997, $(\lambda_{con}, \lambda_{lab}, \lambda_{lib}, \beta)_{1997} = (+1.24, 0.97, 0.0, 0.5)$ so

$$\rho_{lib} = \frac{e^0}{e^0 + e^{1.24} + e^{0.97}} = \frac{1}{7.08} = 0.14.$$

Since the electoral variance is 1.0 on the first economic axis and 1.5 on the European axis, we obtain

$$\beta(1 - 2\rho_{lib}) = 0.36 \text{ and}$$

$$C_{lib} = (0.72) \begin{bmatrix} 1.0 & 0 \\ 0 & 1.5 \end{bmatrix} - I = \begin{bmatrix} -0.28 & 0 \\ 0 & +0.08 \end{bmatrix}.$$

The convergence coefficient can be calculated to be 1.8. Although the necessary condition is satisfied, the origin is clearly a saddlepoint for the Liberal Democrat Party. Note that the second "European" axis is a "principal electoral axis" exhibiting greater electoral variance. This axis is the eigenvector associated with the positive eigenvalue. Because the covariance between the two electoral axes is negligible, we can infer that, for each party, the eigenvalue of the Hessian at the origin is negative on the first or minor "economic" axis. According to the formal model with exogenous valence, all parties should have converged to the origin on this minor axis. Because the eigenvalue for the Liberal Democrat Party is positive on the second axis, we have an explanation for its position away from the origin on the Europe axis in Figure 4.13. However there is no explanation for the location of the Conservative Party so far from the origin on both axes. Schofield (2005) presented a model where the falling exogenous valence of the Conservative Party leader increases the marginal importance of two opposed activist groups in the party: one group "pro-capital" and one group "pro-Britain."

The empirical analysis by Schofield showed that overall Conservative valence fell from 1.58 in 1992 to 1.24 in 1997, while the Labour valence increased from 0.58 to 0.97. These estimated valences include both exogenous valence terms for the parties and the activist component. Recent studies of these elections[186] suggest that when Tony Blair took over from John Smith as leader of the Labour Party, then the exogenous valence, $\lambda_{lab,}$, of the party increased up to the 1997 election. Conversely, the exogenous valence, λ_{con}, for the Conservatives fell. Since the coefficients in the equation for the electoral pull for the Conservative Party depend on $\lambda_{con} - \lambda_{lab}$, Theorem 1 implies that the effect would be to increase the marginal effect of activism for the Conservative Party, thus pulling the optimal position away from the party's weighted electoral mean. The opposite conclusion holds for the Labour Party, since increasing $\lambda_{lab} - \lambda_{con}$ has the effect of reducing the marginal activist effect. Figure 4.14 gives an illustration taken from Schofield (2005) based on an activist model for Britain for recent elections. As in Figure 4.13, there are two dimensions. The Labour Party benefits from resources from two potential activist groups, with preferred policy positions at L and E. The contract

---

[186]For an empirical analysis of the election of 2005 see Clarke, Sanders, Stewart and Whiteley (2004). For discussion of the nature of party competition in Britain from 1992 on see Clarke, Stewart and Whiteley (1997, 1998).

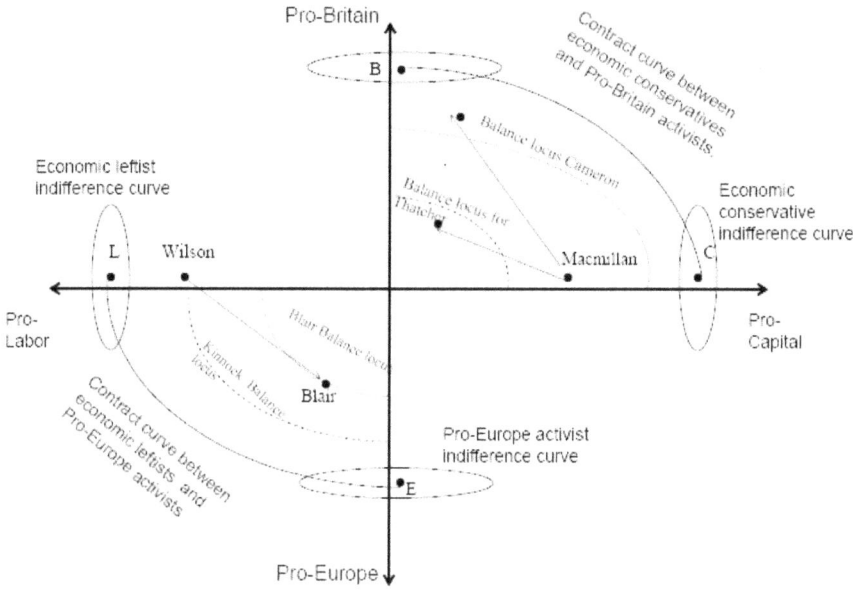

Figure 4.14: Activists in Britain in 1997

curve is the curve connecting these preferred positions of an activist group (L) on the economic left and an activist group (E), supporting a membership of a strong European Union.

The optimal Labour position will be determined by a version of the balance equation

$$\left[\frac{d\mathcal{E}^*_{lab}}{dz_{lab}} - z^*_{lab}\right] + \frac{1}{2\beta}\left[\frac{d\mu_{lab,L}}{dz_{lab}} + \frac{d\mu_{lab,E}}{dz_{lab}}\right] = 0 \tag{4.2}$$

which equates the "electoral pull" against the two "activist pulls," generated by the two different activist functions, $\mu_{lab,L}$ and $\mu_{lab,E}$. In the same way, if there are two activist groups for the Conservatives, generated by functions $\mu_{con,C}$ and $\mu_{con,B}$ centered at C and B respectively, then we obtain a balance equation:

$$\left[\frac{d\mathcal{E}^*_{con}}{dz_{con}} - z^*_{con}\right] + \frac{1}{2\beta}\left[\frac{d\mu_{con,C}}{dz_{con}} + \frac{d\mu_{con,B}}{dz_{con}}\right] = 0. \tag{4.3}$$

Since the electoral pull for the Conservative Party fell between the elections, the optimal position, z^*_{con}, will be one which is "closer" to the locus of points that generates the greatest activist support. This locus is where the joint marginal activist pull is zero. This locus of points can be called the "activist contract curve" for the Conservative Party.

Using Theorem 3.1, we can infer that the reason the Labour Party under Blair was able to move to a position closer to the origin between the elections of 1992 and 1997 was that his increasing valence reduced the importance of pro-labour activists in the party. On the other hand, the declining valences of the Conservative Party leaders, first William Hague, and then Iain Duncan Smith, increased the importance of the marginal activist effect for the party. This appears to have the effect of obliging the party to move to the fairly extreme position shown in Figure 4.13. After Gordon Brown took over as Prime Minister from Tony Blair in 2007, the worsening economic situation dramatically changed the valence balance between Brown and the new Conservative leader, David Cameron. Brown has also been the subject of scorn because of his attempt to push through a law allowing for a six week detention of suspected terrorists. This attempt caused a Conservative, David Davis, to resign and then recontest and then win his parliamentary seat on the basis of a reassertion of liberty. On Thursday, July 14, 2008, Labour lost a safe seat in the by-election in Glasgow East to the Scottish Nationalists.

In Ireland, the leader of Sinn Fein, Gerry Adams, led the successful opposition to the Lisbon Treaty in the referendum on June 14, 2008, arguing that the treaty would undermine Ireland's sovereignty on moral, military and financial matters. This No vote has caused consternation among European leaders,including the Irish Taoiseach, Brian Cowen, and the French President, Nicolas Sarkozy. Many Britons wondered why the electorate had not been asked for a referendum.

4.5   Elections in the Netherlands 1977, 1981 and 2006

Next we consider a multinomial logit (MNL) model for the elections of 1977 and 1981 in the Netherlands (Schofield, Martin, Quinn and Whitford, 1998; Quinn, Martin and Whitford, 1999) using data from the middle level Elites Study (ISEIUM, 1983). There are four main parties: Labor (PvdA), Christian Democratic Appeal (CDA), Liberals (VVD) and Democrats (D'66), with approximately 38 percent, 36 percent, 20 percent and 6 percent of the popular vote in 1977. Table 4.7 gives the valences for an MNL model based on the estimated positions of the parties, derived from the Elites Study, while Figure 4.15 gives the estimate of the density contours of the electoral distribution of voter bliss points based on the Rabier Inglehart (1981) Euro-barometer survey. Table 4.7 also gives the national and sample vote shares for the four major parties (these excluded the small parties, so the four shares sum to 100 percent). The estimated vote shares when all parties are at the origin are derived below, and are given by the column labeled Model in Table 4.7.

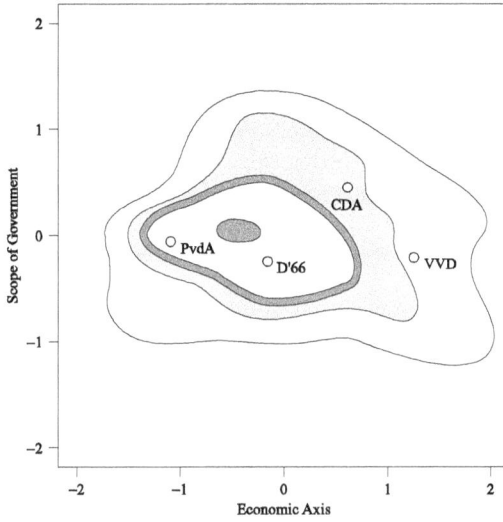

Figure 4.15: Party positions in the Netherlands in 1977

Table 4.7. Estimated vote shares and valences in the Netherlands

Party	National vote % in 1977	Sample vote%	Model %	Valences
PvdA	38.0	36.9	38.6	1.596
CDA	35.9	33.8	31.9	1.403
VVD	20.0	18.9	21.7	1.015
D'66	6.1	10.4	7.8	0
Total	**100.0**	**100.0**	**100.0**	

The estimated exogenous valences were normalized, by choosing the D'66 to have exogenous valence $\lambda_{D66} = 0$. The other valences are $\lambda_{VVD} = 1.015$, $\lambda_{CDA} = 1.403$ and $\lambda_{PvdA} = 1.596$. To compute the D'66 Hessian, we note that the electoral variance on the first axis is $\sigma_1^2 = 0.658$, while on the second it is $\sigma_2^2 = 0.289$. The covariance $(\sigma_1, \sigma_2) = -0.06$ is negligible.

The spatial coefficient $\beta = 0.737$ for the model with exogenous valence. Thus the probability of voting for each of the parties, as well as the Hessians when all parties are at the origin, can be calculated as follows:

$$\rho_{D66} = \frac{1}{1 + e^{1.015} + e^{1.403} + e^{1.596}} = 0.078,$$

$$2\beta(1 - 2\rho_{D66}) = 2 \times 0.737 \times 0.844 = 1.244.$$

$$\text{Hence } C_{D66} = (1.244) \begin{bmatrix} 0.658 & -0.06 \\ -0.06 & 0.289 \end{bmatrix} - I$$

$$= \begin{bmatrix} -0.18 & -0.07 \\ -0.07 & -0.64 \end{bmatrix},$$

$$\text{so } c = 2 \times 0.622 \times 0.947) = 1.178.$$

Although the convergence coefficient exceeds 1.0, so the sufficient condition, given by Theorem 3.4 is not satisfied, the necessary condition of the Theorem is satisfied, and the eigenvalues for the characteristic matrix for D'66 can be seen to be negative. Thus the joint origin is an LSNE for the stochastic model with exogenous valence.

In a similar way, we can compute the other probabilities, giving

$$(\rho_{D66}, \rho_{VVD}, \rho_{CDA}, \rho_{PvdA}) = (0.078, 0.217, 0.319, 0.386).$$

This vector can be identified as the expected vote shares of the parties when all occupy the electoral origin. Note also that these expected vote shares are very similar to the sample vote shares

$$(S^*_{D66}, S^*_{VVD}, S^*_{CDA}, S^*_{PvdA}) = (0.104, 0.189, 0.338, 0.369),$$

as well as the average of the national vote shares in the two elections.

$$(E^*_{D66}, E^*_{VVD}, E^*_{CDSA}, E^*_{PvdA}) = (0.094, 0.199, 0.356, 0.352).$$

These national vote shares can be regarded as approximations of the expected vote shares.

Although we do not have data available on the activist valences for the parties, we can use sociodemographic variables as proxies for the activist group, and use the expression

$$u_{ij}(x_i, z_j) = \lambda_j - \beta \|x_i - z_j\|^2 + \theta_j^{\mathrm{T}} \eta_i + \varepsilon_j. \tag{4.4}$$

Table 4.11 gives the joint MNL estimation with the sociodemographics (as re-estimated by Zakharov and Fantazzini, 2008), using the data from Quinn, Martin and Whitford (1999).[187] From Table 4.11,

$$(\lambda_{PvdA}, \lambda_{CDA}, \lambda_{VVD}, \lambda_{D66}, \beta)_{1979} = (+1.95, -1.53, 0.15, 0.0, 0.63). \tag{4.5}$$

Using this these empirical results we find

$$\rho_{CDA} = \frac{1}{1 + e^{3.49} + e^{1.67} + e^{1.531}} \simeq 0.0,$$

$$\text{and } 2\beta(1 - 2\rho_{CDA}) = 2 \times 0.63 \times 1 = 1.26.$$

$$\text{so } C_{CDA} = (1.26) \begin{bmatrix} 0.658 & -0.06 \\ -0.06 & 0.289 \end{bmatrix} - I = \begin{bmatrix} -0.17 & -0.08 \\ -0.08 & -0.54 \end{bmatrix}$$

$$\text{and } c = 1.19.$$

[187] The sociodemographics are those used by Quinn *et al:* manual labor, religion, income, size of town, education.

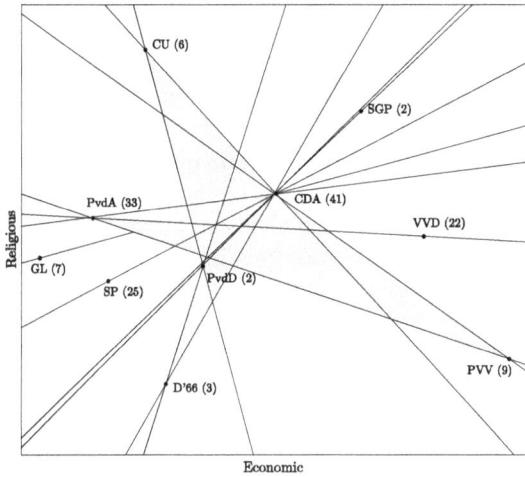

Figure 4.16: The Dutch Parliament in 2006

Again, the eigenvalues for the characteristic matrix for CDA can be seen to be negative. Thus the joint origin is an LSNE for the stochastic model with exogenous valence
and sociodemographic variables.

Quinn and Martin (2002) performed a simulation of the empirical model and showed
that the joint origin was indeed a PSNE for the vote-maximizing model with the exogenous valence values as estimated by the MNL models with and without sociodemographic variables. Indeed, the positions given in Figure 4.15 could not be an LSNE of
the stochastic model with exogenous valence alone. This conflict between the predicted
equilibrium positions of the model and the estimated positions suggest that the activists
for the parties played an important role in determining the party positions. These empirical results indicate that Theorem 3.4 is compatible with the following two hypotheses:

(i) the party positions given in Figure 4.15 are a close approximation to the actual
     positions of the parties;

(ii) each party was at a Nash equilibrium position in an electoral contest involving
      a balance for each party between the centripetal marginal electoral pull for the
      party and the centrifugal marginal activist pull on the party.

Figure 4.16 for the Netherlands in 2006 illustrates the heterogenous location of parties in the Dutch polity (based on the work by Shikano and Linhart, 2007) and shows
an estimate of the legislative heart, bounded by the various median lines. The figure
indicates how small parties can obtain representation in Parliament when the electoral
system is based on proportional representation.

4.6   Concluding remarks

The discussion of politics in Israel, Turkey, Canada, Britain and the Netherlands, together with the results on the 1992 election in the United States, suggests that any centripetal tendency towards an electoral center will be relatively weak.[188] Although there may be some degree of convergence on the economic axis in Britain and the United States, this will be countered by divergence on the other policy axis. The theory, as well as empirical work presented in Schofield and Sened (2006) suggests that activist groups will tend to pull the parties away from the center. Indeed, we can follow Duverger (1954) and Riker (1953) and note that under proportional electoral methods, there is very little motivation for interest groups to coalesce. Consequently, the fragmentation of interest groups will lead to fragmentation in the polity.[189] Fragmentation may be mitigated by the electoral system (especially if there is a relatively high electoral requirement which determines whether a party will obtain some legislative representation). We can express the difference between proportional representation and plurality rule as follows.

Under *proportional electoral methods*, bargaining to create winning coalitions occurs *after* the election. As a consequence, there need be no strong tendency forcing activist groups to coalesce, in order to concentrate their influence. If activist groups respond to this impulse, then activist fragmentation will result in party fragmentation. As Figure 4.16 for the Netherlands illustrates, parties can be scattered throughout the policy space. Activist groups, linked to small parties, may aspire to affect policy outcomes, by gaining access to the governing coalition. This is indicated by the observation that the bargaining domain in the legislature (the heart) often includes small parties. Although party strengths may fluctuate in response to exogenous shocks, it may be conjectured that the structure of the heart is little affected by these changes. The formation of coalition within the policy arena of the heart induces stable expectations about party cooperation. Because relatively small activist groups, and their associated parties, may have veto power, policy choice may be risk avoiding.

Under *plurality rule,* if interest groups do not form a coalition *before* the election, then they will have little impact on political outcomes. Consequently, small parties face the possibility of extinction. Unlike the situation in a polity based on proportional rule, an activist group linked to a small party in a plurality polity has little expectation of influencing government policy. Thus activist groups face increasing returns to size. The activist model of elections presented in Chapter 3 suggests that when there are two dimensions of policy, then there will tend to be at most four principal activist groups. In Britain and Canada, the nature of the electoral contest generally produces two principal activist groups. However, regional preferences, over issues such as Québec in Canada, allows small parties, such as the Bloc Québécois, to survive. The New Democratic Party, with 2,500,00 votes (17%) obtained only 9% of the seats, while the Green Party

---

[188] Recent work by Zakharov and Fantazzini (2008) explores a number of variants of the MNL-sociodemographic model for Israel, the UK and the Netherlands and finds the models to be robust.

[189] See Adams et al. (2006).

of Canada, with over 660,000 votes (or 4.5%) can gain no seats.

In the United States, plurality rule induces the two party system, through this effect on activist groups. Although the two party configuration may be in equilibrium at any time, the tension within the activist coalitions induces a slow rotation, and thus political realignment. Presidential candidates must balance the centripetal electoral effect against the centrifugal valence effect. It is plausible that, in general, the relative electoral effect is stronger under plurality than under proportional rule. On occasion in the United States, the conflict within activist groups is so pronounced that the two party system breaks down. Such a collapse of activist cohesion may herald a major realignment, induced by the creation of a new policy dimension, such as civil rights. The effect of this process of realignment may be to weaken the degree of policy conflict on the economic axis, at the cost of increasing policy conflict on the new policy axis. This change can be interpreted as a manifestation of "political polarization."

The well known relationship between proportional representation and a degree of political fragmentation (as measured by effective number) may be accounted for indirectly as a consequence of the logic forced on activist groups rather than parties themselves.

4.7 Empirical Appendix

Table 4.8. Multinomial Logit Analysis of the 2004 Election in Canada
(Normalized w.r.t LPC)

	Party	Mean	95% confidence Lower Bound	interval Upper Bound
Spatial Coefficient β		0.915	0.756	1.06
Constant λ coefficients	CP	1.812	1.063	2.5607
	BQ	-7.535	-12.835	-3.2731
	NDP	2.296	1.251	3.3574
	GPC	1.332	-0.339	2.93
Age	CP	-0.016	-0.026	-0.0063
	BQ	-0.02	-0.035	-0.0039
	NDP	-0.03	-0.044	-0.0175
	GPC	-0.042	-0.065	-0.0184
Female	CP	-0.059	-0.13	0.014
	BQ	-0.08	-0.213	0.0729
	NDP	-0.022	-0.118	0.0647
	GPC	-0.167	-0.343	0.0031
Education	CP	-0.125	-0.209	-0.0455
	BQ	-0.145	-0.282	0.0029
	NDP	-0.098	-0.188	-0.0105
	GPC	-0.134	-0.289	0.0148
Quebec	CP	-0.768	-1.189	-0.2997
	BQ	10.962	6.65	16.3883
	NDP	-1.147	-1.775	-0.5708
	GPC	-0.442	-1.225	0.3929

p=839	Log likelihood= -1020.45

Table 4.9. Log Bayes factors for Canadian model comparisons in 2004

	$\mathbb{M}_2$	Joint	Spatial	Socio-Dem.
	Joint	na	+130***	+52***
$\mathbb{M}_1$	Spatial	-130	na	-78
	Socio-Dem.	-52	+78***	na

*** Extremely strong support for $\mathbb{M}_1$ against $\mathbb{M}_2$.

Table 4.10. Weighting Coefficients on the Social Axis	
Components	**Social**
How much do you think should be done to reduce the gap between the rich and the poor ?(1=much more, 5=much less)	0.318
How much do you think should be done for women ? (1=much more, 5=much less)	0.334
how much do you think should be done for quebec? (1=much more, 5=much less)	0.313
Only the police and the military should be allowed to have guns. (1=strongly agree, 7=strongly disagree)	0.204
As you may know, Canada decided not to participate in the war against Iraq. do you think this is a good decision (1=good decision, 5=bad decision)	0.244
In politics people sometimes talk of left and right. where would you place yours. (0=left, 10=right)	0.292

Table 4.11. Weighting Coefficients on Decentralization	
Components	**Decentr.**
The welfare state makes people less willing to look after themselves. (1=strongly agree, 4=strongly disagree)	-0.063
The government should: 1= see to it that everyone has a decent standard of living, 2=leave people to get ahead on their own	0.149
If people can't find work in the region where they live, they should move to to where the jobs are ? (1=strongly agree, 7=strongly disagree)	0.389
How much do you think should be done for Quebec ? (1=much more, 5=much less)	0.050
In general, which government looks after your interests better, the federal government or the provincal government ? (1=federal government, 3=provincal government)	0.882

Table 4.11 MNL model for the Netherlands in 1977 with sociodemographic variables, normalized wrt D'66.

p=529	Parameters	Estimates	Std.err	t	Prob
PvdA	valence	1.946	0.602	3.232	0.001
	manlab	1.536	0.631	2.434	0.015
	relig	0.099	0.161	0.612	0.541
	income	-0.055	0.045	-1.212	0.218
	stown	0.350	0.244	1.433	0.152
	educ	-0.207	0.060	-3.476	0.001
VVD	valence	0.148	0.731	0.203	0.839
	manlab	-0.378	0.846	-0.447	0.655
	relig	0.118	0.178	0.667	0.505
	income	0.100	0.050	2.004	0.045
	stown	0.203	0.279	0.727	0.467
	educ	-0.063	0.065	-0.957	0.339
CDA	valence	-1.531	0.728	-2.101	0.036
	manlab	1.303	0.677	1.925	0.054
	relig	1.500	0.186	8.089	0.000
	income	0.011	0.048	0.228	0.820
	stown	0.558	0.265	2.103	0.035
	educ	-0.162	0.063	-2.574	0.010
β	spatial coeff	0.633	0.062	10.269	0.000
Log-likelihood	-434.920				

Chapter 5

The Global Political Economy

5.1 Introduction

A major theme in the pronouncements of the Reagan administration in the United States and of the Thatcher government in Britain during the 1980's was that Keynesian economic theory provided an excuse for the previous governments of these countries to intervene in their own economies in a way which lead eventually to high unemployment and inflation. One version of this argument, due to Buchanan and Wagner (1977), asserts that, once a government implements Keynesian deficit spending strategies, it becomes susceptible to various special interests in the economy. In an attempt to remain in office, the government adopts policies which result in an increase in the money supply and thus in the rate of inflation. A related argument, presented in the literature on the so-called "political business cycle," suggests that governments will seek to bring about those combinations of inflation and unemployment which are "politically optimal" in terms of electoral response at the time of an election, in an effort to assure re-election. These politically optimal combinations will not coincide with economically optimal combinations, but instead will generate, in the long term, increasing rates of inflation and levels of unemployment.

Keynesian economics was based on the assumption that inconsistent expectations of producers and consumers are persistent features of free market economies. The privileged role of benevolent dictator was given to government, so that its spending strategies might off-set the inconsistency of expectations, encourage investment, and increase output and employment. The new conventional wisdom of the 1980's rejected Keynesian economic theory and returned to pre-Keynesian assumptions. In its simplest form, the neoclassical theory asserts that free markets will tend to be in a state of Pareto optimal equilibrium, as long as government restricts itself to a minimalist strategy. Such a strategy includes increasing the money supply at a constant and declared rate, equal to the long term expected rate of economic growth, reducing the government budget deficit to zero, and if possible bringing about a drop in the government share of GNP. This "disentanglement" of government from the economy would reduce the politically induced inefficiencies in the economy and bring about higher

rates of economic growth. As agents and coalitions realize that they cannot expect assistance from government on terms which are economically irrational and politically
motivated, they will increasingly accept their "legitimate" returns, from the free market. According to Usher (1981) this should reduce the level of distributional conflict
in the political economy.

Table 5.1. Twelve Developed Polities December 2007

Country	GDP/cap[a]	B[d]	E[e]	U[f]	T[g]	S[h]
Corporatist						
Sweden	31.0	+2.80	3.40	5.70	+9.30	9.30
Denmark	32.0	+3.80	1.60	3.00	+6.30	1.00
Austria	34.0	−0.60	3.20	4.20	+1.30	9.00
France	30.2	−2.40	1.80	8.10	−1.60	11.40
Average	—	—	2.50	5.25	—	—
Mixed						
Belgium	32.9	-0.10	2.60	11.10	+5.30	10.40
Italy	28.0	-2.40	1.70	6.00	−0.70	11.60
Germany	30.7	-0.40	2.60	8.60	+5.90	10.70
Netherlands	35.1	-0.30	2.50	4.30	+7.40	7.10
Average	—	—	2.40	7.50	—	—
Liberal						
UK	32.8	−3.00	3.00	5.40	−4.50	−0.13
Canada	34.0	+1.00	2.60	5.80	+3.80	+1.22
US	41.8	−1.20	2.00	4.70	−6.00	−0.40
Japan	30.8	−2.60	2.00	4.00	+1.30	+3.20
Average	—	—	2.40	5.00	—	—
Overall Average	—	—	2.40	5.90	—	—

[a] GDP/capita in thousand US dollars.
[d] B=Budget balance deficit (-) or surplus (+) as a percent of GDP for previous year.
[e] E=Economic growth, as percent change in GDP, over previous year.
[f] U=Unemployment, average percent, over previous year.
[g] T=Trade balance (goods and services) as a percent of GDP
[h] S=average savings rate as percent of disposable income.
Source: OECD. http://www.oecd.org/linklist

There were, of course, a number of problems with this view. For example, it is
remarkable that Reagan's policies resulted in much increased federal budget deficits of
the order of $200 billion during the late 1980's. At the same time economic growth
rates were high, so the alleged relationship between a reduction in the budget deficit

and growth appeared unclear. In Britain there was a greater effort to match rhetoric to economic policies. The attempts to control the public sector borrowing requirement and the growth of money supply, while allowing interest rates to reach historically high levels, brought about a substantial drop in manufacturing output. This caused increased pressure on labor and wages, a rapid increase of unemployment, to about 3.5 million, coupled with a drop in inflation to the 5-7 percent range.

It can be argued that the output and employment losses resulting from government strategies in the United States and Britain in the late 1980's and early 1990's were, in fact, necessary to flush out the damaging effects of previous, myopic policies. Indeed Table 5.1 gives some indication that unemployment rates as of the end of 2007 were somewhat lower in the United States and Britain than in other OECD countries, but that economic growth is very similar. By mid-2008, economic growth had dropped considerably everywhere.

It is very likely that the fairly high unemployment rates in a number of the European economies is a consequence of a change in the balance of comparative advantage between the developed economies of the "North" and the developing or less-developed economies of the "South," and that the employment consequences of this change are made even more serious by the so called "Third Wave" of labor destroying micro-chip technology. One early estimate suggested that over 30 percent of all job-types in the OECD countries were at risk as a consequence of this new technology (see Merrit, 1982).

The adoption of a theory which assumes free market optimality makes it very difficult for government to focus on ways in which to ameliorate the effects of these transformations in the "global economy." In Britain in particular, older-established industries, such as shipbuilding, automobiles, textiles, steel, etc. contracted rapidly, and this raised fears of de-industrialization (Blackaby, 1979). Similar fears in the United States have raised the possibility of increased trade protection and limits on immigration.

The questions I wish to raise here may be listed as follows.

(1) Is there any evidence that western governments have, in the past, intervened in the macro-economy for purely electoral reasons, in ways which, in the long run, may be deemed economically irrational?

This is different from asking whether particular macro-economic decisions can be seen, with hindsight, to be economically irrational. It asks whether the logic of the "political marketplace" is such as to produce economically suboptimal consequences. The literature that dealt with the question was based on a simple economic theory that supposed that inflation and unemployment could be traded off against one another in a fairly obvious fashion. This is clearly false; macro-economic intervention always produces unintended, and frequently surprising consequences. Even if governments wished to achieve "socially optimal" unemployment-inflation combinations, they would be unable to do so. Secondly, the analyses supposed that, in terms of electoral response, there were favorable unemployment- inflation combinations. This is equivalent to the assumption that the vote response can essentially be regarded as a social welfare function, and that "socially optimal" government behavior is the optimization of this social welfare function within the feasible macro-economic possibilities.

The model presented in Chapter 3 suggests that although voters respond to economic choices by government, the policy responses by government include non-economic features. This implies that the vote maximizing functions of political agents incorporate many different dimensions. In other words, electoral response to government behavior is affected by transitory political events (as the current situation in Iraq illustrates).

(2) Is there any evidence that political logic forces governments to accede to special interest groups, to the extent that they over-regulate, over-bureaucratize, over-provide public goods and welfare, etc.?

The general mode of argument of the literature that addresses this question, is essentially that the political and economic cost benefit analyses are quite different and that the political calculus leads to an underestimation of the true economic costs of, for example, a public goods project. The difficulty with this kind of argument is that in order to allege overprovision it is necessary to give an indication of the "optimal" level of provision and a method for attaining it. For example, is there a procedure by which public goods could be created and distributed within a free market context and without the intervention of government, in such a way that the outcome is Pareto superior to the outcome when government intervenes? While a number of authors (Nozick, 1974) have argued that public goods can be provided by protective associations, these arguments simply replace the Hobbesian world of every man against his neighbor with one of every coalition (or neighborhood) against every other. In any case, all such arguments depend in one way or another on an equilibrium optimality result. This leads us to the next question.

(3) Is it reasonable to suppose that a free market economy will generally be in a state of Pareto optimal equilibrium?

At the heart of economic theory is the general equilibrium result, that the consequences of rational self-seeking behavior by agents is a Pareto optimal outcome. If this theory had any relevance at all for economic affairs, then one would expect market adaptation to the presence of unemployment not only to eliminate involuntary unemployment but to do it in such a way that the welfare of every individual increases. There is no strong empirical evidence that this is occurring, and it is worth asking whether there is a major flaw in the theory. The assumptions of the theory are of course very restrictive. The preferences of individuals are supposed to be defined on private goods-whether consumption bundles or production outputs. Secondly, complete Arrow-Debreu (1954) markets are assumed to exist in all commodities, so as to eliminate, or rationalize, all future risk. Finally, and most importantly, economic agents are assumed to treat prices parametrically, in the sense that agents treat prices as fixed and optimize on the fixed budget or production sets. This is a reasonable assumption when all agents are "small" relative to the economy. That is, if any agent is removed, then the others may move to a new equilibrium which they prefer at least as much as the original. If this strong "no-surplus" condition fails, for even one agent, then that agent may manipulate the economy to bring about outcomes that the agent prefers (Ostroy, 1980). What this means is that the manipulator attempts to compute the effects its own behavior has on the eventual equilibrium outcome and then behaves in such a way as to produce a different outcome which it prefers. This notion of manipulation developed out of social choice theory and is proving to be of interest to general equilibrium theorists. It seems reasonable to believe that there will be at least one manipulator in any economy, in which case there is no reason to suppose that even a perfect market in private goods will achieve Pareto-optimality. Hahn (1980) has called this feature "the canker at the heart of the theory."

At the same time the notion of manipulation may prove of considerable value in economic theory. It provides a theoretical mode of access to the analysis of monopoly or oligopoly behavior–such as transfer pricing and the construction of entry barriers. Using this theoretical notion, one may analyze national strategies of manipulation, including the erection of tariffs, and domestic redistribution of income to pick up the increasing returns to scale or the benefits of trade of a national economy.

(4) In which aspects of the economy might one reasonably argue that government intervention is necessary for the attainment of long term optimal performance?

Schofield (2006a) suggests that the fundamental argument in Keynes (1936) was that markets in commodities, especially traded goods, may very well be governed by equilibrium theory, by the law of supply and demand. What concerned Keynes, however, was the degree to which instability or speculative bubbles in asset markets (by which he meant markets in stocks, currencies and houses, etc.) could undermine the stability of commodities markets. Given the events that had occurred in Keynes' lifetime, his preoccupation was with effects of this kind not only in the labor market (where the result is persistent unemployment), but also in the international polity (leading to competitive devaluations).

Keynes accepted this weak version of the equilibrium hypothesis (only for commodities markets), because he saw a terrible danger to the Atlantic democracies. In a world of speculative disorder, the returns to capitalists and the wages of labor would have no legitimate basis. To escape this chaos, the citizens of a nation could rationally choose to give up their freedom to the agents of the state. Bound by such a Hobbesian contract to an autocrat, the citizens could at least hope for some certainty in their lives. Keynes was keenly aware that authoritarian state systems could solve the problem of unemployment, by paying the price of efficiency while necessarily depriving their citizens of their freedom. It seemed all too probable in the 1930's that citizens would be willing to pay the double price of inefficiency and loss of freedom to avoid the great and apparent risks of unemployment. We can also speculate that the disorder exhibited by the Russian political economy in the 1990's led the way to the electorate's willingness to accept Putin's concentration of political power in the early part of the 21st century. Keynes' fears of market disorder seem quite justified in view of the currency crash of the late 1990's, the "dot-com" crash of 2000 and the problems in the "sub-prime" mortgage market in the United States in 2007 and early 2008. In December 2007, Central Banks were desperately making capital available for fear of a liquidity crunch. Figure 5.1 illustrates the extent of the drop in house prices and in the stock market in 2008 while figure 5.2 contrasts the loss in confidence in January 2008 with other crashes in

the period from 1973 on. On January 21, 2008,the DAX index in Germany closed down
7.16 percent while the CAC 40 in France lost 6.83 percent and the London stock market
index, the FTSE 100, lost 5.48 percent. The Federal cut its key interest rate to 2.25%
in March, and then to 2% on April 30, 2008, in the face of the possibility of stagflation (see Figure 5.3). Figure 5.4 shows the rise of oil prices (as of March 2008), while
by July the price had risen to about $140/barrel. Clearly this suggests that the 1970's
have returned. (See Phillips ,2006, 2008, for comments on the causes of the interlinked
problems of oil and debt and the probable decline of the United States.)

From this Keynesian perspective, the fundamental purpose of government is to ameliorate the chaos of the marketplace, and to promote the human and economic opportunities available to citizens by curbing the degree of risk that they must face. This
suggests that government does have a significant interventionist role to play. I concentrate on two related aspects of such intervention.

The most important characteristic of a developed economy is the level (and rate of
change) of productivity. This depends, I would argue, on two structural features of the
economy-the social organization and quality of labor and the level of technological innovation and utilization. Both features have fundamental public goods aspects. One
important aspect of labor is the level of problem solving capacity that is exhibited-the
ability to respond in subtle fashion to the micro-difficulties that any economic activity
necessarily faces. This depends, in turn, on the quality of the human resources (education in the broadest sense) and on the way labor organizes itself. As regards education,
an economist might argue that it is up to each individual to compute the extent of that individual's level of education, given the likely costs and anticipated returns. Since there
are high social benefits from education, the aggregate of individuals' calculations need
not be socially optimal. Consequently, there is an important role for government to intervene, so as to facilitate the enlargement of education, particularly in an era of intense
technological competition (Goldin and Katz. 2008). As regards technological innovation, theoretical analyses by Reinganum (1981) and Kamien and Schwartz (1981)
indicate that it is unlikely that the socially optimal rate of investment in innovation will
occur naturally. In a completely competitive market, with many small firms, almost no
investment will occur, since each firm will leave it up to the others and hope to pick up
the benefits later. In an oligopoly, firms will invest but keep the benefits, in a socially
non-optimal way, for themselves. The logical conclusion is for government to guide investment by subsidies, grants, etc., along the lines that it deems socially profitable. One
problem, of course, with such a strategy is that it is not obvious that there is any connection between government preferred and socially optimal patterns of investment in
research and innovation. A strong case can be made that there has been excess concentration by Britain and the U.S. on defense related industries (see for example Freeman,
1979, and Block 1975). In the future, if climate change does turn out to be the major
problem facing humanity, then socially necessary technological innovation to reduce
greenhouse emissions will become vital.

These arguments suggest that government has an obligation to offset the suboptimal
social choices of the marketplace. The "debate" between the European Union and the

"Anglo-Saxon" polities of the United States and the United Kingdom concerns the degree to which intervention in the global economy by government is acceptable. Table 5.1 does suggest that there are some differences between the OECD economies, while Figure 5.5 gives an idea of GDP/capita growth in six OECD countries from 1952 to 1994.

To provide a way of interpreting Figure 5.5, we can use the Figure 5.6, which presents a fundamental economic idea.

This figure is intended to suggest that any developed economy will tend to exhibit logistic change, with very low growth at the start, then high , essentially linear growth in the middle phase, and declining growth in the period of maturity. Figure 5.5 suggests that the OECD countries were, until recently, all in the linear phase of growth. The figure also suggests that the countries are approaching the plateau of limited growth. Where this onset of the plateau occurs will depend on the internal characteristics of the political economy: the extent to which the labor market is free, the age structure of the society, the level of technological training etc. Table 5.1 suggests that the OECD polities may still be in the linear phase of the logistic transformation, but may be approaching their plateau at GDP/capita of about \$31,000 to \$35,000 for the European countries, with the United States on a higher plateau of about \$42,000.

Figure 5.7 gives a schematic representation of GDP/capita to contrast the difference between the successful economies (the United States, Japan and Europe) and much of the rest of the world, caught, as was noted in Chapter 1, in the Malthusian trap. Figure 5.8 shows the relationship between dependence on agriculture and GDP/capita. Recent emphases on biofuels seems to have dramatically increased world food prices (by about 80%). New understanding about the effect of climate change on world food production as illustrated in Figure 5.9 (and discussed in Chapter 10) suggests that the future may bring massive social unrest and population movement.

Keynes was concerned not just about speculation and market chaos, but about the degree to which uncertainty made the equilibrium theorems invalid. As he wrote

> By "uncertain" knowledge, let me explain, I do not mean merely to distinguish what is known for certain from what is only probable ... Even the weather is only moderately uncertain. The sense in which I am using the term is that in which the prospect of a European war is uncertain, or the price of copper and the rate of interest twenty years hence. (Keynes, 1937).

The possibility of positive feedback effects associated with human activity, particularly the rapid increase of energy utilization by growing economies such as China and India, has increased the uncertainty that is presented by the future. The concern that Keynes had about the difficulty of controlling market disorder is now even more pronounced, as controlling climate change will need the cooperative action of all states. This difficulty is made worse, because of the changes brought about in the beliefs of political leaders about the feasibility of controlling the global market (Bobbitt, 2008). We now consider attempts by political leaders to moderate the effects of market forces.

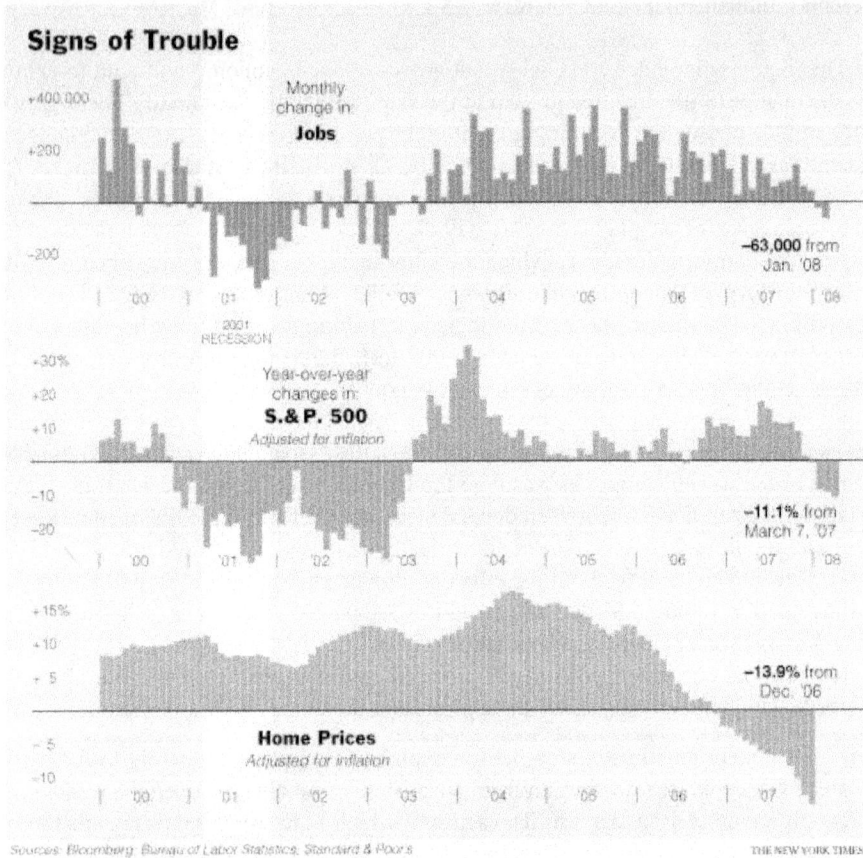

Figure 5.1: Bubbles. (*New York Times*, 8 March 2008).

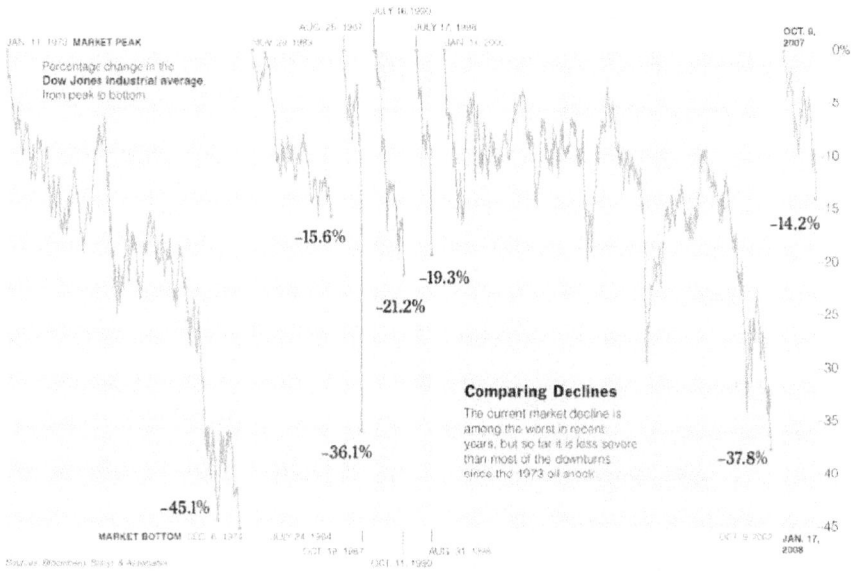

Figure 5.2: Market crashes (*New York Times*, 18 January 2008).

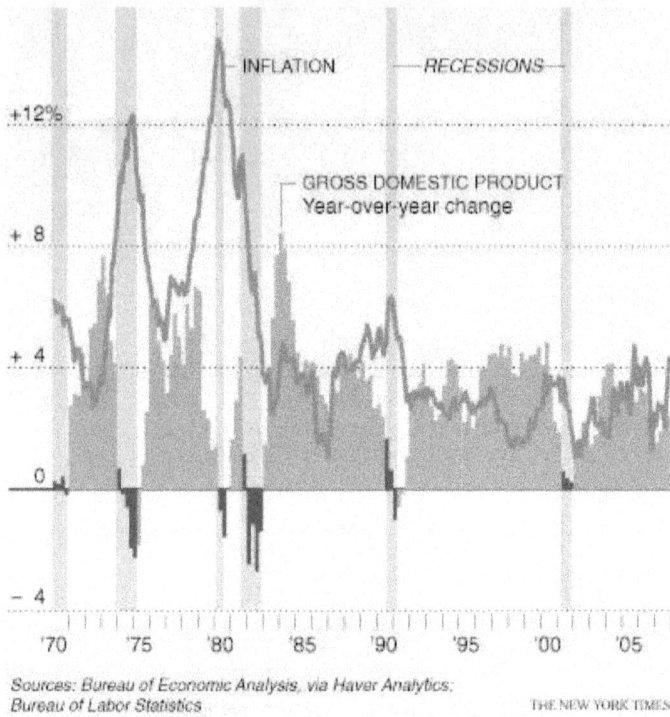

Figure 5.3: The possibility of stagflation (*New York Times,* 21 February 2008).

Figure 5.4: Real Price of Oil. (*New York Times,* 4 March 2008).

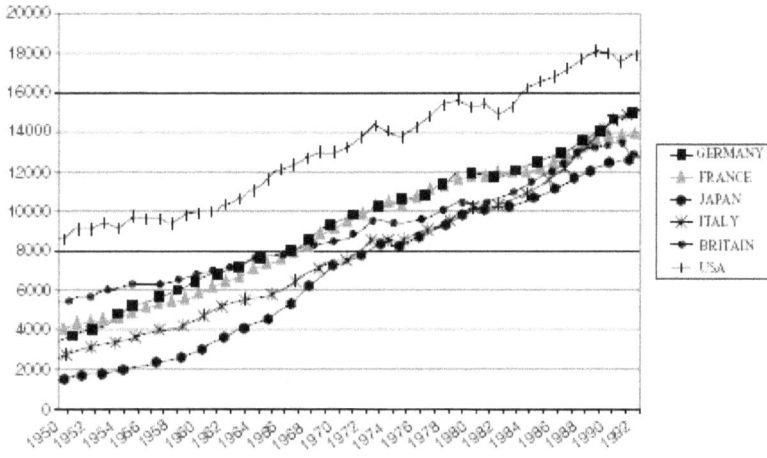

Figure 5.5: GDP per capita in six OECD countries (in 1985 dollars)

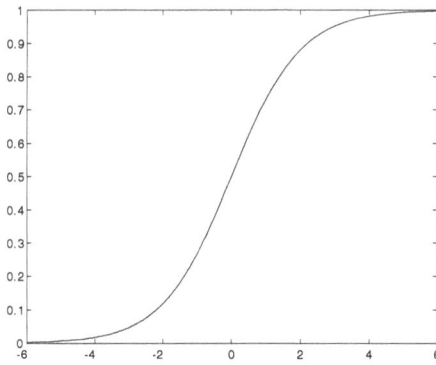

Figure 5.6: The logistic growth curve

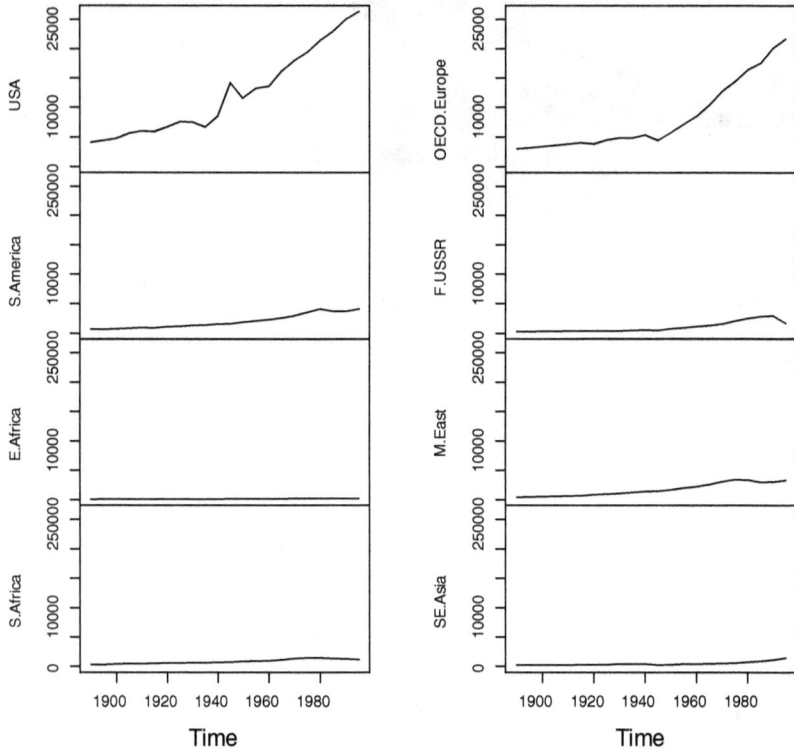

Figure 5.7: The Malthusian Trap facing the Third World

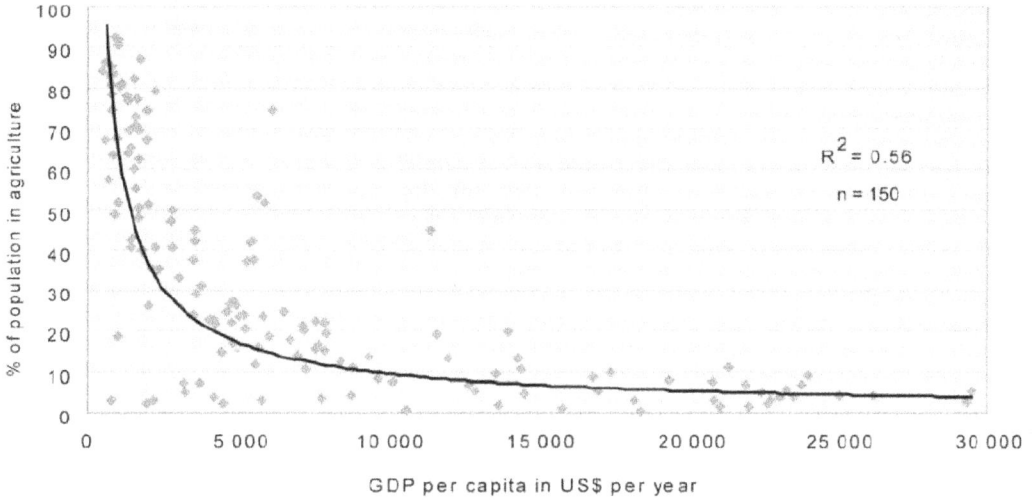

Figure 5.8: Agriculture and GDP/ capita (International Assessment of Agricultural Science and Technology for Development, 2008)

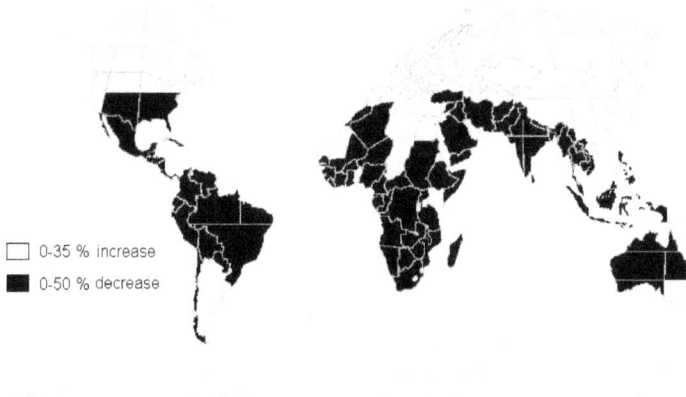

Figure 5.9: The possible effects of climate change on regional agricultural output (W. Cline, 2007)

5.2   The Political Business Cycle

The essential ideas underlying the literature on the Political Business Cycle are three fold:

1. the popularity of a government at some time is effectively determined by the level of unemployment and inflation at that time or in the recent past;

2. government itself can manipulate various aspects of the macro-economy to effect changes in unemployment and inflation within some feasible range;

3. incumbent governments will in fact manipulate the economy to bring about levels of unemployment and inflation which at election times are "socially optimal" in terms of resulting in the maximum number of votes for the party in government.

In their early paper, Goodhart and Bhansali (1970) first correlated government popularity (or the lead over the opposition) in Britain against unemployment and inflation, but were forced to add in cyclical dummies like euphoria and backswing, to account for apparently non-economic changes in popularity between elections. By stimulating the economy in the appropriate manner before an election, the "optimal" combination of unemployment/inflation on the Phillips curve could be attained. However, once inflation was induced into the system, this would trigger inflationary expectations and move the Phillips curve to the right.

As Brittan (1978) has observed,

> over a run of political cycles the short term Phillips curve will drift upwards
> ... democratic myopia and economic time lags will land the economy with an
> excessive rate of inflation.

Indeed as the Phillips curve moved to the right the socially optimal combinations would result in fewer votes, and each incumbent government would find itself defeated. According to Goodhart and Bhansali, "a pure democracy, with all parties seeking to maximize public support, is doomed to increasing inflation and political disintegration."

Further extensions by Nordhaus (1975), MacRae (1976) and Tufte (1978) postulated the existence of a political business cycle (PBC), in which government stimulates the economy near election time and then deflates to increase unemployment and bring inflation under some degree of control in preparation for the upswing at the next election.

These views have clearly been highly influential. The McCracken report to the OECD for example, put the blame for the high levels of inflation in 1973-4 on the bunching of elections in 1972 and the irresponsibility of governments in excessively stimulating their economies in 1971.

These models have been criticized from a number of different perspectives. Of course, it could well be the case that governments attempt to manipulate economic variables for political advantage, but find themselves unable to do so successfully because of events outside their control. However, the relationship between government popularity and economic variables appears to be extremely tenuous. Whitely (1979, 1984), on the basis of statistical analysis of poll data in Britain, has argued that government popularity is best modeled by a process of random fluctuation round a level which is itself subject to external shocks. As he says,

> [A] whole series of adverse events have to occur to change government pop-
> ularity drastically for the worse. Public opinion is 'driven' by a series of on-off
> events which act like shocks to the system over time. The inertia of opinion en-
> sure that when a government enjoys above average popularity, it will retain that
> position for several months. If adverse events make it lose popularity, it will in
> turn remain unpopular for several periods. In this way irregular cycles are gen-
> erated but they have no substantive significance of a political nature (Whitely,
> 1980).

To pursue this however, we have to leave the macro-political economic framework
and consider individual responses to changing economic circumstance. Fiorina (1981)
has used survey data to analyze these individual responses. He assumed "That in making a voting decision the citizen looks at the incumbent's performance, the alternative
platforms of the incumbent and challenger, and (perhaps) imagines a hypothetical past
performance term for the previous challenger." In his analysis Fiorina regressed voting
behavior on party identification or PID (essentially a proxy for past individual evaluations), current comparative evaluations and future expectations. As he says, "Personally experienced and/or perceived economic judgments affect more general economic
performance judgments, both types of evaluations feed into evaluations of presidential
performance, and the more general judgments, at least, contribute to the modification of
party identification."

Fiorina's micro-political economic analysis indicates that individuals behave in a rational way in using their own experience to interpret the political environment and to
make evaluations of policy makers. Further research on the U.S. by Kiewiet (1983)
makes it clear that individuals' personal experiences do matter, in that these affect evaluation of how an incumbent President is handling the situation. This, in turn, influences
the way the individual votes. The importance of this observation is that personal experience is something unique to the individual, and thus one might reasonably expect
"idiosyncratic" response to government behavior, in a sense of a weakening of the relationship between class and voting. This phenomenon of "partisan dealignment" has
been noted in Britain. A related phenomenon is the considerable decline of electoral
support for the two main parties in Britain, even though the political consequence of
this has been reduced because of the operation of the electoral system.

With the decay of partisan voting, the variation in individual experience and evaluation of government policy is likely to be sufficient to produce a kind of instability
compatible with Whiteley's interpretation of government popularity. Since individual
learning is a continuous experience, the popularity of government could be expected to
change fairly continuously but in directions that are largely indeterminate.

For the moment we note that there appears to be no stable relationship between
macro-economic variables by themselves and government popularity. It is true however, that government behavior does appear to produce very different changes in unemployment and inflation rates in the United States, depending on whether there was a

Democrat or Republican administration. Mueller (2003) estimates that unemployment rates dropped and inflation rates increased during Democrat administration (unemployment down by 1.9% and inflation up by 3.2% in 1960-1968; unemployment down by 3.5% and inflation up by 0.3% in 1992-2000). Since Democrat voters are likely to be more sensitive to unemployment increases, and Republican voters more sensitive to inflation. these observations are compatible with the electoral model presented in Chapter 3. In that model, although individual preferences depend partly on the economic axis, on tax rates and the like, they also depend on voter perceptions about the policy declarations that candidates or party leaders make on social issues. Thus the electoral model of Chapter 3 would imply a weak relationship between macro-economic outcomes and government popularity, rather than the determinate relationship indicated by something like the Phillips curve.

To see this,consider Figure 5.10, which gives a version of Figures 1.6 and 3.2. If the model is valid, then, as the second dimension becomes increasingly important, there is a tendency for Democrat and Republican candidates to converge slightly on the economic axis. Of course, these axes are inferred from voter surveys, and need not correlate precisely with the economic variables discussed above. Moreover, as we have intimated, policy choices on the second axis may have economic consequences in terms of increasing budget deficits and the like.

Similarly, Figure 4.13 in the previous chapter suggests that the Labour and Conservative parties have been slowly moving from the positions they held on the economic axes in the 1960's to positions separated by their differences on attitudes to Europe. Figures 5.11 presents an estimate of the party positions in Britain in 1979 (taken from Schofield and Sened, 2006).This configuration is quite different from the Figure 4.13 in the previous chapter, and it suggests that Labour and the Conservative Party have very slightly converged on economic policy over eighteen years. Of course, there are still major differences between the two major parties in both the United States and Britain, and it is very likely that the economic downturn of 2008 will magnify these differences.

5.3   Macro-Political Economy

The literature discussed above essentially concentrated on liberal political systems, where interest focuses on the macroeconomic manipulation by government concerned with the results of infrequent elections. A separate research program has concentrated on the populist mode of government (Riker, 1982), generated by the rational self seeking behavior of political actors as they attempt to deliver "public goods" to particular constituencies. The classical justification of government was that public goods such as defense, etc., cannot, in general, be supplied by the competitive economy (Baumol, 1965). The point here is that a good which is to be supplied to all is subject to various forms of manipulation, the most obvious of which is the free-rider problem-the tendency of recipients of the good to disguise their desire for the good so as to avoid some or all of the costs of production (Olson, 1965).

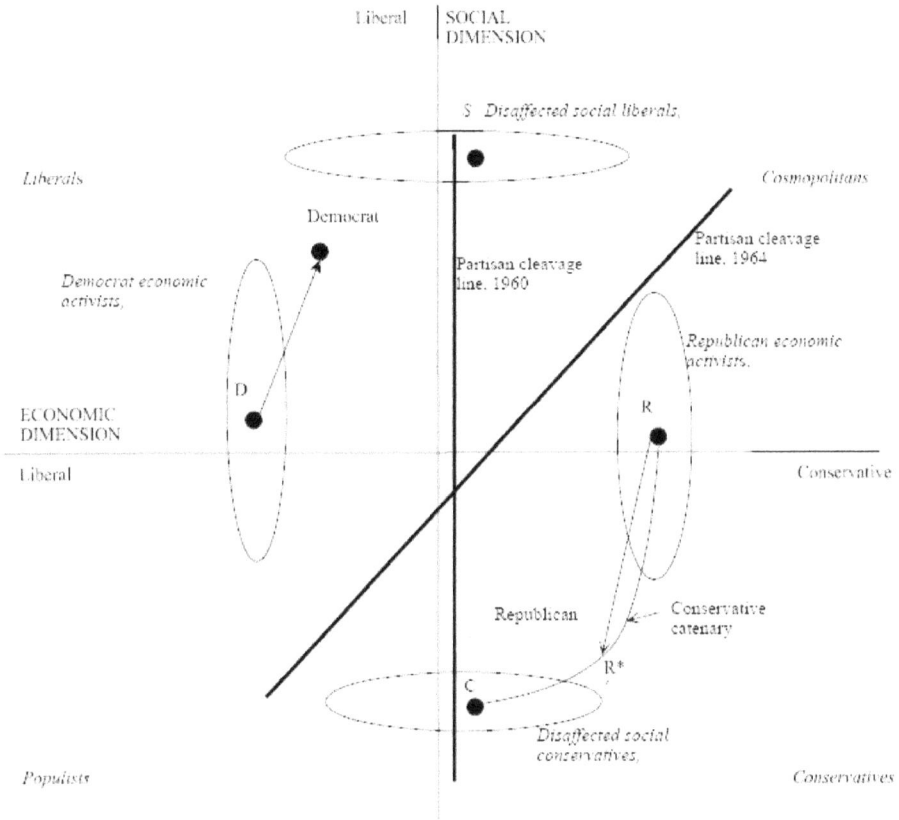

Figure 5.10: Weakening of the impact of economic policy in the US

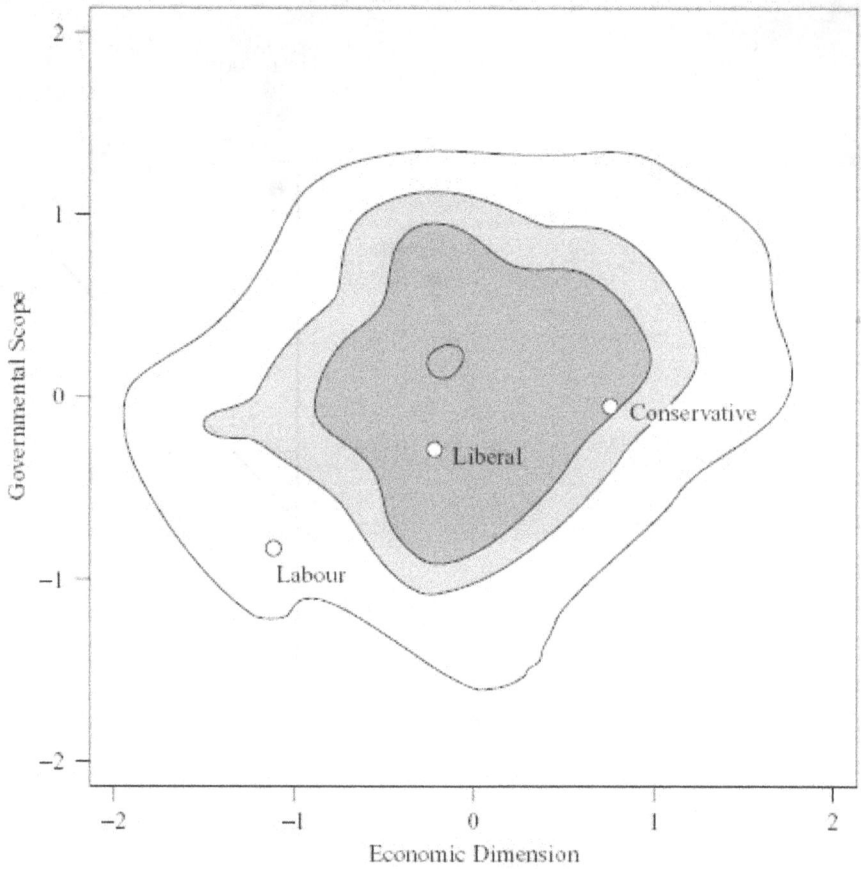

Figure 5.11: Party positions and voter distribution in Britain in 1979

However, very few of the activities of government are concerned with the provision of "pure" public goods, and even then public goods have associated private effects. For example, any public project (a dam, road, defense establishment or whatever) is likely to have geographically local effects on employment and factor costs, as well as more widespread general equilibrium effects. Since any government activity has some distributional consequences, Thurow (1980) is right in one sense to refer to the "zero sum society." While government activity is not entirely distributional, the conflicts of interest that are created are sufficient to bring about the instability effects mentioned above.

A number of authors have argued that political mechanisms, that are devised to deal with these public good conflicts, actually lead to an overprovision of the goods. The typical model has a political representative for each geographical constituency proposing a "pork barrel" project which if carried through, will benefit that particular constituency. The bundle of projects that are accepted are then paid for out of taxes levied on all. Formally this situation resembles a prisoner's dilemma, since each constituency will demand "too much" of its local public goods, since it does not have to meet the full costs of production. If all projects are approved, then the outcome is socially non-optimal. However, to pass any single project a legislator has to logroll with others to form a winning coalition. The instability results, mentioned above, may lead to the inference that, in the absence of formal party discipline, anything can happen.

Weingast (1979) however, has argued that "universalist" coalitions of all, or nearly all, legislators are likely under certain conditions, and this assumption has been used to show the universalist coalitions will over provide public goods (Weingast, Shepsle, Johnsen, 1981). Similar arguments can be made that government intervention, in such areas as regulation and pollution control, is excessive. However without a determinate theory of logrolling based on a good equilibrium notion it is difficult to accept the logical basis of this argument. The second problem is that in the absence of any procedure to truly determine "society's" preference it may as well be the case that public goods are under-provided.

As GNP increases, one might reasonably expect a greater than proportional increase in demand for public goods, and therefore an elasticity of government expenditure with respect to national income in excess of one. Chrystal and Alt (1979) recently argued that one should examine this problem only with respect to public expenditure G, excluding transfers. In their analyses of the case of Britain they find the elasticity of G with respect to national income, I, was significantly less than one. They note for example that government income tends to fluctuate more widely than government non-transfer expenditure. In a many country analysis they found that the elasticity of G with respect to I was essentially unity.

In their original analysis of British government spending, Peacock and Wiseman (1961) suggested that there was a ratchet effect, with government expenditure increasing rapidly during wars, and remaining at a constant proportion to income between wars. Burton (1978) has contested this view and argued that the acceptance of Keynesian economics lead to an increasing budget deficit which was essentially politically motivated.

It is certainly true that government expenditure (G) as a percentage of GDP has tended to increase from an average of about 28% in 1960 in the OECD economies, to around 45% in 1996 Mueller, 2003). Individual countries show wide variation however. In France, G/GDP rose from about 35% in 1960 to 55% in 1996, while in Britain the increase was from 32% to 43%. The United States has a very low ratios (27% in 1960 and 32% in 1996). Government spending also tends to be correlated with government deficits. The budget deficit in France was about 1% of GDP in 1960 but 3.6% in 1996. Although the budget was in surplus in the United States in 2000, an increase of government expenditure on law, order and defence from 5.5% of GDP in 2000 to 6.7%, and a decrease of tax revenue from about 30% of GDP in 2000 to 27% in 2005, has led to an overall increase in government debt from 55% of GDP to 62% of GDP. Thus a relatively small shift in the pattern of government expenditure and income, induced by politically motivated tax cuts and military expenditure, can cause fiscal difficulty.

5.4 Micro-Political Economy

As mentioned above, general (economic) equilibrium theory supposes that agents respond to prices parametrically and shows that with sufficient price flexibility the outcome will be Pareto optimal with all markets cleared. It is obvious that this is an unrealistic assumption, since industrial economies contain organized "interest" groups which behave strategically with respect to the rest of the economy.

The general model proposed by Olson (1982a) supposes that the interaction of these interest groups is essentially a prisoner's dilemma in the following sense. A particular group, a trade union for example, will defend its interests by, say, pushing for higher wage rates or restricting the implementation of new technology to maintain employment for its members. Olson's argument is that such a strategy, while rational for the group, is socially "irrational" in that it effectively reduces total social output in the long run. Government has a small role to play in Olson's model, since government is viewed only as reacting to, or accommodating, these interest group strategies, by increasing the money supply and stimulating inflation. As Mueller (1982) has observed, economic ineffectiveness of this type is likely to lead to an intensification of distributional conflicts and thus to even more extreme socially irrational strategies.

Formally speaking, Olson's argument is based on an assumption that, with the complex externalities (or external effects) that exist in a modern economy, group strategies that are permissible within a pluralistic economy cannot generally result in an "efficient" outcome. This conclusion depends however on the nature of the coalition structure that holds in the economy. As Olson (1982b) says:

> interest organizations that are quite large in relation to the society of which they are a part, will "internalize" much of the benefit of any action they take in the interest of the society, or (more pertinently) much of the cost of any action

they take that reduces efficiency, raises prices, or slows growth in the society.

This suggests that as the concentration of the interest group pattern increases from a purely atomistic one to a single centrally organized structure, the disparity between actual and socially optimal outcomes will widen first of all and then finally fall. Olson contended that those countries that have experienced a severe crisis-such as a defeat in war- will have weakened interest group structures, and therefore exhibit higher than average rates of growth.

An alternative form of analysis is to concentrate on the procedures by which interest groups can bargain together, to recognize the existence of externalities and thus ameliorate the socially harmful effects of non-cooperative strategies. Crouch (1982) for example concentrates on two important variables: consociationalism (or the degree to which bargaining and compromise dominates in the political arena) and centralization (of the trade union structure). (See also Lehmbruch, 1980, and Lipjhart, 1976.)

Consociationalism is a term used to describe a political system where there is a tendency for no single party to command a majority. Crouch's argument is that trade union centralization will occur either in the context of a consociationalist political system or in one where there is a dominant social democratic party that has been in office for considerable duration. In both cases there may exist the possibility for binding contracts between the trade union system and the political system. In Crouch's view, therefore, qualitative characteristics of the political system bring about an institutional framework in the economic system which is conducive to economic "efficiency." One could go further in following Mueller's suggestion and infer that economic "optimality" is in turn conducive to the maintenance of the consociationalist features of the political system.

Any collective action coalition is intrinsically unstable, but under certain favorable conditions cooperation may be possible. Suppose that a relatively large coalition has, for some historical reason, come into existence. If this coalition is sufficiently large vis-à-vis the economy, then it will be forced to internalize the social externalities of its actions. Moreover, the coalition may be able to bargain with other "smaller, non-cooperative" proto-coalitions and which coalesce into cooperative coalitions. The more rapidly the economy is growing, or the less pronounced the distributional features within the social economy, the easier is this bargaining process and the more readily may a corporatist or centralized coalition come into existence. The point is that there is a crucial "size" (determined by "productivity") for a coalition above which it will behave cooperatively. If economic growth slows down, then a cooperative coalition might suddenly fragment. Since its relative productivity declines, it is obvious too that the parliamentary coalition structure is of vital significance in this bargaining process. Although a fragmented parliamentary system may be relatively stable in good times, it is likely to become unstable in bad times.

Table 5.2 presents some data on duration of governments in twelve European polities (Laver and Schofield, 1998). The effective number is a simple measure of the fragmentation of the legislature (Laakso and Taagepera, 1979). Because the electoral system tends to be based on a method of proportional representation, government in these poli-

ties tends to be made up of a coalition of parties. Some of these polities have tended to
have relatively short lived government.

Table 5.2. Duration (in months) of government, 1945–1987

Country	Average duration	Effective number n_s
Luxembourg	45	3.5
Ireland	39	2.6
Austria	38	2.2
Germany	37	2.9
Iceland	34	3.7
Norway	32	3.2
Sweden	28	3.2
Netherlands	27	4.5
Denmark	26	4.5
Belgium	22	4.0
Finland	15	5.0
Italy	13	3.5
Average	**26**	**3.7**

The logic of coalition government can be illustrated by Figure 4.16, for the Netherlands in 2006, as presented in the previous chapter. The theory of elections presented in
that chapter suggests that polities based on proportional representation will tend to encourage the formation of many heterogenous activist groups, linked to particular parties.
These activist groups may exercise some degree of veto power, so that difficult policy
choices (over such issues as protection, immigration and agriculture) may tend to be
avoided. While this risk avoidance may be associated with somewhat lower growth
when times are good, it can be a rational choice, when times turn bad. The cost is
the difficulty of reaching agreement. "Globalization", or the integration of the global
market, has brought about the economic growth shown in Figure 5.5, but this very in-
terconnectedness has deepened the chaotic aspects associated with the collapse of asset
bubbles. We now face increasing market uncertainty, and even greater long-run uncertainty because of climate change and global terrorism, In such an environment, attempts
at risk avoidance are probably rational. The converse strategy of policy makers in the
United States, of accepting risk by acquiescing to global market forces, while simultaneously exercising unilateral military force, could lead to catastrophe. Recent events in
the global economy seem to imply that it is increasingly necessary for government in
the United States to intervene actively both in the domestic sphere, and internationally,
in a number of ways:

(i) to repair the social contract by implementing some form of universal health care
and enhancing the creation of human capital through education innovations

(ii) to facilitate a technological drive to create new energy sources, so as to offset the
problems of the imbalance between demand and supply of carbon-based fuels

(iii) to create of new transportaion systems that are less wasteful of imported oil

(iv) regulate and stabilize economic institutions, including financial services, banking and housing, in an attempt to avoid bubbles and crashes

(v) to find some method of stabilizing or reducing global carbon emissions, although this will be opposed by the newly industrializing nations, such as China and India

(vi) to find some resolution to the potentially chaotic situation in the Middle East, particularly with regard to the nuclear powers of Israel, India, Pakistan and a new nuclear Iran.

The problems over international order are particularly complex, because of the possiblity of instability in Israel, as mentioned in Chapter 4, and revolution in Pakistan.

Any attempt to deal with such a complex world requires some understanding of the nature of authoritarian regimes, such as Iran. The next two chapters attempt to model such regimes, using the general model presented in Chapter 3.

Chapter 6

Modelling Tyranny

Since at least the time of Machiavelli, political theorists have studied how govern-ment structure influences regime durability.[190] Today, with democracy ascendant over dictatorship in most of the world, political scientists have attempted to construct mod-els of the transition to democracy, and have also examined how it is that autocratic regimes can stay in power, and why some apparently democratic regimes can fall back into semi-dictatorhip.[191] Zimbabwe, under the autocratic rule of Mugabe since 1980, currently had hyper-ininflation of over a million percent (as of May, 2008) and unem-ployment well over 80% [192] A country like Zimbabwe is likely to fall into civil war. Whether this may lead eventually to democracy or further debilitating civil war is a matter of debate.[193] While Przeworski has noted that once a political economy reaches a GDP of about $7000/capita (in PPI or purchasing parity terms) it is unlikely to fall back from democracy to autocracy, it is still the case that resource rich economies like Iran (at current GDP/capita of $8400), Kazakhstan (at $8300) and China (at $6800) are autocracies.[194] Perhaps more alarmingly, Russia has invented the institution of "sov-ereign democracy," a kind of oligarchic democracy [195].

This chapter contends that to understand autocracies and the possibility of a trans-formation to democracy, it is appropriate to construct a model that is general enough to be able to incorporate both democratic and autocratic institutions.

We start with the political economic assumption introduced in Chapter 1, that power derives from the control of the factors of capital, land and labor. The alloca-tion of these factors can be described by a point in a high dimensional *economic factor*

---

[190]This chapter was co-authored by Norman Schofield and Micah Levinson.

[191]See Przeworski (2006), Boix (2003, 2006), Boix and Stokes (2003), Bueno de Mesquita et al. (2002, 2003).

[192]A month after Zimbabwe's election on March 29, 2008, the electoral body declared that Morgan Tsvan-girai, the leader of the opposition party, won more votes than President Robert Mugabe, but only 48%, not a majority. It was declared that a runoff on June 27 would be necessary. Mugabe and his supporters ini-tiated a process of murder and intimidation forcing Tsvangirai to withdraw, leaving Mugabe in power. On July 11, 2008, Russia and China vetoed a US led attempt in the U.N. Security Council to impose sanctions on Zimbabwe. On July 26, the Bush administration announced new sanctions against Zimbabwe.

[193]Wantchekon (2004).

[194]Przeworski (2006) estimates that the probability per annum that an authoritarian regime transits to democracy is about 25%, suggesting that a typical authoritarian regime is stable with about a 75% probabil-ity.

[195]See Aron (2007) and the Russian electoral model in section 8.1 below.

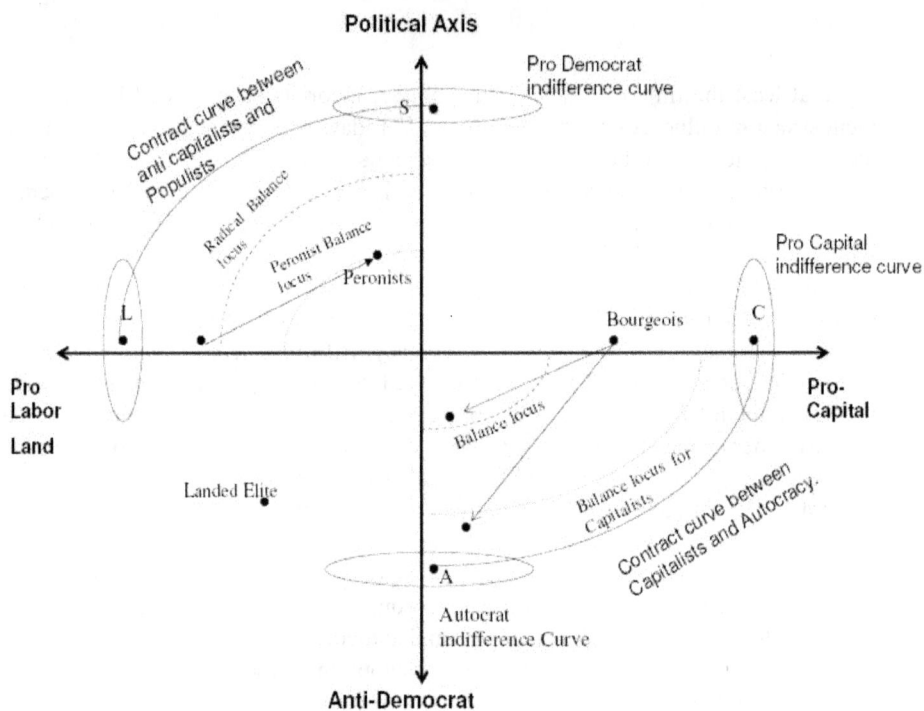

Figure 6.1: The Balance Locus of the Autocrat

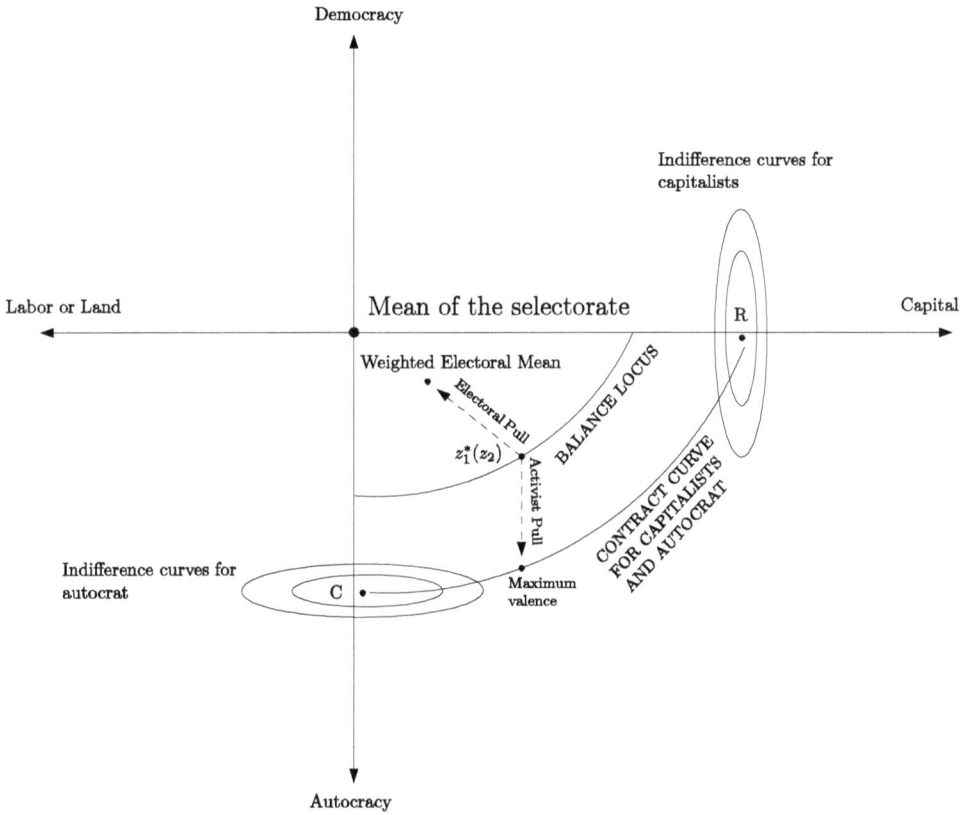

Figure 6.2: The weighted electoral mean and equilibrium position, $z_1^*(z_2)$, of the Autocrat in response to an opposition strategy z_2.

space. For purposes of exposition, Figure 6.1 gives an extreme simplification of this idea, where the factor space of land, capital and labor is represented simply as a horizontal axis with Labor/Land at one end and Capital at the other. Perpendicular to the economic space is the *political space*. Again, for purposes of exposition, we can assume this space is unidimensional. In modern democracies, this axis can be identified with civil and social rights.

The idea underlying this figure follows from the work of North and Weingast, as applied in Chapter 1, to examine the political bargains instituted in Britain in the 1720's and the United States in 1787-1800.[196]

For example, the ability of Britain to deal with the debt associated with its wars with France in the eighteenth century depended on the willingness of the landed and capitalist elite to commit to payment on the escalating interest on the debt. This was done by a complex bargain between Whig and Tories, involving high excise and customs taxes. Since this protected the landed interest, it had the indirect effect of raising the value of land. The second indirect effect was that the poor suffered. Schofield has argued that for this bargain to be maintained, it was necessary to restrict the franchise. The reform acts and the repeal of the corn laws came much later, in response to the fear of starvation and civilian unrest. In the United States in the period up to the election of Jefferson in 1800, capital and landed elites were in conflict over whether a similar bargain could be instituted. A tariff would protect manufactures, thus raising the price of capital incensive goods in terms of the price of land. The contract that was put in place gave the landed interest the upper hand, by suppressing the question of slavery (on the political axis) until at least 1850-1860.

These comments are meant to suggest that the political economic equilibrium in a society is the result of a bargain between the elite holders of factors, and those who govern the institutions. A political leader, whether democratically elected, or holding onto power by force, must have enough support from the elite or the people, or both, to stay in power. The formal model of power is presented in Chapter 3.

Firstly, each factor elite has an ellipsoidal utility function, as illustrated in Figures 6.1 and 6.2, indicating their primary concern with that factor. Similarly the political elite, whether autocrat or prime minister or president, is less interested in the particular disposition of factors, but rather in their utilization in order to maintain power. As Figure 6.1 illustrates, the particular assumption on elite utilities allows the economic and political elite to bargain. Figure 6.2 presents a *contract curve* between the capital elite and an autocrat, representing the set of bargains that are possible. In some autocratic regimes, of course, the "autocrat" can be identified with a military elite. In this case, the contract curve specifies the nature of the resources, military and capitalistic, that can be made available to the political leader. Again, it is not crucial that the bargain be only between capital and the political or military elite. It is quite possible in some regimes that the landed elite control the critical factor. The resources made available by this contract can then used to maintain political power.

In the formal model, each member of the population has a utility function, based

---

[196]See North and Weingast (1989) and Schofield (2003, 2006a)

partly on some preferred position in the factor space, but also on what we call the *valences* of the various political leaders. The formal model distinguishes between exogenous (or intrinsic) valence and the valence that results from the resources made available to the political leader by the factor elite. As an example, film of the crowd's response to Mussolini when he came to power suggests that the people regarded him very highly, at least initially. Revolutionary leaders, such as Castro, also have very high intrinsic valence. Autocrats, like Mugabe may be hated by some of the people, but can keep power through intimidation, precisely because of their control of resources. While the contract curve specifies the locus of actions that maximizes resources, the *balance locus* gives the equilibrium locus of the political leader. In a democratic regime, this will depend on the intrinsic valences of political opponents and the activist contributions. In the model used here, the equilibrium position of the leader will be a weighted sum of the preferred positions of those with some power in the polity (the selectorate). In both models, the leader with greater intrinsic valence will be less dependent on the resource support of activists or the factor elite. Moreover, the greater the intrinsic valence of an opponent, whether a revolutionary or a leader of a democratically chosen opposition, the further will the leader's position be from the center. In Figure 6.2, the point denoted "the mean of the selectorate" is used to denote the center.[197]

One obvious inference from this model is that the "equilibrium" position of the autocrat may be so far from the center that the populace will be induced to revolution. On the other hand, some authoritarian systems have evolved so that the "autocratic equilibrium" is stable. While we cannot overlook culture and historical distinctiveness, the authoritarian government's institutional design almost certainly contributes to its relative durability. By applying the model just proposed, we suggest we can pinpoint which authoritarian systems are more durable and why. Three types of authoritarian regimes have predominated in the twentieth-century: bureaucratic military dictatorship, fascist dictatorship, and the communist party dictatorship.

Applying the model suggests that the military bureaucratic regime seems the least durable, fascism more durable, and the socialist party dictatorship very stable. To illustrate, we examine three regimes: Argentina's military junta (1976-1983) , Francoist Spain (1938-1975), and the Soviet system (1924-1991).[198] We show how the theoretical prerequisites for regime change to democracy were sequentially harder to meet. The prerequisites include:

(1) enough economic and or political inequality to induce an oppositional underclass to demand formally institutionalizing some power redistribution.

(2) not so much inequality in economic or political power that the authoritarian elite is willing to incur almost any cost to keep power

---

[197]The model presented in Chapter 3 can be readily adapted to the situation where the electorate (or selectorate) is restricted in some fashion, so not everyone has equal political weight. See Bueno de Mesquita et al. (2002, 2003).

[198]It is hard to definitively demarcate the formation of the Soviet system. The Bolsheviks did not wield untrammeled power immediately following the October Revolution and the Soviet system only reached its more recognizable form after the Civil War (1922) and the first Soviet Constitution's enactment (1924).

(3) the ability of the regime's opponents to overcome the collective action problem inherent in organizing a revolution

(4) for democracy is to be achieved, reformers within the authoritarian bloc must align themselves with moderate opposition leaders to force authoritarian hardliners into accepting transition.

Argentina's wealth and political power distribution were neither egalitarian nor acutely concentrated. Spain's economic inequality was not profoundly different from Argentina's but its political organization was more centralized. The Soviet system both brutally imposed comparative economic egalitarianism and sharply concentrated political power. This reduced the revolution's economic boon to the citizenry while encouraging the government to spare nothing to defend its power. Francoism's early corporatism raised Spain's hurdle for oppositional collective action higher than Argentina's and Soviet party-oriented social organization raised it higher still.

The Argentine junta could not effectively penetrate or balkanize the organizations that kept their regime in power. This afforded some of the regime's erstwhile supporters enough autonomy to negotiate with the opposition and pressure the authoritarian elite to reach an accommodation with them.

Although Franco's regime also could not effectively penetrate and balkanize certain support organizations, Franco's complete personal control over the cabinet helped him manipulate the power distribution within his elite, hampering any single Francoist faction from attaining enough power to combine with the opposition and tie his hands. Without Franco, the system disintegrated.

Lastly, the Soviet system centralized all personnel decisions, for organizations that propped up the government, within the apparatus of the Communist Party of the Soviet Union's (CPSU). This precluded the emergence of an autonomous Reformist clique within the Soviet political elite without the General Secretary's consent.

Our analysis depends on Przeworki's observation that the ability of the elite and the citizenry to compromise depends on their cohesiveness. Przeworki follows O'Donnell (1978) by dividing society into four political actors: *Hardliners* and *Reformers* in the authoritarian elite and *Moderates* and *Radicals* in the oppositional citizenry. Hardliners have the most vested interest in the regime. In the Soviet Union, the Communist Party apparatus and KGB were prominent Hardliners. Franco himself and the Falange were the Spanish Hardliners and in Argentina the Hardliners were the military brass. "Reformers tend to be recruited from among the politicians of the [authoritarian] regime and from some groups outside the state apparatus: sectors of the bourgeoisie under capitalism, and some economic managers under socialism."[199] Reformers maintain weaker bonds to the regime and some may even gain from regime change if it leads to a [centrist] voter on the economic or power axis closer to themselves. Moderates want regime change but can accept some institutionalized commitments to elites that temper regime change's power redistribution. The Radicals, furthest away from Hardliners on the economic and political axes, oppose most concessions short of thorough institutional over-

---

[199]Przeworski (1991: 68).

haul in their own favor. Clearly, the Hardliners are the elite, Radicals the citizenry, and Reformers and Moderates a "bifurcated" middle class.

Przeworski argues that regime change "can result only from an understanding between Reformers and Moderates" and then only when "an agreement can be reached between Reformers and Moderates to establish institutions under which the social forces they represent would have a significant political presence in the democratic [or successor] system."[200] Reformers and Moderates sometimes secure Hardliners' and Radicals' assent to agreements with convincing rhetoric. However, typically, the Reformers and Moderates must either align themselves with the Hardliners or Radicals to force the remaining members of the autocracy to accept the new political order. Because the Hardliners control the authoritarian regime's repression apparatus, they normally make a more attractive partner. As will become apparent from the discussion below, Hardliner-Reformer-Moderate coalitions were more institutionally viable in Argentina and Spain than in the Soviet Union because the Communist Party apparatus did not depend on a co-opted middle class's cooperation to endure – instead every organization relied on the Party. Such a transition could only take place in the Soviet Union when the Hardliners' leader was himself a Reformer. That happened with Gorbachev. In terms of our model, the exogenous or intrinsic valence of the Hardline leaders of the regime had become very low indeed in contrast to oppositional reformers. Although Gorbachev could retain power through the support of the Communist Party elite, when he tried to adopt a Reformer position, moving nearer the center, he lost to higher valence reformers.

Although Figure 6.2 is not immediately applicable to the fall of the Soviet Union, we can note that the control exercised by the CPSU can be interpreted as a position on the contract curve close to the autocrat position. Similarly, the stability of "sovereign democracy" in Russia at present suggests an equilibrium position for Putin that is characterized by cooperation with, or control over, capital, a high degree of economic inequality, politically sustained by his high valence in contrast to the valences of the fragmented opposition.

6.1 Political Economy Theory

Political economy theory (PET) is based on the postulates of the "new institutionalism," two of which seem of greatest importance. First, political "actors take rational actions to maximize the probabilities of reelection, career advancement, or some other positive benefit."[201] According to Kenneth Shepsle, "a rational agent [or actor] is one who comes to a social situation with preferences over possible social states, beliefs about the world around him, and a capability to employ these data intelligently."[202] Douglass North systematized the second postulate in his inquires into institutional design and economic performance: "Institutions are the rules of the game in a society ... the humanly de-

---

[200] Ibid.
[201] Smith (2005: 140).
[202] Shepsle (1989).

vised constraints that shape human interaction ... they structure incentives in human exchange, whether political, social, or economic."[203] PET can illuminate a political system's institutionally engendered incentive structures to determine whether they are more or less likely to encourage rational agents to behave in ways that render a regime more susceptible to collapse.

In gauging an authoritarian system's susceptibility to collapse, one can ask

(i) how its fundamental de jure and de facto political institutions provide incentives to citizens to oust their autocratic elite?

(ii) what are the institutionally-induced prospects of successful ouster?

Smith wrote that "authoritarian regimes can break down because of external war, economic crisis, social upheaval, or defections from the ruling coalition. Pressures can come from without, from within, or from below."[204] We start with the assumption that, in theory, any regime can be dislodged by a foreign army. This limits the inquiry to the authoritarian elite's power vis-à-vis its subjects and cohesion. The case studies were selected partly because their regimes were not ejected by foreign invasion. It is obvious, however, that certain authoritarian systems, particularly fascist varieties, rely more on saber-rattling nationalism to keep the citizenry mobilized behind the dictator, heightening the chance of war, military defeat, and invasion.

PET identifies two sources of political power. To quote Acemoglu, and Robinson (2005): "The first source of political power is simply what a group can do to other groups and the society at large by using force. [We] refer to this as de facto political power."[205] De facto political power's distribution is not static. "Harvest failures, economic depressions, international financial or debt crises, and wars ... are intrinsically transitory and lead to short-term fluctuations in *de facto* political power."[206] The other source of political power, "allocated by political institutions," is called *de jure* power. The literature identifies three societal groups who exercise those powers: an elite, a citizenry, and a middle class. By definition the elites are a minority and the citizenry the majority. In this body of theory, they have conflicting interests. "For example, if the elites are the relatively rich individuals ... [they] will be opposed to redistributive taxation; whereas the citizens ... will be in favor of taxation that would redistribute resources to them."[207]

As suggested in the introduction, the present study extends this idea and refers to economic elites and political elites,located in distinct policy spaces. The economic factor space is a way of presenting the control exercised by each individual over the relevant factors, and by inference, the individual's utility function. For example, a capitalist (or Capital interest) at C in Figure 6.1 will be obviously opposed to redistribution of capital wealth, but may agree to a redistribution of the factor of land. Capital and the landed interest may also bargain effectively to retain their power (as illustrated by the example above from Britain in the eighteenth century). An individual at L, endowed only

---

[203] North (1990: 3).
[204] Smith (2005: 44).
[205] Acemoglu, and Robinson (2005: 32).
[206] Ibid., p. 21.
[207] Ibid. p.15.

with labor, would prefer capital, and perhaps land, redistribution. Similarly, the political axis represents an individual's policy preferences on the distribution of political
rights. Figure 6.1 suggest that a capitalist at C may not prefer the extreme concentration
of political power implied by A. Again, holders of the labor factor may be conservative
in their views about the rights to be allocated to minorities, for example. Both the elite
"activists" ,who bargain in the political realm, and the citizenry will be characterized by
distribution of their preferred points in the political economic space, X.

In Argentina and Spain, the political and economic elites were allies. In the Soviet
Union, however, because of capital's private ownership's proscription, no traditional
economic elite existed. Instead, there was only a political elite (the CPSU), which
collectively managed all Soviet capital. In some sense, therefore, the political elite was
the economic elite – however they only reaped a political reward from it. Between the
elite and great mass of citizens lies the middle class, which often sees itself as a distinct
group with distinct interests and thus a player in the contest for more de jure and de facto
power to realize its interests. The economic elite, owning a disproportionate share of
capital, will generally be most redistribution-averse, while the citizenry is most in favor
of redistribution. The middle class's capital redistribution preference will generally lie
between the elite's and citizenry's (represented by the position marked Bourgeois in
Figure 6.1).

The greater the concentration of capital and level of inequality, the further will be the
centrist citizen be from the elite preferred position and the more redistribution he will
prefer. However, one can similarly think of the distribution of political power. Certain
individuals, whether CPSU apparatchiki or Argentine generals, will disproportionately
influence state policy while others, like non-party members in the USSR or former
Republicans in Francoist Spain, are underrepresented in policy making.

Centrist redistribution explains why elites oppose democracy. "Nondemocracy, especially compared to the ideal of democracy, is neither egalitarian nor fair. Therefore
... citizens have a constant desire to change the outcome, the policies, and the regime.
What prevents them is the fact that the elites control the political institutions and military power in nondemocratic societies."[208] While the citizens lack de jure power in
authoritarian systems, their majority status confers some de facto power, which they
can use to threaten revolution unless the elite promises greater redistribution. The elite
must always choose an equilibrium, based on cost-benefit analysis, between redistributive concessions and repression to forestall revolution.

Repression is attractive when it is marginally cheaper than concessions. However,
North and Weingast suggest that policy concessions are sometimes insufficient to stave-
off revolution because "commitment problems arise when political power is not in the
hands of the beneficiaries of the promised policies. In essence, those with political
power cannot commit not to use it to renege on promises made in the past."[209] To forestall elite reneging when de facto power's distribution swings back in their favor, the
temporarily empowered citizens regularly demand institutional changes that transfer

---

[208] Ibid., p. 93.
[209] North and Weingast (1989).

some policy-making powers to themselves. While some citizen revolutionaries might call for institutionalizing a dictatorship of the citizenry, such demands are rare because they give the elite the incentive to spare no cost to block the citizens' aims.

The elite's cost-benefit analysis derived response to citizen restiveness also balances the revolutionary threat's credibility against democratization's probable impact on their assets. For the revolutionary threat to be credible, its leaders must overcome revolution's inherent collective-action problems. "... the payoff for not taking part is always greater than the payoff for taking part in a revolution. Therefore, all citizens prefer to free-ride on others' revolutionary activities rather than incurring the costs themselves."[210] Like the elite, the citizens perform cost-benefit analyses to discern whether revolution is profitable. "The simplest way to think of a post-revolutionary society is ... that some of the resources of the economy are destroyed in the turbulence of the revolution and the rest are distributed in some way among the citizens."[211] Some revolutionary leaders successfully impart an ideological utility calculus to their followers, so they receive sufficient reward from serving the group. However,

> [m]ost real-world revolutionaries try to generate private benefits, monetary or otherwise, for taking part in revolutionary activities that the participants can keep, even if the revolution fails ... . In practice, the most common strategy to deal with collective action problems is 'exclusion.' Exclusion limits the benefits from collective action to only those who take part in the action.[212]

Not only the citizens are divided, different members of the elite have different interests, reflecting the nature of their economic resources.

> Turbulence and disruption lead to the breakdown of complex economic relations ... much more important for capitalist production than agrarian production. This is natural because there is less concern about the quality of products in agriculture than in manufacturing. Moreover, the importance of complex relationships between buyer and supplier networks, and of investments in skills and in relationship-specific capital, is far greater in more industrialized activities.[213]

Therefore, repression and revolution's tempestuousness is marginally more costly for industrialists than for landowners, making industrialists marginally more congenial to granting violence-averting concessions. "Because land is supplied more inelastically, when allowed, citizens impose higher taxes on land than on capital."[214] This further widens the difference between industrialists' and landowners' marginal willingness to repress. Likewise, political elites whose power relies more on autonomous organizations, like economic elites and independent technocrats, risk losing more from repression that breaks down complex political networks and alliances.

---

[210] Acemoglu & Robinson (2005: 123).
[211] Ibid., p. 121.
[212] Ibid., p. 124.
[213] Ibid., p. 296-7.
[214] Ibid., p. 300.

Usually, a middle class is an independent political actor in the haggle between the elites and the citizens over the extent of enfranchisement. The middle class's greater income endowment positions it as the citizenry's natural vanguard. However, that greater income endowment simultaneously makes them less inclined towards resource redistribution than the citizenry. Indeed, the elite may enfranchise, and thus co-opt, the middle class if it calculates that the economic cost of the consequent redistribution regime, induced by the new poorer centrist voter, is less than that of repressing an alliance of middle class and citizenry. "A large affluent middle class may act like a buffer between the elites and the citizens in democracy. It does this by simultaneously making democratization more attractive for elites than repression and changing policy enough that the citizens are content not to revolt."[215]

In this chapter, the idea of a middle class is important in both an economic and political context. It indicates that certain economic and political groups are able and willing to align themselves with either pole of the economic and/or political axis. When centrist groups have a lot of latitude, they decide whether the authoritarian regime remains intact or liberalizes. Therefore, when the middle class or part of the middle class has been co-opted to keep the authoritarian regime afloat, the authoritarian regime's survival depends on the cohesiveness of the alliance of the elite and middle classes. In terms of the model illustrated by Figure 2, the stronger the bourgeois, the closer will be the regime's balance locus to the mean of the selectorate.

The second element of an authoritarian regime's durability is its elite's cohesiveness. Smith delineates two types of authoritarian elites, "personalistic and institutional ... personalistic dictatorships are ruled by strong-willed individuals who dominate the political process. Their principal interest is power. They are tyrants. They do not subscribe to substantive ideologies and they do not have programmatic missions."[216] Obvious examples are Trujillo's Dominican Republic and Duvalier's Haiti. Basically, the political elite of a personalistic regime is the tyrant and his coterie. "Institutional authoritarian regimes [are] very different. Power [does] not belong to individuals. It belongs to committees, bureaucracies, or institutions."[217] The juntas of Argentina and Brazil belong to this category. Obviously, this measure is relative. Even personalistic dictatorships have delegated some administrative, and thus some de facto, power to bureaucracies.

Smith contends that

> There are two broad types of change: transition via ruptura, a complete and usually sudden and violent break with the authoritarian past and transition via reforma, a process of give-and-take negotiation between incumbents and dissidents ... gradual and pragmatic changes via 'reforma' tend to be incremental, not revolutionary, and include formal or informal compacts designed to achieve

---

[215] Ibid., p. 39.
[216] Smith (2005: 45).
[217] Ibid., p. 47.

political transformation with a minimum of risks.[218]

Smith illustrates the incentives for citizens to revolt and elites to hold tenaciously to power in order to uncover when transitions either via ruptura or via reforma are more likely. He concludes,

> Personalistic regimes have been most susceptible to sweeping and violent overthrow ... Dissidents usually believed it was necessary to eliminate the tyrant via assassination and that with this accomplishment the entire regime would crumble. There was neither room nor need for negotiations with surviving collaborators: without the dictator they had no remaining power base ... . In dominant-party regimes, as in Mexico, members of the erstwhile ruling party could simply move into the opposition ... . Military regimes also [have] a ready exit: they [can] return to the barracks ... . More than any other autocrats, military rulers [have] a place to go. This often [makes] it easier for them to engage in negotiations with the opposition.[219]

Smith's distinction between 'personalistic' and 'institutional' dictatorships is similar to Machiavelli's distinction between absolute princes (personal dictators who face no real organized opposition) and limited princes (limited by institutions which give some others substantial power to oppose the autocratic leader). Machiavelli argued that absolute princes are more difficult to bring down and violence is probably needed to do so, but once the old regime is upset, the new prince/dictator can maintain his power relatively easily, with the implication that this kind of regime is relatively durable until the next round of violence occurs. On the other hand, Machiavelli claimed that limited princes are easier to bring down because their various opponents can be attracted into a revolutionary coalition by the promise of more power and other benefits, yet the new autocratic leaders will have a relatively difficult time maintaining power for the same reason.

Some of Machiavelli's observations can be related to the idea of valence. An absolute prince may well be strongly loved by the majority, though hated by a minority of the citizenry. Indeed, successful imperial houses can be long -lived precisely because they surround the prince with pomp and circumstance, raising the intrinsic valence, just as it may be raised by media attention in a modern democracy. Limited princes may face much less variance in the valence by which they are perceived by the citizens.

The next section presents the case studies based on this political economic theory.

---

[218] Ibid., p. 63.
[219] Ibid., p. 64.

6.2   Case Studies

6.2.1   Argentine Junta (1976-1983)

O'Donnell (1978) defines bureaucratic authoritarianism as "a system of exclusion of the popular sector, based on the reaction of dominant sectors and classes to the political and economic crises to which populism and its developmentalist successors led."[220] In the 1960s and 1970s, Latin American militaries adopted such systems in Brazil, Uruguay and Argentina. However, unlike earlier exclusions of the popular sector, the military ruled both directly and collegially, not simply supporting economic elites' hegemony. Argentina's 1976-83 experience is paradigmatic.

After the coup of the March 24, 1976, the Argentine military reorganized the government so that the military command selected the president and cabinet, both of whom, acting together, made and executed all laws.[221] The president derived little power from his title and policy decisions required some consensus among military notables.

> Each service had its 'feudal domains' and active duty officers were appointed to a much wider range of subordinate posts, as commanders of the federal police, intervenors of the central labor federation and key unions, and heads of the major state enterprises. Military control, furthermore, also penetrated the provincial level, dividing governorships between the branches, and at times reached all the way down to local government.[222]

There was no umpire who could utilize referee powers to impose stability and mitigate factional acrimony. Thus government decisions reflected the policy preferences of those officers possessing the most de facto power. Wynia (1986) described the junta's governing operation as

> never very neat, no matter how hard the junta work[ed] to appear united behind the president... [and grew] worse when commands [were] rotated... New service commanders [did] not necessarily come from the same factions as those who originally appointed the president, which, when ignored, [could] escalate into agitation for his replacement.[223]

By the time the military installed its first president, General Jorge Videla, the junta had already split into three factions on issues of the longer-term political future. One, headed by Admiral Emilio Messera, wanted to cow the hitherto combative working class by mimicking Peronist populism, but trading economic nationalist rhetoric for anti-Marxist rhetoric and, as effective counterinsurgency and anti-subversive campaigns subsided, reasserting old claims.[224] The second faction, headed by Generals Carlos

---

[220] O'Donnell (1978: 13).
[221] Wynia (1986: 110).
[222] Norden (1996: 64).
[223] Wynia (1986: 111).
[224] In 1977, Argentina and Chile accepted British arbitration on their historical territorial dispute over the

Masón and Mario Menéndez, favored unrelenting war against everything Peronist and leftist and completely replacing Argentina's protectionist trade policy and bloated public sector with market fundamentalism. The third clique, led by General Videla and his successor, General Roberto Viola, wanted economic recovery. Although they deemed greater reliance on markets as a wise recovery tactic, they did not sanction fundamentally dismantling all state enterprises and even reversed some early trade liberalization policies to aid the industrialist elite at the agrarian elite's expense.[225] In October 1979, Menéndez launched a rebellion against what he saw as too moderate a regime. Videla and Viola's military allies squelched the insurrection but, in 1981, the harder-line General Leopoldo Galtieri obtained enough support within the military to threaten a coup against Viola. Politically weakened by economic crisis and perceived softness on the left, attributable to his releasing Isabel Peron from government custody, Viola resigned and Galtieri replaced him.[226]

After the 1976 coup, Videla "went to work right away, unleashing the three [military] services' intelligence and counterinsurgency units to make war on the clandestine military movements whose members had been terrorizing the country with kidnappings and bombings for over three years."[227] The guerillas

> sought the violent overthrow of the government and the institution of a revolutionary socialist regime along Marxist-Leninist lines. They were predominantly middle class and many were university students or recent graduates. [They were] desperately idealistic and deeply alienated by the merry-go-round of Argentine politics.[228]

Videla gave military intelligence and counterinsurgency units wide latitude to arrest, interrogate, and kill virtually autonomously. Many who never committed terrorist acts

> lived in fear, never knowing whether or not they, too, might be taken away from their homes in one of the government's infamous, unmarked gray Ford Falcons, never to be seen again. Suspects were taken to one of 280 clandestine prisons, most of them on military bases in or near the nation's largest cities, where they were tortured and killed without any records of their deaths being kept.[229]

Between 10,000 and 20,000 "disappeared" that way in what is called Argentina's Dirty War.[230]

Like many other Latin American countries, an economically liberal agrarian oligarchy dominated Argentina until the Great Depression-induced contraction of foreign

---

Beagle Channel in Tierra del Fuego. When the British awarded most of the disputed territory to Chile, Massera threatened war, hoping to stir nationalist sentiments and mobilize the population behind the regime.

[225] Rock (1985: 369).

[226] Ibid., p. 370-4.

[227] Wynia.(1986: 264).

[228] Skidmore and Smith (1997: 104).

[229] Wynia (1986: 264-5).

[230] Skidmore and Smith (1997: 103).

demand for Argentine agricultural goods spurred limited industrialization to provide
no longer importable consumer goods. Peron accelerated industrialization during his
Presidency (1946-55), imposing heavy tariffs on foreign manufactured goods and over-
valuing the exchange rate to encourage capital goods' importation.[231]

> In spite of the liberal restoration in 1955, the agricultural capitalists never re-
> gained full political power, and they became even more economically marginal-
> ized in the expansive industrialization of the 1960s.[232]

Peron's bloc included the industrial elite, urban middle class, and working class.
However, between 1955 and Peronism's 1973 resuscitation, foreign direct investment
generated substantial capital accumulation and growth of the industrial elite and urban
bourgeoisie, undermining their political alliance with the working class and increasing
the number of interests they shared with the residual agrarian elite.

In 1975, many labor "unions began negotiating new contracts with 100 percent
wage increases or more."[233] The Peronist government annulled the new contracts, inciting massive strikes, forcing the government to reinstate them. Concurrently, inflation
reached 335 percent and Marxist guerillas staged provocative attacks on the police and
military, assassinating some bigwigs.[234] The military cunningly waited to until Isabel
Peron was thoroughly discredited before attempting her overthrow. Peronism had failed

> due in large measure to the loss of control by the trade union bureaucracy
> over the working class ... . Finally the deepening economic crisis made it im-
> perative to the bourgeoisie to move toward a 'strong state' that could suppress
> the living standards of the masses sufficiently to restore a 'healthy' rate of profit
> for capitalism.[235]

Argentina's economic evolution sundered the industrial elite's and urban bourgeoisie's
Peronist political alliance with the working class and the 1970s "economic situation deprived the bourgeoisie of the maneuvering room needed to grant reforms to the workers
without threatening the profitability of industry."[236] Genuinely socialist labor organizations, outflanking the official unions and coordinating officially unsanctioned strikes
and other collective action, drove the middle class into the military's lap.

The military needed extensive elite and middle class support because of the military establishment's limited expertise. Not only did they need technocrats to formulate
macroeconomic policy, they needed the elite's and middle class's acquiescence to implement the policy. The Argentine junta's key economic initiatives were:

> (i) The reduction of real wages by nearly 50 percent in relation to the previous
> five years, increase in the price of public services, and an end to the subsidy of

---

[231] Wynia (1986: 256).
[232] Munck (1985: 63).
[233] Skidmore and Smith (1997: 102).
[234] Ibid., p. 103.
[235] Munck (1986: 56).
[236] Ibid., p. 56.

social services such as health and housing. . .
    (ii) A program of progressive reduction of import tariffs, no subsidies to non-traditional exports, encouragement of agricultural exports. . .
    (iii) A liberalization of the exchange and financial markets. . .
    (iv) The reduction of government expenditure and employment, the repriva-tization of state owned firms.[237]

The junta's policies contributed to a flood of foreign capital, which started when OPEC's 1973-4 and 1979-81 production halts provided OPEC countries' governments with so many dollars they could not invest them all domestically. The OPEC governments deposited huge sums in American and European banks, lowering interest rates and enticing Latin American borrowers. "Between 1976 and 1980 the [Argentine] financial sector grew by 45 percent. Finance capital, a fusion of banking and capital, became the hegemonic [faction] within the ruling class [bloc]."[238] The new preponderant elite faction soon faced calamity and grew disenchanted with their military partners, no longer trusting them to steward the economy.

In the early 1980s, recession in the developed world depressed demand for Latin America's raw materials and Argentina's obsession with comparative advantage pushed many industrialists into bankruptcy, making raw materials a very high percentage of exports. At the same time, international interest rates rose markedly, stretching Latin American borrowers to the limit. After Mexico defaulted on its foreign loans, the supply of loanable funds to all Latin American countries plummeted. Unable to continue profligate deficit spending, capital flowed out of Argentina to its creditor nations. The Argentine financial elite, with bank failure spreading like wild fire, lost all confidence in the junta. Simultaneously, skyrocketing unemployment and poverty triggered citizen demands for regime change, and increased the popularity of a Reformer-Moderate regime. Schofield and Cataife (2007) discuss the electoral changes in support of Carlos Menem, the candidate of the Partido Justicialista in winning the election of 1989. It is of interest that Menem won the second election in 1995 by instituting the Convertability Plan by linking the peso to the dollar. This generated significant benefits for the bourgeois and capitalists, at significant cost to the working class. In terms of the model deployed here, Menem won the 1989 election because of high intrinsic valence, and then capitalized on activist support to move further away from the electoral center.

6.2.2   Francoist Spain (1938-1975)

No universally accepted definition of fascism exists. In fact, the word fascist is used frequently simply as a pejorative to denigrate regimes resembling those most associated with fascism – Nazi Germany and Mussolini's Italy. Seymour Martin Lipset claims that "mainstream fascism of the Mussolini and Hitler variety sprang from the same secular, petit bourgeois sources as classical liberalism." Lipset sees such "mainstream

---

[237] Ibid., p. 58.
[238] Ibid., p. 59.

fascism" as "a movement of the center... a reaction of the lower middle-class that, frightened by communism, had lost its faith in democracy." Moreover, Lipset divided that movement into a right-wing, "violent reactionaries who use extremist tactics and modern mobilization techniques to defend traditional cultural values," and a left-wing, "anti-democratic anti-Marxist movements that compete with communists for working class support."[239] He would include Portugal's Salazar and Austria's Dolfuss in the former group and Argentina's Peron and Brazil's Vargas in the latter.

Payne (1995) characterizes fascist movements' ideology as an "espousal of an idealist, vitalist, and voluntaristic philosophy, normally involving the attempt to realize a new modern, self-determined, and secular culture" and their goals as creating a "novel nationalist, authoritarian state with an imperialist or assertive foreign policy."[240] He depicts them as anti-liberal, anti-communist, and, although they may temporarily ally with conservative groups out of expediency, anti-conservative. Their anti-conservatism stems from their desire to transform modern society radically through society's militarization, emphasizing emotions and mysticism, and exalting youth over other stages of life.[241] However, Payne concedes that his typology is only a base and that many fascist movements add additional unique elements or do not meet a few of his criteria but are still fascist. He attributes some of the variety to fascism's intrinsic nationalism, which is expressed differently in countries with different histories and cultures. Payne argues "all fascist movements generally ... subordinated economic issues to the state and to the greater well-being of the nation, while retaining the basic principle of private property... [and] most fascist movements espoused corporatism."[242] Politically, he notes "a general tendency to exalt leadership, hierarchy... [and] deferring to the creative function of leadership more than to prior ideology or a bureaucratized party line."[243]

Spain's fascist movement did not enjoy the degree of support accorded other European countries fascist parties in the early 1930s. Previously a marginal political group, even on the right, the fascist corporatist Falange, founded and charismatically led by José Antonio Primo de Rivera, the deposed General Rivera's son, gained prominence after electoral failure of the less radical right in 1936. The country's subsequent lurch to the left discredited politicians committed to democratically implementing a rightist agenda. Falangist ideology "identified the age of Spain's greatness as the 15th century, the heyday of Castilian centralism" and melded imperialism, devout Catholicism, the adulation of military values, and "vague promises to 'redeem' the working and peasant classes"[244] and urged the violent seizure of power.

Even with mainstream rightist parties' discredited, the Falange was too impotent to consider independently toppling the Republic. When the Civil War erupted, Republican forces arrested most Falangist leaders, weakening the movement even more. The weakened Falange joined the Nationalist movement and integrated its militias into the Na-

---

[239]Lipset (1963: 127).
[240]Payne (1987: 7).
[241]Ibid.
[242]Ibid., p. 10.
[243]Ibid., p. 14.
[244]Ellwood (1987: 13).

tionalist army, thereby surrendering its autonomy to Franco. On April 18, 1937 Franco unified, by decree, all rightist organizations. (The new organization – called Falange Espanola Tradicionalista y de las JONS – was more ideologically, symbolically, and organizationally Falangist than anything else.) He assumed the conglomerate's leadership, and outlawed all other political organizations. Franco forced unification with carrots and sticks. He jailed rightist leaders who opposed his takeover but simultaneously gave each faction powers. Most rightists agreed to unite, even if dissatisfied with their role in the Nationalist organization, because the Republicans were still formidable and many, particularly the Falangists, never realistically believed they would have as much power as they then held. They did not want to risk losing it in the pursuit of complete power and ideological purity.[245] Despite Franco's overlordship and need to share power with other rightist groups, the Falange set the ideological tone and ran the corporatist trade syndicates until the end of the Second World War.

Francoist Spain's de jure political institutions developed during the Civil War. After the Civil War's eruption, an imprecisely defined decentralized Junta of National Defense, under a General Miguel Cabanellas's nominal leadership, directed the Nationalist Army, while General Emilio Molo commanded Carlist forces,[246] and the Falangist militias and other anti-Republican forces fought for the most part independently.[247] On August 6, 1936, Franco flew to Seville to set up his headquarters. "By mid-August, it had already become clear that the key to [a Nationalist] victory lay in the tough and disciplined Army of Africa, which Franco himself had done so much to create in his brilliant military youth... And since Franco controlled this impressive weapon, he was already[,] in fact if not in name, the Supreme Commander."[248]

On September 12, 1936, to foster greater tactical unity, ten Nationalist generals and two colonels met outside Salamanca to resolve whether there should be a unified Nationalist command. All present but Cabanellas supported anointing Franco Generalissimo of the Nationalist forces but to keep the decision secret until the National Defense Junta at Burgos could meet and make the public announcement.[249] They then scheduled a further meeting to adumbrate the Generalissimo's powers and appoint a Chief of State. The group reconvened on September 29 and, after heated debate, voted on a compromise decree, which Cabanellas signed as Chairman of the National Defense Committee at Burgos. The decree stated,

> His Excellency Don Francisco Franco Bahamonde has been appointed Head
> of the Government of the Spanish State and will assume all the powers of the

---

[245] Ibid., p. 32-55.

[246] The once conservative King Fernando VII (reigned 1813-33) relied increasingly on liberal ministers in his later years, because they were the only ones able to secure funds in European money markets. As a result, he angered his ultra-reactionary brother Carlos, who only recognized Fernando's claim to the throne so long as he bequeathed the throne to him. However, Fernando left the throne to his daughter Isabella, igniting the Carlist Wars (1833-40, 1847-9, 1872-6). Even after Carlos's death, many conservatives, supporting royal absolutism and expansive ecclesiastical privilege, upheld the Carlist claim to Spain's throne.

[247] Lewis (2002: 75).

[248] Crozier (1967: 201).

[249] Ibid. p. 209.

New State... He is likewise appointed Generalissimo of the National Land, Sea, and Air Forces, and the post of Chief General of the Operational Armies is conferred upon him.[250]

Cabanellas ceremoniously bestowed these powers on Franco on October 1. If the decree did not specifically grant Franco dictatorial powers, he immediately assumed them and commenced issuing decrees as Chief of State. With the Nationalist military victory, every semblance of democracy disappeared. Franco manufactured an irrelevant unicameral Cortes.

> One third of the members were directly nominated by the Generalissimo. A further third were ex officio members – government ministers, members of the Consejo Nacional, the President of the Supreme Court, the Alcaldes of the fifty provincial capitals, rectors of universities and so on – all of whom had also been nominated to their posts by Franco or his ministers. Finally, the remaining third were 'elected by the Falangist syndicates from carefully prepared lists of candidates... Although the 'representative' elements would be widened over the years, the Cortes met very rarely and always approved legislation submitted to it. Ministers were responsible to the Caudillo, not to the Cortes.[251]

The Council of Ministers became the only consequential policy-making body.
Franco established a Council of Ministers on January 30, 1938, with himself as its President, and appointed eleven ministers the following day. Franco "appointed and dismissed [ministers] at will, and could dictate and promulgate laws without previously consulting them. Franco laid down the general guidelines of policy... So long as his ministers stayed within his guidelines they had considerable latitude in running their departments."[252] The Council normally held all-day sessions weekly or biweekly.

> In the regime's early years Franco tended to dominate the discussions, but later he preferred to encourage debate among others while he listened. When he thought the matter had been discussed sufficiently he would call for a resolution. If there was general agreement, the resolution was passed; if not, the ministers were told to study the matter further and try to come to a consensus before the next meeting.[253]

Franco focused on foreign policy, clerical matters, and public order issues and left what he considered mundane administration to his cabinet. His power hinged on preserving right-wing unity but not allowing any single Nationalist faction from preponderating the rest, which would have necessarily sidelined Franco. From the cabinet's opening to Franco's death, three factions: the Alphonsist monarchists,[254] Carlist monar-

---

[250] Ibid., p. 211.
[251] Preston (1994: 489).
[252] Lewis (2002: 76).
[253] Ibid., p. 77.
[254] Alphonsist monarchists upheld the royal claim of the line descended from Fernando's daughter, Isabella.

chists, and Falangists constantly jockeyed for dominant influence. Each faction had a
following in the military and broader Nationalist network and Franco's personal control stemmed from his referee position. As ostensibly impartial as possible, Franco
played a shrewd political balancing game, appointing ministers, who he thought bend-
able to his will, from each Nationalist faction and the military. He subtly encouraged
factional competition for ministries but cultivated enough unity to obviate a Nationalist
coalitional fracture that might draw some leftist groups back into politics.

Franco fostered factional competition and disassembled crystallizing ulterior power
centers through frequent cabinet shake-ups, thirteen in all.[255] Franco's first cabinet included five Alphonsists, one Carlist, three Falangists, and two military officers. Despite
their handsome representation, radical Falangists could not palliate Franco's regime of
compromise and some planned a coup. Franco responded with a cabinet shake-up, appointing more Falangists to the cabinet but more moderate ones loyal to himself, and
stationing potential coup plotters in prestigious but innocuous government posts, such
as the ambassadorship to Brazil.[256] To diffuse power further, Franco trifurcated the military command, creating a ministry for each military branch and handing them to different Nationalist factions.[257] Until the Axis's defeat became apparent, Franco devoted
most energy attending to the Falangist-Monarchist and Military cleavage and sidelining
Falangist radicals vitalized by Hitler's early military successes. However, after World
War II, the Falangists lost their initiative and Franco subordinated them.

Facing critics at home and abroad in the wake of the Second World War, Franco
composed a Spanish bill of rights to temper their censure and obfuscate his recent amity
with Hitler and Mussolini. The bill of rights, the Charter of the Spaniards (*Fuero de
los Españoles*), dated July 16, 1945 and released the next day, did not really change the
contours of power. While proclaiming "respect for the dignity[;] integrity and liberty of
the human person," enshrining freedom from arbitrary arrest, and guaranteeing the right
to education; work; security in distress; and the inviolability of property, it stated that
Spaniards owed loyalty to the Chief of State. Moreover, many rights were abrogated
as quickly as they were given. Article 12 read, "All Spaniards may freely express their
ideas, so long as these do not prejudice the fundamental principles of the State," and Article 16 read, "Spaniards may assemble and associate freely for lawful purposes and in
accordance with the law."[258] Although the rights enumerated in *Fuero de los Españoles*
were picayune to start, the charter lacked internal provisions for ensuring the rights'
protection. Article 34 deputized the Franco-appointed Cortes to pass necessary legislation to protect the rights specified in the Charter. However, the Cortes passed few laws
translating Charter-guaranteed rights into state commitments. Furthermore, Article 35
allowed the government to "temporarily" suspend certain articles detailing citizens' individual rights. The *Fuero de los Españoles* also proclaimed Spain a monarchy but, true

---

King Alfonso XIII, from that line, was expelled at the birth of the Second Republic.

[255]Lewis (2002: 112).

[256]Ibid. p. 83.

[257]Payne (1987: 235).

[258]Crozier (1967: 436).

to his political guile, Franco did not identify its monarch.

As Franco aged, internal pressures mounted to name a successor. That Spain would revert to monarchy after Franco's death was assured but nobody knew whom Franco would choose as king. Alfonso XIII's son, Juan de Borbón, and grandson, Juan Carlos, appealed to Alfonsists, but Franco could not jilt his arch-conservative Carlist allies. Franco thought Juan de Borbón too liberal to meet both his standard. Consequently, Franco passed him over for his Francoist Spanish-educated son, Juan Carlos, whom Franco thought would oversee Francoist absolutism's continuation after proper grooming.[259] On July 21, 1969, Franco informed the Council of the Realm[260] that he had named Juan Carlos his successor. The Council immediately approved the decision and the Cortes joined them the next day. Upon installation as heir-apparent, Juan Carlos began officiating at state events along with Franco and showed no inclination toward democracy. Although, nearer to Franco's death, Juan Carlos met with some exiled opposition leaders, Franco dismissed any possibility that Juan Carlos might betray Francoist political principles.

Descending into dotage and the infirmity of Parkinson's disease , Franco appointed Secretary to the President Admiral Carrero Blanco as vice-President of the Council of Ministers, with the responsibility of supervising the cabinet's daily activities. On July 9, 1973, Franco "resigned as president of the Council of Ministers and turned the job over to Admiral Carrero Blanco... [Franco remained] Chief of State, Commander in Chief of the Armed Forces, and Caudillo of the National Movement, but for the most part he [became] just a figure head."[261]

Spain rapidly industrialized in the first quarter of twentieth century, with over half of the 1929 population employed in industry or the service sector, producing a large proletariat and stark urban wealth inequalities. Concurrently, on the Mediterranean coast, an agrarian elite owned large estates on which masses of rural laborers cultivated valuable exports, including wine, fruit and nuts.[262] The urban and rural wealth inequalities spawned outspoken socialist groups calling for wealth redistribution. Royal governments and General Primo de Rivera (dictator 1923-30) vacillated between repression and concessions to the citizenry, but no policy secured enough support to produce a stable coalition of societal actors. The left dominated the first Republican government and instituted stridently pro-labor policies: "an eight-hour working day, compulsory wage arbitration, security of tenure for leaseholders and sharecroppers, and agrarian reform to redistribute the large estates."[263] Though unbridled labor assertiveness and socialist fractiousness handed the 1933 election to a right-wing coalition, a reunited and revitalized left recaptured power in 1936 and applied redistributive policies even more forcefully than before, rallying the economic elite and even most of the middle class behind

---

[259] Payne (1987: 378).

[260] The 1947 Act of Spanish Succession had established The Council of the Realm, Franco's chief advisory body.

[261] Lewis (2002: 102).

[262] Grugel and Rees (1997: 104)

[263] Ibid., p. 105.

the Nationalists when the coup came.

While Spain's economic elites favored Franco over the Republican socialists and communists, the Nationalists were not wedded to big business's interests. Equating free markets with individualism and destabilizing class warfare, Franco and other Nationalists, bent on consolidating their power, resorted to a limited corporatist command economy.

> The economy was to be run, literally, on military lines; objectives were to be identified and the necessary factors of production brought together ... economic policy before and after the war was placed largely in the hands of the military. At all levels of economic policy-making and implementation men in uniform abounded ... a bewildering array of bodies at national and provincial levels [were] created to supervise every aspect of economic life.[264]

However, the Nationalists returned assets expropriated by the Republicans when they could and imposed an exceedingly pro-elite labor policy.

Franco's labor policy smashed independent trade unions and labor parties and replaced them with official Falangist syndicates for each trade.

> With everyone engaged in each area of the economy enrolled in a syndicate, representatives from both the employers and the employed were supposed to act together to ensure harmonious labor relations. In practice, while all workers were dragooned into the syndicates, employers successfully demanded exemption and the official organizations became devices for disciplining the labor force. With strikes and collective bargaining outlawed, the syndicates controlled employment, and set wages and conditions of work. Not surprisingly, it was the interests of employers that were mainly favored.[265]

Although the syndicates were Falange appendages, the cabinet set economic policy.

Government controls spurred economic inefficiencies and a titanic black market. The economy stagnated and the economic and political authoritarian elites accrued disproportionately large percentages of the formal and black market economies' surplus. By the 1950s, the citizenry's economic position grew so baleful that anti-regime protests and strikes erupted and numerous Falangist syndicate leaders joined them, reasoning that only more balanced syndicate employer-employee mediation, not repression, could avert disruptive revolutionary activity. Realizing many of his economic elite allies would open political transition negotiations with oppositional moderates should he violently repress the anti-regime protestors and keep the status quo, Franco responded with a cabinet reshuffle. In 1957, Franco introduced another faction to the authoritarian elite, Opus Dei affiliated, neoliberal, professionally trained economists. The technocrats liberalized trade, reduced inflation, raised interest rates, curtailed public spending, and liberalized capital markets. However, onerous labor regulations remained, as did extra-

---

[264]Ibid., p. 106.
[265]Ibid., p. 108.

Falange labor organization's proscription.[266]

Spain's neoliberal program benefited physical capital and banking interests more than landowning and the economic elite quickly transformed into a primarily capitalist one. Simultaneously, Spain's stellar GDP growth, averaging 7.5% per annum from 1960 to 1973, manifested itself in a large new middle class of professionals and white-collar employees.

Franco co-opted the new middle class through its very creation and retained their support with continued low taxes and career preferment.[267] Yet, as is so often the case with economic liberalization, wealth inequality grew and the working class and the informal sector bore the brunt. The inequality spurred calls for regime change and a new workers' movement organization. While Francoist Hardliners wanted to crush all dissent, the new economic elite and middle class had little stomach for it and preferred secret negotiations with non-Falange union leaders rather than repression, since this would surely lower industrial productivity. When OPEC reduced petroleum exports, raising petroleum prices and stimulating extensive inflation, Spain's trade declined, unemployment surged, and living standards eroded.

> The paralysis of the regime in the face of these deep economic problems helped convince its own chief supporters that the dictatorship was now an obstacle rather than an aid to the pursuit of their interests. With strikes growing in their intensity and overt political purpose, employers abandoned the official syndical apparatus to deal directly with the 'illegal' unions.[268]

The neoliberal program intended to secure fascist longevity divided the economic elite from their political allies and precipitated a negotiated transition to democracy in the manner discussed by Przeworski. Briefly, in terms of the model, the crisis induced a collapse of the valence of the regime, so that elite support was no longer sufficient to retain power.

6.2.3   The Soviet System (1924-1991)

The Communist Party of the Soviet Union (CPSU) dominated the Soviet polity. The rigidly hierarchical CPSU concentrated authority in the hands of the General Secretary (Gensek) of the Central Committee of the CPSU. While Stalin forged the Gensek dictatorship, which lasted until Glasnost, the CPSU's hierarchical organizational structure emanated from Lenin's notion of democratic centralism. Party statutes stated:

> The guiding principle of party organizational structure is democratic centralism, which means:
> (i) Election of all leading party organs from the lowest to the highest organ.
> (ii) Periodic accountability of party organs to their party organizations and

---

[266] Payne (1987: 450).
[267] Grugel and Rees (1997: 118).
[268] Ibid., p. 122.

higher organs.

(iii) Strict party discipline and subordination of the minority to the majority.

(iv) The decisions of the higher organs are absolutely binding on lower organs.[269]

The emphasis of democratic centralism's on electing party leaders from the bottom up just feigned accountability of top party organs to their subordinate organs. The Gensek and Secretariat (party apparatus) determined who was on the party election ballots. Only democratic centralism-imposed fealty to majority decisions (that is unquestioningly obeying resolutions passed by Gensek approved party assemblies) was practiced unadulterated.

Democratic centralism translated into a branched political hierarchy, founded on the *primary party organization* (PPO). As the basic unit of party organization, PPOs were formed in any Soviet institution or enterprise containing at least three party members. They were "found in factories, farms, schools, universities, research institutes, stores, cultural institutions, government bureaus and offices, armed forces and police units."[270] PPOs implemented party policies and decisions in the institution in which they were embedded. In addition to producing propaganda, organizing workers to meet party economic plans, striving to strengthen labor discipline, and struggling to improve production standards, PPOs were to "promptly inform the party organs of any shortcomings in the work of the establishment or individual workers, regardless of their positions."[271] Thus, party loyalists infiltrated every Soviet organization. PPO members usually did not directly manage PPO activities but elected local party committees, which acted for the PPOs when they were not in session. The committees then elected local party secretaries, who handled the PPOs' day-to-day work.

Above the PPOs, all CPSU units were territorially-based[272] and supervised all party activities in their territories. Each territorial tier of party organization consisted of five organs: (1) the constituent body, "the highest governing organ of party organization," which elected from among its members the next highest constituent body in the party's territorial hierarchy, a committee to exercise power during the constituent bodies' recess, and an inconsequential auditing commission; (2) a committee, which elected from among its members an executive decision-making bureau to govern when the committee was not in session and the territory's party secretaries; (3) the aforementioned decision-making bureau; (4) a secretariat, consisting of several secretaries (including a First and Second secretary at higher levels) and their staffs to handle the party's day-to-day work for the territorial unit; (5) an auditing commission, which inspected the work of the party organization itself.

The CPSU's All-Union constituent body was the Party Congress, elected by the Party Congresses of the 14 non-Russian Republics and the Party Conferences of the

---

[269]Finer, et al. (1968: 526).

[270]Ibid., p. 527.

[271]Ibid., p. 528.

[272]Above the PPOs, the first territorial tier represented rayons, cities, and boroughs. The second territorial tier represented krays, oblasts, and ethnic units. The third territorial tier represented individual union republics. The highest tier covered the entire Soviet Union.

krays and oblasts.[273]

The Party Congress's formal authority remained relatively static throughout the Soviet years.

> The Congress:
> (i) heard and approved the reports of the Central Committee, the Central Auditing Commission, and other central organizations;
> (ii) review[d], amended, and approved the party program and statutes;
> (iii) determined the party line on questions of domestic and foreign policy and examined and decided on the most important problems in the building of Communism;
> (iv) elect[ed] the Central Committee and the Central Auditing Commission.[274]

However, the Party Congress's infrequent convention[275] and the unanimous decisions on proposals offered by the All-Union Central Committee indicate that it was little more than a sounding board for Central Committee, Politburo, and Secretariat initiatives.[276] The Central Committee set the Congress's agenda. The Congress listened to the Central Committee's foreign affairs, domestic affairs, and party affairs report, approved all acts introduced by the leadership and Central Committee resolutions promulgated since the last Party Congress; and elected a new Central Committee.

The Central Committee was a convention of the party elite. It made the fateful decision of October 10, 1917 to seize power and initially served as the Soviet Union's de facto parliament. In the Lenin and early Stalin years, it contained representatives of the party's important pre-revolutionary factions and entrenched interests. However, following the revolution, it mainly rubberstamped Politburo and Secretariat decisions. That is not to say that the Politburo members and General Secretary disregarded the Central Committee members. Responsible for implementing party policy in their localities, state institutions, and the military between plena, Central Committee members wielded some power and collectively held a common interest in preserving their privileges. Although Stalin broke their autonomy after murdering a majority of its members in the 1930s, by the 1960s and until Glasnost, the Soviet system granted "unprecedented personal security and stability of tenure" for Central Committee members.[277] In addition to full voting members, Party Congresses elected candidate members to the Central Committee, who participated in deliberations and filled vacancies in the Central Committee

---

[273]Oblasts were composed of districts (raions) and cities/towns directly under the jurisdiction of an oblast. Historically, a kray was a vast territory located along the periphery of the country. There is no difference in legal status between a kray and an oblast. In the Soviet Union (according to its Constitution of 1977), the only difference between a kray and an oblast was that an autonomous oblast could be a sub-division of a kray or of a union republic, but not of an oblast.

[274]Finer et al. (1968: 533).

[275]The Leninist era saw annual Party Congresses. However, as Stalin consolidated his power, the Party Congress convened less frequently, first biennially, then triennially. Finally, party statutes were amended to require a Party Congress meeting only every four years but Stalin ignored the statute, which was not upheld until 1956. Then, in the 1960s, the interlude between Congresses was raised to five years.

[276]Finer et al. (1968: 534).

[277]Mawdsley and White (2000: 286).

caused by expulsion, resignation, or death.[278] Like the Party Congress, the Central Committee's size increased and it also met intermittently, twice a year for a few days each. Consequently, the Central Committee became nearly as ponderous as the Party Congresses. To make policy in its absence, the Central Committee created three bodies to articulate party policy and manage the party between Central Committee sessions: the Political Bureau (Politburo), Organizational Bureau (Orgburo, which was merged with the Politburo in 1952), and Secretariat.

The Politburo started as the party's most important decision-making organ. Since PPOs were embedded in every important enterprise and most government employees and civil servants were party members, democratic centralism made Politburo directives the ultimate authority. But soon after Lenin died, the Secretariat subordinated it. In 1925, General Secretary Stalin and the General Department of the Secretariat commenced drafting the Politburo meetings' agendas. "Many draft decisions were prepared in the Secretariat under the supervision of the General Secretary and the other secretaries, and discussed in a secretaries' meeting before they reached the Politburo agenda."[279] Often, Politburo meetings consisted solely of confirming the Secretariat authored agenda, a process facilitated by the General Secretary presiding over Politburo meetings.[280] The Politburo could confer assent through majority vote in sessions or by initialing circulated proposals, which were raised in the next meeting if they did not garner unanimous support. However, when Stalin or successive Genseks approached Politburo members individually with proposals already initialed by the Gensek himself, few refused to cosign it. Like the Central Committee, the Politburo had full voting and candidate members.

The Secretariat supervised party policies' implementation in administrative, economic, military, social, cultural, and professional institutions, organizations, and establishments. The All-Union Secretariat implemented all-union policies but, due to democratic centralism, rigidly directed lower-level Secretariats' activities too. The hierarchy of secretaries formed the "party apparatus," the corps of full-time professional party functionaries. The party apparatus

> determined key appointments in all party, state, economic, social, cultural, and military institutions at every level; they explained and implemented the policies of the state and party in all sectors of Soviet life; they checked and ensured the fulfillment of party and state directives; they mobilized and manipulated the energies and pressures required for the implementation of the party's will; they accumulated and organized information and prepared reports and recommendations for action, which [were] transmitted to the Politburo; [and] they [kept] a close tab on public moods and sentiments, reported their impressions to the central authorities, and maintain[ed] an extensive file of dossiers on party

---

[278] Finer et al. (1968: 537).
[279] Löwenhardt et al. (1992: 116).
[280] Ibid., p.117.

members.[281]

Party policy, and thus government policy, was what the party apparatus chose to implement. Moreover,

> as the network of local secretaries was absorbed into the central apparatus and became dependent on it for assignments and promotions, the secretarial hierarchy emerged as a distinct group with vested interests of its own. The drive to stabilize its own position and to extend its authority became an end in itself... The rising influence of the General Secretary symbolized its own aspirations; every effort to delimit his influence was construed as an effort to undermine the power of the apparatus itself.[282]

As democratic centralism made the Gensek the party apparatus's logical standard bearer, the Gensek arrogated power that ensured his indisputable leadership of the party and thus the Soviet Union.

The system of party elections demonstrates the supremacy of the party apparatus, and Gensek. Regional party secretaries, beholden to the Gensek, chose who was on the ballot for elections to the next highest territorial constituent body.[283] Then, the delegates in the relevant constituent body registered their preferences by voting, when party rules were followed, secretly, for or against each candidate selected by the local secretariat.[284] Of course, since the All-Union Party Congress (the CPSU's highest constituent body) elected the Central Committee and Politburo, the Gensek, short of a secretariat revolt, effectively selected those bodies and could pack them with allies.

The Soviet constitutional order, established by the Soviet constitutions of 1924, 1936, and 1977, created a federal institutional structure, parallel to the party, that carried out party promulgated state policy. From 1936 onward, the Soviet Union boasted universal suffrage. The Soviet electorate directly chose delegates for local soviets, rayon soviets, and a soviet for every territorial level parallel to the CPSU territorial bodies, up to the All-Union Supreme Soviet. Most delegates were CPSU members and subject to party discipline and, moreover, elections followed the same process as for party constituent bodies, placing full power in the Secretariat's hands.

> Every soviet elect[ed] an executive committee to function as an administrative and supervisory body, with a chairman who in effect function[ed] as the chief administrative officer of the unit concerned. At the Union, Union Republic, and Autonomous Republic levels, instead of an executive committee, there [was] an elected Presidium and Council of Ministers, each with a chairman.[285]

The executive committees exercised authority during the soviets' recesses. They

---

[281] Finer et al. (1968: 545).
[282] Fainsod (1954: 157).
[283] Hough and Fainsod (1979: 144)
[284] Finer et al. (1968: 530).
[285] Ibid., p. 568.

controlled the legislative, executive, and judicial power in their territories and, like the
CPSU, lower tier soviets and committees were subordinate to those of higher territorial
rank.

The Supreme Soviet was a rubberstamp bicameral legislature, each house holding
equal power. One house, the Soviet of the Union, was directly elected by the citizenry
from single member districts while the other, the Soviet of Nationalities, included representatives of the federal units and gave each national unit equal representation. The soviets had a remarkably high turnover rate, about two-thirds of delegates at each session
being new.[286] Each house had a "council of elders," which was primarily a ceremonial
role awarded for loyally servicing the party. Both chambers devoted most of their time
to listening to Ministers' reports and enacting government legislation drawn up between
Supreme Soviet plena. The Supreme Soviet elected a Presidium to wield its power between sessions and a Council of Ministers (government) to issue executive decrees and
implement the legislation enacted by the Supreme Soviet or Presidium. The Supreme
Soviet also amended the Constitution, elected the Supreme Court, and appointed the
Procurator-General.[287] As party functionaries, the Supreme Soviet's delegates' votes
echoed secretariat decisions.

The Soviet of the Union and Soviet of Nationalities elected the Presidium in joint
session. The Presidium promulgated decrees, which were supposed to conform with
hitherto passed Supreme Soviet legislation, during the Supreme Soviet's recess. While
the Presidium promulgated decrees, the Council of Ministers executed them through
their ministries, making the Council of Ministers the real governing organ. All-Union
ministry decisions filtered down to their Union Republic counterparts, which implemented Moscow's policies at the periphery. The Supreme Soviet's Presidium contained
many Politburo and All-Union Secretariat members and the Council of Ministers was
usually almost indistinguishable from the Politburo. The Council of Ministers, with
dozens of ministers and their staffs, like so many other state and party organs, was un-
wieldy and delegated a lot of its authority to its own small presidium and chairman, who
was often the Gensek.[288]

The economic system Stalin built upon and expanded outlawed money lending and
all private ownership of capital.[289] "Stalin's innovation was to confiscate for his own
purposes almost the total natural and tangible capital stock of the country and then to
use [those] resources to produce a mix of output that was much more intensive in capital
goods and other goods Stalin wanted than would have otherwise been produced."[290]

Therefore, Soviet citizens only earned income by labor. Party technocrats set base
wages very low and consumer goods' prices comparatively high, maximizing the output of goods desired by the authoritarian political elite. To retain natural worker productivity incentives, the system levied "little or no implicit taxation on extra, overtime,

[286]Ibid., p. 577.
[287]"1936 Constitution of the USSR." See PoliticsForum.org 15 April 2006.
[288]Finer et al. (1968: 576).
[289]Hewett (1988: 47).
[290]Olson (2000: 114).

above-the-norm or 'bonus' work and productivity" and made use of progressive piece rates that increased the per-unit payment with the amount a person produced.[291] Stalin applied the system most brutally on the former agricultural landowners (kulaks). Stalin collectivized agriculture in his first five year plan (1928-1933) to make certain kulaks met their output quotas to the state before selling practically untaxed output produced on their tiny CPSU allocated private plots on the market. Put simply, the economy of workers' paradise operated like the slave economy of the antebellum South.

Unlike the antebellum South, the Soviet's relied on CPSU technocrats' direction. Managers needed to collect and exploit a gargantuan amount of information to coordinate their activities with other managers and execute the CPSU elite's decisions. Competition with other managers for greater production to procure promotion and other bureaucrats' incentive to prove to their superiors that fault for any shortages, low quality goods, or less than expected production possibility estimates lay elsewhere discouraged managers from skimming resources, understating production possibilities, and feeding misinformation casting themselves in a more favorable light. Astute superiors could usually uncover shirking or graft by looking for output discrepancies between factories or farms that produced the same goods.[292]

However, the surveillance system foundered once managers forsook competition for collusion. Because all output belonged to the state, managers had no inherent incentive to protect it and deliver all of it. Without Stalinist purges eliminating collusive links, the links metastasized vertically, managers colluding with inferiors and superiors to split stolen output, and horizontally, managers in nominally competing factories or farms colluding. As the collusive links expanded, those colluding pilfered more output, reducing government revenue.[293]

6.3   The Durability of Regimes

Measured by amount of capital owned by the elite, by the middle class, and by the citizenry, it is clear that economic inequality characterized both Argentina and Francoist Spain's institutionally engendered economic systems. Since capital generated the personal income of the elite, while the citizens' income came from labor, wide income differentials existed. Therefore, inequality was always acute enough to provide incentives to citizens to oppose the regime. Moreover, it implied enough of a redistributive reward to make revolutionary activity extremely profitable.

Conversely, in the non-collusive Soviet economic model, almost all income accrued from labor, meaning income differentials emanated nearly exclusively from wage disparities, effectively imposing relative egalitarianism and greatly diminishing the value of redistribution and the economic returns of revolutionary activity. After Khrushchev delivered his 1956 de-Stalinization speech and the Stalinist "Anti-Party Group's" 1957

---

[291] Ibid., p. 116.
[292] Ibid., p. 139-142.
[293] Ibid., p. 141.

extirpation, vertical and horizontal collusive syndicates surfaced that illegally increased inequality. The politically connected had better opportunities to steal state assets and could buyoff or threaten to use their political leverage to harm the politically inconsequential people who protested. However, the criminally based inequality was not nearly as marked as Argentina's and Spain's, and was kept secret.

The CPSU's economic power issued from its dictatorial management of the country's capital stock and its monopoly on privileged information. Later, many Soviet factory and farm managers accrued power by stealing public industrial and agricultural output. Democratization in Argentina or Spain meant a more redistributive tax rate but the economic elites would still survive. Conversely, the Soviet elite's status depended on the nature of the particular system from which it benefited. With democracy, the CPSU could no longer direct the economy and the managers' parasitic syndicates would vanish from competition. Therefore, while the citizenry's economic incentive to topple the system was trivial, the political elites had a strong interest in protecting the system. Consequently, Soviet collective preferences were comparatively less inclined to regime change than their Argentine and Spanish counterparts.

As regards political power, the Argentine military elite lost the least from abdication because power was less concentrated in their hands than in Franco's or than in the apparatus of the CPSU, because it had a place to go (the barracks), and because it retained more de facto power than the other systems. The Argentine military could, and did, negotiate an agreeable transition to democracy, securing painful concessions from the oppositional Moderates. These concessions included the "National Pacification Law," giving amnesty to the "Dirty War's" perpetrators. Moreover, whenever the military brass felt their civilian successors were reneging on their side of the bargain, their institutional autonomy allowed them to threaten another coup.

Unlike the Argentine junta, Francoism concentrated power in one man. While an army can retain a healthy bargaining leverage following extrication, a man loses it. Franco's unparalleled power derived from his exclusive control over cabinet and high military appointments and from his masterful ad hoc political maneuvers to protect his regime. As long as the fascist dictator lived, he would not accede to institutional transition and could only be ejected via ruptura. However, once the fascist dictator dies, PET implies that his frangible coalition may (and did in Spain's case) accede to transition, especially if the members of the new coalition reserve some voice on future choices. Spain's right proved its electability in 1933. After Franco, the right could reasonably assume that it could succeed in democratic elections, especially under a Franco-picked king and with a vigilant politicized military.

The CPSU could have resigned itself to democratic contestation of power. After all, many communist parties have fared well at the ballot box, even in some former Soviet states like Moldova.[294] However, democratization would have stripped the sec-

---

[294]"In February 2001, in elections certified by international observers as free and fair, slightly over half of Moldova's voters cast their ballots for the Communist Party. Under the rules of Moldova's proportional representation system, the Communist faction, which in the previous Parliament consisted of 40 of Parliament's 101 seats, jumped to 71 – a clear majority. The Parliament then elected the leader of the Communist faction,

retariat of control over the CPSU itself. The dictatorship was of the CPSU apparatus, not the CPSU. The power of Gensek and the party apparatus flowed from their control over CPSU elections and personnel distribution. This was only sustainable so long as enforced by a police and military embedded with PPOs. Moreover, unlike in Spain, the elite was self-perpetuating. The Secretariat and entire CPSU maintained reliable electoral succession protocol to choose a new dictatorial Gensek when one died in office. Only Khrushchev was forced out and it was by an antagonistic CPSU apparatus led by the All-Union Second Secretary, Brezhnev, after much furtive plotting. They rebelled because they feared Khrushchev's 1962 decision to divide provincial and local party machines into industrial and agricultural branches would jeopardize their grip on power.[295]

In contrast, Gorbachev was not exactly ousted. Recognizing the Soviet Union's economic duress, he concluded that only economic and political liberalization (glasnost and perestroika) could revitalize the Soviet economy and narrow the growing gap between American and Soviet output. We may conjecture that he hoped that by this liberalization he would win the newly enfranchised masses' political support and recast himself in the public's imagination as a Reformer instead of chief Hardliner, thus becoming the new center of a Hardliner-Reformer-Moderate coalition. Gorbachev could not recreate himself in this way, and the voters chose Yeltsin.

The three regimes examined here could deploy brutal and efficient repression methods against oppositional citizenry's organization and its efforts to overcome the collective action problem. However, the Soviet system stands out for two reasons. First, overcoming the collective action problem requires paying revolutionaries. This becomes marginally harder as wealth inequality abates. As detailed above, Soviet citizens gained less of a payoff from income redistribution than the Argentine and Spanish citizens. Second, many Soviet citizens probably estimated that destroying the hegemony of the CPSU apparatus might wreak economic chaos, especially because few Soviet enterprises could withstand any competition.

The Argentine and Spanish governments could not effectively filter their decisions into non-military and police organizations and enterprises. The Argentine junta relied nearly exclusively on the police and military, through their control over de jure governmental institutions, to enforce their edicts. However, they could not directly enforce these edicts in factories, cultural organizations, and universities. Franco controlled the police and military too and could also tame and fracture the working class through Falangist syndicates.

The Gensek and CPSU apparatus not only controlled the police and military through their command of de jure governmental institutions. They also controlled every meaningful Soviet organization or enterprise, because the territorial party hierarchy's tentacles reached into them through PPOs. democratic centralism and the vested interest in

---

Vladimir Voronin, to be President." See 'Background Note: Moldova, Political Conditions,' U.S. Department of State: Bureau of European and Eurasian Affairs August. 2005.
     <http://www.state.gov/r/pa/ei/bgn/5357.htm#political>.
[295]Löwenhardt et al. (1992: 54-56).

preserving secretarial prerogatives, the secretariats enforced the dictator's decisions.

Argentina's junta and Franco's coterie exited via reforma, the compromise transition, as Przeworski has suggested. In contrast, the Soviet system exploded. When Gorbachev weakened the CPSU for his own benefit, he created incentives for his party subordinates to grab what they could before the center of power collapsed. This led to a rush to appropriate state assets – tearing the system apart by wanton piracy. The key is that no effectual Reformers besides the General Secretary (Gensek) and the CPSU apparatus could exist in the Soviet Union. The economic elites and middle classes that the Argentine and Spanish governments needed to stay in power, did not exist in the Soviet Union. Lenin tried co-option with his New Economic Policy during the Russian Civil War.[296] In contrast, Stalin had no need of co-option because he had expropriated all capital, thus eliminating all who resisted, and enslaving the rest of the population and making them dependent on PPO taskmasters.

An historical analysis demonstrates that party dictatorships are more institutionally durable than military or fascist ones. That conclusion has obvious foreign policy implications. Soviet-like party systems, including China and North Korea, are very unlikely to collapse from internal pressures, though they may fall from external pressure or from reforms from the top. However, Gorbachev's fate suggest that few party dictatorship elites will willingly democratize. China is liberalizing its economy but not its polity, maintaining the dominance of the party apparatus's even as reliance on technocrats increases. Either outright confrontation or détente are viable policy approaches towards those states, but there would seem to be no effective strategy in between these extremes.

6.4   Concluding Remarks

Acemoglu, and Robinson (2005) have offered a compelling model that connects democracy and dictatorship. There are four problems with their analysis that the PET framework presented here attempts to rectify.

Firstly, they work in the Downsian context, where the policy space has only one dimension.[297] This usually means a focus on the conflict between labor and capital, with the median (or centrist) citizen being pivotal between left and right. Various recent empirical studies of elections in developed polities clearly indicate that there is usually a second "social" axis, characterized by citizens' preferences on civil rights, sometimes involving religious beliefs, as in Israel and Turkey. Although the meaning of this social axis varies across different polities, it typically has an interpretation that is consistent with the notion of the political axis shown in Figure 6.1.[298]

Secondly, we use the notion of valence, first proposed by Stokes as presented in

---

[296] Decreed on March 21, 1921 by the 10th Congress of the Russian Communist Party, the New Economic Policy restored private ownership in many sectors of the economy, particularly agriculture, because government ownership of all factories and requisitioning farmers' surpluses had precipitously shrunk output.

[297] Downs (1957).

[298] See Chapter 4.

earlier chapters. Valence has been shown by the empirical studies to be statistically relevant in modelling elections. The valence idea provides a formal reason why the median citizen will not be pivotal. Instead, asymmetries in the perception of the citizens of the autocrat and opposition will cause their "equilibrium" policy positions to be very different. The two varieties of valence that we use are intended to accommodate two different aspects of a leader's appeal. It is entirely possible that a revolutionary leader is blindly supported because of his intrinsic valence, or charisma, so that the policy position chosen by the leader is uncritically supported by the masses. On the other hand, a charismatic leader, such as Castro or Lenin, can gain even more support by articulating revolutionary policies that are opposed to those of the autocrat. This second aspect of valence we formally model by the notion of activist (or policy dependent) valence. An autocrat's response to opposition will depend on the degree to which the opposition is united. For example, a fragmented opposition will tend to be characterized by the low valence of its leaders. An equilibrium response would be to accommodate the demands, by adopting a position close to a weighted electoral mean. This weighted mean takes account of whatever support there is in the citizenry for the leader. The discussion, above, about Gorbachev's strategy suggests that his policy position was adopted due to an incorrect belief on his part about the low valence of the opposition.

The third key point is the high dimensionality of the factor space. We have tended to emphasize the possibility of collusion between the autocrat and capital. In less developed, capital poor economies, a more likely coalition is between the landed elite interest and the autocrat, with a revolutionary leader promising land reform. It is probable that a leader such as Mugabe in Zimbabwe was able to take power initially by such promises. It seems, however, that Mugabe has maintained his control by a strategy based on manipulation of capital. By the device of an artificial exchange rate, available only to his cronies, he has destroyed the wage rate, and probably the factor price of land, even as the citizens were impoverished. While his intrinsic valence has fallen, the fragmented opposition and the support of his clique has allowed him to keep power.

The fourth point is related to the first. In the empirical studies noted above, the intrinsic valence of a political leader is a measure of the "quality" of the leader as viewed by the citizens. This will vary among the population, and it assumed to be distributed in a stochastic fashion. However, in the empirical analyses of elections, it is possible to use sociodemographic characteristics of citizens as an additional source of information in modelling political choice. Formally, this can be interpreted as allowing leader valences to be very different in the various, heterogenous segments of the society. It is obvious enough that, in a fragmented society such as Iraq, with the autocrat removed, the valences of the political leaders may be so heterogenous that civil war ensues. This chapter has not discussed how the intrinsic valence of leaders is generated or determined, though in earlier work has been presented some ideas.[299]

As Collier (2007) has noted, approximately 750 million poor people in the world

---

[299]Schofield (2006a) suggests that valence in a population can be subject to rapid "belief cascades", thus changing the rationality of certain acts. Though presented in a different context, Karklins and Petersen (1993) make a similar suggestion. Fragmenting belief cascades may thus induce civil war.

are either in the midst of, or have recently been exposed to, civil war. A version of
the PET model presented here, consistent with the work of Wantchekon (2004), could
provide some insight into why poor societies are constrained to the Malthusian Trap
(Clark, 2007), often subject to the imposition of autocracy or to the chaos of civil war.

Chapter 7

Authoritarian Regimes

7.1 Dictatorships in the Soviet Union, China and North Korea

Note.[300]

Most of the communist dictatorships collapsed in the late 1980s and early 1990s, while those that survived liberalized their economies to varying degrees, China and Vietnam being examples. North Korea's regime, however, has retained both its totalitarian control over the population and administrative-command economy in heavy industry and other industries prioritized by the regime.[301] Although North Korea implemented some economic reforms in 2002, its score on the Heritage Foundation's Index of Economic Freedom has declined since then. And, its 2008 score of 3 out of 100, pales in comparison with China's 52.8, Vietnam's 49.8, and even Cuba's 27.5.[302] This section has several objectives: (1) outlining a theory of communist regime durability, (2) using that theory to reiterate the previous chapter's discussion why the Soviet regime collapsed in 1989, (3) using the theory to explain how China's regime could liberalize its economy and accord its citizens more civil rights without collapsing, and, most importantly, (4) using the theory to explain how North Korea's regime has preserved its orthodox communist system, and the totalitarian regime that sustains it, while Russia and China have not and determining how stable North Korea's regime presently is.

Four variables explain most of the variance in communist regime durability: (1) the cost and credibility of the regime's economic monitoring system (i.e., the dictatorial elite's capacity to detect shirking workers and workers and officials pilfering state assets and thereby skimming the dictator's rents); (2) how severely those detected are punished; (3) the workforce's human capital endowment; and (4) the value of the assets party notables could buy or seize if the communist regime were to collapse. This

---

[300] This section was written by Micah Levinson.
[301] Yang (2007: 51).
[302] "Index of Economic Freedom 2008," Heritage Foundation, 6 July 2008.
  <http://www.heritage.org/research/features/index.cfm>

section argues that North Korea's strict communist system has proved more durable than the rest because: (1) its industrial organization makes economic monitoring relatively cheaper than it was in the post-Stalin USSR and post-Mao China; (2) North Korea punishes those detected shirking, pilfering, or conducting illegal business activity more severely than other Communist regimes did; (3) North Korea's relative paucity of human capital has cheapened repression and replacing workers while stymieing the rising expectations that workers often exhibit when their level of education rises, which can translate into worker restiveness; and (4) North Korea's abject poverty and limited natural resources limit the potential payoff to party notables of deserting the regime when it looks weak in order to wield their political influence to enrich themselves in the post-communist order.

    This section defines communist dictatorship as any regime that uses the state's coercive powers to impose and sustain an administrative-command economy. Stalin created the first administrative-command economy in the USSR through his First Five Year Plan (1929-33). Throughout this section, "communist dictatorship" refers to the economic model that Stalin innovated, and which persisted in the USSR until *perestroika* in the 1980s, whether practiced in the USSR or elsewhere. Sometimes in their haste to differentiate Leninism, Maoism, and North Korea's Juche ideology, scholars forget that, until the 1980s, the mode of economic organization throughout the communist bloc was very similar despite ostensible ideological conflicts among the regimes. However, by the 1980s, North Korea increasingly differed from the other communist states in ways that enabled a more faithful adherence to communist economic and political organization. Before comparing communist regimes, we must apprehend how they function. Once we understand how communist regimes function, we can infer what could disrupt their functioning, thereby uncovering the communist dictatorship's intrinsic, systemic weaknesses. Thereafter, we can study various communist regimes and discern which are more likely to fall prey to these intrinsic, systemic weaknesses because of their institutional design, the country's culture, or some specific circumstantial factor. The easiest way to comprehend the communist system is to comprehend the one that Stalin built in the USSR because it served as the template for most other states that adopted communism.

7.1.1   The Political Economy of the Soviet Dictatorship

In Stalin's USSR, the dictatorial elite consisted of the top party (CPSU) brass, who served in the Central Committee of the CPSU, its Politburo, and its Secretariat. At the apex was the General Secretary of the Central Committee of the CPSU.[303] Olson (2000) correctly identifies the Soviet dictatorial elite as a "stationary bandit." Stationary bandits are people or groups possessing a monopoly of force over a given territory and who use the force to appropriate the wealth of the people residing in that territory towards their own ends. In a practical context, stationary bandits are governments that tax their

---

[303] Each of the Soviet dictators after Lenin held the position of General Secretary of the Central Committee of the CPSU.

citizens to aggrandize themselves. Although the leaders might invest in roads and factories to expand the economy of the territory they rule, the objective is not to improve the citizens' standard of living for its own sake but to increase the amount that rulers can skim for themselves as rents.[304] But, usually stationary bandits sacrifice some income to enhance political security by appointing slavishly loyal ministers and investing money in raising their subjects' standard of living in order to limit their discontent with the regime. The stationary bandit model of government describes most monarchical and dictatorial constitutions. However, Stalin devised a new modus operandi for appropriating value from the people under his control that enabled more appropriation per-capita over the long-term than any invented before or since and proved sturdy enough to withstand shocks ranging from famine that killed millions in the 1930s to four years of fighting the Wermacht. Similarly, the Chinese regime survived the dislocation of the Great Leap Forward and the North Korean regime survived a famine in the mid-1990s that may have killed 10% of its population.

When Stalin came to power in the mid-1920s, the USSR's economy was still very market-oriented. Although the state owned most large-scale industry, it instructed factory managers to finance themselves through profits and empowered them to hire and fire workers to maximize profits. Additionally, the government rented out or sold many artisan workshops and small factories to individuals. Agriculture, in a predominantly rural Russia, was still private. During the revolution, Lenin nationalized the wealthy magnates' land and transferred it to peasant communes, which subsequently distributed it among their members. With this reorganization, the number of peasant households swelled to 25 million. These peasants had the right to sell their produce domestically to individuals, state agencies, and private traders at market prices. Most retail trade remained in private hands.[305] The peasants' only obligation to the government was to pay moderate taxes. This market economy posed a serious problem for Stalin. To augment his country's wealth and power and thus his own power, Stalin wanted the USSR's heavy industrial output to surpass that of its more developed European competitors. But, the break-up of the large landed estates into peasant smallholdings shrunk the scale of the agricultural enterprises below that necessary to make selling large surpluses profitable at the price the state was willing to offer. The state could increase agricultural production, grain being the most important, to pay for industrialization and feed a growing urban workforce several ways. The regime could allow successful peasants to buy more land until the scale of agricultural enterprises again made selling at the price the government offered profitable. It could also increase the price offered for grain and divert some government investment in heavy industry to manufacturing consumer goods that would make the higher prices attractive because there would be more to buy. However, Stalin could not countenance a wealthy new class of proprietors who would threaten his dictatorship. He also refused to delay his industrialization project by diverting investment to consumer goods and disliked the idea of having to cajole the peasants to sell their grain by offering them prices that would also slow his industrialization project.

---

[304]Olson (2000: 7-8).
[305]Davies (1998: 24-8).

Stalin decided to secure artificially cheap grain by forcing the USSR's peasants onto collective farms that had to sell grain to the state at deflated prices. Essentially, he was forcefully employing the entire agricultural sector to work for the state and paying them low wages for producing certain quotas of produce.

In 1930, as part of the First Five Year Plan, Stalin started forcing the USSR's millions of peasants onto collective farms. When the dislocation reduced agricultural output, peasants' grain reserves were seized leading to a famine that killed over five million people. Peasants resisting expropriation were sent to the Gulag as forced-labor or shot. After the storm of collectivization subsided in 1934, the state ordered each collective to deliver a quota to the state, leaving the surplus to the peasant workers, who could sell it at fixed prices for their own enrichment.[306] Stalin also nationalized all private industry and commercial enterprises and replaced the profit-loss accounting in the factories with national production plans devised by the CPSU elite and supervised by CPSU and state organs. To motivate workers in this new order, state planners set wages very low and prices for consumer goods, in comparison with the pay, relatively high.[307] Then, most workers were put on a piece-rate labor compensation program. They were assigned a quota and if they completed it they earned the base wage.[308] If they completed less, they received less than the base wage. And, if they produced more than their quota, they received progressively more for each unit of output. Clerks, teachers, and whoever else's work did not produce easily quantified output were usually paid according to time rates and could earn bonuses based on the quality of work. However, Khrushchev and his successors gradually raised the base wage, shifted many workers formerly compensated by a piece-rate to a time-rate, and capped the amount piece-rate workers could earn above their base wage. Thus, the CPSU elite monopolized agricultural and industrial capital, had a monopsony on labor, and could use a pseudo-market wage system backed by force to mobilize capital and labor as it wished. This control over the economy conferred awesome political powers on the CPSU elite. Evidence of the CPSU elite's command of the economy is that the amount of grain the state received after collectivization was two and a half times greater than that before despite the fact that the price the state paid for it markedly declined while the supply of grain grew negligibly.[309]

In the communist economy that Stalin built, the state was the employer and the workers the employees. Since the state was the only employer it could set the wages however it wished, enabling the accumulation of gargantuan rents by keeping wages low. The CPSU elite did not need to fear any autonomous economic interests because everyone worked for it and depended upon it for their livelihood as employees do with their employer. And, as Stalin demonstrated with the recalcitrant peasants, any collective action by workers assured fearsome retribution. That is why no workers attempted large-scale collective action until *glasnost*. Whenever a state finances itself by taxing its citizens' and businesses' income, the workers become the employer and the state the employee.

---

[306] Seton-Watson (1954: 156-9).
[307] Olson (2000: 115-6).
[308] Filtzer (1989: 90).
[309] Seton-Watson (1954: 159).

Thus, the direction of accountability switches and the only way that a stationary bandit can sustain its regime and accumulate rents is through finding a happy balance between worker and enterprises' economic interests and repressing political dissent.

Although the communist dictatorship is very stable once created and arguably empowers its elite more than any other kind of dictatorship, its constitution contains intrinsic weaknesses. First, workers are not compensated according to their productivity but according to the appearance of productivity, generating an opportunity to shirk. Piece-rate workers are inclined to produce output of poor quality and as time-rate compensation regimes replace piece-rate ones, workers begin asking themselves what is the least I can do to get my salary? Moreover, workers and enterprise managers might even feel compelled to pilfer state assets for personal consumption or to sell on the black market engendered by price controls. What the state owns only the state has an inherent incentive to protect. The workers only have an incentive not to pilfer so much as to alert suspicion and jeopardize their wages or safety.

This shirking and pilfering not only cuts into the dictator's rents but also threatens his stranglehold on capital and labor and, therefore, on power itself. The leakage of the dictator's rents reduces the reliance on the state for income and livelihood of the beneficiaries of the leaked rents. And, if these newly empowered beneficiaries share a trait, for instance employment in the same industry, they can coalesce into an interest group. Such a group can further empower itself if it includes enterprise managers and *glavk* officials who oversee enterprises in a particular industry or region because they can wield to their political advantage the capital that they were delegated to manage. The emergence of such organized interests capable of autonomous and deliberate action threaten the dictator's power to the extent that they can subvert his will and ultimately terminate his hold on power should he unduly antagonize them. Therefore, the dictator must circumscribe shirking and pilfering to conserve his power.

Only a credible threat of detection and severe punishment will deter most workers and managers from shirking and pilfering. Accordingly, Harrison (2002) argues that the communist dictator must delegate some of his authority to economic monitors to root out shirking and pilfering. However, monitoring costs money and it comes out of the dictator's pocket. Harrison distinguishes between direct and collateral monitoring costs. The direct costs cover actually detecting and punishing the individual shirkers and pilferers. Collateral costs consist of the loss in economic output, and thus the dictator's rents, incurred in punishing those detected.[310] Replacing workers, sentencing them to perform unskilled forced-labor in the Gulag, and executing them reduces overall labor productivity. Consequently, the dictator must calculate the level of investment in detection that maximizes his rents. That is when buying one more unit of detection would marginally decrease the dictators rents because the monitoring cost variable would overpower the shirking-pilfering dissuasion variable.

To discern the optimal level of investment in economic monitoring, the dictator must first know how dissuasive his monitoring system will be, which depends heavily on the

---

[310]Harrison (2002: 404-406).

monitoring regime's credibility. When the probability of detection shrinks, so too does the monitoring regime's dissuasiveness. The USSR boasted many mechanisms for detecting shirkers and pilferers. The CPSU and state each employed control commissions that searched for corruption and failure to meet planned economic targets. The CPSU's Party Control Commission and state's Committee for Soviet Control could investigate anyone and any enterprise and hand those deemed corrupt to the Office of the Public Procurator for prosecution. The State Planning Committee (Gosplan) also combated shirking and pilfering the dictator's rents. Gosplan was the All-Union agency charged with translating the Politburo's and Council of Ministers' economic aims into a coherent economic plan that the ministries would implement. When Gosplan officials felt that enterprises, glavks, and even whole ministries were flouting their plan, they often appealed for legal intervention. For example, in 1933, Gosplan requested that the Committee for Soviet Control investigate "the crude mistakes and noneconomic use of resources of pipe factories in Leningrad" and "in the shortest possible time to find the guilty and turn them over to the courts."[311] Around the same time, Gosplan asked the Committee to investigate the Ministry of Forestry Products' failure to build an electrical station in Arkhangelsk. However, the monitoring by Gosplan, the control commissions, and the Ministry of Justice was complicated by reliance on the ministries, *glavks*, and enterprises for the economic data needed for effective planning and building cases against shirkers and pilferers. Some pivotal branches of industry were more assiduously monitored. In the early 1930s, more than 40,000 Ministry of the Interior personnel monitored military factories, looking in part for accounting violations and construction defects.[312] Yet, in less sensitive industrial sectors, monitoring was largely comprised of Gosplan, control commissions, the Ministry of Finance, and the State Bank (Gosbank) scanning ministry reports for red flags. But, despite enjoying only a narrow independent investigative capability, enterprises, glavks, and ministries often cooperated with economic monitors out of self-interest.

Olson ascribes the cooperation to bureaucratic competition. He avers that, in an administrative-command economy, "each bureaucrat can be constrained by others in the same chain or series of productive activities – that is, by those who manage the activities that either use the output of the activity managed by a given manager or supply an input for this activity."[313] Olson calls these bureaucrats *serial*. He contends that they diminish corruption because

> The managers of activities in series with a given manager's activity are well placed to make pertinent observations that the supervisory hierarchy often will not be able to make. The managers in series with a given manager also have incentives that countervail those of the manager in question. The manager of a construction project should know if the bricks were too few, too poor, or too late, and he normally has an incentive to report (if not exaggerate) such deficien-

---

[311] Gregory (2003: 132).
[312] Ibid., p. 131.
[313] Olson (2000: 138).

cies. If the brick-making manager wrongly claims that he did not receive the needed straw, the supplier of the straw obviously has corrective information and an incentive to provide it to superiors.[314]

An example of serial bureaucratic competition occurred in late July 1932 when the Ministry of Agriculture complained to the Council of Ministers that the Kommunar Factory, which reported to the Ministry of Heavy Industry, was delivering combines missing essential parts to its enterprises. The Council of Ministers then ordered the Ministry of Justice to investigate the complaint.[315] Olson claims that parallel bureaucrats can also expose shirking and pilfering. Parallel bureaucrats are those managing enterprises producing the same good or service. Shirking and pilfering become more visible when one factory produces far more output than a parallel enterprise when each were allocated the same inputs. Some phenomena, however, attenuate serial and bureaucratic competition's effectiveness, and thus credibility, as an economic monitoring device. As the economic plan calls for more light industry and consumer goods, which often require fewer inputs than heavy industry goods, the prevalence of serial bureaucratic competition declines. Likewise, as the economic plan calls for a greater diversity of goods, which often occurs when technology advances and goods become more specialized, the prevalence of parallel bureaucratic competition decreases. Ergo, as economic plans call for more light industry, more consumer goods, and a greater diversity of goods, detecting shirking and pilfering becomes harder. Consequently, direct economic monitoring costs are higher and the credibility of the dictator's economic monitoring regime marginally decreases.

When economic changes reduce the effectiveness of economic monitoring, the dictator may want to offset his diminished monitoring capacity by increasing the severity of the punishment for shirking and pilfering. But, generally, increasing punishment's severity increases its collateral cost because the harsher someone is treated, on average, the less productive he will be. Of course, execution is the extreme. The collateral cost of harshening punishment is correlated to the initial level of worker productivity. The more productive a worker is the more expensive it is to fire, imprison, or execute him for petty shirking or pilfering. So, as the workforce becomes better educated and more technically skilled, and consequently more productive, the collateral cost of severe punishment rises more precipitously. Rising education levels can also breed greater political awareness and familiarity with the living standards in other countries that deflates workers' valuation of their measly labor compensation and enflames resentment of the regime. This devaluation and resentment can translate into workers being willing to risk more to raise their standard of living through shirking or pilfering.

As the communist regime grows frailer due to higher economic monitoring costs, steeper collateral punishment costs, and a myriad of other weaknesses that may range from recessions engendered by inefficient economic planning to the restiveness of subjugated nationalities, party notables may wish to brace themselves for the regime's col-

---

[314]Ibid., p. 139.
[315]Gregory (2003: 145).

lapse. These party notables, with connections to the centers of power and managerial control over state assets, may decide to wield their influence to grab control of state assets before anyone else can do so in order to ensure their comfort and continued importance in the post-communist era. However, the rush to grab state assets before it is too late hastens the collapse of the regime, which is the source of the party notable's power. It is too late to grab assets when other party notables have already seized them all or the regime's collapse eliminates one's political leverage for obtaining state assets. Since the communist regime is already very frail, thereby minimizing the probability of the regime regaining its footing and punishing those who abandoned it, and any single party notable's loyalty is usually insufficiently significant to affect the regime's stability, loyalty to the regime is the less attractive option. And, loyalty grows increasingly unattractive the more valuable the assets ripe for seizure are. In an impoverished state exhibiting minimal economic activity, the profit available to those who desert the regime to secure their future in a capitalist economy by wielding their political influence to grab state assets is relatively less than in a wealthier state. Therefore, the incentive for a party notable to abandon the communist regime is marginally lower the poorer the state.

Now that we are armed with a theory of communist dictatorships that highlights their inherent weaknesses, we can compare the institutional and circumstantial features of various communist regimes to determine which guarded best against the inherent weaknesses. The USSR, China, and North Korea responded to the weaknesses in three distinct ways. The Soviet strategy failed,which led to its communist regime's abrupt collapse. China's approach preserved the Chinese Communist Party's (CCP) political control but diluted its political power. And, North Korea's gambit sustained, until recently, an economic and political regime more faithful to the administrative-command economy that Stalin constructed in the USSR's First Five Year Plan than any other regime since the 1980s.

The Collapse of the USSR   The Soviet system started its long demise soon after Stalin's death. First, economic monitoring costs began to rise. Dowlah and Elliot (1997) argue that, by the late 1950s, the economic returns on investment in heavy industry were precipitously diminishing, spurring Khrushchev to shift more resources towards light industry and consumer goods.[316] The production of more light industrial and consumer goods meant the production of more goods, such as furniture, pots, and many household appliances, requiring fewer inputs, thereby entailing less serial bureaucratic competition and higher economic monitoring costs. Similarly, Khrushchev's emphasis on diversifying production marginally decreased the prevalence of parallel bureaucratic competition. Because serial and parallel bureaucratic competition encourages enterprise managers to report the shirking and pilfering of other enterprises to the authorities, the decreasing prevalence of each type of bureaucratic competition raised direct economic monitoring costs, thereby lowering the credibility of the economic monitoring system. Khrushchev and his successors could have tried to deter potential shirkers and pilferers emboldened by declining direct economic monitoring costs by increasing the severity

---

[316]Dowlah and Elliot (1997: 121-126).

of punishment of those caught. However, Soviet initiatives to raise worker productivity, pursued concurrently with the increased production of light industrial and consumer
goods, raised the cost of punishing shirkers and pilferers.

Stalin invested mostly in equipment and factories for unskilled labor. As returns on
such investment sagged in the 1950s, the CPSU elite turned to technological improvements and creativity of labor, each of which required a better-educated Soviet workforce, to reinvigorate their economy.[317] The Cold War rivalry between the USSR and
the United States added further urgency to the CPSU elite's aim to advance the state of
Soviet technology. Accordingly, the CPSU elite marshaled the USSR's resources to accumulate human capital. The 1959 budget alone increased education spending to 94.3
billion rubles from 56.9 billion the previous year. Between 1939 and 1970, the percentage of Soviet citizens with higher or secondary education rose 447%.[318] The amplified
investment in education paid dividends in the form of worker productivity. The productivity of each industrial worker tripled between 1940 and 1960.[319] As the workers
grew more productive, their imprisonment and replacement for minor offences became
more expensive. In the less-skilled Soviet workplace of the 1930s and 40s, Stalin made
even occasional lateness to work and absenteeism criminal offences. Khrushchev, in the
1950s, on the other hand, found imprisonment for occasional lateness and absenteeism
uneconomical. He ended the large-scale use of forced-labor and repealed harsh labor
laws. Then, Brezhnev increased job security for enterprise managers and other officials, reducing the likelihood of dismissal for lackluster performance.[320] The concurrent
growth of direct monitoring costs and collateral monitoring costs invited omnipresent
shirking and pilfering of state assets. Shirking and pilfering began consuming the dictator's rents at an alarming rate in the Brezhnev years as enterprise managers and other
officials enriched themselves in the growing black market. Education and human capital
accumulation posed another threat to the regime. Deutscher (1967) predicted that as the
USSR invested more in human capital and education levels rose, Soviet citizens would
come to devalue their meager compensation for their labor and reach for more.[321] By
the 1980s, the Soviet regime faced "rising expectations of Soviet consumers no longer
isolated from the world" and aware that their standard of living was falling increasingly behind that of the democratic West.[322] This realization fomented more worker
dissatisfaction with the prevailing system of labor compensation, inciting workers, for
whom revolutionary spirit was a historical abstraction, to rebel against the system by
shirking and pilfering. However, while the escalating economic monitoring costs and
widespread disillusionment with the administrative-command economy weakened the
CPSU elite by devouring more of their rents and spawning black-market economic interests capable of autonomous political activity, Gorbachev's economic and political
reforms that ultimately destroyed the Soviet regime.

---

[317]Ibid., p. 125.
[318]Hahn (1978: 551).
[319]*The National Economy of the USSR* (1962: 166).
[320]Harrison (2002: 407).
[321]Harrison (2002: 407).
[322]von Laue (1993: 166).

Gorbachev hoped to close the widening gap between the American. and Soviet GDP, attributable to increasing shirking and pilfering along with the standard inefficiencies of the command economy, by liberalizing the economy of the USSR (*perestroika*). He wanted to grant enterprises more operational autonomy, scale back the state's economic plans, and permit enterprises to sell all of their output above a smaller government quota at free market prices to any customer. Gorbachev reasoned that, if enterprises could earn substantial profits by selling output exceeding their centrally planned quota and the workers shared those profits, workers would have a motive to be productive, not just look productive in order to receive their wages. Under Gorbachev's plan, the dictatorial elite would extract more of its rents from taxing increasingly productive workers than from the workers' labor itself, as had been the case in the past. However, Gorbachev met resistance to his reforms from members of the CPSU elite, who feared that economic liberalization would make the regime too accountable to workers and enterprises' economic interests to retain its dictatorial powers. Rather than striving to allay his colleagues' concerns behind closed doors by assuring them that he would preserve the state's repressive apparatus for political crimes and liberalize the economy slowly so that the process never would spin out of the government's control, Gorbachev decided to liberalize the political regime enough to seek a popular mandate for economic reform that would force the CPSU elite's hand (*glasnost*). Gorbachev invited political exiles home, relaxed censorship, and empowered state institutions (particularly the Supreme Soviet) to act independently of the CPSU elite. The *glasnost* media bestowed Gorbachev with a mandate to liberalize the economy. He passed legislation that put into motion his plan for allotting more decision-making powers to enterprises and increasing their profit-making opportunities. Additional legislation empowered workers to elect their enterprise's manager.[323] For all intents and purposes, the CPSU had selected enterprise managers up to then. Economic and political liberalization frightened enterprise managers and other CPSU notables. They feared losing their power due to either losing elections for manager or the whole communist dictatorship collapsing. Since no one knew how far Gorbachev would take political liberalization, doubts began surfacing as to whether the regime would forcibly protect the CPSU's interests and its paramount political position, to which enterprise managers and their superiors owed their jobs. A crisis of confidence in the regime commenced, galvanizing enterprise managers and other CPSU notables to begin hedging against the regime to secure importance and comfort in a post-Bolshevik Russia.

As decreasing certainty that the regime would defend itself joined high economic monitoring costs and growing worker dissatisfaction as factors weakening the Soviet regime, enterprise managers and other connected communists had to decide whether to wield their still preponderant influence to grab and privatize state assets in order to ensure their importance and comfort after the regime collapsed. But, a run on the state's assets by the connected and powerful in the CPSU would hasten the dictatorship's collapse. Whether a CPSU notable should choose fidelity to the regime over

---

[323] Dowlah and Elliot (1997: 189).

grabbing assets depends on the perceived weakness of the dictatorship and how valuable the available assets are. If the regime appears weaker, the incentive to grab assets is marginally higher. The incentive to grab assets is also marginally higher when the assets are marginally more valuable and promise a richer future.

In 1989, the CPSU's power to enforce its will lost most of its credibility. The March elections for the Congress of People's Deputies for the first time allowed those not belonging to the CPSU to run and voting was by secret ballot. Although the CPSU retained its majority, many sitting CPSU members lost their seats to dissidents.[324] Then, in July, more than 100,000 miners went on strike to protest low pay and poor working conditions. Labor unrest had not reached such proportions since Stalin began constructing the administrative-command economy back in the 1920s. But, rather than resorting to Stalinist terror to reinforce the credibility of the state's repressive apparatus and thereby discourage further collective action against the regime, Gorbachev negotiated with the miners. These events convinced many CPSU notables that the Soviet dictatorship was irreparably weak and to abandon the regime by wielding their influence to obtain state assets. The only alternative was forcibly reversing the reforms that had already garnered acclaim in the Soviet media. From the get-go, few considered forcibly restoring the fading communist dictatorship feasible. And, after the failed August coup against Gorbachev, its chances died. Yet, enterprise managers and other CPSU notables did not desert the dictatorship only because of the regime's frailty. The wealth of Soviet assets, from factories to commodities, also tempted them. If one boasted weighty CPSU connections when the USSR disintegrated, many opportunities to enrich oneself arose.

Kotz and Weir (1997: 117) describe how, during the death throes of the USSR, CPSU connections rather than technical knowledge contributed to success in business because word of prospective business opportunities rarely reached workers and only those connected to individuals running Soviet enterprises or organizations managing lots of money could procure financing. Before the emergence of a private banking sector, the only source of credit was state and CPSU organizations handling large amounts of cash. They would only lend it to people they knew and trusted, who were invariably CPSU notables. Mikhail Khodorkovsky participated in organizing Komsomol's (the CPSU's youth wing) Center for Scientific and Technical Creativity. In 1988, Khodorkovsky and some associates founded a bank. They lacked the equity to finance the project themselves so they each brought the CPSU and state agencies that they worked for into the venture as investors. Khodorkovsky obtained equity from the Center for Scientific and Technical Creativity while other parties committed the State Committee for Science and Technology (part of the state's central planning apparatus) and Zhilsotsbank (part of the state banking system).[325] Thus, Khodorkovsky and his colleagues invested CPSU and state money in a private bank whose success would shake the CPSU and state's monopoly of finance and consequently their economic and political power. Many managers of state banks merely privatized the ones they managed, transforming them into joint-stock companies in which they owned the largest or even a controlling

---

[324] Ibid., p. 215.
[325] Kotz and Weir (1997: 120).

share. The pattern of managers privatizing the enterprises they managed extended beyond banks to most industries. Former managers of state enterprises headed 68.1% of the 267 Muscovite businesses in a 1993 random sample.[326] Many CPSU notables enriched themselves in this flood into the market at the regime's expense. However, if the USSR lacked the industrial and natural wealth it had, the marginal benefit of abandoning the regime would have been lower. The scope of wielding political influence to obtain assets reached the scale of grabbing entire republics. In 1993, the leaders of eleven former Soviet republics were formerly high-ranking communists and five had once served in the Politburo. So, the prizes dangled in front of CPSU notables as the Soviet regime atrophied encouraged sabotaging their own dictatorship rather than trying to salvage it.

7.1.2   China's Economic Liberalization

Maoist China's economic and political organization closely resembled that of Stalin's Soviet Union. Like Stalin, Mao hoped to develop his country's heavy industry rapidly in order to catch up with the West. Albeit, China's Five Year Plans and the Great Leap Forward (1958-60) were not as successful in industrializing China as Stalin's first two Five Year Plans were in the USSR. After Mao died in 1976, Deng Xiaoping, like Khrushchev and his successors, wanted to develop his country economically so that it could eventually catch up with and then compete with the Western democracies. And, again like his Soviet reformist counterparts, Deng realized that long-term economic development required shifting some investment in heavy industry towards light industry and consumer goods, diversifying the economy, and investing more in technological improvements and creativity of labor. Mao Zedong, like Stalin, favored heavy industry at light industry and consumer goods' expense.[327] However, as shown above, greater emphasis on light industry and consumer goods diverts more resources to less input-intensive industries, thereby reducing serial bureaucratic competition. And diversifying economic output decreases parallel bureaucratic competition. So post-Maoist China, like the post-Stalinist USSR, would have to trade higher economic monitoring costs for brisk economic development. Human capital accumulation would have the same implications for China as it did in the USSR.

China's dictatorial elite, however, decided to forestall the shirking and pilfering that eroded the Soviet regime by gradually liberalizing China's economy as it refocused on light industry, consumer goods, and human capital accumulation. By privatizing parts of the economy, the Chinese regime had to monitor fewer industries, enabling it to spend the residual on monitoring the industries that remained state-controlled and enhancing the security apparatus. Because most of the Soviet hierarchy feared the political repercussions of economic liberalization, Gorbachev felt that he had to liberalize unilaterally the USSR's political institutions to effect economic liberalization by popular mandate over the objections of his own Party colleagues. Most of Deng's colleagues, on the other hand, were more daring and supported the incremental introduction of free-market re-

---

[326]Ibid., p. 117.
[327]Krishnaswamy (1987: 64-5).

forms, obviating the need for democratization. By reforming the economy very methodically and reversing reforms when they proved undesirable, the CCP maintained
its continuing grip on economic and political power, disillusioning anyone who might
speculate that the regime's hold on power may slip and economic reforms spiral out of
control.[328] Thus, throughout the reformation process, no one doubted that the Communist Party would remain in complete control of the country, and the crackdown on the
1989 Tiananmen Square protests dispelled any doubt. Very methodically the state dis-
banded the communes and cooperatives and leased agricultural land to private families,
allowed private ownership of capital, established Special Economic Zones on China's
southern and eastern coast,where trade and foreign investment were encouraged, and
permitted private enterprises to compete with public one's, which were reorganized to
operate on a profit-making basis.[329] These reforms broke the state's monopsony of labor
and switched the state's role from employer to employee, more reliant on the workers in
the market for revenue than workers are on the state for wages. And, as predicted above,
to maintain it dictatorial control after this role reversal, China's government needed to
find a happy balance between accommodating the burgeoning worker and business interests and repressing political dissent. The CCP's commitment to building a "harmo-
nious society" by improving education, medical care, and social security represents the
accommodating face of the balance while the 2008 crackdown on Tibetan rioters represents the repressive face.

7.1.3   The North Korean Regime of Kim Il Sung

The North Korean communist regime remained true to orthodox Stalinist economics
until very recently. Kim Il Sung began imposing an administrative-command economy after the Korean War. And, in 1958, the Korean Workers' Party (KWP) completed
collectivizing agriculture and owned all North Korean industry, cementing itself as the
national employer and its citizens as its employees.[330] At this point, North Korea's economy closely resembled the USSR's after the First Five Year Plan. Like Stalin, Kim Il
Sung prioritized heavy industry at the expense of light industry, consumer goods, and
agriculture. And, North Korea experienced phenomenal economic growth throughout
the decade following its adopting an administrative-command economy.[331] The North
Korean regime's singular emphasis on heavy industry ensured ample serial and parallel
bureaucratic competition that restrained direct economic monitoring costs. But, North
Korea diverged from the USSR and China's trajectory when,facing substantial diminishing returns from investment in heavy industry in the 1970s, Kim Il Sung refused to shift
investment from heavy industry to other sectors. Thus, he kept direct economic monitoring costs down by not employing more workers in less input-intensive industries, which
would have reduced serial bureaucratic competition, and did not diversify production,

---

[328] Hunter and Sexton (1999: 73).
[329] Wright (2000: 168).
[330] Kim (1973: 205).
[331] An (1983: 118).

which would have reduced parallel bureaucratic competition. With less opportunity to shirk or pilfer, workers enjoyed fewer chances of obtaining means beyond government wages. In fact, until the 1980s, the North Korean regime even banned cultivating private kitchen gardens so that even farmers on the collectives would be completely dependent on the state for food rations and therefore more obedient to the state.[332]

The North Korean regime also deters shirking and pilfering rents more effectively than the post-Stalinist USSR because it punished and continues to punish such behavior more severely. Although North Korea's isolation conceals most of what occurs inside, defectors and refugees paint a clear picture of the regime's penal system. Many speak of "daily executions of 'criminals' who had stolen two pounds of maize or a couple eggs."[333] Additionally, between 150,000 and 200,000 people are estimated to perform forced-labor in the North Korean Gulag.[334] All reports from defectors and refugees relate that "North Koreans are under tight surveillance" and "believe that various forms of political surveillance agents always surround them."[335] Not only are the punishments for shirking and pilfering rents extremely severe, but no one feels immune from them. This perpetuation of Stalinist terror strays from Khrushchev's dismantling of the USSR's archipelago of forced-labor camps and Brezhnev increasing job security for enterprise managers. The primary reason that North Korea's punishment can be more severe than its counterparts in the later USSR or China is North Korea's paucity of human capital.

North Korea's dearth of human capital translates into lower worker productivity, which makes it marginally cheaper to replace, imprison, or kill a North Korean worker than a post-Stalinist Soviet or post-Maoist Chinese one. That means that the collateral economic monitoring costs are lower in North Korea. The poverty of education and resulting deficit of human capital in North Korea is palpable. Hunter (1999) estimates that "only about 30 to 40 percent of middle school graduates go on to high school" and "less than 10 percent of high school graduates go on to college (two-year) or university (four-year)."[336] And, undoubtedly, the few who attend college gained admission because they are the next generation of the dictatorial elite and therefore have the least incentive to undermine rent collection. Another indicator of North Korea's poverty of human capital is that, while China has produced five Nobel Laureates and the USSR seventeen and each country boasts many internationally-acclaimed physicists, chemists, and economists, North Korea has neither produced any Nobel Laureates nor even any scholar of international standing in any field. North Koreans' isolation from and ignorance about the rest of the world also contributes to the regime's durability. In the USSR and China, widespread knowledge of Western living standards fomented worker dissatisfaction with the prevailing system of labor compensation, inciting workers to rebel against the system by shirking and pilfering. However, in North Korea, until recently, workers have had

[332]Lankov (2006: 111).
[333]Becker (2005: 37).
[334]Lefkowitz, "Remarks to Henry Jackson Society," 24 Jan. 2007.
    <http://www.state.gov/g/senk/80152.htm>.
[335]Suh and Lee (1998: 205-6).
[336]Hunter (1999: 214).

fewer reference points with which to gauge their wellbeing relative to the rest of the world. North Korea's isolation reached proportions unrivalled by the USSR and China. Only the highest echelon of the dictatorial elite may own foreign books or magazines and citizens still must report purchases of radios and televisions. The regime censors the stations and channels and sometimes inspects sets unannounced to ensure that they are not tuned to anything but official programming.[337] Possession of radios that can pick up foreign signals and illegal telephone calls outside North Korea can result in imprisonment, forced labor, or death. Geography traditionally exacerbated the isolation. The 2.5-mile Korean Demilitarized Zone blocks North Koreans' access to South Korea while the Yalu River, whose shore is dotted with North Korean snipers ordered to shoot to kill people fleeing the country, limit contact with China and Russia. However, North Korea's insularity has decreased in the last decade. When China started importing DVD players and newer VCRs at the turn of the millennium, North Korean smugglers bought up many of the obsolete VCRs and illegally sold them in North Korea. The most popular videos in North Korea are South Korean television dramas.[338] These soap operas depict a rich South Korea, an image that conflicts with the regime's unfavorable rendering of the world outside North Korea. If a sizeable number of North Koreans come to believe that the television dramas accurately portray the South Korean standard of living, North Korean workers could grow increasingly dissatisfied with the regime and more prone to abandon it. North Korean workers can also deduce the relative underdevelopment of their country by comparing the shoddy consumer goods made in North Korea with the increasing number of goods being smuggled in from South Korea that are of superior quality.[339]

North Korea's low standard of living may actually shore up the regime. The North Korean economy's weakness promises fewer riches to those who might abandon the regime should it totter in order to wield their influence to grab as many state assets as possible. While the USSR boasted the industry of a superpower and vast reserves of natural resources, North Korea's GDP equals only about $40 billion.[340] Consequently, if the regime started to flounder, members of the dictatorial elite probably would be more reticent to abandon the regime than their Soviet counterparts were, thereby giving the North Korean regime a larger window of opportunity to regain its balance than Gorbachev had.

The North Korean regime has proved the most durable communist dictatorship because (1) its economic organization held direct and collateral economic monitoring costs below those in the late USSR and contemporary China; (2) it kept its population relatively more ignorant of living standards in the rest of the world; and (3) it generated a relatively smaller economic pie. However, circumstances have begun to force Kim Jong Il to reform North Korea's economy to finance his regime. South Korea's central

---

[337] French (2007: 46).
[338] Lankov (2006: 103-4).
[339] Ibid., p. 108.
[340] "North Korea," *CIA Fact Book*, 13 July 2008.
   <https://cia.gov/library/publications/the-world-factbook/geos/kn.html>.

bank estimates that North Korea's economy contracted throughout the 1990s, particularly severely in the middle of the decade when a famine may have killed up to 10%
of the population.[341] The economic contraction forced the regime to scale back its budget from $19.19 billion in 1994 to $9.13 billion in 1997 and it has moved little since.
With less revenue to spend, the regime had to relinquish its command over swathes of
the economy. The state manages priority industries, including munitions and heavy industry while entrusting light industry and the manufacture of consumer goods to the
market.[342] Most importantly, the state has abdicated responsibility for food production
and rationing. During the famine, North Korean farmers had to violate the restrictions
on private agriculture to survive. The rationing system collapsed and workers had to
pilfer assets to pay for food, as the authorities could not muster the money to pay their
salaries. Extreme conditions impelled North Koreans to risk severe punishment to steal
the dictator's rents and quit working for the government to trade in the black market.

Presented with a *fait accompli*, the North Korean regime adapted itself to the breakdown of the strict command economy. On 1 July 2002, the North Korean government
passed reform measures that granted enterprises more operational autonomy, including a more self-supporting accounting system, and gradually abolished the rationing
system for food and other daily necessities.[343] Like Gorbachev, when the North Korean regime needed to contain rent leakage, they turned to markets. In 2003, the North
Korean government legalized most black market activity by sanctioning the trade of industrial in addition to agricultural goods. Kim Jong-il hoped that by legalizing the black
market and taxing it, he could stimulate economic growth and recapture rents by taxing the market. But, as his regime grew more dependent on taxing markets to fill his
coffers, his regime transformed itself from employer to employee. Like the USSR and
China when they made that transition, North Korea's leadership needed to decide how
to balance accommodating the economic interests of its subjects with military repression. Kim Jong-il's Military First policy has gravitated toward the latter and the regime
displays no willingness to reform its Gulag. However, Kim may make some concessions to his people. Each January 1, North Korea's dictatorial elite articulates its policy
objectives for the coming year in an editorial. The 2007 editorial emphasized raising
North Korea's standard of living more than its predecessors, which focused more on
the military aims. The editorial said, "We should decisively improve the production of
consumer goods by waging a revolution in light industry" and "steadily increase the
quality and variety of consumer goods."[344] This new emphasis on increasing the quan-
tity, quality, and diversity of light industry and consumer goods portends less serial and
parallel bureaucratic competition, weakening the dictatorial elite's command over the
economy, which is already reeling from privatizing part of the economy. Throughout
the 1990s and early 2000s, despite international speculation that the North Korean communist regime would collapse and plummeting state revenues, there was no exodus of

---

[341]"Gross Domestic Product of North Korea in 2007," *Bank of Korea* 14 July 2008.
[342]Yang (2007: 49-51).
[343]Ibid., p. 53.
[344]Lee (2007: 5).

communist notables. This in part because there was so little to grab that most members of the regime probably assumed that few opportunities for enriching themselves would exist in a post-communist North Korea, especially if it united with the South. Consequently, after more than a decade of uncertainty the North Korean regime is regaining foothold and may try to suppress some of the economic freedoms granted to survive through the toughest years. In October 2005, North Korea proscribed private sales of grain and reconstituted the centralized food rationing system.[345] If Kim Jong-il succeeds in reasserting the state's monopoly of capital and monopsony of labor, the North Korean regime will regain most of the stability it lost during the famine, the only lasting effect being a public less ignorant of the living standards elsewhere in the world.

7.1.4   Concluding Remarks

Communist regimes must reform or collapse when they can no longer collect enough rents from their administrative-command economy to finance the essential command apparatus. Therefore, any political or economic decisions made by the dictatorial elite that reduces confidence in the regime's capability to collect rents and crush dissent, forcibly if need be, can bankrupt a regime. For just fear that a regime cannot collect its rents is sufficient to spark a panic amongst its communist notables, who will want to grab what assets they can from the party and state before the regime collapses, which otherwise would leave them politically and economically broke. The run on the communist state's assets resembles a bank run and each usually results in the institution's failure. Fears that *perestroika* and *glasnost* would eliminate the regime's capability to collect rents and crush dissent forcibly brought down the Soviet regime. The CCP's transparent willingness to destroy any challenges to their clearly demarcated political and economic prerogatives has spared the CCP from the CPSU's fate. Also, a secure stream of revenue from an ever-growing Chinese economy improves the credibility of the CCP's capacity to finance its apparatus of control.

As long as North Korea can finance its administrative-command apparatus, Kim Jong-il has nothing to fear. Although he has become more reliant on taxes to finance his regime, Kim Jong-il can reduce that reliance by dismantling part of his nuclear program. North Korea has already proved that it can supplement the income it generates from narcotics trafficking, counterfeiting, and dealing conventional weapons, by demanding payments from the U.S., South Korea, and Japan in exchange for dismantling part of his its nuclear program. If those payments are large enough to reduce substantially the regime's reliance on its population to finance what remains of the administrative-command apparatus, not only will it increase the regime's capability to collect rents and crush dissent but also to use its more secure footing to reassert state ownership over some of the market enterprises, which would safeguard the regime for the foreseeable future.

---

[345]"North Korea," *CIA Fact Book*, 13 July 2008.
    <https://cia.gov/library/publications/the-world-factbook/geos/kn.html>.

7.2 Spain and Cuba in Comparative Perspective

On February 19th 2008, when Fidel Castro announced that he would no longer return as the president of Cuba, it seemed that Cuba had finally reached the end of an era.[346] The long awaited resignation seemed imminent after Fidel's brother Raul assumed presidential duties two years earlier, and yet it was this moment in history that marked an official turning point for the country. The question on everyone's minds: is Cuba finally ready to become a democracy? While scholars have speculated a great deal about the consequences of a democratic Cuba, few have examined the nature of such a transition. How will the processes of liberalization, democratization and consolidation manifest themselves in a country that has lived under strict socialist rule for over forty years? In order to better understand Cuba's prospects for a democratic future, it is important to place it within the larger context of the other so-called "third wave" democracies. In this paper, I look at Cuba in comparison to both the traditional theoretical model and the case of Spain, acknowledged by political scientists[347] as the classic example of a pacted transition to democracy. The goal is to examine the extent to which Cuba's trajectory parallels that of post-Francoist Spain and to analyze the impact of their similarities and differences on the outcomes that may result.

The existing literature concerning transitology varies greatly in its approach to the subject of democratic transitions. While scholars differ in opinion as to how exogenous factors catalyze, define and contribute to the movement from one phase to the other, they have reached a broad consensus on the model for approaching democratic transitions. Political scientists have defined three stages of the transition process: liberalization, democratization and consolidation.

The first stage of any transition to democracy is liberalization. Liberalization is a political opening taken usually by the authoritarian government itself that guarantees the rights of individuals and the autonomy of social groups.[348] Moreover, it allows political groups and political parties to organize. Key features of liberalization may include both social and political changes including the extension of amnesty to citizens, the release of dissidents from prison, the writ of habeas corpus, the return of exiles and increased freedom for the media. While liberalization cannot be measured by a simple checklist, it must be a marked change from the status quo ante in terms of the protection received by individuals and groups against violations of basic human rights. It is the regime's willingness to tolerate at the very least the existence of some form of opposition that truly characterizes the move to liberalization.

Unlike the characteristics that define it, the causes of liberalization tend not to be so easily categorized. In some cases, authoritarian leaders believe that liberalization is a strategy for consolidating, legitimizing and increasing their monopoly on power. In other cases, liberalization is the only path for the exiting regime to control the pace of an inevitable transition to democracy. In yet others, military defeat or coup d'état

---

[346]This section was written by Zharna Shah.
[347]Linz and Stepan (1996: 87).
[348]O'Donnell and Schmitter (1986: 7).

lead to extreme dissatisfaction or regime collapse. Przeworski proposes four possible factors that can contribute to the breakdown of authoritarian regimes and the initiation of liberalization: lack of functional purpose, loss of legitimacy, conflict within the ruling bloc and compromise as a result of foreign pressure to democratize.[349] These factors are not mutually exclusive by any means. Rather, they are indicative of fissures in the power base of the authoritarian regime that may force liberal change.

While liberalization does not necessarily lead to democratization, it does lower the cost of individual and collective action.[350] In doing so, it allows for the development of more than one type of political actor. These can roughly be classified at this stage as hardliners and softliners. Hardliners are staunch supporters of the status quo authoritarian regime, while softliners, as the name would indicate, are more open to reform and a broader dictatorship. Softliners can themselves be divided further, as we will see during the democratization phase of the transition. It is important to emphasize that while liberalization is ideally a precursor to democratization, this is not always the case. As we have seen in post-Salazar Portugal, liberalization can occur concurrently with democratization. It can also, in a few rare cases never progress to democratization, as seen after the Tiananmen Square massacre, where liberal protest led to severe repression. However, in most cases, the regime is forced to either incorporate a few autonomous groups, repressing everyone else to return to the authoritarian equilibrium or open the political agenda to consider the possibility of democracy.[351] The choice depends largely on the cost of repression, whether it will successfully produce the results necessary to return to the authoritarian status quo, and whether that status quo is a desirable or advantageous one for the hardliners. Additionally, hardliners and softliners alike must have full and accurate information about each other's preferences. If softliners prefer a full transition and not just liberalization but do not indicate this to hardliners, chances for repression or revolution are high.

Assuming liberalization moves forward and a democratic transition is still plausible, we are now at a stage where actors must come forward and identify themselves as significant interest holders in the formation of a new regime. The game is one of credible threats and credible promises. Interest groups must be willing to compromise but they must also be able to contribute significantly to the negotiation process, enough that their lack of participation would be indicative of an incomplete or flawed transition. The best process for distinguishing these groups is through elections, which are the true marker of the movement into the democratization phase of the transition process. Unlike liberalization, democratization places emphasis on choosing institutions and developing the new "rules of the game."[352] Democratization, as defined by Linz and Stepan "requires open contestation over the right to win control of the government, and this in turn requires free competitive elections, the results of which determine who governs."[353]

---

[349]Przeworski (1986: 50).
[350]Ibid. p. 7.
[351]Ibid. p. 110.
[352]Linz and Stepan (1996: 5).
[353]Ibid. p. 3.

After elections have been held and all major players have been identified, it is possible for these players to engage in a pact making process. As Linz and Stepan have
emphasized, pacts are not necessarily required for a democratic transition, nor are they
always democratic by their very nature.[354] Whether relevant political actors are able to
engage in the pact making process depends on two factors: the transition path undertaken and the role and type of the exiting authoritarian regime. The classic negotiated
transition path, also known as reforma pactada-ruptura pactada (agreed reform-agreed
rupture), is impossible in both totalitarian and sultanistic regimes as there is no room for
democratic opposition and no regime moderates are allowed to organize or voice their
discontent. In fact, only a mature post-totalitarian regime that believes that elections are
a way to consolidate their support base could progress to negotiations. However, this
transition type is ideal for authoritarian regimes where a reasonably active civil society
and some form of political opposition allow for pacts between pro-regime moderates
and pro-opposition moderates. It is this scenario that we will focus on in this paper.

For other transitions paths, including defeat in war, regime collapse, extrication from
rule by hierarchically led military and interim government after coup by nonhierarchical
military, armed insurgents or mass uprising, the likelihood of a pacted transition is contingent upon a variety of variables which depends on regime type.[355] While we will not
be focusing on these other transitions paths, it is important to note that pacts require that
party leaders are not only able to organize and form coalitions between themselves, but
that they are also able to convince their followers to abide by the terms of the pact.[356]
When regime conditions are not conducive to either of these elements, it is unlikely that
a pact will be maintained after it is formed.

Now that we have limited our scope to reforma pactada-ruptura pactada transitions
in authoritarian regimes, we can examine the process of democratization in such cases.
As previously mentioned, the pact making process must involve all relevant political actors in order for the resulting pact to be acceptable to all voting citizens. O'Donnell and
Schmitter have distinguished four types of political actors: hardliners, radicals, reformers, and moderates.[357] Hardliners are those who prefer the authoritarian status quo, and
they "tend to be found among the repressive cores of the authoritarian bloc."[358] On the
opposite end of the spectrum are radicals, who favor sweeping political and economic
reforms. In between these two groups are moderates and reformers. Przeworski distinguishes reformers from moderates by placing reformers within the authoritarian bloc
and moderates within the opposition block along with Radicals. Reformers, he says
"tend to be recruited among politicians of the regime and some groups outside the state
apparatus: sectors of the bourgeoisie under capitalism, economic managers under socialism."[359] They are more likely to work with the authoritarian regime in producing
centrist-oriented reforms. Moderates are less willing to cooperate with the hardliners,

---

[354] Ibid. p. 56-61.
[355] Ibid. p. 58-60.
[356] Ibid. p. 61.
[357] O'Donnell and Schmitter (1986: 40).
[358] Przeworski (1992: 17).
[359] Ibid. p. 117.

although they are more likely to do so than radicals. In fact, this is what distinguishes them most from radicals. "Moderates and radicals need not represent different interests...Moderates may be those who fear hardliners, not necessarily those who have less radical goals"[360] In terms of their risk preferences, both hardliners and radicals are risk-insensitive while moderates and reformers are more risk-averse.[361]

Given the risk preferences of all actors involved, "extrication"[362] from the authoritarian regime can take place under three conditions[363]:

(1) Reformers are able to neutralize the threats posed by hardliners and incorporate their interests

(2) Moderates are able to neutralize the threats posed by radicals and incorporate their interests

(3) Reformers and moderates are able to reach an agreement to establish democratic institutions under conditions favorable to all four parties

This process is accomplished via bilateral and multilateral negotiation, often in the context of a constitutional assembly or constitutional congress. The pact that results, usually a constitution, is an official statement of the rules of the democratic game that all players have agreed to abide by.

But once these rules are adopted, how can we be sure that democracy has in fact been achieved? In other words, how do we determine whether democracy has consolidated, or that democracy is the "only game in town?"[364] Before answering this question, we must first define what constitutes a consolidated democracy. The term consolidation refers to the solidification and institutionalization of democracy. More specifically, it means that all players acknowledge the legitimacy of democratic governance as the best and only option. Linz and Stepan define this concept further by delineating three types of consolidation: behavioral, attitudinal and constitutional.[365] That is, those who lose agree to continue to stay involved in the political process (behavioral), all players agree that democracy is the best system despite the results of any one election (attitudinal), and everyone accepts the results of the democratic process as legitimate (constitutional). They define five arenas of a consolidated democracy, which must exist in order for a functioning democratic state. The first is a free and active civil society that is granted freedom of association and communication. Secondly there must be an autonomous political society, chosen by free and fair elections. There must also be rule of law, guaranteed by the constitution, to ensure basic rights and freedoms are respected. Fourth, there must be a state bureaucracy in order to enforce democratically sanctioned laws. Finally, there must be an institutionalized economic society, which consists of a series of norms, regulations, policies and institutions, whose goal is to produce the surplus necessary to carry on the functions of government and provide a financial base

---

[360]Ibid. p. 117.
[361]Przeworski (1986: 54).
[362]Przeworski (1992: 116).
[363]Ibid. p. 117.
[364]Linz and Stepan (1996: 5).
[365]Ibid. p. 6.

for democracy.[366] Przeworski outlines similar conditions, citing an institutional framework for contestation, a competitive representative regime, the channeling of economic
conflicts via democratic institutions and a military under civilian control, as necessary
elements of a consolidated democracy.[367]

Of the three stages of the democratic transition, consolidation is in many ways the
most difficult to identify and achieve. Its onset is usually marked by the adoption of a
constitution, and the peaceful transition of power from one party or ruler to another. It
is also important to emphasize that consolidation can easily be reversed. Many nations
revert to nondemocratic regimes, despite reaching the consolidation phase. In many
ways it is the most vulnerable stage because it is the period during which institutions are
tested for their strength and ability to withstand shocks, such as economic and political
crises.

We will now apply the general model for democratic transitions to the case of Spain.
Spain is widely acknowledged by political scientists as a classic example of a reforma
pactada-ruptura pactada transition to democracy.[368] Because of this it provides an interesting comparison to modern day Cuba, which is very similar to Spain in 1975, immediately after the death of Franco. A reforma pactada-ruptura pactada transition by its very
nature involves a pact between the exiting regime and the incoming democratic forces.
It is most likely to occur in authoritarian regimes, where a relatively independent civil
and political society is available after some liberalization. In the case of Spain, this transition was largely led by elites, because these individuals were capable of mobilizing
their groups for negotiation.

Historically, Spain had made attempts at democracy throughout the nineteenth century. The Second Republic, which lasted from 1931-1936, was a highly leftist, anti-
monarchist, socialist, secular and federalist state. This was abruptly put to an end by a
military coup led by General Francisco Franco, which led to civil war and a new regime
under Franco which lasted from the end of the civil war in 1939 until Franco's death
in 1975.[369] Franco's regime was the polar opposite of its predecessor. It was a right
wing, centralized, unitary state that very much supported the role of the monarch and
the church. But unlike many authoritarian regimes, it was highly civilianized as well.
The military remained an institution outside of government, and government structure
was not systematically aligned with military ranks, although many government personnel were recruited from the armed forces. In addition, the government was structured
and institutionalized. Franco served as head of state, while his second-in-command Luis
Carrero Blanco served as prime minister. There was also a corporatist parliament, the
Cortes, which represented only those sectors of society that Franco deemed important.
While there was no constitution, a set of seven fundamental laws served as a substitute.
In many ways, Franco was institutionally limited by the regime he had created. The
structure of his government outlined a certain decision making process that allowed for

---

[366] Ibid. p. 7-15.
[367] Przeworski (1992: 106).
[368] Linz and Stepan (1996: 87).
[369] See Chapter 6.

a degree of predictability. It was then no surprise when in 1973, the assassination of Carrero Blanco by Basque separatist group ETA, this framework simply allowed for the insertion of a new figure into an old position. Carlos Arias Navarro, seamlessly replaced Carrero Blanco just as two years later, King Juan Carlos was chosen to replaced Franco after his death. This fluidity in the system allowed the transition to take place from within, as few questioned the positions themselves but rather the individuals who filled them. It also assisted the new democratic regime to withstand threats to its stability later in the transition process.

Spain's transition to democracy can be clearly divided into three stages of liberalization, democratization and consolidation. The liberalization process began once Adolfo Suárez was appointed prime minister. Suárez replaced Arias Navarro, whose lack of progress towards reform led to a series of strikes and protests that discredited him. Juan Carlos, keen to initiate reform but unable to do so himself because of his position as a national figurehead, submitted to the Cortes the names of two radical leaders and Suárez, a relatively unknown moderate from the old Franco regime. Suárez was immediately chosen and soon thereafter he began to meet with representatives of the opposition, most notably Santiago Carillo, the leader of the left wing Communist Party of Spain (CPE), Felipe González, leader of the Social Party of Spain (PSOE), and Josep Tarradellas, the exiled president of the Catalán regional government. This political opening was precisely the first step necessary for a gradual and almost invisible liberalization.

Along with the granting of traditional liberal freedoms such as the right to associate or the freeing of political prisoners, Suárez also achieved three key reforms that allowed for the transition into democratization. First, he was able to legalize the CPE, which had previously been banned from participation in politics. This incorporated the interests of a large population of demobilized voters into the negotiation process, while offsetting a sizeable threat posed by the CPE, which was the former legitimately ruling group prior to the 1936 coup. In exchange for their reentrance to politics, Santiago Carillo on behalf of the CPE willingly abandoned radical ideas for true Stalinist communism, which in turn allowed Suárez to accomplish yet another key reform, the Moncloa Pact. The Moncloa Pact "pledged the government to a continuing program of reforms of political institutions, the social security system, and the regressive taxation system inherited from the Franquist regime; to government controls on price increases; [and] to democratization of the education system."[370]

The CPE and PSOE agreed to use their influence to keep strikes at a minimum, to limit the demand for pay increases and to accept certain restrictive monetary and expenditure policies. The pact served as a signal to the international community that Spain had no intention of becoming communist, especially at the height of the Cold War era, while also allaying the fears of Franquist hardliners that incorporating the CPE was not a return to the Second Republic. Finally, Suárez was able to pass the Law for Political Reform, which effectively called for reform, namely elections, of the Cortes itself.

---

[370]Gunther (1992: 55)

The 1977 elections set the stage for the second phase of the transition to democracy, bringing to the foreground the leaders of each group large enough to pose a credible threat and deliver a credible promise. Within the model of O'Donnell and Schmitter's four player game, the hardliners were represented by the military and other staunch Franquists from the revolution, the reformers were represented by Juan Carlos, who served as a representative of the Franquist state but who also acknowledged the need for political reforms, the moderates represented by Suárez, whose party the Union of the Democratic Center (UCD) had been reelected with a majority, and the radicals represented by Carillo and González of the CPE and PSOE.

The pact-making process can be divided into two categories: the first between the reformers, moderates and members of the opposition, and the second between the reformers, moderates and hardliners within the ruling bloc. Within the first category of pacts, we see the interaction between what Colomer calls "openists" and "rupturists." As evidenced by the Moncloa Pact and the agreement to legalize the communist party, both players are motivated to cooperate in order to maximize their payoffs.[371] Suárez's success in nullifying the radical elements of the CPE and PSOE platforms allowed him to incorporate a significant threat that would have threatened the stability of any future democratic regime.

If we consider the second category of pacts as a game with a single force-vulnerable equilibrium between what Colomer calls "reformists" and "continuists," we see that both players are again ultimately motivated to cooperate in order to equalize their payoffs as much as possible.[372] In short, they are motivated to pursue "reform by agreement." However, once there, continuists are more motivated to abandon the outcome because their payoffs are slightly lower, and so it is the reformists who must utilize threats and promises to secure the agreement. If we take Suárez and Juan Carlos as the "reformists" and the military and staunch Franquists as "continuists," we see that both leveraged a series of threats and promises to yield this outcome.

Within the ruling bloc Suárez eliminated the hardline military threat by working with Lieutenant General Manuel Gutiérrez Mellado in calling for all military commanders to abstain from politics under penalty of expulsion. At the same time, Juan Carlos was able to maintain his authority over the military by sheer virtue of his legitimacy as commander of the armed forces, ensuring that the military would not interfere in the pact making process. Suárez also addressed hardline Franquist fears of military uprising and concerns over separatist movements in the Basque and Catalán regions and the reemergence of communism. He promised the Franquists the continuation of the monarchy, the preservation of Spanish unity and the elimination of radical opposition from politics. At the same time, the legitimacy of the new regime was solidified by the fact that a sanctioned head of state using existing Franquist institutions had initiated political change. The active role undertaken by elements of the former regime in creating the new one assuaged hardline concerns and allowed Suárez and Juan Carlos to neutralize and eliminate significant hardline threats while incorporating this bloc into an

---

[371] Colomer (1991: 1290).
[372] Ibid. p. 1290.

agreement for reform.

The result of these two types of pacts can be seen in the 1978 Constitution, which replaced the seven fundamental laws. The new constitution adapted many of the existing structures and institutions into its framework, maintaining the king as head of state and establishing a secular parliamentary democracy based on a market economy with strong elements of social welfare. The constitution also marked the onset of consolidation. The Spanish democracy established by the 1978 constitution saw its first democratic elections under that constitution in 1979. It survived an attempted coup by a dissenting sector of the military in 1981 and witnessed a socialist party victory in 1982, marking a peaceful transition of powerful from the ruling UCD party of Suárez to an opposition party. It also allowed the Basque and Catalán regions to gain autonomy in mid 1981. The absence of any significant protest, unrest, coups or challenges to government during this period is indicative of attitudinal, behavioral and constitutional consolidation. Institutional legitimacy and electoral results were widely accepted, as democratic structures became the primary conduits for social, political and economic conflict.

Given both the theoretical and Spanish models, we now turn to Cuba. In many ways, Castro's Cuba is very similar to Franco's Spain. Although the two leaders differ in ideology, both were anti-democratic rulers who relied heavily on repression of dissent and opposition.[373] Their autarchic policies, harsh treatment of civilians, and suppression of independent labor organizations and any political opposition also had tremendous consequences on the governments and economies they left behind. In the case of Spain, rigid bureaucratic controls had disastrous effects on the economy, while Castro's widespread expropriation of property also hurt production. Additionally, both economies suffered foreign exchange crises, which prompted short, oftentimes restricted openings of the economy to full investment.[374]

Given these similarities between the Franco and Castro regimes and the social and economic conditions that have resulted, is it possible for us to predict a democratic transition via reforma pactada-ruptura pactada in Cuba? In the late 1980s, Cuba too underwent a period of liberalization similar in many ways to the theoretical model. A sharp decline in gross domestic product and a loss of the majority of its trading partners and Soviet subsidies sparked an economic crisis that forced Fidel Castro to adopt market-oriented reforms. Cuba was opened to tourism and foreign investment and self-employment was allowed for certain occupations. In addition, farmers were allowed to sell their products above certain production quotas at free market prices. Liberalized agricultural markets, new taxes and a stronger Cuban peso contributed to an increase in GDP growth rates after 1994. At the same time, relations with other Latin American nations and the European Union also improved. These economic reforms were also accompanied by certain political openings. Two party congresses were convened during this time in 1991 and 1997 to discuss the authorization of Cuban-owned private enterprise and other reforms that would liberalize the economy, perhaps through the creation of a single national party, such as Mexico's PRI, or the normalization of relations with

---

[373]Cuzán (2003: 11).
[374]Ibid. p. 12-13.

the United States.[375] While these did not succeed, the mere allowance of such open
debate was a first since the Cuban Revolution took place in 1959.

Unfortunately, liberalization was short lived, as Cuba returned to non-democracy in
2002 after Castro pulled in the reins on discussion of economic reforms. A referendum
in 2002 declared socialism irrevocable as the National Assembly moved to amend the
constitution to reflect this proclamation. In truth, both the referendum and the constitutional amendments were "an overstated, hyperactive and theatrical response"[376] the
Varela Project, championed by Oswaldo Payá Sardiñas, who presented a petition with
over 11,000 signatures in favor of a referendum on political and economic changes,
more than the 10,000 minimum stipulated by Article 88 of the Cuban Constitution. The
declaration was a victory for Castro, who proved that above all, it was he who was responsible for directing Cuban economic policy. True to this notion, no party congress
was called between 2002 and 2003, when it was customary to do so.

With the recent resignation of Fidel Castro as president of Cuba in 2008, we now see
the reemergence of debate on economic reform. Fidel's younger brother Raúl, who assumed the presidency a few months later, has begun to implement new liberal economic
policies. His agricultural reforms, removal of wage limits, housing reforms and lifting
of the ban on the purchase of electrical goods including cellular telephones and personal
computers seem to indicate that he too is willing to consider reform. The Cuban Communist Party has also shown signs of liveliness, as the party secretariat was restored for
the first time since 1991 and a plenary meeting of the Central Committee was held in
July 2006 under Raúl's caretaker regime. The shift in emphasis from a highly personalistic leader to the head of a political party, in addition to the socially and economically
liberal reforms is indicative of perhaps another period of liberalization. While no political openings have been made and opposition groups are certainly not allowed, it seems
that Raúl may be open to more than just a short list of reforms.

In many ways, the present day situation in Cuba is comparable to that in post-
Francoist Spain. The presence of a hardline threat from Fidel Castro and staunch members of the Cuban Communist Party known as the "Havana Taliban"[377] and the emergence of Raúl Castro, a potential reformer from within the system with a great deal of
legitimacy are strikingly similar to the hardline Franquists and reform-minded Juan Carlos. The question then turns to the remaining two political actors: the radicals and the
moderates. Thus far, the leaders of these blocs have yet to emerge. While Raúl certainly
commands his own bloc of loyal followers, it still remains to be seen whether there will
emerge from their ranks an Adolfo Suárez. And although there are illegally active political parties, most operate outside of Cuba within the exile community, as public political
activities on the island by any party other than the Communist Party are not permitted.

However as the wait for the opposition to organize itself continues, many factors
need to be considered when weighing the possibility of a democratic future for Cuba. It

---

[375] Pérez-Stable (2007: 33).

[376] Ibid. p. 34.

[377] J.-F. Fogel in "Le Dernier Carré Du Pouvoi Castriste," *Le Monde*, 26 Octobre 2003.
    <http://coranet.radicalparty.org/pressreview/print.php?func=detail&par=7044>

is here that we may take into account the differences between Francoist Spain and Castro's Cuba. We can divide these factors into problems of democratization and problems of consolidation. Problems of democratization pose specific threats to the formation of pacts and the development of a consensus on the rules and institutions of the new regime. While the lack of a clear, unified opposition is certainly the first obstacle to democratization, there are also issues concerning the role of existing actors, namely the military, the Cuban Communist party, and Fidel Castro himself.

The Cuban Armed Revolutionary Forces (FAR) is a highly professionalized and politicized body. The rate of participation in the Cuban military, including the reserves, has been higher than any other Latin American country since the 1960s.[378] Cuba's conscription standards, close to universal military service, make the military truly a "people's army."[379] While the professional nature of the military reduces the likelihood of a coup,[380] the inclusiveness of the armed forces also blurs the line between civilian and military affairs. The armed forces continue to be a wild card in any pact making process. While a passive role in government constitutes a reduction in power, they may value an option that allows them to maintain their institutional integrity.[381]

Similarly, the Cuban Communist Party is also an uncertain element in the democratization process. As a body that relied so heavily on Fidel Castro as the face of their movement, in is unclear whether the party will be able to stand on its own two feet in competitive elections. Its institutionalization certainly provides it with a comparative advantage over other, less well-known opposition parties, but at the same time places it at a disadvantage if it cannot effectively implement reform. The party must also find a way to incorporate an increasingly disaffected younger generation[382] who no longer believe in the cause of the socialist revolution. Finally, it must also develop a new role for Fidel himself, who now only serves as a symbol of a revolutionary era that once was. While Fidel Castro may never cease to play the role of figurehead, it remains to be seen how long his persona will be able to counter the tide of liberal reform.

This leads us to consider problems of consolidation, challenges a newly democratic Cuba may face after democratization. Chief amongst these are an aging population and the need for economic reforms. Unlike other Latin American countries, Cuba's population structure is inversely related to its degree of development.[383] Its rapidly aging population is not accompanied by a higher average income or greater economic development. Instead, the size of its labor force is decreasing, placing a strain on government to provide services to its elderly at a time when resources should be focused on jump-starting the economy. The economy itself is also in dire need of reform. Low productivity rates, a small private sector, widespread corruption and no rule of law prevent the existing economic structures from functioning optimally.[384] Additionally, expropriation

---

[378] Domínguez (2007: 49)
[379] Ibid. p. 50.
[380] Ibid. p. 53.
[381] Pérez-Stable (2007: 45).
[382] Gonzalez and McCarthy (2004: 40).
[383] Ibid. p. 72.
[384] Ibid. p. 83-93.

claims against the government launched by Cuban exiles will also pose a significant strain on Cuba's already record-high hard-currency foreign debt, which was reported by the Banco Central de Cuba to have reached US$12.210 billion in late 2002.[385] The issue at hand of course is the need for social and economic decentralization, which comes at a high cost to a regime that is unwilling to relinquish control.[386]

A secondary challenge to consolidation is the future role of the international community and the United States. A stable Cuba is in the interests of both the United States and the Organization of American States. Past interactions between Cuba and the United States have hardly been cordial and yet, Raúl's reforms now give Washington an incentive to reestablish ties with the country. Whether the international community or the United States will directly intervene in Cuban politics to push for a transition to democracy is unclear. In many ways, this could be potentially destabilizing, as a new regime may not be able to control migration or drug trafficking as well.[387] On the other hand, foreign assistance to Cuba may help the country's economy adjust better to liberal reforms, facilitating its integration into a regional and perhaps global market economy.

Given these problems of democratization and consolidation, what does the future hold for Cuba? While it is entirely possible that Cuba will undergo a classical reforma pactada-ruptura pactada transition, following in Spain's footsteps, there are a great number of issues that must first be resolved. A large part of Cuba's future will rest on Raúl Castro's shoulders. If he is capable of controlling the liberalization process, Cuba may continue to remain a socialist state. If however, he cannot stabilize the regime after implementing liberal reforms and a unified opposition forms, a political opening may become likely.[388] If Raúl maintains his role as a reformer in the negotiation, and the political elite commit to rule of law and the extension of civil liberties, Cuba may see its first elections in over fifty years, followed by a process of democratization and institution building. If however, Raúl loses control of the process, it is very likely that extreme reforms will be implemented and Cuba may become very much like China or Vietnam,[389] communist only in name, with Castro as it's new Mao. Alternatively, as Linz suggests, frozen post-totalitarian regimes only witness transitions via mass uprising.[390] The challenge to this transition path in Cuba is a weak civil society and a strong likelihood of repression.

The democratic future of Cuba continues to remain largely indeterminate. However, in considering whether a transition to democracy is possible, we can learn a great deal by comparing Cuba's current social, political and economic climate to that of a theoretical model and to the classical example of Spain. While Cuba does not grapple with many of the issues that Spain did, namely, the presence of a strong opposition threat, and disagreement over national economic policy and separatist territories, they do have a

---

[385]United States, Department of State, Cuba's Foreign Debt, (Washington: Bureau of Western Hemisphere Affairs). <http://www.state.gov/p/wha/rls/fs/22743.htm>

[386]Gonzalez and McCarthy (2004:108).

[387]Pérez-Stable (2007: 42).

[388]Ibid. p. 42.

[389]Ibid. p. 40-41.

[390]Linz and Stepan (1996: 58).

great deal in common. Both Franco and Castro left similar legacies, and as a result, we see comparable political situations in both countries. The presence of a strong hardline threat and the emergence of a reformer from within the system lead us to believe that Cuba may also progress along similar lines as Spain. Additionally, Cuba too must reconsider its economic structures and the means by which it desires to reform them. However, before it can proceed, a unified opposition must mobilize, and Cuba must tackle the challenges of a changing demographic, an undefined military, and a central party from the Fidel Castro era. How Cuba's leaders and citizens proceed to respond to these issues will determine the extent to which it liberalizes and ultimately whether it will undergo the classic reforma pactada-ruptura pactada transition to democracy.

7.3   Chavez, Bolívar and the Neoliberal Dilemma

Fragile democracies tend to fall into one of two categories–they are usually either newly-formed democracies or regimes under the constant strain of political or economic crisis.[391] According to the argument of one political scientist, in such fragile democracies popular support for democracy in itself tends to be linked more readily to the performance of the political system in place and often the political incumbents themselves. Damarys Canache (2002) argues that because of the fragile state of Venezuela's democratic system after decades of coups, economic crises and overall regional instability, popular support for democracy is not particularly strong. Failures of particular political systems or even the incumbent politicians have a greater impact on the popularity of democracy itself than it would in strongly democratic regimes.[392] Therefore any perceived weakness in a democratic regime leads to a shift in support away from democracy itself to more radical and autocratic systems of government – of which Chavez and his Bolivarian Revolution are considered the epitome.

   Canache and other critics of the Bolivarian/Chavismo movement tend to make the mistake, however, of assuming Chavez's lack of respect for the democratic process and dismissing Chavez supporters as the poor, uneducated and gullible followers of a charismatic autocrat. Canache for one points to surveys taken in Venezuela in1995 (as Chavez's movement was gaining ground nationally) that demonstrates that the lower the support for democracy as a political system, the higher the probability that the person surveyed supports Chavez. It wasn't merely opponents of the previous incumbents or opponents of the bipartisan Punto Fijo regime that supported him, but "opponents of democracy" that turned to Chavez and his party, she concludes. Others dismiss the Movimiento Quinta República (MVR) as a "not much more than Chavez's [personal] party, despite his failed attempts to turn it into a party of the masses and the predominance of a leftist orientation in its ranks."[393] This is perhaps to simplistic approach to understand the popularity of Chavez and his Bolivarian Revolution.

---

[391] This section was written by Sofia Medina.
[392] Canache (2002:150).
[393] Molina (2004: 39).

While Chavez's 1992 coup can certainly point to his "opposition to democracy", the previous democratic regime (led by Acción Democrática, a social democratic party) also came about through the process of two coups led by sympathetic military leaders in both 1945 and 1958 – and was institutionalized in a power-sharing agreement removing electoral competition from what was otherwise a democratic regime. By the logic presented the previous regime could also be construed as anti-democracy, but such a reductionist theorization hardly captures the nuance in the circumstances leading to the Chavez's rise–or his opposition's fall. The economic prosperity propped up by high oil prices on the international market and a deep institutionalization of the bipartisan consensus of 1958 created conditions that encouraged highly "risk-preferring" behavior typically found in oligarchies or autocratic regimes.[394] The artificial stability of Latin America's "exceptional democracy"[395] led to an artificial sense of security in the status quo that encouraged risky policy decisions and political insularity that led to the system's loss of legitimacy and ultimate downfall by the 1990s – leaving room for "democracy's opponent" to enter office in the 1998 presidential election.

Latin America's economic stagnation and tendency towards political instability has long been a subject of academic inquiry, and a look at Latin America's history over the nearly two centuries since independence from Spain hardly encourages positive views of their prospects. The past two hundred years of Venezuela's history, like the history of the rest of Latin America, is rife with attempts at establishing constitutional government interrupted by military coups and long-lasting dictatorial regimes. The current era of democratic rule and the origin of the political system preceding Chavez's election can be traced to the post-war period after the ouster of the dictator Juan Vicente Gomez in 1945.[396] The recently-formed social democratic party AD (Democratic Action) led the coup with the help of sympathetic military officers and introduced a constitutional democracy that lasted a mere three years. Within this short-lived democratic period AD dominated the political landscape with its pro-democracy leanings and its support for urban labor unions and the rural working class. Of the other three major parties only one, the center-right Christian democrats (COPEI), proved to be a significant political rival in what was mostly an AD-run government. The honeymoon period for Democratic Action was barely over before the army staged yet another coup in 1948 and dismantled the constitutional government, installing the Carlos Andrés Pérez dictatorship that lasted for the next ten years.

By the time the four former parties (calling themselves the Patriotic Junta) could overthrow Jiménez and return democracy to Venezuela, AD could not hope to return to its short-lived position of dominance within the system again. Facing this prospect the party ultimately decided to come to an agreement with COPEI, their biggest rival party, and in 1958 AD, COPEI and URD (Union of the Democratic Republic) signed a power-sharing agreement called the Pacto de Puntofijo (Fixed Point Pact), agreeing to form a coalition government that essentially cancelled out any chance of an opposition party

---

[394]See the discussion in Chapter 1.
[395]Ellner et al. (2007).
[396]Molina (2004).

gaining ground against them. The agreement also forced AD and COPEI to moderate their positions and move their ideological and policy positions towards the center.

In agreeing to this coalition pact the parties' ideological shifts were following traditional election theory. In sharing power and combining forces they were essentially combining the electoral power of their respective constituencies, representing the interests of a "super-bloc." When parties representing large swaths of interests join forces, the party members begin to moderate their positions because they hope to appeal to an ever-widening base of diverse interests in order to win the broadest base of support. The assumption, however, that a consensus of power means a consensus of interests is a false one. A distinction must be made between the policy preferences and beliefs of the electorate. The parties' consensus thus assumed the representation of a populace whose interests were rendered artificially monolithic. The relative competency valence was exceptionally high for the AD/COPEI alliance due to Venezuela's lack of experience with democracies led by any other political parties–giving the impression of a policy mandate that would turn out to have much narrower support as years passed under the consensus.

Venezuela's unprecedented economic growth and the stability of its seemingly functioning democracy encouraged foreign policy experts and political science scholars to dub it the "exceptional democracy." The international economic boom in the post-war era and militarization responding to Cold War tensions increased demand for oil, and instability in the Middle East by the mid-1960s only added to this, bringing unprecedented growth to the Venezuelan economy. Compared to the political instability and dictatorships rising to and falling from power through the 1960s and 70s, Venezuela's prosperity and stability seemed to be a happy anomaly. Even during this time period, however, the country's dependence on oil revenues for much of their growth left the nation's economy at the mercy of the international oil market – and the government relying too heavily on oil revenues to keep their economy and their political support afloat. While Venezuela's oil had been a chief export since the discovery of the first deposits in the 1920s, it was with the 1958 consensus that the government and its electorate explicitly linked the success of the ruling regime to the successful distribution of oil rents and the guarantee of an increasingly better living standard.[397] Unfortunately the democratic process in and of itself does not guarantee this goal, and a strong rentier state was Venezuela's guarantee. As long as the oil flowed and the state could distribute rents, whether through transfer payments or other social programs, the coalition could hold together. Whenever the economy showed signs of slowing down, the government's legitimacy would be questioned and deep-seated class divisions and greater political polarization would bring unrest. For a time, however, an abundance of oil and good prices allowed the government to operate as it wished.

With the solidity of the Puntofijo coalition and a booming economy as a result of consistently high oil prices, both AD and COPEI began to further entrench themselves into civil society and government institutions. The parties became increasingly

---

[397]Romero (1997: 2).

involved with labor unions, making deals with union leadership to give them greater control. Greater collaboration with foreign oil companies to maintain consistent access to Venezuelan oil led to high levels of corruption, and without a substantial opposition to blow the whistle or pose a threat to the coalition's reelection the problem only continued to worsen.[398] Even in the decades preceding this tense period, the Venezuelan government felt acute anxiety over giving the impression of such strong ties to foreign oil corporations, for example requesting that the State Department not make announcements publicly about the content of trade deals and the government's concessions to oil companies, particularly before close elections.[399] Instead of solving deeper inequalities in the socioeconomic structure, an abundance of oil revenues merely masked the problem by providing enough revenue to keep its social programs afloat. Price increases caused by crises in the Middle East in 1973 simply perpetuated the situation, allowing successive administrations to establish more and more programs and sink the country deeper into debt without immediate consequences.[400] An increase in a nation's wealth does not necessarily turn a regime from an autocracy to a democracy–it merely insulates current democracies from devolving into autocracies.[401] By the same token, poor democracies are far more fragile than poor autocracies, particularly if they are recently established or otherwise under strain preventing the establishment of a stable democracy–"fragile" by Canache's definition (Canache, 2002).

Oil revenues allowed the relatively new democracy to maintain power and achieve a sense of stability (however illusory it was) not possible in the rest of Latin America.[402] Still, for all the praise of Venezuela as an exceptional case in comparison with the rising totalitarianism in Latin America in the 1960s and 70s, the country's growth was nevertheless constrained by the lack of competition in the new democracy. Instead of consolidating a democracy in Venezuela, the power-sharing agreement of 1958 created an electoral bargaining system, effectively preserving the image of a democracy while removing the potential for actual competition and excluding new parties in the process. As Aníbal Romero explains, "Neocorporatist pacts predicated on gratifying utilitarian expectations may be useful as tools for compromise... [but] they do not necessarily entail a deep normative commitment to democracy per se."[403] When a governing regime is so stable that it does not risk a loss of power without a severely obvious blow to legitimacy, calling the system open and democratic is difficult. In addition, in such a system corruption begins to run rampant which not only privileges one class at the expense of another, but also hides the true costs of particular policy gambles, putting the country's economic welfare at risk. Japan's one-party democracy for example led to a level of economic manipulation that hid the costs of economic gambles the government took, resulting in an unanticipated collapse in the property market in the 1990s. The Black Friday economic crisis of 1983 resulted in a drastic devaluation of the bolí-

---

[398]Ellner (2007: 77)
[399]Tinker Salas (2007).
[400]Romero (1997).
[401]Prezeworski et al. (2000).
[402]Prezeworski et al. (2000).
[403]Romero (1997: 11).

var currency, but the bad rentier habits of previous administrations continued, sinking the country even further into debt and causing a rise in economic inequality. By the late 1980s, Venezuelans were increasingly disappointed with the government's ability to deliver on its promises and the extent of the patronage and corruption in the government, and pressure mounted.

The most infamous event symbolizing this total collapse of the Punto Fijo consensus and institutionalized party system was the 1989 uprising known as the Caracazo (so named for the city of Caracas where it initially broke out). Falling oil prices and the resulting fall in national income led to an economic downturn in the late 1980s after nearly three decades of relative prosperity, and the reelection of AD's Carlos Andrés Pérez as president in 1988 brought an unexpected deviation in government policy. Forced to abandon his party's usual social democratic platform due to the state of the economy and the extent of the country's debt, he began to introduce a series of wildly unpopular neoliberal reforms. A population that had become so accustomed to this system of rent distribution suddenly faced a government forced to renege on their policies, and the anger suddenly exploded. When transportation fare hikes were announced in Caracas, protests and riots broke out which were put down by military police, resulting in the deaths of hundreds of protesters (Morgan, 2007) While President Pérez went on to institute a scaled-back version of the reforms, the Caracazo was the first toll of the death bell for Pérez and his AD party. By the beginning of the early 1990s, the party system was beginning to fail entirely as Venezuelans increasingly defected from the parties, declaring themselves as independent in the 1993 election cycle. Two coup attempts in 1992 by disaffected military leaders, including a young lieutenant colonel named Hugo Chavez, only accelerated the collapse.

The deterioration of the consensus due to the excesses of power and risk-preferring behavior has been explained as the result of the lack of electoral competition institutionalized in the 1958 Puntofijo Agreement and the enabling effects of oil rentierism on the nation's economy. Both of these elements worked together to decrease the financial solvency of the lower classes, which Leonard Seabrooke theorizes is a source of legitimacy for the national financial system – and the nation's standing internationally. A government that provides for the interests of lower-class groupings (LIGs) and empowers them to establish credit systems creates an environment where the financial system as it exists is accepted by the population at large as a legitimate structure that governs the economy.[404]

A financial system is inherently a social construct governing economic interaction, and the conception and legitimacy of the system is dynamic and heavily dependent on how it is used to exchange benefits. When a government manipulates the financial system in such a way that it more directly benefits the lower classes, their access to credit and property legitimizes the financial system in their eyes and begins to translate into more overall satisfaction with the economic and political system that manipulates it. The financial solvency of LIGs thus constitutes a "social source of financial power"

---

[404] Seabrooke (2006: 1-8).

for the country that legitimizes the political system and legitimizes its good standing in the international finance market.[405]

Conversely, a government that begins to shift its attentions more towards "rentier interests" (landowners, corporations and wealthier investors) and away from the interests of lower-income groups will often risk a loss in domestic legitimacy. While it may pay off in the short-term to serve wealthier interest groups by preserving the status-quo financial system, the maintenance of such a structure ultimately costs the government the financial solvency (and trust) of its people, which translates into lost political influence. This loss of domestic legitimacy and the narrowing base of financial solvency in turn both affect their standings in international financial markets. It comes as little surprise that this leaking legitimacy, both domestic and international, feeds into itself and becomes a downward spiral that can result in deeper political and economic troubles for a country. In the Venezuelan context, the economic crisis in 1983, the devaluation of the bolívar and the decline in the country's financial standing can be traced back to the growing patronage system as a result of rentier state policies. At first there had been enough oil wealth flowing into the country to allow for concessions to be made to foreign oil companies, investors and landed elites while still serving its lower-income groups with a social policy system that temporarily served their needs. When the economic bubble burst, however, forcing the AD government to make the choice between its "rentier interests" and its poor, President Perez and AD prioritized foreign and domestic elite rentier interests and deregulated the economy. This provoked a reaction of immense proportions that destroyed much of the incumbent government's credibility, paving the way for the entrance of the socialist MVR and its charismatic leader. A poor political decision was the turning point that shone the light on long-standing, long-ignored class tensions, and the balloon finally burst.

Hugo Chavez's attempt at a coup was more than the mere seizure of opportunity in the political system's weakness. Lieutenant Colonel Hugo Chavez had aspired to military and political leadership from his humble childhood, and earned a spot in Venezuela's military academy.[406] Inspired by military theorists like Mao, Chavez and three other mid-ranked military officers formed a paramilitary organization which by 1982 was named the Movimiento Bolivariano Revolucionario 200 (MBR-200, or the Bolivarian Revolutionary Movement) in honor of the bicentennial of revolutionary Simon Bolivar's birth. They were already well-connected to the political elite historically – recall their role in the counter-coups to bring AD to power in 1945 and 1958 – and had developed sympathies with leftist guerrillas they were fighting in the rural areas. Disaffected with their army's use to put down popular rebellions, especially in light of the 1989 Caracazo, Chavez and the members of MBR-200 developed increasingly close ties with left-wing political organizations aspiring to power, such as Causa Radical (Causa R)[407] Ironically enough, military involvement in the crackdowns may have inadvertently contributed to the conditions allowing for the politicization of the military and the rise of

---

[405] Ibid. p. 51.
[406] Chavez Frias (2005).
[407] Almao (2004: 64-66).

the MBR-200.

With the coup attempt and arrest of Chavez and his compatriots in 1992, the move-ment gained national attention, and true to the height of apathy with the current regime, the coup provoked little public outcry either for or against the regime. By the time of Chavez's release from prison in 1994 (thanks to a back-room deal struck with the AD and COPEI), the legitimacy of the current system was sinking to its lowest point – so low, in fact, that Rafael Caldera, former president and founder of COPEI, won reelec-tion in 1993 in part because he defected from his own party and ran as an independent candidate. In light of this low popular support, Chavez decided to confront the gov-ernment through electoral grassroots support. By 1997 the MBR-200 would become a legal political party, the Movimiento Quinta República (5th Republic Movement, or MVR), in time for the 1998 presidential elections. However, before his election in 1998 he represented a "minority electoral alternative" that rose to power largely because of the stunning weakness and perceived incompetency of the incumbent parties.[408]

Traditional electoral models usually predict that, given an electorate with little pref-erence variation, electoral candidates would gravitate to the center of the spectrum of ideological and political choices. The resulting government would remain risk-averse because of the balance that had to be maintained in an effort to preserve the widest base of support possible. However, the theory makes the mistake of assuming a ho-mogeneous belief in the competence of the government in power, regardless of voter preferences on specific policy issues.[409] The Venezuelan "exceptionalism thesis" made this mistake as well, assuming a consensus on beliefs where in reality the polity was much more stratified. Economic and political stratification coincided (and to this day still overlaps) with belief in the competency of the system, and in a rentier state where legitimacy of the ruler is explicitly tied to competence and delivery of expected policy result, a regime that does not deliver on its promises to a particular group loses their support.

In addition, as is the nature of democratic political systems, risk-preferring behav-ior did not become most apparent until years into the rule of the coalition. It is certainly not in the nature of democratic regimes to display such risk preference given the natural instability of democracy with its election cycles ("a crisis of political survival" insti-tutionalized if you will). However, risk adversity only comes into play when there is sufficient electoral competition for government seats to encourage more cautious moves, especially in countries where governments are routinely toppled and replaced in military coups. The AD and COPEI's entrance into power via a military coup and the concilia-tory measures in the Puntofijo consensus, however, left their competition limited which left them room in which to take measures that gambled with their legitimacy and their ability to deliver on political promises.

Democracies naturally face "threats to political regimes" via elections, but more fragile democracies such as those in Latin America usually also have to compensate for the threat of a military coup as well. One particular survival strategy for regimes in this

---

[408] Ibid. p. 67.
[409] See the formal model of Chapter 3.

scenario is to pacify military interests with increases in the military budget, whether
in absolute terms or proportional to the rest of the government budget. This can often
succeed in avoiding military coups, but in the process this allocation can often decrease
funding for social and economic programs that solidify electoral support when the threat
of another regime change comes via elections (in democracies this "electoral crisis"
is built into the system, but makes it no less of a threat to the political survival of a
regime).[410] In Venezuela, not only did the government manipulate fiscal policies to
distribute rents and social program funding to a population expecting the government
to increase their living standards, but they also took political support from the military
for granted. After the 1945 military coup bringing the first era of AD-style democracy
to Venezuela, the same military turned again in 1948 and deposed the government,
installing a dictator until the return of the political parties again in 1958. Despite such
shifts in political support within the military during this time, the incumbents began
to take the military's support for granted as they were asked to provide the muscle
against the government's rivals, far-left rural guerrillas and the protesting masses of
the Caracazo. The use of military forces for partisan ends angered the officers and
encouraged the conditions for a political mobilization of the military, as did the suffering
and frustrations of a people under the supposed protection of the system.[411]

The failures of the previous Punto Fijo consensus aside, the agency of Chavez and
the Bolivarian Revolutionary Movement (MBR-200) also have to be taken into account
in this transition. Too great a focus on the fall of the previous coalition contributing to
Chavez's ascent has the danger of implying a lack of agency on the part of the movement
and those who support it. This also would seem to imply that such a movement would
have no traction without the absolute collapse of the current regime to leave a political
and ideological vacuum for Chavez's party to fill. While the collapse may have left
a power vacuum open, Chavez and his fellow founders of MBR-200 could not have
seized the opportunity to come to power democratically had there not been previous
organizing efforts and planning taking place. Their leftist political ideology appealed
to a disaffected voting public tired of the corruption and economic inequality present
in the system devised in 1958. The attempted coups in 1992 raised the profile of the
movement and gave Hugo Chavez national recognition, setting the foundation for a
campaign that turned MBR-200 into a legal political party with a broad base of support
among those demanding a change in government – "anti-democratic" or not. By the
time of his presidential election in 1998, Hugo Chavez and the MVR were introducing
a new constitution for a popular referendum.

For decades the 1958 constitution and Puntofijo Pact had been the rules by which
democracy was played, resulting in a system that promised far more than it could deliver
and entrenched systems of patronage that ultimately brought more harm to the government. In fragile democracies, the electorate's support for or criticism of an incumbent
government has more of an impact on their views of the utility of the political system
itself, and with the previous political system being a "constitutional democracy" with

---

[410] Ames (1987: 43-47, 98-99).
[411] Almoa (2004: 65).

power-sharing resembling more of an oligarchy rotating in and out of power, there is little surprise that a new constitution was seen as necessary. The intensely partisan political culture in Venezuela now is a symptom of the larger class tensions that existed long before Chavez came to power – and were covered up for decades with government largesse enabled by an abundance of oil revenues and a power-sharing agreement masking ideological divides.

The years following the constitutional referendum have been filled with successes for the Chavez regime, including the consolidation of Venezuela's oil in the government-owned PDVSA (Petróleo de Venezuela) and a series of confrontations with the United States over its neoliberal trade policy and attempts to form the Free Trade Area of the Americas (FTAA). Despite such setbacks as multiple coup attempts against Chavez in 2002 and a defeated recall election in 2004, only recently has his widespread support begun to falter somewhat with the most recent electoral defeat of a constitutional amendment – one allowing for lifetime presidency.

The stability of the AD/COPEI party system in place had inspired a sense of over-confidence leading to more risk-preferring behavior from the ruling coalition. While democratic in name, the government's increased entrenchment of the party system and the Pacto Punto Fijo was creating an atmosphere of government excess preparing the ground for increased corruption. While reliable evidence of actual corruption is scant given the taint of media bias and political motivations behind most accusations (unfounded or not), we can at the very least note the laying of groundwork conducive to such improprieties – especially in the form of legal patronage and clientelist networks developed through the 1960s and 70s. Even so, it was the lack of attention to the dynamics of popular support, rising socioeconomic tensions and changing political circumstances that were most significant in the collapse of the AD/COPEI consensus. The rentier state system and the good graces of the post-war international oil market insulated the government from a breakdown, but the regime's dependence on the spending of oil revenues, the corruption and clientelist patronage systems that resulted from such government largesse and the misuse of (and lack of control over) the military that sealed the fate of Venezuela's centrist power-sharing democracy. Until Chavez's election in 1998 and the passage of the new constitution the following year, attempts at reforming the system were simply "rearranging the deck chairs" on a sinking ship – the damage was done from the very beginning.[412]

Signing the "Fixed Point" Pact ultimately laid the foundation for the regime to sign their death certificate and leave a power vacuum wide open for a former coup leader to be elected as a newly-minted constitutional democrat – and in the process usher in a new era of leftist politics in South America. Much to the chagrin of the United States, the conditions under which the neoliberal model prevailed in the "exceptional democracy" of Venezuela were the very conditions that contributed to that democracy's downfall.

---

[412]Romero (1997).

7.4 Iranian Autocracy

The1979 Iranian Revolution is something of an anomaly globally.[413] Like many other states in the later half of the twentieth century, Iran was shaped by the fallout of the Second World War. It faced external challenges resulting from the breakup of the European colonial system as well as an internal struggle for greater popular representation. After 1945, many such states saw mass revolution against repressive autocratic regimes, typically resulting in either a move toward democracy and the West or Communism and the East. However, the Iranian Revolution resulted neither in democratization nor a leftist regime; rather, it created a cleric-dominated autocracy based on religious precepts.[414] Understanding the forces responsible for the creation and maintenance of the Islamic Republic of Iran is essential to a theoretical understanding of autocratic regimes. Although the Islamic Republic may appear to be an unexplained anomaly, it is the contention of this chapter that not only does Iran conform to the predictions of past theories of autocratic institutions, it allows for further generalization and improvement thereof. To this end, a detailed analysis of Iranian autocracy will be applied to the model of autocratic institutions outlined in the body of this chapter.

The model of authoritarian regimes attempts to incorporate both democratic and authoritarian institutions into a single model in order to understand the stability of autocracies and the possibility of a transformation to democracy. This model rests on an analysis of the political and economic space within a given state. It assumes two dimensions; the first is an economic dimension, in which power is derived from the factors of capital, labor and land; and the second is a political dimension concerned, in modern democracies, with civil and social rights. The entire populace of a given state is distributed across this two-dimensional space. For any form of government, the leader is chosen by a subset of the populace referred to as the selectorate. Autocracies are distinguished from democracies in that the selectorate is a small minority of, and not responsible to, the general populace. Consequently, it is possible that the equilibrium position of an autocrat will be so far from the political center of the populace as to induce revolution.

The Iranian government fits the definition of autocracy both prior to and post the 1979 revolution. Consequently, the story of Iranian autocracy since the Second World War is, in fact, the story of two very different regimes. The first is the autocracy of Mohammad Reza Pahlavi, which lasted from roughly 1941 to 1979, and the second is the clerical autocracy of the current Islamic Republic, which has ruled since 1979. The modern autocracy of the Islamic Republic cannot be properly understood without first understanding the authoritarian monarchy which existed under the shah and the events leading to its collapse.

The shah's autocracy and the resulting revolution were fairly typical of modern, western autocracies. The ruling selectorate of the autocracy was an alliance of western-leaning capital interests backed up by US military aid and the 'bureaucratic bourgeoisie'"

---

[413]This section was written by Paul Bender.
[414]Panah (2007: 14).

of the state.[415] Between the end of World War II and 1979, the shah's government increasingly allied itself with Western, particularly US, interests against the moderate and radical elements of the populace. The seminal conflict in this period came in the early 1950s when the shah's popular Prime Minister Mohammad Mosaddeq nationalized the Iranian oil industry and forced the shah to flee the country. Mosaddeq's nationalization program posed a threat both to Western oil interests, who feared Iran's potential withdraw from the capitalist market as a dangerous precedent that could be followed by other non-aligned states.[416] In response, the United States engineered a coup via the CIA which removed Mosaddeq and re-installed the shah as authoritarian monarch. This interference by American and other western forces ingrained nationalist resentment of foreign intervention while at the same time causing shifts to ward a western, capitalist economy. Both factors would have a profound impact on subsequent Iranian history.

The shah's ruling selectorate was opposed by an alliance of the disenfranchised proletariat, who allied with clerics and their traditional, conservative bourgeoisie allies. They were joined by members of the new, western-leaning middle class disenchanted by the economic downturns of the mid-1970's. This coalition grew as a result of several events during the course of the shah's reign. Land reform policies undertaken in the 1960s and 70s transferred land from landed elites to small farmers in an attempt to establish capitalist relations in rural areas. While this initially succeeded in creating a class of small land-owners, this group quickly collapsed. Many of the newly-landed farmers were unable to subsist off of the land and were therefore forced to sell their land to large agribusinesses. The resulting landless then moved to the cities, most notably Tehran, and formed a disenfranchised proletariat. The government also alienated sectors of the Iranian economy in the urban areas. Policies meant to aid industrial and financial capital did so at the expense of the traditional middle class of commodity producers. This also impacted the religious establishment, which drew taxes from these traditional sectors of the population. Finally, although the new, modern middle class originally supported the shah and were recipients of some of the new wealth created by government policy, they lost faith in the shah's regime following economic downturns in the mid-1970s. The resulting resentment of the government and the new middle class against the shah and paved the path for revolution.

From the broad-based anti-shah coalition of the late 1970s emerged a cleric-dominated autocracy based on the legal principles of shi'a Islam. This unexpected transformation of the government was the consequence of a variety of factors. Prior to the revolution, the non-clerical revolutionaries in 1979 underestimated the possibility of clerical rule. Khomeini repeatedly claimed to be uninterested in rule prior to and during the beginning stages of the revolution, and his writings advocating a cleric-dominated state were suppressed.[417] Furthermore, due to his anti-western ideals, his movement was able to initially ally with leftists who distrusted middle-class revolutionaries as tools of the west. During the chaotic period immediately following the overthrow of the

---

[415] Ibid. p. 27.
[416] Ibid. p. 19.
[417] Keddie (2006: 240).

shah, Khomeini made use of anti-US and anti-imperialistic rhetoric in order to cement his hold on power. He endeavored to stir up resentment against foreign interference by co-opting the legacy of Mosaddeq and preaching against US interference and military support of the shah.

This ideological strength on the part of the clerics and their allies proved crucial to the outcome of the revolution. Although US-Iranian relations were improving in early 1979 under the interim government, they soon crumbled in a flood of anti-American sentiment. When the now-exiled shah was allowed into the US for medical treatment, the Iranian interim government came under attack from both the right and the left as anti-US sentiment soared. This crisis was prolonged by Khomeini's supporters, who took advantage of the weakness of other revolutionary factions to consolidate power and pass a new constitution enshrining clerical rule. Liberal revolutionaries who had contact with the US were prosecuted or forced to resign, thereby sealing the clerical hold on the state.[418] After clerical consolidation of power, some leftist parties attempted to start minor uprisings in outer areas of the country. However, they were soon defeated and their leaders executed. Meanwhile, the remaining leftist parties backed the government, which they still saw as the best protection against imperialist interference. From that point onward, Khomeini saw few serious threats to his cleric-lead government.

The model presented in this chapter identifies various political actors in terms of their position in the political-economic space of the state. The ruling selectorate is made up of a core of Hardliners who, via their control of certain factors of production, derive the most utility from maintaining the autocracy. They are joined in the selectorate by Reformers, who also benefit from the stability and policies of the autocracy but are more amenable to compromise. Outside of the selectorate, the general population consists of Radicals, who have the most to gain from the dissolution of the autocratic system, and Moderates, a middle-class of citizens who are less stridently opposed to the autocratic regime. In order to effect revolution, the Reformers and Moderates in the middle class must overcome the inherent collective action problem and align themselves either with either the Hardliners in the regime or the Radicals in the populace.

In terms of the model of autocratic institutions, the shah's autocracy looks very much like a typical post-war dictatorship. His selectorate was a coalition between the Hardliners, represented by the shah himself, and the new capitalist middle-class. This arrangement was opposed by the typical alliance of leftist Radicals fueled by the growing urban poor who had suffered from the shah's land redistribution policies. However, in Iran, these economic Radicals were also joined by rightist Radicals on the political axis; the clerical establishment and their economic traditionalist allies, the "bazaar bourgeoisie." A symbiotic relationship had existed between the shi'a clerics and the socially traditional "bazaaris" for several centuries; the clerics would bless their day to day commerce and give them the good will of the lower classes, while the bazaaris would financially support the clergy by paying religious taxes and other fees.[419] Governmental support of foreign investment and infrastructure development under the shah

---

[418]Panah (2007: 57).
[419]Moslem (2006: 56).

had undermined the economic base of this class by shifting the focus of Iran's economy toward modern capitalist interaction. Thus, this second group of Radicals represented a traditional, Islamic upper class in Iran whose livelihood had been harmed by the shah's modern, pro-capital policies.

The shah's government collapsed because the middle-class Moderates abandoned his coalition and allied with the Radicals. The social Radicals were able to hijack this revolutionary coalition and establish an autocracy of their own. The selectorate of the current Islamic Republic is an alliance between the clerics and the traditional sectors of the economy, that is, the religious/conservative end of the Iranian social axis. Ultimate political power rests with a set of "religious supervisory bodies" made up of shi'a clerics, which are the highest ranking set of institutions in modern Iran. They hold overriding authority over all decisions made within the political system and serve to ensure the power of the ruling clerical Hardliners.

To a lesser extent, both the poor and the modern capitalist middle classes also support the regime. Since the revolution, the loyalty of the poor has been maintained through their identification with the clergy and their hostility to the upper classes, which they see as "western." The regime's support among the capitalist middle classes is significantly more tenuous, and stems almost entirely from its anti-imperialist rhetoric. After the revolution, Khomeini worked to cultivate an image as nationalist successor to Mosaddeq. Allies of Khomeini argued that, if the populace did not remain behind Khomeini, western powers would repeat the 1953 coup and install a western-leaning autocrat to the further detriment and shame of the Iranian people. This tactic of appealing to nationalist images of Iran's past has continued to be successful even since Khomeini's death due to the incredibly high resonance of anti-imperialist, nationalist sentiments. This tactic has quite successfully allowed the socially and religiously conservative clerics to overcome reservations regarding reactionary positions on democracy and women's rights.

Although the clerical autocrats in Iran have occasionally used economic leverage to ensure the loyalty of the economic left and right, their leeway in this respect is limited both by their reliance on the support of the bazaaris and their need to balance the interests of a wide range of groups with competing economic interests. Recently, the Iranian government has attempted to balance minor liberalization with continued social programs aimed at the poor. However, any substantial reforms are blocked by the clerical establishment, as they will hurt the power base of the clerics and their bazaari allies. Furthermore, Iran's relative isolation from the Western world due to the impact of US sanctions also affects Iranian economic policy. During the mid-1990s, Reformers in the Iranian government attempted to move toward market-based economic change which would benefit the capitalist middle class. However, internal conflict with the left made this effort difficult, and increased US sanctions in 1995 led to the near collapse of the attempted reforms.

The structure of autocracy in the Islamic Republic of Iran can now be analyzed according to the precepts of the model of autocratic institutions. Unlike the case studies presented earlier in this chapter, the clerical selectorate in Iran is located near the center of the economic dimension. The ruling clerics and their bazaari supporters represent the traditional Iranian middle class, which derives utility from the maintenance of a traditional Islamic social order. This turns the traditional model "on its side," so to speak. In the body of the chapter, it was argued that the response of the elite depends on the cost-benefit analysis of the balance between the revolutionary threat's credibility against democratization's probable impact on their assets. Yet in Iran, the Hardliners do not explicitly fear the redistribution of economic resources as such; rather, they fear the redistribution of political and social power. Any move toward the political center will necessarily deprive the clerics of a portion of their social influence and therefore the economic rents they extract from the bazaari class. It is essential, however, to understand that the clerical Hardliners do not benefit from the control of a specific economic factor of production. Instead, they benefit from the maintenance of a specific social order.

Turning the model on its side in this fashion explains why the Iranian regime has been willing and able to court both the economic right and left. The regime has traditionally been able to adopt relatively centrist economic policies in terms of wealth redistribution without harming its traditional economic base. However, as discussed above, the regime has generally been relatively more willing to ally with the economic left than the capitalist middle class. However, this preference for the left has relatively little to do with an inherent preference for leftist redistribution on the part of the autocratic elites. Rather, it is a direct consequence of the Hardliners' reliance on anti-US nationalism to support the dominance of a religious selectorate, a message much more compatible with leftist economics than the US-style capitalism of the middle class. Indeed, with the rise of hard-line president Ahmadinejad in 2005, Iran has increasingly pursued a brand of ultra-conservative populism and promoted efforts toward leftist reforms.

The Iranian regime does not lie at or even near the political center of the populace. Nevertheless, the elites in the clerical hierarchy maintain power through their continual manipulation of Iranian nationalism, and promote themselves as the only alternative to further interference by the west in general and the US in particular. "The events of 1953 have created an emotional barrier for Iran's masses and have made them inherently suspicious of American motives and conduct."[420] This has allowed the ruling Hardliners to use US actions against Iran to further their political dominance. Statements made by the United States against the Iranian regime have thus "had the opposite effect from what they intended – they strengthened the hard-liners and create suspicion of those who want better relations with the United States."[421] The continued stability of the autocracy therefore requires continued antagonism with the West as a nationalist tool to manipulate the political preferences of the Iranian populace.

The prospects for internal regime change in Iran require the opposition to overcome the revolutionary collective action problem discussed above. In the mid to late 1990's, the growing number of educated and professional men and women in Iran began to discuss human rights, greater freedoms, and democracy. This group represents primarily

---

[420] Takeyh (2006: 84).
[421] Keddie (2006: 284).

Moderates in the general populace who support and are loosely allied with Reformers in the government. Aside from the Reformers and the governmental Hardliners, there is a third group who want to see the government overthrown in a popular movement and re-placed by a secular liberal democracy. This group represents the Radicals in the Islamic Republic; that is, those far to the left on the social/political axis who support the sec-ularization of governmental institutions and the liberalization of civil rights. However, this group currently lacks sufficient cohesion and support at to be effective. Further-more, these Iranian Radicals are plagued by unwanted support; the Bush administration has regularly called for the internal ouster of the Iranian regime and has offered mone-tary aid to anti-regime movements. However, the rhetoric and financial support of the Bush administration makes life significantly more difficult for the democratic advocates it is intended to buttress, for it ties them to the US and spawns fears among Moderates that they would aid in the creation of an American-dominated government.

Unlike many traditional autocracies, the clerical elites of the Islamic Republic of Iran derive utility from the support of traditional social roles. Several interesting con-cluding points can be made in light of this characterization. First, the clerical leaders of Iran increase their valence and therefore popular support by capitalizing on popular fears of US interference in Iranian affairs driven by the memory of the 1953 coup. US support of anti-government factions therefore serves to aid the political elites at the at the expense of their opponents. Second, in this model of Iranian autocracy, the social position of the ruling elites drives their preference for economic policy, rather than the reverse. It has been shown that the Iranian elites are willing to support both leftist and capitalist economic policies insofar as they do not interfere with the Islamic/nationalist ideology of the ruling clerics. However, given the current political climate, the Iranian regime is more amenable to leftist economic policies due to the association of capital-ism with the US (and likely as a result of the left's association with US antagonists such as Venezuela). Third and finally, Iran provides an interesting case study for "chain-autocracy." That is to say, a state in which a ruling autocracy is overthrown via popular revolution is then replaced with further autocracy. This scenario unfolded in Iran be-cause a high-valence individual, Khomeini, was able to leverage his popularity into widespread popular support in spite of his significant distance from the center of the general populace. We cannot yet tell whether the Hardliners in the Iranian regime will continue to benefit from hostile US rhetoric in order to maintain their control of the Iranian selectorate.

Chapter 8

Modelling Elections

8.1 Ideology and Putin's Approval in Russian Elections

8.1.1 Introduction

What was the main factor behind the pro-Kremlin United Russia winning the December 2007 State Duma election with 64% of the seats?[422] The party's centrist ideology, association with Vladimir Putin, as well as media bias, administrative pressure, and vote-rigging have all been suggested as the primary cause behind the party's success. This work tackles the question by estimating a multinomial logit model of voter choice based on survey data from May 2007. The present analysis finds the approval of President Putin tends to be the single most important factor affecting the voter's choice in favor of United Russia. [423] The personal ideological preferences was a major factor affecting the vote, so the party's centrist position improved its electoral performance. The opponents' appeal to older voters also was a contributing factor. Voter's income, education, and the rural/urban status were found to have little effect on the vote.

There have been a number of attempts at quantitative voter research on newly democratic countries such as Russia.[424] Colton and Hale (2008) compared the effects of positions on various ideological and policy issues on the 2000 and 2004 Presidential vote. They found that the role of such positions (including the left-right self-identification) declined in 2004. Only two issues (foreign policy and presidentialism) were found to be important for the election that year. According to the "transitional model" of economic voting, the economic evaluations of voters in post-Communist countries are more long-term. The voters compare the current economic conditions

---

[422]This section was written by Alexei Zakharov and is based on Zakharov (2008c). See
http://www.polit-econ.ru/zakharov/statii/ideological_voting.pdf
[423]Putin's popularity has been sustained for a number of years. See Andrew Harding, "Why is Putin Popular?", BBC News, (8 March, 2000).
<http://news.bbc.co.uk/1/hi/world/europe/669247.stm>.
[424]See Fidrmuc (2000, a,b), White, Oates and Mac Allister (2001), Hesli and Bashkirova (2001), Mishler and Willerton (2003) and Wegren and Konitzer (2006).

with the pre-transition economy. Those who believe that the economic conditions have deteriorated should support the parties that are associated with the pre-transition Communist regime. Owen and Tucker (2008) tested this theory against data from Poland, with some evidence in favor of both the transitional model and the conventional model of economic voting.

The present work tests several theories of voter motivation using Russian survey data. According to the Downsian voting model, forward-looking voters evaluate candidates or parties based on the expectations of the policy that they will deliver. This proposition can be tested with survey data that estimates the positions of the voters on various policy issues.[425] One can then use factor analysis to calculate the position of each voter in the policy space. This approach was used to analyze data from Netherlands and Germany (Schofield, Martin, Quinn and Whitford, 1998) and Great Britain (Quinn, Martin and Whitford, 1999) and extended to Israel and Italy (Schofield and Sened, 2006; Giannetti and Sened, 2004).[426] The second approach is to include in the voter utility function a separate term for each policy issue. This is used, for example, by Thurner and Eymann (2000) for German Bundestag elections and by Colton and Hale (2008) for Russian Presidential elections.

Here we test whether sociodemographic factors such as age, income, education, or gender affect partisan preferences of Russian voters.[427] In addition, we examine the influence of the voter' approval of President Putin and other federal structures. A voter's approval rate of president Putin may be used as a proxy for the voter's positive retrospective economic evaluation. There is indirect evidence to support this claim. For example, Treisman (2008) found that the approval rate for Russian presidents (Putin and Yeltsin) closely followed the electorate's perception of economic performance.

8.1.2   The Data

The results of this section are based on a survey conducted by VCIOM (Russian Public Opinion Research Center) in May 2007. Some 1588 adult citizens were interviewed in 46 Russian regions, out of a total of 83 regions. Over 66% of the respondents indicated that they would vote for some party if the election were held at the time of the survey (Table 8.2). The distribution of vote in the sample is similar to the distribution of actual vote in the election of December 2, 2007. Most of the vote went to the pro-Kremlin United Russia party.[428]

It is commonly believed that the United Russia received an unfair advantage due to the lopsided coverage on the state television channels and political pressure. The party also enjoyed an open endorsement by the then President Vladimir Putin. It is also

---

[425]For example, a common measure of ideology is the voter's self-identification on a left right economic axis.

[426]See the analyses in Chapter 4.

[427]See Brader and Tucker (2007) on partisanship in Russia.

[428]The United Russia party was formed in April 2001, and is a pro-presidential political party. Most scholars view the party as a political tool for the reconciliation of the country's ruling elite. The party's policy program — the so-called "Putin Plan" — is vaguely defined and makes broad allusions to claiming credit for the "return of Russia to the world stage."

believed that some form of election fraud had taken place (see, for instance, Harding, 2007). The support for the pro-Kremlin United Russia actually declined from 45% in the May sample to 40% in the December election. According to some sources, the decline may have been due to the popular dissatisfaction with the rising food prices in the third and fourth quarters of 2007.[429]

Most of the rest of the vote, both in the elections and in the sample, went to the three runner-up parties. Support for Vladimir Zhirinovsky's Liberal Democratic Party (LDPR) increased from 4.2% to 5.1%; for Fair Russia (SR) it has declined from 6.2% to under 5%; for the Communist Party (CPRF), it has remained constant at 7.1-7.3%. The share of votes for most minor parties was also similar in the survey and in the elections.

Some 54.7% of the respondents were female, and 45.3% male. The age of the respondents varied from 18 to 92 years, with the mean of 44.7 years. Rural residents consisted of 26.7% of the sample. The mean self-reported level of education (on a scale of 0 to 1) was 0.56. For income, the figure was also 0.56 (see Appendix A to this section for the index details).

The approval rate for President Putin is noticeably higher than for other federal government institutions (Table 8.1). Only a small part of the population (12%) disapproved of Putin, and an even smaller part (8%) was undecided. For other insititutions, the disapproval rates were much higher. The share of the respondents who answered "don't know" was also greater, suggesting that the attitudes are weaker.

The respondent's ideological preferences were measured by two survey questions. In the first question, the respondent was read a list of 40 words. After each item, he/she was asked to identify whether he/she felt positive toward the concept it represented. The second question was identical, except that the negative feelings were recorded (see Table 8.3). "Order" was positively identified by the largest number of respondents (57%), followed by "justice", "stability", and "well-being". The largest number of negative responses was given to "elite" (41%), followed by "non-Russians" (29%) and "West" (23%)

For each concept, a variable was constructed that took the value of -1 if the respondent's feeling was negative, +1 if the feeling was positive, and 0 otherwise. A Karhunen-Loeve transform was used to construct the two-dimensional ideological space as well as the positions of the respondents. Figure 8.1 shows the positions of the respondents in the ideological space, while Table 8.3 shows factor loadings for each of the 40 concepts. Each factor loading is proportional to the correlation between the values of the ideological factor and the feelings toward the concept. The concepts with high absolute factor loadings are "ideologically integrated" (Basinger and Hartman, 2006). The first ideological factor (or the position along the first dimension) can be interpreted as the degree of a voter's general *satisfaction (or dissatisfaction)*. High values of the first factor correspond to negative feelings toward "justice" and "labor", and, to a lesser extent, "order", "state", "stability" and "equality". Also, those with high values on this first

---

[429] See, for instance, Babich, "Rising Food Prices in Russia" *Russia: Beyond the headlines* (Nov. 14, 2007) <http://rbth.rg.ru/article.php?id=10046>

factor tend to feel neutral toward "order", "elite", "West", and "non-Russians". Low
values of the first factor correspond to positive attitudes to "order", "justice", "stability" and "equality", and negative attitudes toward "elite", "West", and "non-Russians".
The second factor can be called the voter's degree of *economic liberalism*. High values
correspond to positive feelings to "freedom", "business", "capitalism", "well-being",
"success", and "progress", and to negative feelings toward "communism", "socialism",
"USSR", and related concepts.

One can see that the supporters of different parties tend to have different ideological
preferences (Table 8.2). The supporters of the United Russia tend to have a centrist
position on both dimensions. This is partly due to the fact that they constitute 45% of
the sample, and the sample means are zero for each ideological factor. The supporters
of the Communist Party and Fair Russia have similar ideological profiles, with negative
values along each factor. The LDPR supporters tend to have low values along the first
ideological factor (suggesting dissatisfaction), but high values along the second factor
(suggesting support for economic liberalism).

8.1.3   The Multinomial Logit Model

As in Chapter 3, we denote by P the set of parties and by N the set of respondents.
Each voter i is characterized by the vector η_i of observable individual-specific nonpolicy
factors, and by the observable positions, (x_{i1}, x_{i2}), on the two ideological dimensions.
Each party j is characterized by the ideological position (z_{i1}, z_{i2}).

We use a variant of the model described in Chapter 3, and suppose that the utility of
voter i with regard to party j is

$$
\begin{aligned}
u_{ij}(x_i, z_j) &= \lambda_j - \beta_1(x_{i1} - z_{j1})^2 + \beta_2(x_{i2} - z_{j2})^2 + \theta_j^{\mathsf{T}} \eta_i + \varepsilon_{ij}. \\
&\equiv u_{ij}^*(x_i, z_j) + \varepsilon_{ij},
\end{aligned}
$$

where $\{\lambda_j, \theta_j\}$, β_1, β_2 are unobservable parameters, and $\{\varepsilon_{ij}\}$ is the set of unobservable independent random variables distributed according to the Type I extreme value
distribution

$$
\Psi(\epsilon_{ij} \le h) = e^{-e^{-h}}.
$$

Assume that the respondents votes for party j if that party provides maximum utility.
Given that the error terms are distributed according to Ψ, the probability that voter i will
support party j is

$$
\rho_{ij} = \frac{\exp u_{ij}^*(x_i, z_j)}{\sum_{j \in P} \exp u_{ij}^*(x_i, z_j)}.
$$

Denote the likelihood of the model by $\mathbb{L}$. The estimation problem is to find the
values of $\{\{\lambda_j, \theta_j : j \epsilon P\}, \beta_1, \beta_2 \}$ that maximize the likelihood $\mathbb{L}$.

Ascertaining $\{z_{j1}$ and $z_{j2}\}$, the ideological positions of political parties, as they
are perceived by the voters, is a methodological problem. There are several ways to
do it, such as expert survey of party elites (as in Quinn, Martin, and Whitford, 1999),

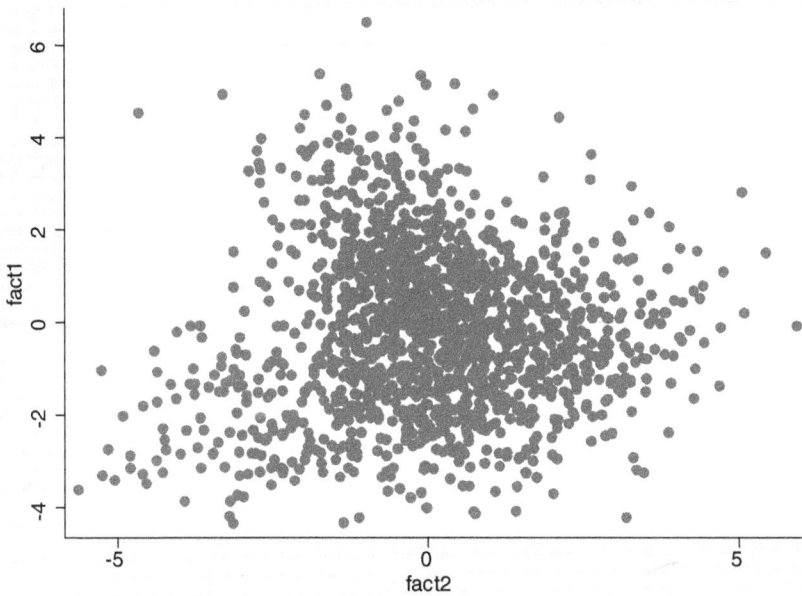

Figure 8.1: Distribution of voter ideal points for all respondents.

expert judgements (as in Schofield and Sened, 2006; Benoit and Laver, 2006), or a systematized analysis of party manifestos (Budge *et al.*, 2003). For the present analysis, the party positions $\{z_{j1}$ and $z_{j2}\}$ of party j are taken to be equal to the average positions of respondents who intended to vote for that party.

8.1.4   Empirical Results

The multinomial models of voter choice generally perform poorly when some parties have very limited support. For this reason, the estimation was limited to four parties — United Russia, the Communist Party, LDPR, and Fair Russia. (In order to check the robustness of the results, the model was also estimated with seven parties, adding Yabloko, SPS, and the Agrarian Party, but the results are not reported here, as the two models were compatible.)

   Several variants of the four-party model are examined.

 1. The full set of expanatory variables is used. These include ideological positions, age, gender, rural residence, income, education, approval and efficacy. (See Table 8.4).

2. All of the above, except ideological positions.

3. Model 1 with significant explanatory variables retained.

4. Model 1 less approval and efficacy.

5. Model 4 less age and gender.

6. Model 5 less education, income, and rural residence ($\theta_j = 0$ in the utility equation).

The findings show overwhelming support for the hypothesis that ideology affects voting. For the four-party and seven-party models with the full set of other explanatory variables, adding the two spatial terms improves log likelihood by 45 and 50.8, respectively. The estimated values of both β_1 and β_2 are approximately equal for the four-party and the seven-party models.

The ideological preferences of a voter strongly affect the predicted vote. Tables 8.6 and 8.7 give the probabilities of a female / male voter supporting the four large parties (based on the estimation of the four-party model with the full set of explanatory variables). One can see that the support for the high-valence United Russia can vary from 45% to 83%, depending on ideological position. The support for low-valence parties varies by a greater extent — from 1% to 31% for the Communist party, for example.[430]

The approval of President Putin had a significant and negative effect on the support for all parties other than United Russia. The effect was the strongest for the CPRF and weakest for the Fair Russia (see Table 8.4). Hence an increase in one's approval is likely to increase a voter's probability of voting for United Russia at the expense of the other three parties, with CPRF being hardest hit. This signifies the fact that Russian voters clearly perceived United Russia as a pro-Putin party even in May 2007, well before it was announced that Putin would head the United Russia party list on October 2001.[431]

The approval the Prime Minister and Cabinet did not have any significant effect on the vote. Approval of the State Duma had a small, negative and marginally significant effect on the LDPR vote; for other parties, that effect was not significant. The term for the approval of the upper house of the Russia parliament, the Federation Council, was significant only for the Fair Russia party. It was also positive, as the party leader, Segei Mironov, is also the head of that legislative body.

The magnitude of the 'Putin effect' on the level of support for the United Russia can be estimated by setting the approval scores equal to zero for all respondents, then re-estimating the probabilities of voting according to the four-party model with the full set of explanatory variables. The expected voteshares for each party by can be obtained by averaging the estimated probabilities for each party across all respondents in the four-party subsample.[432]

---

[430]In all estimations, the constant terms for all parties except United Russia are negative and significant. This means that there are other factors, besides gender, income, age, education, rural residence, approval, efficacy, and ideology, that bias the preferences of the voters toward United Russia.

[431]This result is robust with respect to the deletion of other explanatory variables, including the spatial terms.

[432]The expected voteshares for the unaltered subsample are equal to the actual voteshares in that subsample.

Table 8.5 indicates that the high approval of President Putin affected the support for the United Russia to a very large extent. In the original four-party subsample, 72% of the votes went to that party. If the approval for Putin uniformly decreased to 0.5 (equivalent to a "don't know" answer to the question whether the respondent approved of Putin), the support for the United Russia would decline to 61%. If everyone completely disapproved of Putin, United Russia would receive only 43% of the vote that went to the four parties, or only 27.2% of the popular vote, if we assume that the share of the abstaining or undecided voters, as well as the vote share of the small parties, remained constant. The main beneficiaries of the decrease in approval would be the Communist party and LDPR, with more modest gains by SR.

Thus this work corroborates what have been common knowledge: the popularity of United Russia was due to the high approval rating of Vladimir Putin, and to the party's perceived connection to the popular president.

The respondents who supported parties other than the United Russia also had lower internal efficacy scores. One can see that an increase in one's efficacy score will increase the probability of supporting United Russia, at the expense of all other parties for the four-party model, where all three efficacy terms are negative and significant. For the seven-party model, the efficacy terms for the three small parties were not significant.

Education was found to have no effect on the political preferences of the voters. For all models, the education terms were individually insignificant, with the exception for SPS, where it was significant at the 10% level. Education was the only significant individual nonpolicy factor found to affect the voter's latent utility for SPS. A voter with a higher education is more likely to support SPS, at the expense of all other parties.

For the four-party model, the income effect is significant only for the LDPR. A voter with a higher income will be more likely to support LDPR. The effect is quite large in magnitude. An increase in self-reported income by one level (from "medium" to "high", for example) will have approximately the same effect on the voter's likelihood to support LDPR as a change in approval from maximum to minimum. For the seven-party model, it was shown that income also had a positive effect on the preference for the Agrarian party.

Gender was the one of the most important factors that affected party preferences. Out of 67 LDPR supporters in the sample, 55 were males. The United Russia had slightly more female supporters (414 out of 726), while the Communist party and the SR has an equal number of male and female supporters. When controlling for all other factors, male voters are more likely to support the Communist Party and especially LDPR at the expense of the SR and the United Russia. For the extended dataset including the supporters of the three small partues, female voters were more likely to support Yabloko and equally likely to support either SPS or the Agrarian party.

Age was also found to have a significant effect for almost all parties. The effect (relative to the United Russia) was largest for the CPRF. Indeed, the average age of CPRF supporters was 59.0 This finding suggests that the factors that make CPRF more popular among the older population are not captured by either ideological preferences, the approval of government, or indernal efficacy. The high age of CPRF supporters also explains the gender bias: in 2006, the average life expectancy of Russian males was only 60.3 years compared for 73.2 years for females. The age effect for the SR was similar (with the average age of the supporters being 54.9 years). For LDPR, the age effect was negative and significant; at the average age of 36.8 the LDPR electorate was the youngest from among the seven parties in the large sample. The age effect for SPS was positive and marginally significant.

The final sociodemographic factor was whether the respondent lived in a rural or urban area. There were no rural residents among Yabloko supporters and only one among the SPS. The proportion of rural residents among the CPRF, United Russia, SR supporters, and the general population, was almost equal (30%, 28.5%, 29.5%, and 30%, respectively). As a result, rural coefficients for neither CPRF or SR were significant. This corroborates the claim that the Communist Party lost the support of rural voters (Wegren and Konitzer, 2006). The only party to have a significantly smaller proportion of rural voters was the LDPR (23.8%).

Tables 8.6 and 8.7 examine the effects of ideology on the voter's probability of supporting each of the four major parties for the four-party model. The analysis suggests that poorly educated, low-income, young females who approve of the federal government and have centrist ideology, are most likely to support United Russia, with probability 96% according to the model. The most likely supporters of LDPR are young urban men with above average income, who disapprove of the government, have low efficacy scores, profess liberal economic ideology and are dissatisfied. The most likely supporters of CPRF and SR are dissatisfied elderly males with below-average income who disapprove of the government, have low efficacy scores, and have anti-market economic views. A voter belonging to this group is expected to support CPRF with probbility of 48% and SR with probability 22%.

There are two remarks with respect to the model's capacity to predict individual votes. First, most types of voters are expected to support the pro-Kremlin United Russia with a large probability. For various sociodemographic profiles with neutral ideology, the figure is above 22% and usually is much higher. For the other three parties, the voting probabilities are usually below 10% for most voter profiles. This auguments the claim that the voters have a strong pro-United Russia bias that is not accounted for by ideological and non-ideological voter characteristics measured in the survey. The source of this bias is the most likely the mass media.

The second thing to note is the model's poor ability to differentiate between CPRF and SR votes. The ratio of probabilities of voting for the two parties is relatively constant across the voter profiles, since the model coefficients are approximately equal for the two parties, and the supporters of the two parties have similar ideology.

8.1.5   Discussion

A number of other model specifications were also tried. A first hypothesis was that certain factors — such as the willingness to discuss politics, education, or internal efficacy — can affect the importance of ideology in an individual's evaluation of a political party. The importance of ideology was found to be unaffected by any of these variables, in contrast to some earlier studies.[433]

A second hypothesis is that regional economic conditions affect the vote.[434] The survey did not contain questions on retrospective self-evaluation of economic conditions, either in the short or long term. As a substitute, ttwo measures of actual economic conditions were used: the absolute level of mean disposable income, and the percentage change in that level from 2000 to 2006. There were two statistically significant effects. First, the support for the Communist party was higher in the regions with lower economic growth. Second, the support for Just Russia was higher in the regions with the higher absolute income. However, the magnitude of either effect was small compared to the effects of either approval or internal efficacy.

A third hypothesis is that ideological preferences affect voter abstention. There are two testable theories of voter abstention due to ideology. First is voter indifference: A voter will support any one party only if he likes the party significantly more than all other parties. The second theory is voter alienation: A voter will support a party only if it offers a payoff that is above certain minimum level.[435] There was no support for either theory. The ideological preferences of the abstaining respondents are located in the center of the ideology space and occupy roughly the same position as the United Russia supporters. This is inconsistent with either voter indifference (the abstaining voters should occupy the ideological gaps between the positions of the political parties), or alienation (the abstaining voters must have positions far away from those of all parties). Instead, several of the individual nonideological factors are highly correlated with abstention. The most important of these are approval and efficacy. Out of 284 respondents who indicated that they would not vote, 104 (or 37%) do not approve of any federal institution, including the President. The corresponding figure for the whole sample is 23% (376 out of 1588). Approval for Putin and for the cabinet of ministers are the most important factors. For the efficacy scores, the difference is similar, with 64% and 43% of the respondents having the internal efficacy score of zero. Testing a multinomial logit model with abstention as one of the options, showed that abstaining voters tend to be of higher self-reported income, have lower education, be younger, and are less likely to live in the rural area. Gender is the only factor that is found not to affect the likelihood of turnout.

There were several reasons why only two ideological factors were used. First, the eigenvalues for the first two factors were much higher than for the other factors. Second, it was not possible to give a transparent interpretation to the minor factors. Finally, the inclusion of additional factors did not improve the fit of the model. (In the four-party case, the log likelihood was 768.5 for zero factors, 759.9 for one factor, 721 for two

---

[433] Zakharov and Fantazzini (2008) found that education significantly increased the weight of ideology for UK and Netherlands; similarly, Hellwig (2008) in his study of European workers found that the importance of left-right policy dimension depends on the sector of individual's employment.

[434] See Owen and Tucker (2008) for economic voting in Poland.

[435] Indifference and alienation were first suggested as a possible explanation of abstention by Hinich, Ledyard, and Ordeshook (1972). Positive empirical evidence for abstention due to indifference and alienation can be found, for example, in Adams, Dow and Merrill (2007). See also Zakharov (2008a,b).

factors, 714.1 for three factors, and 711.8 for four factors.)

The work does not control for several other factors that affected voter preferences. Most importantly, the parties' access to local mass media outlets, and the degree to which the law is selectively applied in favor of United Russia. There is variation across regions in parties' access to local mass media outlets, and in the degree to which the law is selectively applied in favor of United Russia.

However, this consideration does not alter this key message of this work. Certainly, neither media bias not vote-rigging (Myagkov, Ordeshook, Shakin, 2005) can be over-looked as factors that contributed to the success of United Russia in the December, 2007 election.[436] However, this work shows that the principal role in the election was the high approval rating of President Putin. Although this work does not examine the origins of Putin's popularity, most accounts, scholarly or not, suggest that the country' economic performance was its primary source.

8.1.6   Appendix to Section 8.1.

Appendix A: Question wording

Age. What is your age in full years?

Education. "What is your education? 1 — Primary education or below, 2 — Incomplete secondary education, 3 — Secondary education, 4 — Vocational school, 5 — Less than 4 years of higher education, 6 — 4 or more years of higher education." Those who responded "Don't know" were assigned the value of 3.5.

The variable education was obtained as follows: (response-1)×0.2

Income. "To which income group does your family belong? 1 — Cannot afford to buy food, 2 — Can afford food but cannot afford clothing, 3 — Can afford alothing but not durable goods, 4 — Can afford all durable goods but cannot afford real estate, 5 — Can afford real estate." For the variable income, those who responded "Don't know" were assigned the value of 3.

The variable income was obtained as follows: (response-1)×0.25

Approval. "Do you approve of A. President, B. Prime Minister, C. Government, D. State Duma, E. Federation council." Each question was coded as follows: "1 — Yes, 2 — No, 1.5 — Can't answer."

Each of the approval variables was obtained as follows: 2 – response.

Size of township. "Where do you live? 1 — Moscow or St. Petersburg, 2 — City over 1 mln., 3 — 500 thousand to 1 mln., 5 — 100 thousand to 500 thousand, 6 — 50 thousand to 100 thousand, 7 — urban-type settlement, 8 — village."

The variable is_village was generated by assigning the value of 1 for "8 — vil-

---

[436]See *The Guardian* Dec. 4, 2007.
    <http://www.guardian.co.uk/world/2007/dec/04/russia.lukeharding>

lage" and 0 otherwise.

Ideological attitude. There were two questions: "Please say if you feel positively (negatively) to each of the following concepts." For each question, a list of 40 words was given (see Table 8.3).

Internal efficacy. "Do you think that the ordinary voters like you have a say in who will be in power in the future, and on the country's future policies? 1 — Yes, a lot depends on the regular voters, 2 — A few things depend on the voters, 3 — Nothing depends on the voters, all main decisions will be made without their concent". The "can't answer" response was coded as 2. The variable efficacy was generated as 1.5 − 0.5×response.

Appendix B: Tables

Table 8.1: Approval of various federal institutions (percent of the sample).

	President	Government	Prime Minister	State Duma
0 (disapprove)	12.72	42.54	29.88	54.24
0.5 (don't know)	8.55	21.66	26.48	22.49
1 (approve)	78.73	35.80	43.64	23.26

Table 8.2: Factor averages across the supporters of each party.

Party	Sample	Vote	Fact 1	Fact 2
Agrarian Party (AGR)	0.63	1.47	-0.16	-0.92
United Russia (ER)	45.72	40.96	0.05	0.30
Communist Party (CPRF)	7.12	7.37	-0.76	-1.59
Liberal Democrats(LDPR)	4.22	5.13	-0.53	0.69
Patriots of Russia	0.25	0.57	0.22	-0.10
Fair Russia (SR)	6.17	4.93	-0.60	-0.87
Civilian Power (Free Russia)	0.69	0.67	-0.43	0.31
Union of Right Forces (SPS)	0.57	0.61	-0.47	1.14
Yabloko	0.76	1.01	-0.56	0.20
Russian Republican Party	0.25		-0.16	1.36
Democratic Party of Russia	0.19	0.08	-0.25	0.75
"Will not vote"	17.88		0.23	-0.06
"Can't answer"	14.92		0.43	-0.04
Did not vote		36.3		

Table 8.3: The frequency of positive and negative responses and factor loadings.

	Concept	Percent pos.	Percent neg.	Fact. 1	Fact. 2
01	Nation	0.21	0.08	0.11	-0.08
02	Order	0.57	0.01	-0.18	0.01
03	Freedom	0.37	0.03	-0.13	0.20
04	Market	0.10	0.15	0.26	0.08
05	Russians	0.34	0.02	-0.15	0.03
06	West	0.02	0.23	0.21	0.10
07	Socialism	0.11	0.11	-0.13	-0.28
08	Communism	0.07	0.19	0.05	-0.32
09	Democracy	0.15	0.09	0.11	0.07
10	Tradition	0.29	0.01	-0.06	-0.04
11	Patriotims	0.34	0.01	-0.14	-0.15
12	State	0.26	0.03	-0.17	-0.03
13	Competitiveness	0.05	0.07	0.07	0.12
14	Sovereignty	0.07	0.05	-0.08	0.01
15	Elite	0.02	0.41	0.30	0.04
16	Party	0.02	0.16	0.04	-0.14
17	Power	0.09	0.18	0.26	-0.09
18	Justice	0.49	0.02	-0.30	0.02
19	Opposition	0.01	0.17	0.12	-0.06
20	Business	0.07	0.13	0.17	0.27
21	USSR	0.12	0.08	-0.01	-0.34
22	Church	0.21	0.02	-0.13	-0.01
23	Revolution	0.01	0.22	0.13	-0.26
24	Property	0.14	0.04	0.13	0.14
25	Success	0.31	0.00	-0.16	0.21
26	Liberalism	0.01	0.14	0.15	-0.01
27	Reform	0.06	0.14	0.23	-0.02
28	Stability	0.38	0.00	-0.16	0.00
29	Labor	0.31	0.00	-0.26	-0.08
30	Individualism	0.02	0.12	0.05	0.10
31	Non-Russians	0.02	0.29	0.25	-0.12
32	Equality	0.18	0.02	-0.18	-0.06
33	Collectivism	0.06	0.09	0.02	-0.22
34	Morality	0.22	0.03	-0.05	-0.07
35	Human rignts	0.32	0.02	-0.15	0.12
36	Wealth	0.12	0.01	0.15	0.25
37	Russia	0.28	0.00	-0.03	0.07
38	Well-being	0.37	0.01	-0.11	0.25
39	Progress	0.21	0.01	-0.03	0.27
40	Capitalism	0.15	0.02	-0.09	0.22

Table 8.4: Estimation of the four-party MNL model 1. ER is the base outcome.

	Parameters	Est.	Std. Err.	t	Prob
β_1	coefficient	0.154	0.034	-4.44	0.000
β_2	coeefficient	0.150	0.020	-7.43	0.000
CPRF	education	0.409	0.507	0.81	0.420
	income	0.490	0.784	0.63	0.532
	age	0.046	0.008	5.53	0.000
	is_village	-0.179	0.274	-0.65	0.513
	gender	-0.617	0.251	-2.46	0.014
	efficacy	-0.754	0.374	-2.02	0.044
	approve_putin	-2.051	0.389	-5.27	0.000
	approve_pm	0.246	0.387	0.64	0.524
	approve_gov	-0.194	0.389	-0.50	0.617
	approve_duma	-0.205	0.473	-0.43	0.664
	approve_sf	-0.406	0.509	-0.80	0.426
	valence λ	-0.057	0.697	-0.08	0.934
LDPR	education	0.084	0.610	0.14	0.890
	income	2.650	0.886	2.99	0.003
	age	-0.021	0.009	-2.19	0.029
	is_village	-0.526	0.333	-1.58	0.114
	gender	-1.899	0.344	-5.51	0.000
	efficacy	-0.531	0.424	-1.25	0.211
	approve_putin	-2.047	0.460	-4.45	0.000
	approve_pm	0.195	0.483	0.40	0.686
	approve_gov	-0.094	0.496	-0.19	0.849
	approve_duma	0.830	0.537	1.54	0.123
	approve_sf	-0.711	0.607	-1.17	0.242
	valence λ	-1.296	0.806	-1.61	0.108
SR	education	0.519	0.482	1.08	0.282
	income	0.152	0.758	0.20	0.841
	age	0.037	0.007	4.95	0.000
	is_village	-0.135	0.261	-0.52	0.604
	gender	-0.328	0.238	-1.38	0.168
	efficacy	-0.523	0.348	-1.50	0.133
	approve_putin	-1.064	0.441	-2.41	0.016
	approve_pm	0.511	0.359	1.42	0.155
	approve_gov	-0.387	0.350	-1.10	0.270
	approve_duma	-1.059	0.389	-2.72	0.007
	approve_sf	0.639	0.411	1.55	0.120
	valence λ	-1.193	0.705	-1.69	0.091
	n	1004			
	Log-likelihood	-694.2			

Table 8.5: Predicted voteshares in the four-party subsample — original sample and the altered zero-approval sample.

	ER	CPRF	LDPR	SR
Original sample	0.723	0.112	0.066	0.097
Neutral Putin approval	0.609	0.163	0.112	0.116
Zero Putin approval	0.430	0.253	0.194	0.121

Table 8.6: Predicted probabilities of voting depending on the ideological preferences, according to model 1. Female voter, income, education, approval, is_village, age, and efficacy are set at mean values.

Fact 1	Fact 1	ER	CPRF	LDPR	SR
0	0	0.861	0.042	0.019	0.076
+3.4	0	0.924	0.020	0.011	0.043
−3.4	0	0.758	0.082	0.030	0.128
0	+3.4	0.936	0.006	0.031	0.025
0	−3.4	0.609	0.202	0.009	0.178

Table 8.7: Predicted probabilities of voting depending on the ideological preferences, according to the four-party model 1. Male voter, income, education, approval, is_village, age, and efficacy are set at mean values.

Fact1	Fact2	ER	CPRF	LDPR	SR
0	0	0.725	0.074	0.107	0.092
+3.4	0	0.835	0.038	0.069	0.056
-3.4	0	0.577	0.131	0.151	0.139
0	+3.4	0.784	0.011	0.173	0.030
0	−3.4	0.452	0.314	0.044	0.189

8.2 Voting Power and the Electoral College of the United States

Downs's book, *An Economic Theory of Democracy* (1957) sparked an extensive body of literature concerning the optimal strategy of candidates in two-candidate elections, with numerous variations, including the study of two-candidate elections with the threat of third candidate entry, elections with "negative voting," and so on.[437] However, there is still no literature concerning the effect of the electoral college in the United States on candidate strategy. The 2000 U.S. presidential election magnified the electoral college's peculiar transformation of individual votes into a solid state vote, of varying weight according to the state population. Al Gore took the popular vote, with 51,003,926 votes (48.38%) against the 50,460,110 (47.87%) for G.W. Bush, but Bush won the election, with 271 electoral votes, 5 more than Gore. Moreover, Ralph Nader took 2,883,105 votes and Patrick Buchanan 449,225. Bush's electoral victory depended on Florida which gave Bush 25 electoral votes as a result of a majority of less than 1000 votes out of over 5.8 million).

It is this transformation of individual votes into state votes, and the effect this process has on candidate strategy which is addressed in this section. Specifically, can the traditional median voter theorem model apply in the context of the electoral college, and if not, then what is the optimal positioning of candidates, and what model do we then use?

Many scholars have used the median voter theorem to predict electoral strategies in the past century.[438] The main thrust of the theorem is that given an election in which there are two candidates, the candidate with the more centrist policy, and thus the most attractive to the median voter, will garner the majority of the votes, and hence, win the election. As attractive and useful as this theorem can be, the reality is that it simply fails to accurately predict the outcome of presidential elections in the United States. The theorem predicts that for a candidate to be successful, he should assess all of the voters' preferences, look for the voter in the dead center of the voter distribution, and copy that voter's policy preferences. Aside from the obvious problem of accurately assessing every voter's policy preferences, we find that candidates with centrist policies do not necessarily win, and candidates with more extreme policies can sometimes find themselves in the oval office.

The purpose of this section is not to delve into all of the factors that may get votes for an extremist candidate, like personality or TV appearances, nor to discover the magic process by which a candidate could successfully discover the median voter's preferences. Rather, we shall specifically, address how the electoral college forces candidates to choose policies which are strategically noncentrist in order to win the U.S. presidential election. Further, we shall provide a way in which to model the disaffected voter, abstention and candidate strategy.

---

[437]This section was written by Lexi Shankster.
[438]See Black (1948) and Downs (1957) for a full formulation of the median voter theorem.

8.2.1   Individual Vote and State Vote

As just mentioned, the 2000 U.S. Presidential election was almost unique: one candidate won the majority of popular votes and the other won the majority of electoral votes (by five electoral votes). This anomaly is, in fact, not an anomaly to the mechanism of the electoral college, but rather, an anomaly to the popular vote. Historically, the electoral college has merely magnified the plurality by which a candidate won the popular vote.[439] However, when the popular election is as close as 2000's, the electoral college can "choose" the popular vote loser.

In simple terms, the electoral college forces candidates to attempt to maximize electoral votes rather than individual votes. In close elections, it is particularly crucial that candidates make this distinction between the two. For instance, Bush did not need to campaign in Washington D.C. to maximize his popular vote as there was no chance he would win their electoral votes. Rather, he needed to campaign in those states where the probability of winning the electoral vote outweighed the cost of garnering individual votes.[440]

Cost refers to the political and monetary costs of campaigning in states which have historically shown heavy partisan favoritism for the opponent's party. In other words, Bush would have needed to vastly change his platform, facing costs in terms of votes in other states, and spend a significant amount of campaign money in Washington D.C. to garner its three electoral votes. Obviously, this would not have been an optimal strategy to pursue.

To help visualize the distinction between individual votes and state votes we use a version of the model presented in Chapter 3 and construct a highly simplified model of the electoral college using two dimensions. The literature on spatial modelling has determined that the two dimensions which are necessary to accurately place candidates and voters in a spatial model in any given election are social and economic. Figure 81, adapts the model proposed in Chapter 3 and aggregates the individual votes into states. Thus, each state is represented by an elliptical distribution of voter "ideal points", centered about a state mean (or median voter).

The dimension, labeled "Social Issues" on Figure 8.2, depicts the candidates' and voters' positions on the relevant social issues, such as civil rights, and abortion, for example. Democrats are placed on the "north" of this dimension ; Republicans, on the "south. " The second, horizontal dimension, labeled "Economic Issues," depicts the candidates' and voters' positions on the relevant economic issues, such as tax reform or government spending, for example. Democrats are placed on the "left" of this dimension and Republicans on the right. Therefore, when the two dimensions are combined, the Democratic candidates will occupy the upper left quadrant, and Republicans, the

---

[439]Throughout this section, the term "plurality" refers to the difference between the number of votes the winning candidate garners and the number of votes garnered by the candidate placing second in the election.

[440]The term "state" refers to any area assigned electoral votes; in other words, Washington D.C., although not a state in the technical sense, is assigned three electoral votes and is therefore included in all of the analyses.

lower right.

The cleavage line represents the division between the Republicans and Democrats on both of these dimensions, and it is this line in Figure 8.1 that determines to which candidate a state's individual and electoral votes fall. In the figure, two states, comprised of five voters, and carrying an electoral vote of one, each choose the Republican candidate. One state, of five voters, with one electoral vote, chooses the Democratic candidate. Three states, however, split their votes; in each of these states, two voters chose the Republican candidate, and three, the Democratic. However, in all three of these states, the electoral vote fell to the Democratic candidate, as the candidate who wins the majority of individual votes in these states, wins the entire electoral vote of each state. Therefore, although the Republican candidate garnered 16 individual votes to the Democratic candidate's 14 individual votes, the Democratic candidate garnered two more electoral votes than the Republican, and thus won the election.

This figure provides an illustration of what occurred in the 2000 election, where Al Gore won the most individual votes (and, we assume represented the most voters), and yet George W. Bush was able to take the election because he won more states. We can deduce from the plurality by which Bush won Florida that the state mean was very close to the dividing line between Bush and Gore. The election was close in all of the swing states, but because the winner takes all Bush was able to win the election.

To further explore the implications of the winner-take-all characteristic of the electoral college, we now turn to a discussion of voter power.

8.2.2   The Electoral College and Voter Power

The idea of varying amounts of "voter power" is the belief that individuals in different states have different probabilities of affecting the outcome of the U.S. presidential election. For example, an individual in Florida, in the 2000 election, had a much greater chance of affecting the outcome of the presidential election than anyone else in the nation; that is, due to Florida's intense political competitiveness in the 2000 election, an individual voter in Florida was much more likely to cast the "tie-breaking" vote than an individual in, say, Washington D.C. Furthermore, should a voter in Florida cast the tie-breaking vote, he or she would send 25 electoral votes to the candidate of his/her choice. Clearly, then, the more politically competitive the state in which a voter lives, the more "voter power" he or she has. When calculating whether or not that voter's state will swing the entire election, we must then look at the number of electoral votes at stake in that state.

In an often-cited paper, Banzhaf (1968) attempted to explain voter power in the electoral college by proportionally relating voter power to the probability that a vote changes the outcome of an election within his district times the probability that his district will change the overall outcome.

Banzhaf ran a combinatorial analysis to determine how many times any given state's electoral votes would determine the outcome of the U.S. presidential election. Then, using Sterling's approximation (using the normal rather than the binomial distribution),

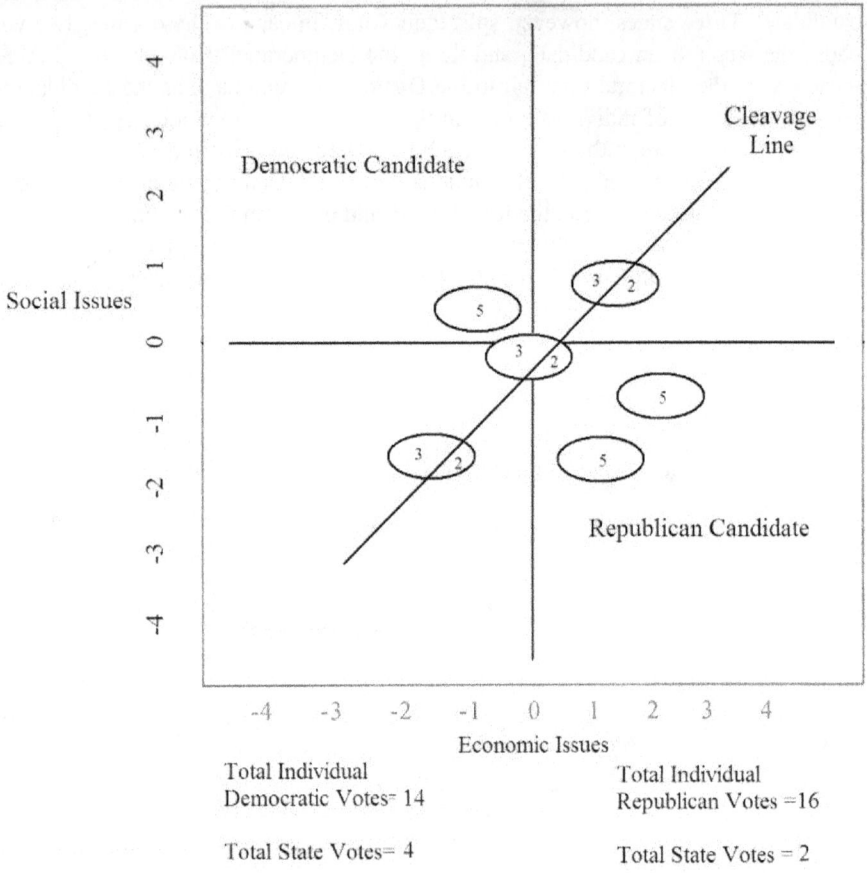

Figure 8.2: Individual and State votes

he calculated the probability that a tie would occur in any given state. This probability is approximately inversely proportional to the square root of $2\pi n_t$, where n_t is the population of state t. Then $\Pr(\text{tie in state } t) =$

$$\Pr(t) = \frac{1}{2\pi n_t} \qquad (8.1)$$

His method of computing voter power, then, was

$$\Pr*(t) = \Pr(t)C_t \qquad (8.2)$$

where C_t is the number of combinations in which state t is able to determine the outcome of a given election, and $\Pr(t)$ is the probability of a tie occurring in state t. Because C_t is directly proportional to the size of the state, and the probability of a tie decreases only by the square root of its size, the larger states will hold a distinct advantage over smaller states in this model.

As Margolis states, however, Banzhaf could only have arrived at (8.1) by treating "$\Pr(t)$ as proportional to the fraction of all possible combinations of voter choices that yield a tie" (Margolis, 1983: 322-323). The fallacy inherent in Banzhaf's claim is that he treats voting combinations like "coin tossing experiments."

> Since, a priori, all voting combinations are equally likely and therefore equally significant, the number of combinations in which each voter can change the outcome by changing his vote serves as the measure of his voting power (Banzhaf 1968: 307).

This statement is obviously false. All voting combinations are not equally likely, which is why Republicans may count on the support of voters in Utah, and Democrats on voters in Washington D.C. As Rabinowitz and MacDonald state in their paper on state power in the presidential election of 1986, "Based on the Shapley value, the Banzhaf formulation does not take into account the political competitiveness of the states" (Rabinowitz and MacDonald 1986: 77). This section develops this point and argues that the Banzhaf formulation fails because he treats the probability of a voter selecting one or the other candidate in all states exactly the same; that is, $\frac{1}{2}$. In fact, when Margolis made only slight changes to this probability, he found that the Banzhaf ratio disappears. Similarly, Rabinowitz and MacDonald explain that when slight alterations are made in this probability, the divisor (square root of n) may become inappropriate, rendering the Shapley value less than truly representative of voter power (Rabinowitz and MacDonald, 1986, p. 85). Therefore, it seems that a more accurate measure of voter power would take into account the plurality by which a candidate wins a particular state in a particular election, or more succinctly, the political competitiveness of a state.

A simple equation taking into account the variation in political competitiveness among states is found in Kallenbach (1960). Kallenbach's formula looks at the number of electoral votes in each state, along with the plurality by which a candidate wins an election in that state. His formula is thus

$$s_t = \frac{E_t V_t}{P_t} \tag{8.3}$$

where V_t is the total popular vote for all candidates in state t , P_t is the plurality of the winning candidate in state t, E_t is the number of electoral votes at stake in state t, and s_t is the definition of the resultant *state norm* of t. Therefore, we divide the total popular vote by the plurality by which a candidate won that state, and multiply that number by the number of electoral votes in that state. For example, to calculate Alabama's state norm, we take the total popular vote in Alabama, V_t =1,672,444 and divide that by the number of votes G.W. Bush garnered over Gore, P_t =247,085. In this example, $s_t = \frac{E_t V_t}{P_t} = 1,672,444/247,085 = 6.769$.

The number of electoral votes of Alabama is nine, so $s_t = 6.769 \times 9 = 60.925$.

In order to make state-by-state comparisons, we define S by summing all of the values of s_t, and dividing by the total number of electoral college votes $E = \Sigma E_t$ =538. Thus

$$S = \frac{1}{E}\Sigma s_t \tag{8.4}$$

The relative power of state t is then

$$S_t = \frac{1}{S}s_t \tag{8.5}$$

In the 2000 election, $S = \frac{1}{E}\Sigma s_t = 1,934,029.300/538) = 3,594.850$. Therefore, Alabama's relative voting power, computed using (8.4) is 60.925 /3,594.850 = .017. This figure represents the power of an individual voter in Alabama relative to national average voter power.

Another measure which may be used to make state-by-state comparisons can be obtained using average values in (8.1).

Let P_* be the average state plurality, E_* the average number of electoral votes at stake and V_* the average total popular vote , P is the average state plurality, E is the average number of electoral votes at stake, and T is the the average number of electoral votes at stake (E_*) multiplied by the average total popular vote per state (V_*) divided by the average plurality (P_*). That is,

$$T = \frac{E_* V_*}{P_*} \tag{8.6}$$

The second measure of relative voting power , or RVP, of a state is

$$T_t = \frac{1}{T}s_t \tag{8.7}$$

In the 2000 election, T= (2,028,574.451 /237,341.471) $\times$ 10.549 = 90.163.

Again using Alabama as the example, an individual in Alabama has a relative voting power of 60.925 /90.163 = 0.676 (from 8.7). This figure also represents the power of an individual voter in Alabama relative to average national voter power. The difference between the two measures of voter power in Alabama arises from the difference between the two variations in calculating national average voter power.

Some of the usefulness of this analysis is that, unlike the Shapley value (which Banzhaf used), it does not require that only two candidates compete. Therefore, we may use these equations to examine relative voting power in the 2000 election, taking into account all of the candidates that garnered any voters. Table 8.8 lists all of the states, the total number of popular votes of each state, the state norm as well as the two measures of relative voting power.

Table 8.8 Voting Power in the 2000 U.S.Election

State	Total Popular Vote for All Candidates	Plurality of Winning Candidate	Electoral Votes	State Norm	Relative Voting Power (S_t)	Relative Voting Power (T_t)
Alabama	1672444	247085	9	60.925	0.017	0.6757
Alaska	230667	71816	3	9.636	0.003	0.107
Arizona	1405311	79382	8	141.625	0.039	1.571
Arkansas	926938	51696	6	107.583	0.03	1.193
California	10679577	1283638	54	449.268	0.125	4.983
Colorado	1740842	145577	8	95.666	0.027	1.061
Connecticut	1419741	249907	8	45.449	0.013	0.504
Delaware	327870	43557	3	22.582	0.006	0.25
Florida	59574234	930	25	160146.8	44.549	1776.191
Georgia	2574234	305330	13	109.603	0.03	1.216
Hawaii	367799	67424	4	21.82	0.006	0.242
Idaho	488472	197945	4	9.871	0.003	0.109
Illinois	4741748	569628	22	183.134	0.051	2.031
Indiana	2176362	342536	12	76.244	0.021	0.846
Iowa	1313899	4130	7	2226.947	0.619	24.7
Kansas	1059729	223962	6	28.39	0.008	0.315
Kentucky	1540667	232428	8	53.029	0.015	0.588
Louisiana	1759809	134833	9	117.466	0.033	1.303
Maine	646783	31385	4	82.432	0.023	0.914
Mass.	2691107	733269	12	44.04	0.001	0.488
Maryland	1925256	322433	10	59.71	0.017	0.662
Michigan	4192375	194621	18	387.742	0.108	4.3
Minnesota	2438297	57900	10	421.122	0.117	4.671
Mississippi	966047	148581	7	45.513	0.013	0.505
Missouri	2355142	78695	11	329.202	0.092	3.651
Montana	410798	102491	3	12.024	0.003	0.133
Nebraska	653732	193103	5	16.927	0.005	0.188
Nevada	608899	21590	4	112.811	0.031	1.251
New Hamp.	566796	7282	4	311.341	0.087	3.453
New Jersey	3110721	493654	15	94.521	0.026	1.048
New Mexico	598605	366	5	8177.664	2.274	90.7
New York	6301201	1531833	33	135.746	0.038	1.506
N. Carolina	2865214	370517	14	108.262	0.03	1.201
N. Dakota	289875	79272	3	10.942	0.003	0.121
Ohio	4569961	176426	21	543.963	0.151	6.033
Oklahoma	1234277	270009	8	36.57	0.01	0.406
Oregon	1528292	6460	7	1656.044	0.461	18.367

State	Total Popular Vote for All Candidates	Plurality of Winning Candidate	Electoral Votes	State Norm	Relative Voting Power (S_t)	Relative Voting Power (T_t)
Pennsylvania	4875969	201103	23	557.661	0.155	6.185
Rhode Island	160062	121965	4	5.249	0.001	0.058
S. Carolina	1415430	226683	8	49.953	0.014	0.554
S. Dakota	316023	71765	3	13.211	0.004	0.147
Tennessee	2064135	78691	11	288.54	0.08	3.2
Texas	6399487	1367521	32	149.748	0.042	1.661
Utah	765845	310434	5	12.335	0.003	0.137
Vermont	290559	28893	3	30.169	0.008	0.335
Virginia	2734518	210560	13	168.829	0.047	1.872
Washington	2468809	138681	11	195.823	0.054	2.172
Wash. D.C.	189590	144984	3	3.92	0.001	0.044
W. Virginia	636617	38620	5	82.421	0.023	0.914
Wisconsin	2589881	5396	11	5276.594	1.479	58.556
Wyoming	213426	87253	3	7.338	0.002	0.081

It is clear from Table 8.9 that it is in those states in which candidates win by a small plurality that voters have the most power. An interesting result of this analysis is that voters in the smaller states can have much more voter power than those in larger states if they are more politically competitive, in the sense of a small winning plurality For instance, voters in New Mexico, a state with only five electoral votes, had roughly eighteen times as much power as voters in California, a state with fifty-four electoral votes. It is important, then, that we look not only at state size for attractiveness to candidates, but also the political dynamic within the state to determine just how much a vote is "worth." Even though Florida was clearly the outlier in this election, diminishing the worth of a vote in every other state across the board, the effect of Florida's unusually large voter power in this last election only serves to exemplify the point: A high degree of political competitiveness combined with a large number of electoral votes is extremely politically powerful.

When constructing models, it is important that the axioms of the model hold in the real world, or the model loses much of its power. In this case, it means that since the possibility of a tie in any state is not 0.5, we cannot state that voters in New York necessarily have an advantage over voters in smaller states, such as New Mexico, nor can assume that the median voter of the nation is the most attractive voter to candidates. In fact, it appears that a vote in New York was worth, at most, one and a half times as much as a vote anywhere else in the nation, worth less than two percent of a vote in New Mexico, and less than a tenth of one percent of a vote in Florida. Therefore, we should expect that those states in which heavy partisan favoritism has consistently been shown, there will be a much lower probability of a tie vote than in those which have historically been labeled as "swing states." It is in these swing states that true voter power lies, and Florida had the most powerful combination: a large number of electoral votes and an extremely high degree of political competitiveness. Of course, the weakness of the Kallenbach model lies in its inability to predict which state will be the most important in future elections; however, we may still predict that those states which have historically shown a high degree of political competitiveness will be disproportionately important to candidates in current and future elections.

8.2.3   Representing electoral competition

We can position the states along a political spectrum, finding their position on the spectrum by first noting which candidate won that particular state (states won by the Democratic candidate lie to the left of the spectrum, and states won by the Republican candidate lie to the right of the spectrum).

For each state, divide the plurality of the winning candidate, P_t, by the total number of popular votes, V_t, cast in the state, and define

$$x_t = \frac{P_t}{V_t} \tag{8.8}$$

Then x_t is the distance of state t from the "center space" along the spectrum.

Mapping this information onto a spectrum is rather easy: We may now view the states' positions along this spectrum as their positions are determined by the political competitiveness of each state, which is determined by the plurality of the winning candidate divided by the total popular vote. To use Alabama as an example again, we would determine its position by dividing the number of votes by which G.W. Bush won the popular vote (247,085) by the total popular vote (1,672,444), so $\frac{P_t}{V_t}$ = (247,085) / (1,672,444) = x_t =0.1477.

The number of electoral votes the state holds determines the height, or weight, of the state. Thus, Figure 8.3 displays the political distribution of states (and hence, votes) in the 2000 election.

This model, which takes into account both political competitiveness and number of electoral votes, does extremely well, post facto, as a way of determining whose vote was "worth" the most. However, for a model to be truly appealing, it must also hold some degree of predictive power. Therefore, in an attempt to display the degree of political competitiveness among the states, Table 8.2, in the Appendix to this chapter, depicts the political positioning of the 51 states in elections dating back to 1968.

States with potential to swing (which we can call LPS states), such as New Hampshire, tend to choose a specific party in elections, though the entrance of a strong third candidate (such as Perot in the 1992 and 1996 elections), or an extremely weak candidate from the state's historically favored party, may "swing" the state to the opposition. In other words, though voters in the LPS states may not punish a candidate for straying too far from traditional party stances by voting for his opponent, the movement away from these stances may create a pool of "negative voters;" that is, it may create a pool of disaffected voters who abstain, or allow for entry of a third candidate, thus increasing the probability of losing the state. In the 1992 presidential election, this occurred to some extent with the entry of Ross Perot. In 1992, Perot took 18.9% of the popular vote which, in turn, gave many Republican LPS states, such as Kentucky, Louisiana, Montana, Nevada, and New Hampshire to Clinton.

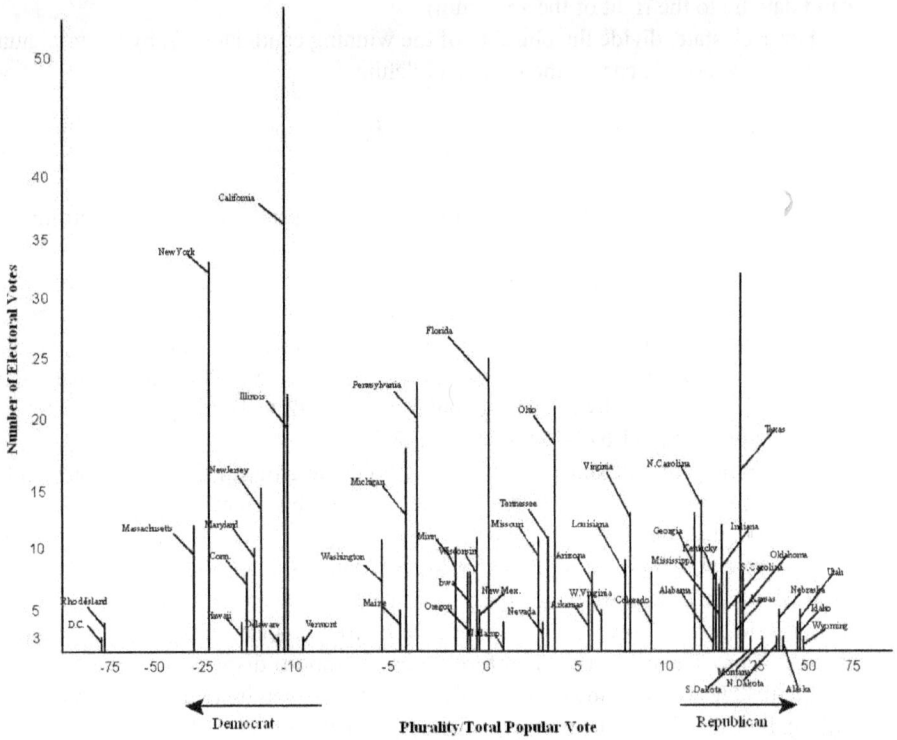

Figure 8.3: State positioning in the 2000 U.S.Presidential Election

Landslide elections have the effect of pulling the spectrum in the direction of the winning candidate so that all swing states become the winning candidate's states, and his opponent's LPS states also either become his, or he loses them by a an extremely small plurality. The extremely loyal states may slightly shift their positions, moving closer to the winning candidate, but will remain loyal to their party. For instance, in 1972, a landslide election in Richard Nixon's favor, Nixon took 520 electoral votes to McGovern's 17 (Leip, 2002). All of the swing states went to Nixon; Minnesota, a Democratic LPS state, went to Nixon, as did New York. Washington D.C., however, an extremely loyal Democratic state remained Democratic, with a political positioning of –56.54.

The analysis above is given in an attempt to gain insight into the political dynamic in states so that predictions about future elections and more accurate statements of voter power may be made. Of course, however, there is no method that would allow absolutely precise and accurate long-term forecasting as both demographics and the importance placed on ideological dimensions in the states change over time. For instance, the Southern states rather consistently voted Democratic in elections until the emergence of civil rights issues in the 1960's. The prominence of these issues eventually turned many of the Southern states, including Alabama, Mississippi, and Louisiana into loyal Republican states. However, excepting major changes in ideology, in the 2008 election, we may expect Washington D.C. to once again fall to the Democratic candidate, and Utah to once again vote Republican. Therefore, we may make fair predictions about optimal positioning of candidates and optimal expenditure of campaign moneys in future elections based on the historical positioning of the states. For instance, one may look at Table 8.2 and confidently assert that Rhode Island will vote for the Democratic Party in the 2008 election, and Wyoming, Idaho, Utah and Alaska will vote for the Republican Party. Excepting a landslide election, Iowa, Missouri, Minnesota, Ohio, Oregon, Michigan, New Mexico, Pennsylvania, Tennessee, Washington and Wisconsin will display continued political competitiveness.

8.2.4   Strategy in the Context of the Electoral College

In the 2000 election, it was essential that a candidate not only retain his party-loyal states, but also be politically attractive enough to win the swing states. Was it merely Gore's neglect of states supposedly "in-the-bag," such as Tennessee, that cost him the election? Or did Bush do a better job at balancing policies geared towards LPS states and those towards the swing states? Though we can confidently assert at this point that a vote in Florida was worth much, much more than a vote anywhere else, Bush would have lost the election had he geared his policies only to the swing voters in Florida. Therefore, it is essential that we see all of the states as individual actors, each with differing power, but all holding some power over at least one of the candidates:"at least one" because extremely loyal states do not necessarily hold much appeal for the candidate to whom support is not likely. For instance, instead of concentrating on Kansas or Nebraska, a Democratic candidate would be wiser to craft his policies based on the preferences of the voters in his LPS states (Minnesota, Maryland, etc.) and those of voters in the swing states, (New Mexico, Florida, Iowa and Wisconsin). Furthermore, the candidate is not necessarily restricted to the median position of those states.

Additionally, in "real-world" politics, we observe that candidates do not have enough flexibility in terms of party and financial support to adjust their positions so that they are able to "win away" loyal states from the opponent. Rather, there is a region of acceptability within which candidates may adjust their platforms in an effort to attract votes in the politically competitive states. Therefore, a strategically competitive candidate should observe the political spectrum and truncate the spectrum so that his new map includes only his loyal states, LPS states, and the swing states. On this new, truncated spectrum, the candidate should position himself so that he maximizes state share, activist support, and attraction to individual swing voters in the competitive states.

Again, presidential candidates do not want to choose the median voter's policies, as this would, in reality, be an arbitrary choice. Rather, he wants to choose policies which will allow him to win his loyal states. In the 2000 election, Bush needed to situate himself so that he won Florida, while maintaining Indiana, for example. It is important that when attempting to choose those policies which will garner a candidate the swing states, he not alienate voters in the LPS states by straying too far from partisan stands on core issues. For Republicans, this might mean preserving traditional stances on land tax and gun control; for Democrats, civil rights issues and the environment. The key argument is that a candidate must pick his battles, so to speak. It would have been a gross misjudgment for Bush to campaign hard on the environment, as Gore (or Nader) had already secured those votes (or states).

Furthermore, Bush would have alienated those states for which environmental protection is considered a threat, such as Alaska. Instead, a winning constellation is one that takes loyal states' strongest preferences into consideration and then maneuvers around them in order to garner the bare majority of votes in the swing states. Additionally, though the entrance of a third candidate into the U.S. presidential election does not necessarily enter the candidates into a chaotic cycle, it will force candidates to pick new policy constellations (or at least slightly alter their existing ones) in order to maximize their share of states.

8.2.5   Concluding Remarks

The notion of equilibrium in the traditional median voter theorem is that both candidates will converge to the center because neither candidate can do better given his opponent's position. However, both candidates can do better by moving away from the center and attracting the "disaffected" voters, party support from activists, and perhaps even winning the swing states by garnering votes from the more extreme voters in those politically competitive states. For even though Florida lies in the center of the political spectrum, it is not a politically neutral state; rather, it is extremely politically competitive, with voters almost evenly divided between the two parties.

The median voter theorem is still a highly useful tool, for very simple situations;

however, the U.S. presidential election process is anything but simple. Varying voter power due to the winner-take-all aspect of the electoral college gives rise to significantly different strategies than would be suggested by the traditional median voter theorem. Though the median voters in the swing states still hold some power in any given election, the median voter of the nation holds little value for candidates.

The implications of these results for the electoral college and representation in the United States are substantial, for policies directed at the national median voter will greatly differ from the policies candidates will attempt to pursue in the context of the electoral college. As we saw in this most recent election, an arguably noncentrist candidate won the election by strategically appealing to voters in both his loyal states, and the key swing state, Florida. It remains a normative question as to whether we should maintain the electoral college, as presently structured, or if it allows for the greatest representation of the people or merely selective representation of those states forming a winning combination. But it is entirely clear that the target in the presidential election is not the national median voter as the traditional median voter theorem suggests.

Table 8.9. Positioning of States in U.S.Elections

State	1968	1972	1976	1980	1984	1988	1992	1996	2000
Alabama	47.13	46389	-13.11	1.3	22.26	19.3	6.77	6.97	14.77
Alaska	2.64	23.51	22.25	27.94	36.79	21.21	9.17	17.53	31.13
Arizona	19.76	31.26	16.57	32.36	33.88	14.18	1.95	-2.22	5.65
Arkansas	*8.10	38.18	-30.06	0.61	22.18	23.32	-17.72	-11.02	5.58
California	3.08	13.46	1.78	16.77	16.25	3.57	-13.39	-12.89	-12.02
Colorado	9.14	28.01	11.47	24	28.32	7.78	-4.34	1.37	8.36
Connecticut	-5.16	18.44	-5.17	9.63	21.9	5.1	-6.44	-18.14	-17.6
Delaware	3.51	20.41	-5.41	2.33	19.85	12.4	-8.2	-15.25	-13.28
Florida	9.6	44.12	-5.28	17.02	30.66	22.36	1.89	-5.7	0
Georgia	*12.43	50.39	-33.78	-14.83	20.39	20.25	-0.59	1.17	11.86
Hawaii	-21.15	24.96	-2.53	-1.9	11.28	-9.52	-11.4	-25.29	-18.33
Idaho	26.13	38.2	22.55	41.27	45.97	26.07	13.61	18.54	40.52
Illinois	2.92	18.52	1.97	7.93	8.25	2.08	-14.24	-17.51	-12.01
Indiana	12.3	32.77	7.62	18.35	23.99	20.16	6.11	5.59	15.74
Iowa	12.19	17.13	1.01	12.7	7.39	-10.22	-6.01	-10.34	-0.31
Kansas	20.13	38.15	7.55	24.56	33.67	13.23	5.14	18.21	21.13
Kentucky	6.14	28.6	-7.19	1.38	20.61	11.64	-3.21	-0.96	15.09
Louisiana	*20.11	36.97	-5.78	5.45	22.6	10.21	-4.61	-12.07	7.66
Maine	-12.23	22.99	0.84	3.36	22.05	11.45	-8.38	-20.86	-4.85
Maryland	-1.64	23.9	-6.04	-2.96	18.99	2.91	-14.18	-15.99	-16.75
Mass.	-30.12	-8.97	-15.67	0.15	-0.18	-7.85	-18.52	-33.38	-27.25
Michigan	-6.73	14.39	5.39	6.49	5.49	7.9	-7.4	-13.21	-4.64
Minnesota	-12.53	5.51	-12.87	-3.94	2.79	-7.02	-11.63	-16.15	-2.37
Mississippi	*40.44	58.57	-1.88	1.32	24.26	20.82	8.92	5.13	15.38
Missouri	1.13	24.53	-3.63	6.81	20.05	3.98	-10.15	-6.3	3.34
Montana	9.01	20.08	7.44	24.39	22.3	5.87	-2.51	2.88	24.95
Nebraska	28.01	41	20.74	39.53	41.74	20.96	17.19	18.7	29.54
Nevada	8.16	27.36	4.36	33.81	33.88	20.94	-3.44	1.02	3.55
New Hamp.	8.18	29.12	11.28	29.39	37.69	26.12	-1.22	-10	1.28
New Jersey	2.13	24.8	2.16	13.42	20.89	13.64	-2.37	-17.86	-15.87
New Mexico	12.1	24.47	2.45	18.18	20.48	4.96	-8.56	-7.33	-0.06
New York	-5.46	17.33	-4.42	2.67	8.01	-4.1	-18.44	-28.31	-24.31
N. Carolina	8.25	40.58	-11.04	37.66	24	16.26	0.79	4.69	12.93
N. Dakota	17.71	26.28	5.85	38.03	31.04	13.06	12.03	6.81	27.42
Ohio	2.28	21.56	-0.27	10.6	18.76	10.85	-1.83	-6.36	3.86
Oklahoma	15.7	49.7	1.21	25.53	37.94	16.55	8.62	7.81	21.88
Oregon	6.05	10.12	0.17	9.66	12.17	-4.67	-9.95	-8.09	-0.42
Pennsylvania	-3.57	19.98	-2.66	7.11	7.35	2.32	-9.02	-9.21	-4.12
Rhode Island	-32.25	6.19	-11.28	-10.47	3.65	-11.71	-18.02	-32.89	-76.2
S. Carolina	5.79	43.06	-13.04	1.24	27.99	23.92	4.23	5.84	16.02
S. Dakota	11.31	8.63	1.48	28.83	26.47	6.34	3.52	3.46	22.71
Tennessee	3.83	37.95	-13	2.9	16.27	16.34	-4.65	-2.41	3.81
Texas	-1.27	32.97	-3.17	13.86	27.5	12.6	3.48	4.93	21.37
Utah	19.42	41.25	28.79	52.21	49.83	34.17	18.71	21.07	40.53
Vermont	9.22	26.2	11.2	5.94	17.11	3.52	-15.7	-22.26	-9.94
Virginia	10.87	37.72	1.34	12.72	25.19	20.5	4.37	1.96	7.7
Washington	-2.11	18.28	3.88	12.34	12.97	-1.59	-11.44	-12.54	-5.62
Wash., DC	-63.64	-56.54	-65.12	-61.49	-71.66	-69.21	-75.55	-75.85	-76.47
W. Virginia	-8.82	27.22	-16.13	-4.5	10.51	-4.74	-13.02	-14.75	6.07
Wisconsin	3.62	38.54	-1.68	4.72	9.18	-3.62	-4.35	-10.33	-0.21
Wyoming	20.25	9.67	19.49	34.67	42.27	22.52	5.6	12.98	40.88

Chapter 9

Topics in Political Economy

9.1 Why People Vote

Note.[441]

Although many of the traditional discussions in economics focus on the production, consumption, and transfer of wealth, an equally suitable definition of economics is "the science which studies human behavior as a relationship between ends and scarce means which have alternative uses." (Robbins, 1932). The fact that humans are the actors behind the aggregate models used by economists makes it rather counterintuitive that psychology does not inform economics (Camerer, 1999). Camerer points to the history of both fields to explain this discrepancy, namely the different conceptualizations of a theory that led economists in the 1940s to justify ignoring psychology. To an economist, a theory is a body of mathematical tools and theorems; whereas to a psychology, a theory is a construct that organizes experimental findings. Called the "f-twist" after its main supporter Milton Friedman, economists saw that theories with even potentially false assumptions could lead to surprisingly accurate predictions, leading to the replacement of psychology with a set of assumptions in economic theory. Because of this history, "economics assumes that the economic actor is rational, and hence he makes strong predictions about human behavior without performing the hard work of observing people." (Simon, 1959, pp. 254).

The assumption of rationality has led economists to use rational choice theories to formally model economic behavior. Although models of rational choice vary, all assume that individuals choose the best action according to a set of stable preferences and constraints facing them. Most economic models also employ methodological individualism, assuming that collective behaviors are the aggregate of individual actions. Other assumptions are often added, for example that an individual has full or perfect information about the consequences of his/her available choices and that an individual has the cognitive ability or time to rationally consider the relative utility of each choice.

In 1957, Downs used a rational choice theory to model voting behavior. He defined

---

[441] This section was written by Mindy Krischer.

his model as:

$$R = \pi B - C$$

where R corresponds to the result of the utility calculus one makes when deciding to vote. If $R > 0$ an individual votes, if $R < 0$ then the individual abstains. B is the difference in utility that a voter perceives between his most and least preferred candidate, π is the probability that a voter will bring about benefit B by voting, and C is the cost of voting. Therefore, the only way for R to be greater than zero, is for πB to be greater than C. However, as the number of voters increases the likelihood that one individual's vote determines the election declines so that P declines rapidly as the number of voters increase. Therefore, B has to be very large or else a rational individual abstains. Given this, even a small cost to vote should be a large deterrent (Simon, 1959). Since voting is costly in both information costs and the actual act of going to the polls and voting, a rational individual should abstain.

The conclusion that a rational individual should almost never vote coupled with the fact that individuals do vote presents a problem for the reliance on rational choice models to explain behavior. For a democracy to function, citizens must vote, therefore the decision appears to require a choice between serving ones own self-interest and the social good (Acevado & Krueger, 2004). Inability for theory to account for practice, has led economists and political scientists to turn to psychology to explain this behavior. Although psychological principles are beginning to be included in voting research, researchers appear to be selectively choosing principles to apply, thereby neglecting the more comprehensive view psychology can provide to explain the individual decision to vote. This section attempts to identify how economists and political scientists have expanded on the Downs (1957) rational choice model through operational defining of terms and exploration of potential psychological variables. It then addresses other psychological constructs that can further explain findings and fill in the gaps in this research. Lastly, an attempt to combine both paradigms into a potential model is explored.

To explain why his rational choice model predicts lower turnout that actually occurs, Downs suggested that voters may vote because of a desire to support democracy and ensure the survival of the democratic process. Along the same viewpoint, Riker and Ordeshook (1968) added a variable D to the original Downs equation. To them, D represents the utility that a citizen receives from the act of voting itself, regardless of who wins the election. Thus, D is conceptualized as a long-term utility investment, a sense of civic duty or utility from affirming partisanship. Their model is, therefore, stated as:

$$R = \pi B - C + D$$

Riker and Ordeshook (1973) found that there was empirical merit to adding this term. When voters expect an election to be close (when π is relatively large) as well as when there is a high B (voter perceives a large difference between the candidates) voter turnout is higher, however these effects are minor relative to the effect of "citizen duty scores." When D declines, the percent voting declines much more rapidly than when B

or π decreases.

The Riker and Ordeshook findings essentially reduce the model to $R = D - C$. However, this makes the decision to vote independent of the particulars of the election, which is contrary to empirical findings. Also the Riker and Ordeshook model does not explain how the combination of these variables could predict whether an individual votes or abstains. This has precipitated two directions in the voting calculus literature (i) how to conceptualize the terms and on their relative importance and (ii) a search to find variables to explain and predict whether an individual chooses to vote in any given election.

An significant problem with the Riker and Ordeshook model is that they assumed the cost was small to the point of being inconsequential (Sigelman & Berry, 1982). Downs had argued that the returns from voting were so low that even tiny variations in cost could have large effects. Other researchers have used demographics to proxy for cost or assumed the cost of voting was equal; two assumptions which Sigelman and Berry argue are incorrect. They therefore attempt to use a clearer and more direct measure of the cost of voting to analyze the validity of Riker and Ordeshook's model. In their study, cost was a dichotomous variable consisting of whether an individual affirmed the statement that "voting personally takes a lot of time and effort." Also included were survey responses to the importance of voting, how close respondents' thought the election would be, and belief of which candidate could better handle two different situations. A discriminant analysis was performed on these survey responses to the 1968 presidential election with voting or abstaining as the grouping variable. Although those who voted were more likely than those who abstained to look upon voting as a worthwhile activity, the cost term clearly dominated the discriminant function with 35.5% of the abstainers reporting high cost to voting while only 8.4% of the voters reported high cost.

Katosh and Traugott (1982) explored the relative importance of a short term, election specific, versus long-term, civic duty, motivations to vote. They conceptualized participation in a similar manner to the Downs and Riker and Ordeshook - as a function of the difference between the value from and cost of voting. He predicts that long-term value from voting is primarily associated with the decision to register to vote, as opposed to the decision to actually vote in a given election. Given that turnout is measured in terms of percentage of registered voters that vote, and turnout varies from election to election, a theory that predicts that a long-standing feeling of civic duty solely influences turnout does not make sense. The argument could then be made that a certain amount of "civic duty" or long-term investment in the democratic process is necessary for an individual to choose to register to vote. Therefore, short-term election specific motivations should account for variability in turnout. Katosh and Traugott found such a conceptualization to be empirically valid. This finding implies that theorists can not simply use and assume away the problems with the rational voting model by saying the act of voting itself gives some utility.

Sanders (1980) attempted to measure the terms differently, in order to examine the relative importance of the terms. In this model D was assessed by a person's response to the statement that "a person should not vote if he doesn't care how the election turns out"; π was assessed by the perceived closeness of the election in the state, B was assessed by the sum of strength of party affiliation, degree of interest in the campaign, and different in feelings of the two candidates, and C was approximated by an index comprising of rural-non-rural residence, educational level, income, length of residence in the community. Using cross-tabulated results from the 1972 election survey, Sanders found that B, the perceived utility difference, was of primary importance.

Findings from a longitudinal study of voting attitudes suggests that turnout is better when there is one candidate that one cannot stand, supporting the importance of short-term election characteristics in decisions to vote (Krosnick, 1988). Along this line, strategic voting also demonstrates why B should be important in a model of the decision to vote. McKelvey and Ordeshook (1972) created a model whereby a voter might be willing to vote for his/her second most preferred party if the more preferred party was unlikely to win and if there is a close contest between the second and third ranked parties. Alvarez and Nagler (2000) use a multinomial probit analysis to examine full choice set while allowing voters to see some parties as close substitutes. A voter's utility for each party is therefore conceptualized as a function of the voter's position on issues relative to the parties position on issues, as measured by the mean of the party placement on an eleven-point issue scale by all respondents, where the distance is measured in absolute value. Using this model, Alvarez and Nagler found that 7.2% of the voters in the UK election of 1987 voted strategically.

Although it may seem that the 'B' term should be highly weighted, Ledyard (1984) raises caution to doing this, arguing that the probability of a pivotal vote is important in the calculus. Palfry and Rosenthal (1985) use game theory to look at voting turnout when candidates take different and fixed positions. They find that high turnout occurs when there are nearly identical numbers of voters supporting each candidate, however when supporters were randomized to candidates there was a low probability of turnout. Thus, uncertainty about the number of voters led to a low turnout equilibrium.

The aforementioned studies have elaborated problems with the rational choice models. The inability of these different conceptualizations of the variables and measurements to both explain and predict whether an individual chooses to vote in a given election has made the need to bring other explanations of human behavior into the equations.

One possible explanation stems directly from the expected utility standpoint. Strom (1975) explains that there are four relevant electoral outcomes based on how a citizen says he/she would feel if he/she votes/abstains and his/her preferred/not preferred candidate wins. The magnitudes of utility for these outcomes are not symmetrical because individuals take into account the subjective estimated probability that an outcome will occur if he/she votes and an outcome will occur if he/she doesn't vote. Therefore, if the difference between a citizen's expected value of voting and of abstaining exceeds the cost of voting, he/she will vote (see also Kanazawa, 2000).

This theory has been understood as belief in personal relevance, where individuals speculate about the potential outcomes of the election and how they would feel about their behavior in light of these potential outcomes. As described by Strom, an individual can choose to vote or abstain and their preferred candidate can either win or lose. Thus, each individual is faced with four different potential outcomes. The idea is that an individual deciding to vote speculates that if they did not vote and their candidate lost they would think- "what if my behavior were different?" From this logic, they will believe that their vote will not be wasted and therefore, vote.

A similar theory has been proposed by Kahneman and Tversky (1984) called the voter's illusion, where a voter projects his/her intention to voter or abstain to similar others. Because this projection differential inspires greater optimism regarding the election outcome when voting rather than abstention- many people choose to vote. In their supporting study, participants were asked to identify with one of two parties seeking to govern the country of "Delta." Some participants learned that the electoral outcome depended on each party's ability to mobilize its supporters. Others learned that the election depended on the ultimate behavior of unaligned voters. Thus, only participants in the party-supporters condition could use their own intentions (vote or abstain) to predict the outcome. All participants predicted the electoral outcome under the assumption they had voted, and under the assumption they had abstained. The results indicated a voting illusion. Kahneman and Tversky suggest that when considering voting, and an individual expects that their preferred candidate will win, he/she may be tempted to abstain, thinking that his or her individual vote is not needed. If the person then decides to abstain this state of mind may also be projected to like-minded others, resulting in a new expectation of defeat. One way a person can avert a cycle of changing forecasts is to vote.

Acevado and Krueger (2004) use the same basic experiment as Kahneman and Tversky to test both a belief in personal relevance and the voter's illusion. They add a manipulation of timing of voting behavior to explore the possibility that the voters illusion is stronger among earlier voters suggesting that voters believe that their own personal decision to vote might induce others to do the same. For each of the possible scenarios about their voting and expected outcome of the election, participants rated the degree to which they would experience a sense of having wasted a vote, their confidence in voting in the next election, and the extent of their regret and satisfaction. Only a modest voter's illusion effect was found. However, a belief in personal relevance was found to be robust and not related to the voter's illusion.

This research suggests that perceived closeness of the election and perceived feelings at the conclusion of the election based on behavior and election outcome are important variables. The voter's illusion seems improbable in a situation where the electorate is large and diverse, because it does not explain research that turnout decreases as the electorate increases (Harkins & Latane, 1998). Belief in personal relevance, however, explains this empirical finding that turnout increases for closer elections and decreases for a larger electorate. It also explains why some voters act strategically. Despite the failings of the voter's illusion, it does suggest that a social desirability or a social influence variable might be a useful consideration.

Sigelman (1982) reports that the percentage of survey respondents who say that they voted in a particular election is consistently larger than actual voter turnout by five to twenty percent. He uses the results from the 1978 CPS National Election Survey to discover the characteristics of the misreporters, those who feel the influence of social desirability enough to lie about voting but not actually vote. In the election being considered, 12.8% of respondents misreported voting then they originally abstained. Misreporters tend to be less interested and less emotionally involved in politics and less inclined to think it is their civic duty to vote as voters, but have more of these qualities than the admitted nonvoters. This shows that although social desirability is important, it does not by itself produce voting behavior.

Fowler attempted to explain voting behavior by saying that people who vote are "discriminating altruists," where voters have altruistic preferences toward specific groups Therefore they vote because they get utility from emphasizing the preferences of their group. However, Parfit (1984) suggested that voters act rationally if they care about the benefits of voting to others. They calculate that the total number of people benefiting from the victory of the 'superior candidate' offsets the costs of voting. Under both these theories, turnout would be consistent from election to election, which is inconsistent with research (Harkins & Latatane, 1998).

The attempts to add social influence to the models have led to an interest in a "group-based" model of voter turnout. In these models, group members participate in elections either because they are directly coordinated and rewarded by group leaders or because they believe themselves to be ethically obliged to act in a manner that is consistent with the group's interest. The first motivation is described by group mobilization models, which assume groups of ideologically similar individuals with leaders who coordinate turnout. In these models, group leaders determine the level of turnout by allotting resources to members. Since buying votes is illegal, the models assume that leaders exert social pressure on members. The social pressure encourages members to vote and exert social pressure on other members to do the same. Thus, the model requires leaders and members who have regular contact and communication.

The other main group-based model is an ethical voter model where voters are motivated by ethical concerns for the welfare of others. Ethical agents evaluate alternative behavioral rules in a Kantian manner by comparing the outcomes that would occur if everyone who shares their preferences were to act according to the same rule. Second, the receive a positive payoff for acting according to a behavioral rule they determine is best given their preferences and their evaluation of alternative rules. Harsanyi (1977) modeled this idea and concluded that rule-utilitarians get a payoff larger than their cost of voting if they act according to the welfare-maximizing rule, thus, turnout will occur if there are many rule-utilitarians in the population.

Feddersen and Sandroni (2006) introduce preference diversity into Harsanyi by assuming that there is a continuum of voters that can be partitioned into those who believe that candidate 1 will produce a better outcome and those who believe candidate 2 will produce a better outcome. Each group consists of ethical voters and abstainers, under the assumption that ethical voters receive a payoff greater than their cost of voting for acting ethically while abstainers have a negative utility from voting and choose to abstain. They find that turnout and margin of victory are positively correlated but this correlation is not caused by changes in the pivot probabilities. However, as the relative size of the two groups of voters become more equal, turnout increases and the margin of victory decreases. Feddersen (2004) argues that not only does such a model not provide any extra information about why people vote, but also it raises the questions of whether group membership, if important, is endogenous or exogenous to interest in the political process. In addition, the group mobilization model yields concerns about the reasons that people join groups and the influence that groups can have.

The fact that empirical studies have consistently found persistence in voting to be robust has led researchers to speculate as to why this is the case. Campbell et al. (1960) refers back to Downs' original conceptualization of civic duty and suggests that the psychological draw to vote is enduring such that people have long-standing feelings of their duty to vote which exert themselves over each election. Stated more generally, people make similar choices when faced with similar situations. Similarly, it may be that certain people are always encouraged by campaigns and other contextual effects. Another explanation for this effect is that voting is habit forming (Gerber, Green, & Shachar, 2003)). According to this theory, psychological reasons might cause an individual to initially vote or not vote, but the behavior itself then is the primary influence on subsequent behavior. Brody and Sniderman (1977) report that past voting behavior predicts current turnout when controlling for a large number of individual-level traits, most importantly, age, race, income, education, sex, and psychological involvement in politics. Proponents of this theory cite the "foot in the door" theory of Freedman and Fraser (1966) where participation makes one more likely to participate in the future, even though the events are independent.

This theory has important predictions because variation in the political environment has the potential to produce long-term effects. Gerber, Green, and & Shachar (2003) caution that what may be called habit may merely reflect the inability to account for persistent causes of voting, especially since previous research in this area has been based on a correlational design. To explore this idea, they conducted a large field experiment prior to the November general election of 1998 in New Haven, Connecticut. Subjects were randomly assigned to treatment conditions where they were encouraged to vote through personal canvassing or mailings prior to the election. This was done because canvassing has been shown to increase turnout in a number of other studies. They then used public records to track voting behavior for the 1998 and 1999 elections. They also looked at the individual's past voting behavior in the 1996 election to separate the effects of habit or unobserved heterogeneity. They found that personal canvassing and direct mail had significant effects on voter turnout in 1998, with 10.2% more turnout in the personal canvassing condition and 1.5% more turnout in the mail condition, than in the control. This effect is particularly robust given the fact that the election was an uneventful reelection of a democratic incumbent in a mostly democratic city and only 39.2% of all registered voters voted. Voting in the 1998 election raised the probability of voting in the 1999 election by 55% and this effect was more robust when controlling for voting in the 1996 election.

These results are certainly encouraging for the 'voting as habit' theory. One possible explanation is that voting is reinforcing, parties target voters and perhaps the party attention encourages one to vote again. Also, voting might lead to an increase in feelings of civic obligation and interest in politics. Gerber also suggests that voting makes attitudes about engaging in the act of voting more positive, which is supported by research on attitude change by Fishbein and Ajzen (1975). A non-voter who may be apprehensive about going to the polls however, may become more comfortable with the process once he/she votes. Voting may also become part of one's self-concept, therefore becoming the 'default' behavior on election day.

Kanazawa (2000) postulates that voters take a win-stay/lose-shift approach to voting. Therefore, they look at their past voting behavior and election outcomes when deciding when to vote, redefining 'p' as a stochastic learning variable. Although his methodology has been criticized (Martin & Shieh, 2003), it raises an interesting question of whether voting becomes a habit only after a favorable election.

The use of a cost/benefit rational choice model to examine voting behavior predicts that voting is irrational in situations where the electorate is big and therefore the probability of an individual vote influencing the outcome is very small. The fact that costs cannot be ignored bears the question of why do people vote. Researchers have distinguished between short-term influences and long-term motivations for voting, where long-term motivations are conceptualized as a sense of civic duty, long term interest in elections, or habit. Short-term motivations are large difference in perceived utility between the candidates, or other election-specific influences. Expected utility from counterfactual thinking has also been identified. This counterfactual thinking will only influence one's voting behavior, however, if one cares about the outcome of the election. Social desirability of voting also appears to be important in light of group-models and the fact that personal canvassing/mail does influence turnout.

There are a few particular psychological concepts that may help to shed more light on the ideas of why people vote that have been considered, especially with respect to groups, belief in personal relevance, and the assumption of rationality.

Groups have special psychological and social traits that separate them from just an aggregate of individuals. Many psychologists have an operationally defined definition of groups stressing the cohesiveness in identity or values. While Gordon Allport (1954) emphasized the notion of a common fate, or experience, Asch (1956) stresses that no matter how different, each member possesses a common characteristic, idea, or purpose. Other psychologists emphasize the mutual influence exerted among members (Wilder & Simon, 1998). Individuals gain a large part of their identity and self-concept from the groups in which they belong (Simon, 1998). The social-categorization theory specifies that the predominance of the social identity over the personal identity guides a person's perceptions and behavior as the person will perceive his world as the group does (Turner, 1987). Group norms emerge out of the expectations about dynamics and focus of the group itself. This suggests that groups can have a large influence on the behavior of members which does not have to be the direct influence of leaders, as the mobilization theories of voting suggest. Rather, if people in an individual's social group place importance on voting, one might vote to remain connected to the other group members.

Belief in personal relevance assumes that one looks at an expected outcome and how that outcome would make one feel if they had/had not voted. Along similar lines, habit theories postulate that voting occurs because of past voting behavior. Behaviorism offers an alternative explanation to these theories of voting, that of superstitious behavior. Superstitious behavior can be defined as behaving in a manner as if there is a contingency between one's behavior and a given outcome, although no contingency really exists. One continues to do the behavior, because one does not test out the alternative and therefore, one does not actually learn that no contingency really exists. Thus, superstitious behavior occurs when the outcome is important to the individual so that he/she does not 'risk' testing the contingency (Skinner, 1948). Therefore, superstitious behavior explains why athletes have "lucky socks" even when they cognitively know that the socks do not make a difference in their performance. Superstitious behavior can also explain much of voting phenomenon. If the outcome of the election is important to an individual, then they will vote because they do not want to 'risk' an outcome if they do not vote, even if they know their vote will have little effect on the outcome. In behavioral terms, habitual behavior results from an association between a behavior and an outcome. Therefore, if individual X votes in a given election and the result is positive, they will perceive a positive contingency between their behavior and the outcome. If subsequent elections are important to the individual, he/she will not test the alternate contingency (outcome if don't vote), and therefore he/she will vote again. Similar to theories of voting as a result of habit or learning, this bears the empirical question of whether those who vote and their candidate wins are more likely to vote in future elections.

Taken with the prior research it seems that a combination of a long-term interest in politics or a feeling of civic duty combined with a social influence variable leads people to register to vote. The characteristics of an individual election, possibly also with social influence, will lead a person to begin voting, and superstitious behavior may explain dynamic patterns in voting. The question of rationality is of crucial importance for trying to combine these variables to both explain and predict turnout.

Fortunately for the economists, it appears that the rationality assumption can remain, whereas a good decision is characterized as one in which the best available course of action is chosen in the face of characteristic uncertainty about the consequences. Neuroscientific studies have found evidence supporting the conceptualization of the expected utility hypothesis as the result of multiplying the alternative's subjective value by probability. Some neuroimaging studies have used dopamine neurons to study responses to earned rewards. Other studies have suggested that the part of the brain used for probability estimation is separate from the reward areas, supporting the utility hypothesis. Experimental neuroimaging with animals has revealed brain areas that appear to directly encode the utility of a stimulus. These areas are often characterized as a motor preparation area, supporting the idea expected utility leads to behavior (Sanfey, 2007).

Thus, it seems like researchers' suggestions that relaxing the assumption of rationality in economic models will make models more psychologically valid is false (see Simon, 1959, Camerer, 1999). In fact, Shapiro (1969) argues that a rational choice model is not by definition inconsistent with a model that looks at attitudes and beliefs.

According to him, rational choice models only assume deductive inference, simply that an individual chooses those actions that will give him/her the highest utility. On the other hand, psychological models address inductive rationality, emphasizing the subjectivity of perceptions and beliefs. Shapiro used a quasi open-ended interview technique to investigate the rationality of voters by using the information and voting criteria that the voter suggests is important in his/her decision. Shapiro postulated a two-part model, of which the first part is the normal utility maximizing function where expected utility is equal to the multiple of the utility from the outcome and its probability of resulting, summed over all possible outcomes. Shapiro modeled the inductive part of the model as

$$A_j = B_i a_i$$

where A_j refers to an attitude towards object j, B_i refers to the strength of belief about 'i' , a_i is the evaluative aspect. This is summed over all beliefs about j. The roles of each part of the model are hypothesized to correspond roughly to the process of "prizing and appraising;" assessments of the relative desirability of various outcomes and assessments of the events that are likely to contribute to those outcomes. The belief and values are thus considered independent information units on which a rational utility-maximizing decision is made. Shapiro studied the validity of such a prediction using voters' perceived attributes of the candidates and perceived positions of the candidates in the 1968 presidential election, finding that including the interrelationship between psychology and economic approaches yield a more comprehensive overview of voting behavior.

The combination of both psychological and economic paradigms suggests that individuals make rational utility calculations based on subjective estimates of the utility of events and their chance of occurrence. There has been a plethora of work in psychology demonstrating that individuals are particularly inaccurate in estimating probabilities, especially when a situation is complex. Prospect theory, proposed by Kahneman and Tversky (1979), is an attempt to integrate standard utility theory with an individual's tendency to make mistakes in perceiving probabilities. This theory describes a decision process in two stages called editing and evaluation. In the editing stage, people arrange alternatives on an continuum, where outcomes lower than a middle "neutral" point are seen as losses and outcomes higher are seen as gains. During the evaluation stage people compute a utility based on the potential outcomes and their respective probabilities. The probabilities are weighed to show that people tend to overreact to small probability events. Also the utilities are weighted to express that there is a bigger impact of losses than gains. In a voting setting this model would predict that people would overestimate a probability that their candidate would lose if they did not vote, and therefore they would be motivated to vote. Therefore, a perceived π can be much larger than Downs suggested (Quattrone and Tversky, 1988). Also, as the race gets closer to a tie, voters perceive that their vote has a much higher probability of affecting the outcome, which is consistent with empirical findings.

A model of voting should relate turnout and perceived differences between the candidates in the form of a subjective utility analysis. Consider the model

$$R = \pi DE - C + S.$$

Here R refers to the utility calculus such that when it is positive an individual votes and when it is negative an individual abstains. D refers to a voter's perceived utility difference between the candidates, or how much he/she favors one candidate over the other and therefore, cares about the outcome of the election. E is perceived closeness of the election, while π is a measure of superstitious belief in personal relevance. One could obtain a superstitious belief in personal relevance from counterfactual thinking (thinking one will have disutility if one does not vote and one's preferred candidate loses from wondering what the outcome would be if one's behavior had been different) or from habit (from one's preferred candidate having won the election when one has voted in the past), therefore one does not want to test the other contingency. The terms π, D, E are multiplied together because if one of them is zero, the others will be irrelevant to the decision. S refers to a perceived social utility from voting either external, from pleasing those in a group which support voting, or internal, from fulfilling ones "civic duty" for the perpetuation of democracy. Subtracted is an individual's cost to vote in terms of direct voting costs and the opportunity costs.

This model appears to support the theories of voting addressed throughout the section. An individual is more likely to vote the more personal interest he/she has in the outcome of the election, especially if the election appears to be close and he/she has a utility for voting because of either a personal sense of duty to vote or perceives voting as socially desirable. This is offset by the cost of voting itself or the opportunity cost to vote. The fact that voting diminishes as the electorate gets larger is admittedly a bit more difficult to explain using this model. However, the fact that one cognitively knows that their vote has a tiny influence may reduce any superstitious belief in personal relevance and the fact that the electorate is large may reduce perceived external social influence to vote since it becomes more difficult for other group members to know if an individual voted, hence why some individuals resort to lying about their voting behavior.

Although this model is not subjected to empirical analysis in this section, it provides a thought experiment on how psychology and economics can combine to explain behavior without having to relax the fundamental assumptions behind their respective paradigms. This section shows that individuals may have different and, in some cases, inaccurate perceptions,but may well act rationally on the basis of these beliefs Decision making is a thus a complex interaction between internal and external processes.

9.2   Liberty versus Security

Today we hear a lot about the threats of terrorism and diminishing civil liberties in society as a response to these threats.[442] There is much debate not only at the level of the

---

[442]This section was written by Martha King.

national government[443] and media[444] but also in the academy[445] concerning the challenges terrorism presents for the preservation of civil liberties. The debate, of course, is not a new one and can be boiled down (admittedly rather simplistically) to an argument over the seeming trade-off between the values of "liberty" and "security." In the past, philosophers seemed to examine these societal goods not only in terms of intrinsic worth both also in terms of their instrumental value in the lives of the members of a society.[446] The "trade-off" was indeed complex. For much of current scholarship, however, liberty and security are for the most part treated only as intrinsic goods.[447] Those who favor national security argue that security is of principal importance since, they argue, liberty itself cannot be enjoyed without a base level of security. Those who favor civil liberties argue that to restrict liberty for the sake of security defeats the purpose of supposedly needing security in order to maintain liberty. Borrowing Jeremy Waldron's terminology, these "security partisans" and "civil liberties partisans"[448] relegate the debate to an unsolvable argument of the extremes. In this section I shall argue that by treating liberty and security as intrinsic goods in the midst of the current debate concerning potential trade-offs is thus a theoretical dead-end, and that, alternatively, we should look to the instrumental values of both liberty and security and use this as a measuring rod for evaluating policy decisions.

In discussing a potential trade-off between liberty and security, it is important that we gain some sort of grasp of what is at stake. The concept of liberty is indeed highly complex and to explore it completely is by no means the task of this section. Not only can the evaluation of liberty involve the philosophical discussion of liberty as a concept by itself, but it also involves the discussion of different individual liberties.[449] Here I simply intend to summarize some of the fundamental conceptions.

Fundamental to today's discussion of liberty is Isaiah Berlin's distinction between "positive" and "negative" liberty. Positive liberty, for Berlin, is an active principle. It is the possibility of freely acting out one's ends, or self-realization, and "derives from the wish on the part of the individual to be his own master."[450] Negative liberty, on the other hand, is the absence of constraints to one's will. This is the conception affiliated with the Classical Liberal tradition in which liberty is seen as 'freedom from interference,' provided that one's will does not impinge on the rights of others.[451] In a sense, negative

---

[443] See Dept. of the Air Force (2002); *Hamdi v. Rumsfeld*; Subcommittee on National Security (2006); U.S. Dept. of State (2005).

[444] See Carlson (2004, 2005); Clymer (2002); Kristoff (2002).

[445] See Dershowitz (2002); Humphreys (2004); Lewis (2005); Aradau (2007); Waldron (2003, 2007).

[446] See Mill (1910); Hobbes (1998) and (2001); and Strauss (1987).

[447] See Cohen (2002); Griffiths (1983); Humphreys (2004); Ignatieff (2004); Posner (2006); Leone and Anrig (2007); Southwood (2004).

[448] Waldron (2006).

[449] See Pettit (1997); Becker (1984); Griffiths (1983). Berlin's negative liberty conception is also quite similar to Benjamin Constant's "liberty of the moderns" in terms of their viewing liberty as a freedom from interference. See Constant (1988).

[450] Berlin (1997: 203).

[451] For instance, Mill wrote that "the only purpose for which power can be rightly exercised over any member of a civilized community, against his will, is to prevent harm to others." Mill (1910: 73).

liberty can be seen as an absence of constraints on positive liberty. In looking at the situation in the world today, considerations of freedom in Berlin's terms require us to evaluate the liberties of citizens and non-citizens. In light of threats of terrorism, liberty needs to be considered not only in a positive sense, but especially so in the negative one. For example, potential terrorists who are U.S. citizens are guaranteed rights that accompany that status; however when the will of a suspected terrorist is to harm others, a discussion of a restriction of that person's liberty may have to be undertaken. Likewise, considerations of wiretapping, data mining, and other restrictions on civil liberties need to be considered in terms of how much these measures restrict everyone's right to self-determine.

Berlin's negative conception is essentially a freedom from interference, but as "Philip Pettit has forcibly reminded us, not all forms of interference are on the same liberty-infringing footing."[452] Pettit's "third" conception of liberty is that of liberty[453] as non-domination, where "[f]reedom as non-domination is defined by reference to how far and how well the bearer is protected against arbitrary interference."[454] This conception is a response to Pettit's objection that it is possible to face domination without interference and also possible to be interfered with, without being dominated. For example, he argues that one could be enslaved but basically let alone (domination without interference) or, alternatively, one could be subject to just laws that restrict complete freedom without facing domination (interference without domination).[455] Pettit's conception helps to expand the meaning of liberty by adding that it "needs something more than the absence of interference; it requires security against interference, in particular against interference on an arbitrary basis."[456]

In the discussion of liberty, it often seems that liberty is considered as equivalent to license. In this sense, liberty simply means the freedom to do absolutely anything one wants, whenever one wants, without facing any restrictions or potential punishment. Early political philosophers, however, recognized that liberty amounting to nothing more than license could in fact lead to a reduction in liberty. As Locke considered,

> Freedom then is not what Sir Robert Filmer tells us . . . 'a liberty for every one to do what he lists, to live as he pleases, and no to be tied by any laws.' But freedom of men under government, is, to have a standing rule to live by, common to every one of that society, and made by the legislative power erected in it; a liberty to follow my own will in all things, where the rule prescribes not; and not to be subject to the inconstant, uncertain, unknown, arbitrary will of another man: As freedom of nature is, to be under no other restraint but the law

---

[452]Southwood (2004: 29).
[453]"Freedom" and "liberty" are used interchangeably in this essay.
[454]Pettit (1997: 109). See also Pettit (2005).
[455]Pettit (1997: 80).
[456]Ibid., p. 51.

of nature.[457]

Locke's "freedom from nature" is what Hobbes and others called (in another context) the "state of nature"–"a state of lawlessness [and] a condition in which we are free from the binding force of any agreed human laws."[458]

Law, Locke recognized, was indeed an impingement on license, but liberty within civil society allowed men the freedom to pursue their own ends. Rousseau makes a similar distinction to Locke, calling the two states of liberty "natural liberty" (license/the state of nature) and "civil liberty" (liberty within the bounds of civil society). For Rousseau, man surrenders his natural liberty when he enters into the social contract in order to secure civil liberty for himself: "What man loses by the social contract is his natural liberty and an unlimited right to everything he tries to get and succeeds in getting; what he gains is civil liberty and the proprietorship of all he possesses."[459] Ironically, liberty (as license) had to be restricted by law for the sake of liberty itself.[460] Bentham too recognized this in 1843 when he wrote:

> By creating obligations, the law to the same extent trenches upon liberty. It converts into offenses acts which would otherwise be permitted and unpunishable. The law creates an offense either by a positive command or a prohibition. These retrenchments of liberty are inevitable. It is impossible to create rights, to impose obligations, to protect the person, life, reputation, property, subsistence, liberty itself, except at the expense of liberty.[461]

"There is therefore a sense in which, in agreeing to give up our natural condition, we must be deciding to give up a form of liberty."[462] However, if everyone were "free" in the sense of being totally unrestrained, would this constitute a complete conception of freedom? Raphael (1983:1) argues that it would not, because "[c]omplete freedom soon leads to no freedom at all. . . . [since] complete freedom for all means the absence of order; the absence of law; [and thus]anarchy, chaos." In discussing the trade-off between liberty and security, then, it is important that liberty be considered as something much

---

[457]Locke (2001: 631, Ch. IV).

[458]Skinner (1990:133). See also Rousseau (1993: 196–197).

[459]Rousseau (1993: 196).

[460]One example of liberty restricted for the sake of liberty in practice is cited by Herbert Hoover, writing in 1934:

"The American system has steadily evolved the protections of Liberty. In the early days of road traffic we secured a respect for liberties of others by standards of decency and courtesy between neighbors. But with the crowding of highways and streets we have invented Stop and Go signals which apply to everybody alike, in order to maintain the same ordered Liberty. But traffic signals are not a sacrifice of Liberty, they are the preservation of it. Under them each citizen moves swiftly to his own individual purpose and attainment. That is a far different thing from the corner policeman being given the right to determine whether the citizen's mission warrants his passing and whether he is competent to execute it, and then telling him which way he should go, whether he likes it or not. That is the whole distance between Liberty and Regimentation." Hoover (1934: 199–200).

[461]Bentham (1931: 94, Part I, Ch. I: "Objects of the Civil Law.")

[462]Skinner (1990: 133).

more complex than license.[463]

In expanding the concept of liberty, it is important to also consider that there may be prior needs that must be fulfilled before a society can enjoy—or even desire—liberty. In A Theory of Justice, John Rawls argues for the principle of the "priority of liberty" in which "liberty can be restricted only for the sake of liberty itself."[464] However, Rawls does admit that there may be certain social conditions that must be satisfied prior to a society being able to enjoy its liberty. Indeed Rawls does explain that although liberty does take precedent, it can be sacrificed for a short while in order to satisfy other needs of a society before liberty (above all else) can be pursued.[465] This of course seems logical, for example, given that without the ability of a society to provide (through its wealth) for its citizens, the full exercise of civil liberties might be of secondary concern (at least temporarily). In order to better explain Rawls's ideas about the priority of liberty, Barry builds on Rawls's idea of effective liberty to better relate the relationship of wealth to liberty. "Effective liberty" is thus the type of liberty that is meant in understanding the priority of liberty. The idea is that no amount of basic liberty, however great, produces any effective liberty unless it is combined with some minimum level of wealth. In other words, it does not matter if you have a maximum amount of freedom if you have no money. Likewise, no amount of wealth, however great, produces any effective liberty if it is not paired with some basic liberty. Thus you could have a great deal of wealth, but without basic liberty, it is of no use to you. Effective liberty Barry has determined to be a product of basic liberty and wealth.[466] Thus "once some minimal level of economic development has been achieved by a society (that is, once it gets to a feasible set of combinations of wealth and liberty which lies some distance from the origin) the pursuit of further equal liberty has absolute priority over the pursuit of increased wealth (that is, the optimal path has become parallel to the 'liberty' axis)."[467]

Apart from the discussion of a minimum level of wealth being necessary for a society to pursue the full exercise of civil liberties it is also certainly possible that a minimum level of security be necessary in order for liberty to be "effective" in the Rawlsian sense. William Miles has written on Chad's failed attempt at pursuing democracy in the early 1990s due to problems of societal instability and a lack of overall security. Miles writes that in 1993, 800 delegates gathered for the Conférence national souveraine "to chart a new political future for the nation. Participants and onlookers alike shared the hope that, as a result of the CNS, democracy and development would replace dictatorship and civil

---

[463] Adam Smith and Immanuel Kant both rejected the idea of considering true liberty as a form of license since they argued that "freedom as license" amounted to people merely being slaves to their passions, in which case they would not truly be free. See Smith (2000) and Kant (1996, 2006).

[464] See Rawls (2001, §39). "The ideal is that of a public-spirited citizen who prizes political activity and service to others as among the chief goods of life and could not contemplate as tolerable an exchange of the opportunities for such activity for mere material goods or contentment." Hart (1973: 554).

[465] "If the persons in the original position assume that their basic liberties can be effectively exercised, they will not exchange a lesser liberty for an improvement in their economic well-being, *at least not once a certain level of wealth has been attained.*" Rawls (1971: 542). Note that Rawls removes this italicized clause in his revised edition. See Rawls (2001: 474–475).

[466] Barry (1973: 79). Liberty and wealth are defined in aggregate terms.

[467] Barry (1973: 82).

war."[468] While hopes were apparently high for a transition to a society with increasing civil liberties, the reality of "widespread insecurity ... [rendered] meaningless the formal exercise of political freedom."[469] Although scattered militias attempted to control various territories, an effective system of justice was not in place, making crimes virtually unpunishable and therefore quite lucrative. For these reasons, Miles argues that a minimum level of security is therefore necessary before a society can meaningfully attempt to secure civil liberties.

Returning to the concept of assigning liberty an absolute priority, it is important that we consider whether or not liberty is something that people are indeed willing to sacrifice. Davis and Silver (2005) have found that people are more willing to sacrifice civil liberties the greater the sense of threat they face. They also found that Americans tended to favor civil liberties over security when these values were presented in the abstract, and that trust in government in general was a major factor in whether or not people were willing to sacrifice liberty for enhanced security. Consistent with Davis and Silver, Lewis (2005) also found that Americans were unsympathetic to sacrifices in civil liberties when presented with specific potential policy measures. (For example, a majority of Americans thought that "detaining people at airports solely because of their religion" and "making it easier for intelligence and law enforcement agents to monitor people's private telephone conversations and e-mail" "go too far" in terms of a sacrifice of liberty.[470]) The perception of threat seems to be a major factor in whether people are willing to surrender their civil liberties. A few months after September 11, 2001, a Gallup poll showed that 47 percent of Americans thought that "the government should take 'all steps necessary' to prevent future acts of terrorism in the United States, even if it meant violating people's basic civil liberties."[471] As time passed after September 11th, however, fewer Americans tended to agree with this proposition.

Like liberty, the concept of security is complex, and if we are to examine a potential trade-off between the two, it is important to understand exactly what is at stake. Perhaps the most well-known discussion of security in political philosophy is that of Thomas Hobbes. The Hobbesian conception of security, of course, is centered around the preservation of life.

> The end for which one man giveth up, and relinquisheth to another, or others, the right of protecting and defending himself by his own power, is the security which he expecteth thereby, of protection and defense from those to whom he doth so relinquish it. And a man may then account himself in the estate of security, when he can foresee no violence to be done unto him. . . ; and without that security there is no reason for a man to deprive himself of his own advantages, and make himself a prey to others. And therefore when there is not such a sovereign power erected, as may afford this security; it is to be understood that

---

[468]Miles (1995: 55).
[469]Ibid., p. 57.
[470]Lewis (2005: 24).
[471]Carlson (2004).

every man's right of doing whatsoever seemeth good in his own eyes, remaineth still with him.[472]

In transitioning from the state of nature to civil society, people submit themselves to the state for the protection of their lives. The sovereign's primary function, therefore, is the protection of the lives of his subjects. According to Hobbes, if a person relinquishes his personal sovereignty and submits to the sovereign for the preservation of his life, a government is only legitimate insofar as it protects him. Should the sovereign cease to protect a person's life, the social contract is thereby abrogated. To require self-incrimination would be to force one to deny himself the very thing he submitted to the sovereign in order to acquire—the assurance of security. (This is the same reasoning behind the Fifth Amendment in the Bill of Rights.[473])

The concept of security considered only in terms of the preservation of one's life, however, is incomplete. As Waldron (2003) has argued, security entails not only personal safety, but also concerns such as the preservation of one's way of life, an absence of fear of threats to one's safety and well-being, and the assurance of such a security. As mentioned earlier, the perception of threat is a major factor in determining whether people are willing to sacrifice their civil liberties for enhanced security. "To sustain security, therefore, it is not enough that the threats [such as threats of terrorist attacks] be repelled. There must be an assurance that they will be repelled, an assurance that people can count on and build upon in advance of the outcome of any particular attack."[474] The assurance of personal security (including to one's life, property, and way of life) is therefore perhaps one of the important elements in the concept of security in general since security by itself would not seem to satisfy anyone's fears unless it was known that one would persist in being secure.

Those who favor security in the trade-off debate argue that freedom itself cannot be enjoyed without the assurance of security.[475] There seems to be some truth in this, recalling the situation in Chad discussed earlier. For example, Miles (1995: 58) notes that, "[in]security undermine[d] democratization in both general and specific ways. In general, the free movement of persons and property without risk or fear of molestation is a precondition for all other expressions of democracy and did not exist in the period following the *Conférence national souveraine.*" Here we see that the lack of security to life and property turned people away from concerns of democratization, despite how strongly that democratization was desired.

In order to better evaluate the nature of the trade-off, it is helpful to it in terms of its extremes. Considered this way, the "extreme" of liberty would be to maximize liberty for all. In this sense, maximal liberty is like the license conception of liberty where all people are free from any restrictions (thus, all legal restraint) to their individual wills.

---

[472] Hobbes (1999: 111. De Corpore Politico, Part II, Ch. XX).

[473] See Skinner (1990) and Hobbes: "If a man be interrogated by the sovereign, or his authority, concerning a crime done by himself, he is not bound (without assurance of pardon) to confess it; because no man … can be obliged by covenant to accuse himself." Hobbes (2001: 653).

[474] Waldron (2003: 317).

[475] See Ullmann (1983); Howard and Sawyer (2005); Lansford and Pauly (2006); Posner (2006, 2007).

Liberty in the extreme thus just is the state of nature.[476] Without law and any hindrances to one's free will, there is no assurance of security, however, and thus "there is also a sense in which every man has very little freedom in the state of nature; for if you have to go in continual fear of your neighbors, if your wishes are always liable to be frustrated by the acts and plots of other men, and in particular if you are always in danger of death, the last thing you want, then you have very little freedom, you have very little real opportunity to do as you like. Complete freedom for all means little effective freedom for anyone."[477] These, then, are the consequences of maximal freedom.

To maximize security for all, on the other hand, is to strive to protect each person from his neighbor in every possible way. To maximize security necessarily greatly diminishes liberty for all, since with even a minimal amount of liberty allowed, the risk of danger to life and property is enhanced. To minimize these risks and maximize security, therefore, ultimately leads to a sort of totalitarianism.

Considered in the extremes, both liberty and security do appear to be inversely related. How can this be so, however, if some are able to argue that security is necessary for liberty? As Berlin argued,

> it remains true that the freedom of some must at times be curtailed to secure the freedom of others. [But upon] what principle should this be done? If freedom is a sacred, untouchable value, there can be no such principle. One or other of these conflicting rules or principles must, at any rate in practice, yield.[478]

Because liberty and security are usually treated as absolute values, we are left at an impasse. As Waldron writes,

> [t]he civil libertarians emphasize the liberties that matter to us, and certainly it is right to point out that those liberties require security for their meaningful exercise. The partisans of security point out that they are trying to protect our way of life (as well as our lives themselves) against attack, and certainly it is right to point out that you cannot do that if you treat our liberties as unimportant. But still there is a genuine trade-off. Even if it is not a trade-off between one set of values and another quire distinct set of values, it is a trade-off between the importance of protecting certain values in one way and the importance of vindicating certain values in another way.[479]

For a government to have any legitimacy, we must also strike a fair balance between security and liberty. Indeed,

> [n]o government is legitimate if it does not promote security, and we may

---

[476]Hobbes recognized this when he wrote: "For if each man allowed to others, as the law of nature requires, the liberty which he demands for himself, the state of nature would return, in which all men may rightly do all things; and they would reject that state as worse than any civil subjection, if they knew it." Hobbes (1998: 121, On the Citizen, Ch. X).

[477]Raphael (1983: 4).

[478]Berlin (1997: 198).

[479]Waldron (1996: 352).

say that this word 'security' captures the pattern of impact on safety that governments are supposed to have as far as that elementary legitimacy is concerned.[480]

Without providing security, as Hobbes also recognized, the state loses its legitimacy all
together; but likewise without liberty, in submitting oneself to the authority of government, one ought to be able to expect that the arrangement is an improvement upon one's
status without government. The solution to the trade-off dilemma, therefore, must be
one in which a compromise is struck between these values that takes into account each
value's role in the legitimacy of the state.

One of the major problems with approaching the dilemma in terms of one absolute
value versus another absolute value is that we cannot help but place the two in an inverse
relation—'if you wish to live in a society with security for all, you must of necessity
sacrifice some of the liberty of all, including your own liberty'—and—'if you wish to
live in a society with maximal liberty for all, you must of necessity be putting your
life at risk.' Partisans of neither side can ever be satisfied with a compromise in such
terms, for each 'compromise' requires at least one side to yield something, which, as an
absolute value, is non-negotiable.

For example,

> [l]iberty ... for Rousseau, is not something which can be adjusted or com-
> promised: you are not allowed to give away now a little of it, now much more of
> it; you are not allowed to barter so much freedom for so much security, so much
> freedom for so much happiness. To yield 'a little' of your liberty is like dying
> a little, dehumanizing yourself a little; and the belief which is most passion-
> ately held by Rousseau, one of the values to which he devoted more eloquence
> than to almost any other, is this notion of human integrity. ... In short, human
> freedom—the capacity to choose ends independently—is for Rousseau an ab-
> solute value, and to say of a value that it is absolute is to say that one cannot
> compromise over it at all.[481]

In looking for a solution to the dilemma, we should not explore only what differ-
entiates liberty and security each as absolute goods, rather we should look at what, if
anything, these values share. For example, Waldron (2006: 310) argues that

> [p]artisans of security may need to face up to the fact that what most people
> (in this country) want to secure is not just life, but their American way of life,
> which has traditionally been associated with the enjoyment of certain liberties.
> Equally, partisans of civil liberties need to face up to the fact that what people
> want is secure liberty, not just liberty left open to abuse and attack.

Seemingly, proponents on both sides of the debate have something to learn from the
other.

Although the discussion of the dilemma tends to focus on liberty and security as ab-

---

[480]Skinner (1990: 338).
[481]Berlin (2002: 33).

solute goods, we see that, in practical usage at least, partisans of both sides make their case based in some measure on the instrumentality of these goods.[482] Both liberty and security—while they may be prized as absolute goods—are desired for something.

Approaching liberty and security as instrumental, instead of only as absolute goods, is not new. Rather, in today's discussion of these issues the approach has been somewhat abandoned. Thus I propose we return to this approach of considering the instrumentality of liberty and security in order to better evaluate potential trade-offs in society. Both liberty and security are desired in general because they are instrumental to the human desire for the "good life." Considered as instrumental goods, then, both security and liberty derive their worth from the degree to which they do or do not conduce to the ends toward which their use is directed.

For example, liberty for J.S. Mill was significantly instrumental. Since he argued that happiness is humanity's chief aim, he came to the conclusion that this happiness is best achieved in civil society where people are left free to pursue their own interests.[483] Thus liberty for Mill was instrumental to happiness. We need not limit ourselves to thinking that the instrumental value of liberty and security is hedonistic, however; rather we can think of these values belonging to a number of different conceptions of the good life. For example, a person's conception of the good life could be directed by attachment to the values of Utilitarianism, Epicureanism, or even Stoicism.

One of the more recent considerations of liberty as an instrumental good is found in Rawls, where he counts various liberties as among what he calls "primary goods"

> something that a person has instrumental reasons to want, no matter what else they want; something that promises results that are likely to appeal to them, no matter what they value and pursue.[484]

Like Mill, Hobbes acknowledged security as instrumental to human happiness:

> By safety one should understand not mere survival in any condition, but a happy life so far as that is possible. For men willingly entered commonwealths which they had formed by design in order to be able to live as pleasantly as the human condition allows.[485]
>
> Regarding this life only, the good things citizens may enjoy can be put into four categories: 1) defense from external enemies; 2) preservation of internal peace; 3) acquisition of wealth, so far as this is consistent with public security; 4) full enjoyment of innocent liberty. Sovereigns can do no more for the citizens' happiness than to enable them to enjoy the possessions their industry has won

---

[482] See, for example, Ullmann (1983); Charters (1994); Posner (2006, 2007); Dershowitz (2002); Paterson (1877); and Ignatieff (2004).

[483] See Magid (1987).

[484] Rawls (2001: 90). We can think of the instrumentality of security in the same way as Rawls considers the instrumentality of the other primary goods.

[485] Hobbes (1998:143, On the Citizen, Ch. XIII).

them, safe from foreign and civil war.[486]

Machiavelli, too, thought that both security and liberty had instrumental value.

> The common benefit gained from a free community is recognized by nobody
> while he possesses it; namely, the power of enjoying freely his possessions with-
> out any anxiety, of feeling no fear for the honor of his women and children, of
> not being afraid for himself.[487]

Liberty and security may also be instrumental in the practice of each other. For instance, security can certainly be argued to be instrumental to effective liberty (as mentioned earlier). Likewise, liberty can be instrumental to security. For example, the
values of political liberty which allow for openness in government can be instrumental
in enhancing security for individual in society who, by having access to these political
liberties, are protected from potential abuses (and potential breeches in personal safety
and the security of property) by government.

Looking at the instrumentality of security and liberty does not make the dilemma
of a potential trade-off any less serious, although it may help us to find compromises
where previously the 'partisan absolutists' would have been unwilling to budge. The
usual question asked is: "How much liberty will be lost and how much security gained
(or vice versa) by this new NSA measure?" Instead we should ask: "Will this new
measure enhance people's ability to self-direct their lives (provided that their wills do
not infringe on the rights of others) in terms of the amount of freedom and security
necessarily to reasonably pursue their ends?"

Considering liberty (or security) as an instrumental good could lead some to the
conclusion that—thus as 'one good among many'—to trade or sacrifice liberty/security
is no different from sacrificing any other societal good, especially if we think that the
good life can be achieved without liberty and security.[488] My argument, however, is
not that liberty and security have no inherent value, simply that they do indeed have
instrumental value.

So far as today's debate goes, both extremes place inherent value on security and
liberty. If this is how we approach issues of terrorism, we may never come to a meaningful compromise and will instead, because of increasing fears, tend to err on the side
of security. Thus my argument is in some sense a pragmatic one. The only way to solve
dilemmas of a sacrifice of either liberty or security for the sake of the other is to approach issues by considering these goods as instrumental. Indeed, there is a purpose to
our enjoyment of liberty and to our enjoyment of security, and we must not forget that
both liberty and security are desired for the sake of something else. We may prize these
as ideals and lose out on both.

---

[486]Ibid., p. 144.

[487]Machiavelli (1965: 236).

[488]These objections are made by Doug den Uyl (2003) who argues that we should consider liberty only as
an absolute good.

Chapter 10

Social Choice and Political Economy

Note.[489]

A theme of this book is that the purpose of social choice theory is to provide a grand theoretical framework for designing human institutions. Once theoretical work had shown how markets optimally aggregated preferences, attempts were made to extend the theory from markets to politics. The early work in rational choice theory or social choice in modelling elections and collective action produced relatively poor predictions, but impelled game theorists to generalize preference-based theories to include belief formation. A consequence of this change is that the theory is no longer purely axiomatic, but draws on insights about human behavior from other disciplines and empirical analysis of the role institutions play in determining beliefs.

In their book, *Pathologies of Rational Choice Theory,* Green and Shapiro (1994) contend that it is pathological for social choice theory to attempt to provide a grand theory of political behavior. An aspect of this alleged pathology is the inattention paid by rational choice theorists to empirical falsification or confirmation of their theories. The assumption underlying this critique is that political science is fundamentally an empirical discipline. If this assumption is accepted, then practitioners of political science have reason to ignore social choice theory.

Green and Shapiro assume that social choice theory has its roots in economic theory, and they suggest that, for this reason, it is method-driven rather than problem-driven. Moreover, they question whether a theoretical framework "designed for the different purpose of explaining the behavior of market prices" (Green and Shapiro, 1994:194) need have any relevance for the understanding of political behavior. I infer that Green and Shapiro view the development of rational choice theory in political science as an act of colonization by economists.

In my view what gives rational choice theory coherence is precisely that it is an attempt to construct a grand theory of human behavior. That is to say, the theory is a conceptual framework through which to analyze the interplay and consequences of human incentives within institutions. This may explain why, long before rational

---

[489]This section discusses some arguments originally presented in Schofield (1995a).

choice theory migrated from economics into political science, it had been used by the Marquis de Condorcet in late-eighteenth-century France to provide a framework for the design of good government and society.[490] A universal theory of human behavior should be equally applicable in either politics or economics. To assess the merits of rational choice theory, then, requires an understanding of how it has evolved, regardless of which discipline served as the site of the various stages of its evolution.

I shall argue that the primary motivation for practitioners of rational choice theory, in the course of its evolution since the 1950s, has been to create an integrated, empirical theory of market and polity that would serve the normative purpose of designing good institutions. It has become increasingly obvious that to create such a theory, it is necessary to understand how individuals form beliefs about empirical reality and how they act in response both to their normative preferences and their beliefs. As this theory evolved, it led to changes in our understanding of how to devise good political and economic institutions, inasmuch as the economists' equation of good with Pareto optimal no longer appeared adequate. Given that people's beliefs – their empirical models of the world, their private information, and so on – vary so much, the aggregation of people's preferences (or values) so as to achieve Pareto optimality could no longer be the normative basis for design. This realization has led to a return to Condorcet's original desire to evaluate human institutions as devices both to aggregate preferences and integrate beliefs.

Green and Shapiro's critique has little weight when rational choice theory is seen as primarily normative, not empirical. Even concentrating on applications within political science, there are reasons to judge their critique to be misdirected. Most of the works that command Green and Shapiro's attention have their origin in the attempts by two economists, namely Downs (1957) and Olson (1965), to deal with questions of preference aggregation in the political economy. In my view, this work should be seen as part of the effort, originating in economics, to gauge whether the theoretical optimality of the market could be extended to the political economy. However, the early work in the research tradition represented by Downs and Olson was never intended to be a substantive analysis of political systems. On the contrary, the conceptual framework underlying these models was designed to be compatible with economic theory. I shall discuss in some detail below how only one component of Condorcet's concern, namely preference aggregation, was developed by economists, and particularly Kenneth Arrow (1951), in laying the foundation for a rational choice theory of political economy. Whereas the work in the Downs-Olson tradition had the virtue of simplicity in construction and prediction, the more recent efforts have shown that the predictions of these preference-based models were not corroborated, in general, in the behavior of real polities.

---

[490]The period 1759 to 1788 saw the publication of major works on "social design" in Britain and the United States as well as France. These include Adam Smith (1759, 1776), Condorcet (1785, 1795), and *The Federalist Papers* (1787). See Lasch (1991) for the notion of "progress" in Adam Smith. See also Commager (1977) for the influence of the French philosophes and Beer (1993) for the influence of Harrington (1656) and other British writers on the debate in the United States. I emphasized the importance of Condorcet's *Essai* of 1785 in Chapter 1.

In this chapter I shall consider the various attempts to construct a closed (or consistent) preference-based theory of human behavior in both economics and politics and show, in each case, why there were logical reasons to extend the theory beyond preferences to beliefs. As the discussion proceeds, I hope to make it clear why the normative economic criterion of Pareto optimality began to appear less appropriate than the Condorcetian criterion of truth. I use "truth" as a shorthand for the property of a human institution to efficiently aggregate the dispersed information held by its individual members.

The earliest effort in this direction was Condorcet's demonstration that, among a jury judging the innocence or guilt of a defendant, a majority vote will more often be correct than the response of an average juror. As the size of the jury, or society, becomes very large, the probability that the majority will be right approaches unity. This theorem seems to justify democratic procedures for belief aggregation (of a certain kind) as optimal.[491] Below 1 shall mention attempts to derive analogous results for markets.

As rational choice theory has evolved, it has been obliged to become less axiomatic in structure. Indeed, the increasing emphasis on beliefs suggests that it will, of necessity, have to draw on insights from other behavioral sciences, including anthropology, linguistics, and psychology. Since the theory also includes the role of institutions in determining human choice, it is likely that there will be continuing interaction between empirical and theoretical research on this topic.

Let me amplify these remarks by briefly discussing how the rational actor theory employed by economists in the 1950s was later obliged to address larger questions of social choice that were anticipated by Condorcet.

Neoclassical economic theory can be viewed as the analysis of human incentives in a particular restricted context of fixed resources, private goods, and a given technology. As such, it is a theory of preference aggregation. Contrary to Green and Shapiro's assertion (quoted previously), the theory does not explain the behavior of market prices. The work of Arrow and Debreu (1954) and of McKenzie (1959) did assert, however, that, in this restricted context, the competitive price equilibrium would be Pareto optimal. In discussions of market behavior, economists often go on to assert (a claim that, as far as I know, is unproven) that only a competitive market can efficiently aggregate the diverse beliefs of the members of a heterogeneous economy. If this were true, then nonmarket, planned economies would be inadequate to the task of integrating the dispersed information that underlies these divergent beliefs.[492]

---

[491] As discussed in Chapter 1, the theorem assumes that the average juror probability of being correct exceeds one-half, and that the jurors' choices are made independently. Recent results by Ladha (1992, 1993) indicate that the independence condition may be weakened, yet still preserve the Condorcet Jury Theorem.

[492] See for example the "calculation" argument of von Hayek (1976). It should be noted that the recent collapse of the economic system of the USSR may be viewed as corroboration that such a system is, in the long run, not well adapted to the generation of technological innovation, one key aspect of information aggregation. This theoretical argument concerning markets is identical in form to the Condorcetian argument concerning democracy. Thus the underlying question is how, exactly, different political economies aggregate information.

Since the difference between preferences and beliefs is important, but subtle, it is worthwhile briefly discussing how market institutions do aggregate beliefs. Foreign exchange markets, futures markets, financial markets, and so forth may seem to be driven by the preferences of buyers or sellers, but in truth the motivations of the agents are derived from their own private information and their expectations of commodity price movements. Rational expectations, or the convergence of agents' expectational beliefs, can be thought of as the appropriate type of truth in markets. However, this convergence in beliefs need not occur.[493]

Thus, in an attempt to develop the analysis of human incentives, rational actor theory has been forced to go well beyond the preference-based study of private-goods markets. The intimate connection between preferences and beliefs has necessitated an attempt to reconstitute a general theory of rationality; this is exactly what game theory is about. Moreover, some goods are public, and jointly produced and consumed. Some such public goods (like technological innovation) may be produced and consumed within the economic system, but others, such as national defense and domestic security, are more traditionally created through the political system. Since one method of political choice is by some form of democracy, the need to extend the theory to public goods translates into a requirement to analyze democratic polities to determine not only preferences for such goods, but the incentives to produce them, given people's beliefs about others' willingness to pay for them. It should be noted here that the distinguishing feature of rational choice theory in its market-based form was its emphasis on the connection between preferences, equilibrium, and optimality. The attempt to enlarge the domain of the theory from economics to political economy retained these key concepts. Moreover, the non market institutions that constrain human behavior are obviously important for the way individuals construct their preferences and beliefs, and for the methods by which these are aggregated. The need to examine this question has become more important in the last few years, as research has attempted to model different political institutions. The general theme underlying this research has been, I believe, a desire to determine whether or not democratic political institutions are compatible, in some sense, with market efficiency.

A very extensive public choice literature, particularly in the 1970s and 1980 argued that democratic political choice was not compatible with market efficiency.[494] The various arguments are too numerous to list here, but in general they asserted that democratic polities created the context for political rent-seeking that constrained economic growth. Indeed, political representatives were viewed as creating rents for themselves, with the consequence that government growth was accompanied by deleterious economic consequences. The debate is, of course, still being carried on, and it underlies many of the tensions that exist between the anglo-saxon polities of the United Kingdom and the United States and the member states of the European Union. The public choice literature, while influenced by theoretical, rational choice models, was also directed at explaining empirical facts (such as stagflation). This mix of theoretical and empirical

---

[493]Brian Arthur (1997) has recently shown the failure of models of rational expectations.
[494]These arguments were discussed in Chapter 5.

reasoning I shall term positive theory. Since positive theory attempts to explain facts of the world, it must address questions of empirical corroboration or falsification.

Early positive attempts to apply economic theory were based on a model of market behavior which assumed that agents are completely characterized by their preferences, and that they respond non-strategically to prices. To some degree the inferences of this model have been corroborated in relatively simple situations. However, this preference-based theory has had little success in modelling choice under either strong uncertainty[495] or large-scale economic change over time.[496] More importantly, the attempt to use rational actor theory as a basis for macroeconomics has not been particularly successful. Although macroeconomics purports to describe the real economic world, it often appears to be a tower of Babel, populated by Keynesians, monetarists, supply-siders, etc. On the other hand, most macroeconomists would accept, in general terms, the postulates of microeconomic theory, and the notion of rationality in particular. The empirical weakness of microeconomics has not led economists to reject this theory, but rather has led them to attempt to develop more complex models of rationality. As I suggested above, the imperative for game theory has been to extend simple models based on preferences so that agents' beliefs are made more explicit.

Is political science more like macroeconomics or microeconomics? Green and Shapiro assert that, like macroeconomics, it is fundamentally a problem-driven rather than a method-driven discipline, and on this basis they attack the rational choice recourse to formal modelling over empirical research. I accept that political science is problem-driven, but do not agree that, like macroeconomics, this makes it necessarily dependent on empirical analysis. Political science is driven by the age-old problem of how we are to be governed. The Founding Fathers and particularly the authors of *The Federalist* , were concerned precisely with the normative problem of the proper form of government. I would go so far as to suggest that Hamilton and the other Federalists were rational choice theorists of a kind. To substantiate this I might mention the recent observation of Gordon Wood that the Federalist notion of government rested completely "on the assumption that most people were self-interested and absorbed in their private affairs."[497] Of course, the Founding Fathers did not engage in empirical political science, as we would understand the term "empirical" today. Nonetheless, they were men of practical reason who made intelligent guesses about the way self-interested individuals were likely to behave under different systems of government. As discussed in Chapter 1, Madison argued n *Federalist X* that

> the greater number of citizens and extent of territory may be brought within the compass of Republican, than of Democratic Government; and it is this circumstance principally which renders factious combinations less to be dreaded in

---

[495] See Denzau and North (1994).
[496] See the discussion of North's work in Chapter 1.
[497] Wood (1991: 264).

the former, than in the latter.

Not only does Madison essentially apply a Condorcetian[498] form of argument in *Federalist X*, but he distinguishes between opinions (i.e., beliefs) and passions (i.e., preferences).

If we distinguish the normative political theory of the Founders from the current study of American, comparative, and international politics, and if we call the latter political science as opposed to political theory, then it is true that political science is now predominantly empirical, just as macroeconomics is. This by no means entails that empirical political science is epistemologically superior in any way to political theory (whether normative or rational choice). My own view is that if political science focuses principally on empirical relationships rather than on the evaluation and design of government, then it is seriously wanting. An attempt within social choice theory to construct a normative basis for evaluation based on Pareto optimality will be discussed in the next section.[499]

Although rational choice theory is predominantly a theoretical discipline, the work presented in this volume has been concerned with empirical corroboration. The mix of problem-based concerns and empirical testing displayed by rational choice theory has contributed significantly to its increasing importance in political science. It might also be mentioned that rational choice theory has had an impact on, or has at least excited the interest of, sociologists, philosophers, and mathematicians, as well as economists and political scientists. Although Green and Shapiro emphasize the significance of rational choice theory for the study of U.S. politics, the theory has been applied in most of the substantive subdisciplines of political science.

The progenitors of these attempts at positive reasoning, the seminal works in rational choice theory by Downs and Olson, on which Green and Shapiro focus, were certainly predominantly theoretical. While Arrow (1951) was concerned with the normative task of aggregating preferences, the problem addressed by both Downs and Olson was to use microeconomic tools to explore the provision of public goods through voting and collective action. Neither Downs's prediction (that, in two-party competition, the parties will tend to converge) nor Olson's claim (about the failure of collective action when private incentives are absent) have been empirically substantiated. The reason is that while both Downs and Olson focused on preferences, it is evident that elections and collective action situations are games that cannot be fully described without modelling the beliefs of the participants. A number of the previous chapters in this book have emphasized that to model elections it is necessary to model the beliefs of voters about the quality or valence of the political candidates.

More generally, it is important to model the way agents form beliefs about other agents' beliefs, and thus their behavior. This is often described as the common knowl-

---

[498] See also McLean and Urken (1992) and Urken (1991) for a different view on whether Condorcet influenced Madison..

[499] Important work in normative political theory by Rawls (1972) and Gauthier (1986), etc., is influenced, to some degree, by social choice theory. See also Binmore (1994) for an attempt to base normative political theory in game theory.

edge problem. In my view, it is at the heart of an understanding of economic as well as political behavior, and indeed all collective action [500]

Preference-based models, whether of markets or elections, are relatively simple, with fairly clear predictions. Beliefs, on the other hand, are anything but simple: they involve, at the very least, some description of how people learn, update, and model the world they live in. Condorcet, known both for his work on the aggregation of beliefs (the so-called Condorcet Jury Theorem) and for work on the aggregation of preferences, was unable to combine these two modes of analysis. In his honor, I shall call the venture of developing an integrated model of politics that includes both preferences and beliefs the Condorcetian research program. In the next sections of the chapter I shall present my view of the evolution of the preference-based models (what I call the Arrovian research program, in honor of Kenneth Arrow) to incorporate beliefs.

10.1 The Arrovian Research Program

Table 10.1: A Classification of Economic and Political Theories

	Economics	Political Economy	Politics
Normative	Welfare economics	Social choice	Normative political theory
Theoretical	Market (equilibrium)	Game theory	Rational choice theory
Positive	Public economics	Public choice	Theory of institutions
Empirical	Macroeconomics	Institutional political economy	Political science

Table 10.1 sets out my view of the relationships between the various branches of economics, political economy, and politics. As the table suggests, rational choice theory as applied to politics is only one among a number of different research activities, all characterized by their varying degrees of emphasis on the normative, the theoretical, the positive and the empirical.[501] The table is also meant to emphasize the close connections between game theory and the adjacent theoretical and positive subfields.

Market theory utilizes the idea of equilibrium to relate economic parameters (resources, preferences, technology) to an outcome or choice. Welfare economics and public economics (research fields that are subsidiary to market theory) are designed to address normative and positive aspects of the relationship between government behavior and the economy. Public economics deals with the appropriate relationship between government and the economy, while macroeconomics covers the empirical aspect of this relationship.

---

[500] See Schofield (1985a), Hinich and Munger (1994).

[501] I distinguish here between empirical research and positive research. The latter is based on theoretical arguments but attempts to make assertions about the empirical world.

In an attempt to provide a formal basis for public finance and government, the economist must determine whether the domain of market theory can be enlarged to include
non-market phenomena, such as preferences for public goods. Arrow took the first
step in this program by asking if the preferences of the individuals making up a society could by aggregated to construct a measure of social welfare. Although his social
choice theory addressed certain concerns that economists regard as essential, including
the compatibility of the market and democracy, nothing about that theory restricts it to
either welfare economics or political theory. Still, for an economist, the question of the
compatibility of the market and democracy must be expressed in a formal language that
is general enough to include economic theory.

Economic theory *circa* 1954 used assumptions on the preferences and resources
of individuals to demonstrate the existence of a market equilibrium. To enlarge its
theoretical language so as to model democracy, the nature of citizen preference was
extended from private goods to public goods. However, the fundamental concept of
preference had to be retained. Since the question involved the degree to which the
market equilibrium result could be generalized, it was necessary to pose it in terms of
the existence (or otherwise) of equilibrium.

Microeconomics adopts the postulate that individual preferences are consistent. However, a variety of consistency axioms can be adopted. The most restrictive one, common
in microeconomics, is that each individual's preference can be represented by a (nu-
merical) utility function. This strong assumption implies that both strict preference and
indifference are transitive: if a and b are equally preferable, as are b and c, then so are a
and c. The standard example of non-transitive indifference, however, is a cup of coffee
with no sugar, which is "indifferent" compared to a cup with a single grain of sugar, to
one with two grains, and so on, but not to one with a thousand grains. A weaker consistency assumption is that of the transitivity of strict preference, but not of indifference.
Even weaker is the assumption of acyclicity: if a is strictly preferred to b, b is strictly
preferred to c, c to d, and so on to x, then x cannot be strictly preferred to a. Acyclicity
guarantees that an individual may always make a "choice," that is, select an alternative,
such that if a is chosen , none of the other alternatives can be preferred to a .

While economic theory concentrates on preferences, it usually adopts the postulate
that individuals' behavior will be given by their choices (if such exist). Where the
outcomes are uncertain, or involve risk, behavioral predictions may associate a list of
probabilities with the final eventualities. Theorists often assume that preferences under
risk behave as if they were weighted by these probabilities. Yet it is entirely possible
that real individual preferences in the presence of risk may fail acyclicity, leading to
apparently "irrational" or inconsistent behavior (Kahneman and Tversky 1979). In my
view the postulate of acyclic consistency is reasonable in the absence of risk, but is less
tenable in its presence.

Rationality postulates combine with various structural assumptions about the nature
of the economic system to yield an economic equilibrium that is Pareto optimal in the
sense that no other allocation of resources is preferred unanimously. In the absence
of a price mechanism,as in politics, rational choice theorists utilized the notion of the

"core."[502] An outcome is in the core if no coalition of agents is able and willing to bring about a different state. The concept of a core was devised, in part, to cover situations involving public goods.

Green and Shapiro seem to assume that Arrow's Impossibility Theorem is simply concerned with democratic rules of collective decision. But in truth, the genius of Arrow's result is that it suggests that, in general, a social utility function cannot be defined, negating the assumption that individual preferences could be aggregated so as to describe an optimal provision of public goods. In a sense, Arrow showed that the assumptions economists typically employ in modelling individual behavior are unlikely to hold where public goods are concerned. For while it is reasonable to assume that individuals prefer more rather than less of a private good, it is entirely possible that among them, individuals can have extremely complex preferences in the public domain. More of my public good may be more of your public bad. While I may want extensive military expenditure, you may loathe the military and prefer good schools, parks, environmental protection, and so forth. Since there is no obvious a priori restriction on the possible set of public preferences that individuals may have, Arrow adopted the unrestricted domain assumption. That assumption allows each individual to have any preference, as long as it satisfies transitivity of both strict preference and indifference. Under this assumption, the only social rule that satisfies the unanimity condition must be dictatorial. More generally, any social utility that can be used to make social choices based on individual preferences must necessarily be dictatorial.

If preferences could be equated with utilities, then social utility could be obtained simply by summing individual utilities. But economists believe in general that interpersonal comparisons of utility are scientifically meaningless, since it is impossible to "extract" the information required to construct such comparisons. Certainly markets and voting mechanisms, when viewed as methods of preference aggregation, do not provide the means of obtaining such information. However, if markets and polities are modelled as devices for aggregating both preferences and beliefs, then it is possible that the negative inferences of the Arrow impossibility theorem could be avoided. As Arrow (1987) himself observed, before this could be attempted, it would be necessary to deal with the question of *common knowledge* – the foundation of our beliefs about the beliefs of others.

Duncan Black (1958) reintroduced Condorcet's work to a modern audience and thus contributed. to the extension of preference-based theory to include the analysis of beliefs. Although Green and Shapiro devote little attention to Black, almost all the elements of what has come to be known as spatial voting theory are present in Black's *The Theory of Committees and Elections*. Just as Arrow had investigated whether individual preferences could be aggregated into a social utility function, Black investigated the possibility of equilibrium in voting systems. In this context an equilibrium is a point or outcome that is unbeaten (although it need not beat every other conceivable point). Suppose that three voters have distinct preferred points on a left-right political contin-

---

[502]This idea was used in Chapter 4 to study legislative bargaining.

uum, and that each voter has single-peaked preferences (preferences that are maximized at a single point). Then the middle (or median) voter's preferred point cannot be beaten under majority rule, where a majority requires two out of three. Black called this equilibrium a "majority motion" in his book. In more recent work, the voting equilibrium is known as the *core*.

Suppose now that the decision problem involves more than a single continuum. For example, preferences for social liberalism or conservatism might be independent from preferences for economic liberalism or conservatism. Under such conditions, even with single-peaked individual preferences, the likelihood of the existence of an equilibrium is negligible. As Black writes, "the conditions that must be satisfied before there can be any majority motion are highly restrictive. The frequency of occurrence as a fraction of the total number of cases possible . . . is infinitesimally small or 'practically zero'" (Black 1958:139). Earlier in the book Black seemed to equate cases without an equilibrium with the occurrence of cycles, so he apparently took it for granted that when there is more than one dimension to voters' preferences, voting cycles will occur. Economics postulates that any observed behavior must express an actor's preference. A voting equilibrium, therefore, would be expected to manifest collective preferences. If there is no equilibrium, however, the economist can make no behavioral predictions. The term "instability" is used for this situation. Green and Shapiro object to the "vagueness with which instability is conceptualized." But there is no formal ambiguity about the meaning of instability, since it is defined as an empty core or equilibrium. Over two decades of theoretical work have made it clear, however, that, in general, democratic procedures of the kind examined by Black generally possess no core. In the absence of a behavioral prediction based on preference theory, the natural step was to account for observed outcomes by modelling the way beliefs influenced behavior. To be more specific, it appeared plausible that the outcome would depend on the expectations of agents, their ability to bargain by making guesses about other agents' behavior, and so on. One of the important results in the purely preference-based theory of voting was that voting cycles could, in principle, go everywhere in the policy space.[503] Yet this occurrence of theoretical indeterminacy or chaos did not necessarily imply behavioral chaos, since there existed no belief-based model about what voters would actually do in the context of theoretical chaos. Indeed, experimental work by Fiorina and Plott (1978) and by Laing and Olmsted (1978) seemed to demonstrated "that coreless games do not produce markedly more unstable outcomes than do games with cores" (Green and Shapiro 135). Green and Shapiro inferred that this empirical work vitiated the logic of preference-based voting theory. This is incorrect, since the formal voting model implied that voting outcomes would be restricted to a small domain, called the *heart*, when there were only two dimensions of policy.[504] The empirical work did suggest that a rational choice theory that incorporates beliefs should smooth out the difference between games with and without a core.

The work on theoretical voting chaos during the late 1970s induced a period of in-

---

[503] Chapter 1 gives more details about these formal results.
[504] Chapter 4 uses this concept in examining outcomes in the Knesset in Israel.

tense debate within rational choice political theory. As Green and Shapiro observe, two of the protagonists in this debate, Riker (1980, 1982, 1986) and Tullock (1981), drew quite different conclusions concerning the significance of chaos results for the study of legislatures (see also the essays in Ordeshook and Shepsle 1982). Because Green and Shapiro view politics as an empirical science, they fault both Riker and Tullock for the inadequate empirical basis of their respective arguments about the relevance or irrelevance of the chaos theorems. My own criticism of Riker and Tullock is more fundamental. Formally, the chaos theorems on which they drew apply only to committees, where there is some foundation for supposing the voters have well-specified preferences. It is not at all clear that representatives in a legislature can be assumed to have "preferences" that are similar in kind to the members of a committee. It may be intuitively plausible that each legislator seeks to provide certain kinds of "goods" to constituency members. But until the voter-legislator connection is modelled in detail, there is no formal rational choice basis for the study of a U.S.-style legislature.

I have argued (Schofield (2008b), however, that it is plausible that the models of committee voting are applicable to European-style legislatures involving well-disciplined parties. In particular, it appears reasonable to me to assume that party leaders in such legislatures do have preferred policy outcomes, and that they attempt to construct legislative majorities to implement these policies. There is an extensive empirical literature on coalition formation in European legislatures (Laver and Schofield 1990) and recent attempts to use rational choice theory in this context do produce empirical predictions that have been substantiated. One insight that comes out of this work concerns the possibility that a large non-majority party may form a minority government when its preferred point is at the core or equilibrium position in the policy space.[505]

Rational choice theory also provides a logical framework within which to make some sense out of some well-established empirical relationships that have been noted in multiparty political systems. For example, the fragmentation of parliamentary systems into many small parties is highly correlated with government brevity in the European systems (Dodd 1976). It should be obvious that in the absence of a core or policy equilibrium, any government that does form may be defeated by another majority coalition with a counter-policy proposal. Thus a connection between political fragmentation and the remote probability of a core would give insight into macropolitical" relationships. In my view, the United States Congress is fundamentally different from European multiparty systems for a number of reasons.[506] Below I shall address some of these issues in the context of the observations by Green and Shapiro on rational choice theories of elections.

There is a venerable tradition on the connection between proportional representation and political fragmentation (Duverger 1954). The empirical work by Taagepera and Schugart (1989), for example, provides a detailed examination of this connection. European polities in general use proportional representation and typically have more than two parties. Duverger (1954) and Popper (1945) argued that this tends to result in weak

---

[505] See again the discussion of bargaining in the Knesset, presented in Chapter 4.
[506] Chapters 3 and 4 make a number of observations on these lines.

government. By the same token, there is some evidence that (plurality) systems based on single-member constituencies tend to produce two parties and thus a clearer electoral choice. The British electoral system, for example, which clearly is a plurality, or first-past- the-post arrangement, has always tended toward two dominant parties. While this is consistent with some rational choice models of elections, Duverger's argument, that small parties will wither away under plurality, is confounded by the continued presence of small British parties such as the centrist Liberal Democrat party in the United Kingdom. On the other hand, although the United States is usually regarded as having a two-party system, its parties appear less disciplined, in general, than European-style parties. In particular, members of Congress are generally more heterogeneous in their voting behavior than one would expect within a European-style party system. The political science literature, from Duverger onwards, is even more inadequate in terms of the theoretical (rather than empirical) analysis of these relationships. My own view is that the formal analysis of elections should start with a general conception of electoral laws and deduce facts about the number and nature of political parties.

There are two distinct classes of models of electoral competition. The first class assumes that voting is *deterministic*. That is, the candidates make promises and each voter picks a candidate depending on which promise the voter prefers. Within this class of models, policy blind models assume that the candidates gain no utility except from winning, and that they attempt, therefore, to gain the maximum number of votes. Green and Shapiro (in Chapter 7) refer to such candidates as purely "election-seeking." Just as in the committee model examined by Black, if the space of possible promises is one-dimensional, then two rational candidates will make the same promise, attempting to occupy the point at the median voter position.

As an economist, Downs (1957) could be justified in viewing this as a solution to the equilibrium problem in political economy. From the perspective of public finance, two-party competition could be assumed to provide a "median" tax schedule which could then be used to cover the provision of the public good in question. Obviously, however, government provides more than one public good, so individual voter preferences must be described in more than one dimension. The results from the committee voting model imply that, in such cases, there will be no core. In other words, no matter what one candidate promises, an opponent can promise something else that will obtain a majority. From the perspective of non-cooperative game theory, the nonexistence of a core means there is no pure strategy Nash equilibrium (PSNE) in the two-candidate game. For public economics, this is a serious problem.

The obvious theoretical response is to develop a more general notion than the core. Kramer (1978) showed that there will be a mixed strategy Nash equilibrium (MSNE) where candidates make ambiguous promises. The nice feature of the so-called *uncovered set* (McKelvey,1986) is that the support of the MSNE will belong to this set. Thus, the political economist can assert that actual political outcomes will lie in the uncovered set. To some extent, at least, the theoretical problem of equilibrium is thus solved.

However, the motivation for this modelling strategy comes from economics, not political science. Its sole purpose is to solve the formal requirements of public economics, not to describe actual politics. Indeed, any model that predicts that candidates will make identical promises cannot be considered to have made any effort to characterize real politics. It was this realization, perhaps, that led Wittman to observe that "the research on formal models has been almost devoid of empirical content."[507]

Wittman, and others, have attempted to inject some political reality into the model by assuming the candidates are policy motivated, in the sense that the candidates' own policy preferences are reflected in the promises they make.[508] A candidate may, for example, contract with a group of supporters to constrain his or her personal policy objectives in a certain way in return for campaign contributions. Green and Shapiro observe that "a policy-motivated candidate is at a disadvantage when confronted by a pure election-seeking opponent."[509] This observation is not at all self-evident and is likely to be false. A policy-motivated candidate may find a way to be more credibly committed to supporters' objectives, and thus raise much greater campaign contributions, than a pure election-seeking candidate. In any case, the possibility of a trade-off between contributions and voting suggests that a PSNE can exist where the candidates make quite different promises. The formal model presented in Chapter 3 suggests that this is the case.

The second class of electoral models assumes that voters are *probabilistic* rather than deterministic. Once the candidate promises are made, a voter in the deterministic model chooses one of the candidates with certainty (except when the two candidates are identical in all respects). In the probabilistic model, on the other hand, the voter's behavior, after the candidate promises are known, is a random variable which is based on the voter's beliefs about the likely consequences of the choice. In particular, such beliefs should deal with the estimates each voter makes concerning the likelihood that the candidates will deliver on their promises.

The advantages of the probabilistic model are two-fold. First, if voter preferences and candidate promises (or positions) are known, then it is possible to model the voter response econometrically. The early empirical work concentrated on two-candidate models (Enelow and Hinich 1984), but recent research, discussed in Chapter 4, has modelled multicandidate and multiparty competition (Schofield and Sened, 2006)).

It is important to note that the probabilistic model is continuous in voter and candidate positions, and the chaos theorems (mentioned above) do not apply. Because the total vote for each candidate is a random variable, it can be characterized by its expectation and variance. Probabilistic models typically assume "pure-election seeking" candidates who make promises to maximize their expected vote. The usual result in models of two-candidate competition is that there exists a PSNE where both candidates propose the mean rather than the median position (Lin, Enelow and Dorussen, 1999; Coughlin 1992). This result solves the equilibrium problem of public economics very neatly.

However, there are a number of theoretical and substantive problems with this prob-

---

[507] Quoted in Green and Shapiro (1994: 148).
[508] See also Wittman (1977, 1995).
[509] Quoted in Green and Shapiro (1994: 107).

abilistic model. Even policy-blind candidates make promises under risk, and the degree of risk depends not just on the expectation of voter response, but on the variance of this response. The models implicitly assume that the variance is independent of candidate positions, and this is untenable in the absence of a clear model of the formation of voter beliefs. The models also assume that each voter's behavior is statistically independent of the others'. This is unwarranted for the same reason. More importantly, however, the conclusions of the model are not empirically substantiated. The analysis presented in Chapter 5 of elections in Israel showed the existence of a PSNE where the parties cluster into two groups. In fact, all the parties maintained separate identities and declared quite different policies to the electorate.

I infer that a more realistic variant of the probabilistic model must assume that candidates, or parties, are policy motivated, at least to the extent of choosing positions that balance their policy and electoral objectives. As one would expect, the Nash equilibrium causes party leaders to make very different promises (Cox 1997).

My observations about these models are intended to highlight the differences in the requirements of public finance and formal political theory. For public finance, the motivation is to extract predictions about political choice that can be used to evaluate the optimality of public decisions concerning taxation and public goods provision. The need to add greater political verisimilitude has obliged political theorists to address questions of belief formation (particularly regarding what voters believe the winning candidate will do after the election) and candidate commitment. From the perspective of public finance, the more refined model appears untidy and less parsimonious. The political theorist, however, faces the quite difficult task not just of comparing predictions with reality, but of evaluating how reasonable the assumptions about belief formation are. It is only recently that these belief-based models have been developed to a degree sufficient to offer plausible predictions.

I have tried to suggest, in this section on elections, why the simple unidimensional two-candidate model of electoral competition is both theoretically and empirically inadequate. On the theoretical side, the attempt to base the analysis purely on techniques of preference aggregation has proved to be unsatisfactory. As I have implied above, Downs paid considerable attention to questions of risk or uncertainty in elections, but the formal techniques to address those problems were not available at that time. The observation that these simple models were also empirically unsatisfactory gives greater weight to the theoretical attempt to model both preferences and beliefs. In the next section, I shall attempt to enlarge the discussion about the nature of beliefs, and show the connection with Condorcet's Jury Theorem.

10.2 The Condorcetian Research Program

From the point of view of pluralistic political theory, no individual preference can be privileged over another. This could be taken to imply that no fundamental agreement may be reached among individuals who differ in their preferences. A Nash equilibrium in a game, or a voting equilibrium in a committee, specifies the nature of the compromise (rather than agreement) that individuals will accept given that they attempt to maximize what they prefer. In contrast to preferences, people with differing empirical beliefs about how the world works may come to agree with each other if they communicate and share information. Economists have recently attempted to model this process when beliefs are uncontaminated by preferences (Aumann 1976; McKelvey and Page 1986).

To some extent, political decision making is a matter of aggregating beliefs. Thus, while people may disagree about what action to take, debate may lead to an agreed solution. When two candidates offer differing courses of action (based on their own beliefs about the world), it is perfectly reasonable to suppose that the probability that a given voter chooses one candidate over the other is determined by the relative degree to which (s)he agrees with the two candidates' beliefs. From this point of view, the paradox of voter turnout does not exist, since voting is not based on the desire to implement one's preferences but on the attempt to ascertain the truth.[510] Moreover, convergence of candidates to the same (Nash equilibrium) position is no longer a problem but a virtue, inasmuch as the equilibrium position is the one that has the highest probability of being correct, given the distribution of beliefs in the society. Thus the Nash equilibrium result solves the optimality problem for political-economic theory.

Admittedly, this argument depends on the validity of the Condorcet Jury Theorem, which in turn depends on the assumption of the statistical independence of voter behavior (see Ladha and Miller 1995). This assumption may not be warranted when votes are determined by voters' beliefs. Moreover, if the candidates or voters are policy motivated, their policy concerns will contaminate the process of belief aggregation. Similarly, parties strong enough to impose policy objectives on candidates will also contaminate this process. Nonetheless, since the empirical evidence suggests that party discipline in the U.S. Congress is weak, there may be a basis for inferring that successful congressional candidates at least approximate the belief optimum of their constituents.[511]

The Jury Theorem depends on beliefs that are, in turn, determined by the configuration of activist factions in the political economy. It should be possible, therefore, to use a more complex version of the theorem to resolve some of the questions raised by the Founding Fathers about the relationship between factions, institutional rules, and good government. On the other hand, the optimality question that formal democratic theory may now pose is whether institutional rules and legislators' and activists' private preferences will intrude on the formation of the outcome that best represents the diverse beliefs of the members of the society.

Pursuing these issues will require the development of rationality models that incor-

---

[510]The preference-based problem of voter turnout is due to the fact that the cost of voting exceeds any likely effect from actually voting. See the discussion in Chapter 7.1. This need not be the case for belief aggregation. A single juror may sway the remaining jurors and change the entire verdict.

[511]The point of Chapter 3 was to examine a model of voting that showed how activists would affect the way that voter beliefs are aggregrated by political candidates.

porate both preferences and beliefs.[512] It is obvious that the interrelation between beliefs
and preferences is fundamental in the context of social dilemmas (discussed by Green
and Shapiro in Chapter 5). Olson's (1965) attempt to analyze the problem of collective action (including voluntary provision of public goods and voter turnout) adopted
the simpler perspective of preference aggregation. In this context it is traditional to use
game theory to model the situation, and indeed to describe it as a prisoner's dilemma.[513]

The paradox of the n-person prisoners' dilemma, of course, is that the dominant or
best strategy for each individual is to defect rather than cooperate. This inference was
used as the basis for the argument that public goods would not be provided, or that interest groups would collapse in the absence of private incentives. Green and Shapiro point
out that this argument flies in the face of reality. But they make no reference to the last
decade of theoretical work on the prisoner's dilemma. This work has suggested that it is
far too simplistic to infer that defection will always occur. One possibility is that a dominant player may bribe or persuade the other members of a group to form a cooperative
coalition. It seems to me that these theoretical observations provide the basis for the
positive literature on hegemony in international relations (e.g., Gilpin 1987). However,
the possibility that cooperative coalitions can form entails that they may also collapse.
Indeed, Richards (1990) has demonstrated the occurrence of chaos, or unpredictability, in the experimental prisoner's dilemma. More recent analysis has emphasized the
importance of modelling the beliefs agents hold about the beliefs of others.[514] Because
the analysis of an agent's choice necessarily requires a model of what the agent thinks
others will do and why they will do it, analysis of the relationship between beliefs and
preferences must deal with the common knowledge problem.

While capitalism and democracy were initially viewed by rational choice theorists
simply as methods of preference aggregation, the more recent work has had to view
rational agents not simply as preference maximizers, but as rational modelers of other
agents and the world in which they live. To model another agent means modelling how
that agent models others. The problem of common knowledge is whether there can be
a formal basis for this hierarchy of individual knowledge. Although the question of
why voters vote or why soldiers fight may seem very similar from the point of view of
preference-based game theory, no plausible understanding of their behavior can ignore
voters' or soldiers' beliefs. In these two cases, the relationship between beliefs and
preferences could, in principle, be very different.

10.3 Cultural and Linguistic Evolution

As the Arrovian and Condorcetian programs have intermingled over the last 50 years,
two aspects of the resulting research program have been become increasingly obvious.
First, the attempt to extend closed, preference-based economic theory to the political

---

[512] See work by Nyarko (1997) and Bicchieri (1994).
[513] Hardin (1971, 1982), Taylor (1976), Axelrod (1980).
[514] See Kreps, Milgrom, Roberts and Wilson (1982), Sugden (1986), Young (1993).

economy has encountered a number of theoretical difficulties. The motivation of this economics program seems very similar in a sense to that of the Hilbert program of logically closing mathematics. Just as Gödel (1931) showed the Hilbert program to be impossible[515], so, I believe, did Arrow demonstrate the inadequacy of the preference-based rational choice program.[516] A theory of rationality based on both preference and belief is likely to be open, both in the sense that it is not completely mathematized, but also in the sense that it incorporates non-rationalist or at least non-logical, aspects of thought and language.[517]

Penrose (1994) makes a strong case that the Gödel-Turing problem forbids any purely formalistic or computational account of self-awareness. Penrose's argument suggests that there must be fundamental constraints on our ability to model our own behavior. However, I feel these constraints apply not only to theoretical work, but even more importantly to all empirical accounts of behavior.

As the inadequacy of the formalism of pure preference-based game theory is increasingly appreciated, I predict that the flow of ideas between the theoretical and empirical aspects of political economy will increase. This is already evident in attempts to relate the positive theory of institutions to empirical work in political economy. For example, while North's (1990, 2005) ideas on institutions and economic performance grew out of his earlier empirical work in economic history (North 1981), they were also informed by the developments in game theory that I have mentioned above. Researchers on the positive aspects of political economy are increasingly aware of the way different institutions, whether economic or political, determine the "rules of the game" and thus the formation and maintenance of beliefs. This, in turn, can create the context for work of a predominantly empirical nature, but situated in political economies very unlike those of developed societies. Thus while political economy will retain the normative and theoretical focus of the Condorcetian and Arrovian research programs, it will also increasingly sustain empirical work of a truly comparative nature.

These remarks are to remind the reader that our ability to juxtapose theoretical and empirical analysis of human behavior is limited by the fundamental Gödel-Turing constraints on the consistency and completeness of self-knowledge. These theoretical observations attest to the following remark:

> [T]he fundamental theoretical problem underlying the question of cooperation is the manner by which individuals attain knowledge of each others' preferences and likely behavior. Moreover, the problem is one of common knowledge, since each individual, i, is required not only to have information about others' preferences, but also to know that the others have knowledge about i's own pref-

---

[515]See Wang (1987) for a discussion of Gödel's work.

[516]See Binmore 1993 and Schofield (1995b) for a discussion of connections between rational choice theory and the work of Godel 1931 and Turing 1937. In fact, both the game-theoretic assumption that agents learn about their opponents and that they choose their best response have recently been shown to be incompatible because of the Turing halting problem.See Nachbar (1997, 2001, 2005) and Foster and Young (2001).

[517]. See Margolis (1987, 1993) for some interesting views on such a possibility.

erences and strategies. (Schofield, 1985b)

As regards the cultural or informational basis of cooperation, Pinker and Bloom (1990) have pointed out that

> humans, probably early on, fell into a lifestyle that depended on extended cooperation for food, safety, nurturance, and reproductive opportunities. This lifestyle presents extraordinary opportunities for evolutionary gains and losses. On the one hand it benefits all participants by surmounting prisoners' dilemmas. On the other it is vulnerable to invasion by cheaters. The minimum cognitive apparatus needed to sustain this lifestyle is memory for individuals and the ability to enforce social contracts ... .

They argue that the logic of surmounting the prisoner's dilemma provided the selection pressure for the evolution of language. Recent research suggests that there was a fairly rapid increase of technological and cultural efficiency somewhere between 30,000 and 60,000 years before the present (BP), that led to a diaspora of humans out of Africa (Mellars, 2006). A plausible conjecture is that this cultural transformation was based on the coevolution of language and cultural techniques to avoid the costs of the prisoner's dilemma. On the other hand, Choi and Bowles (2007) present a game theoretical simulation of altruism in prisoner dilemma like situations that seems to indicate that altruism-"benefiting fellow group members at a cost to oneself"- cannot be evolutionary stable. Choi and Bowles suggest, on the contrary, that altruism can coevolve with parochialism-"hostility towards individuals not of the same group." (See also Bowles, 2006).

One obvious way that people can determine whether others are of the same or different group is whether they speak the same language. At the same time it seems quite clear that language tends to exhibit rapid evolution (Kenneally, 2007). For example, Anthony (2007) argues that all Indo-European languages evolved in a few thousand years from a single population originally inhabiting an area north of the Black Sea.

Putting these various ideas together suggests the hypothesis that altruism-parochialism and language coevolved. Within a single speech community, cooperation is enhanced by mutual intelligibility, but conflict between speech communities drives group competition and war.

As Calvin (1991, 2006) has argued, human cultural evolution has been dramatically influenced by the chaotic climatic changes that have occurred since the end of the Ice Age, about 16,000 years BP. At about 7,600 BP, the end of a mini ice age caused the flooding of the fresh-water Euxine Lake to create the Black Sea. This may have been the trigger for a flow of agricultural communities into Western Europe. Drought in the Aegean about 3,200 BP destroyed the Hittite empire in Anatolia and the Mycenean late bronze age civilization. Fagan (2004) suggests that the longevity of the Roman Empire was a function of the stability of the Mediterranean climatic or ecological zone from 2,300BP to 1,700BP. A climatic change around 1,600BP (400CE) may have shifted this ecological zone and precipitated the movement of peoples into Western Europe, bringing the Roman Empire to an end. The Medieval Warm Period, 900CE to 1200CE, tended to benefit Western Europe, and led, for example to the colonization of Greenland about 985CE. However, it also brought drought and collapse to the Mayan civilization (750CE to 1025CE) and the Mesa Verde,Chaco Canyon and Mimbres cultures in North America (1276-1299CE).[518] A cold period, the little ice age, after 1200CE, brought widespread famine in Europe. It is also thought that this climate change contributed to the virulence of the black death about 1340CE.[519] After the end of the little ice age, about 1740CE, agricultural productivity started to increase. As we discussed in Chapter 1, this had important ramifications for the beginning of the industrial revolution.

We may reasonably call these climatic changes *chaotic* because they are caused by complex feedback loops, involving, among other things, the North Atlantic Oscillation, the El Nino Southern Oscillation and the Great Ocean Conveyer Belt. Fagan calls this the "dance of air and ocean," the interaction of periodicities in the orbit of Earth, solar radiation, and deep ocean currents generated by the Coriolis force. Rapid transformations are possible in these dynamic systems, to the extent that they can become structurally unstable: a relatively small perturbation can induce a qualitatively very different system.

In our time, a small humanly induced increase in CO_2 concentration in the atmosphere could enhance the green house effect, inducing catastrophic collapses of the Greenland and Antartic ice sheets. The Greenland collapse would turn off the Gulf Stream, freeze Europe and flood the low-lying land where great cities lie. Drought would cause massive fires in Asia and probably destroy the Amazon forest, causing further positive feedback and increased green house effects.[520] The theoretical and empirical evidence strongly suggests that this threat to the survival of the human race is far more severe even than the threat of nuclear war in the last century. The problem is that we desire economic growth, and the most readily available energy sources to sustain this growth are oil and coal, whose use exacerbates the green house effect. Reliance on markets seems only to bring about chaos.

As drought and famine occur throughout the world, attempts to deal with this global problem will become increasingly ineffective.[521] The leaders of oligopoly capitalism may be able to avoid the pain that the poor and underprivileged will be forced to bear. They may even benefit from the chaos that globalization seems to have created (Klein, 2007).We, however, shall be caught in the last and most terrifying threat of a chaotic prisoners' dilemma, and *the end of history*. Even though the nature of this enviromental "tragedy of the commons"[522] is well understood, it is not at all clear that the divergent perspectives of developed economies, the growing economies of China and India, and

---

[518]Diamond (2005).

[519]See the various books by Fagan (1999, 2000, 2004, 2008).

[520]See Calvin (2008).

[521]It has been conjectured that climate change already contributes to the widespread stress and civil war currently seen in Africa (Miguel, Satyanath and Sergenti, 2004). Recent books by Khanna (2008), Rashid (2008) and Zakaria (2008) discuss aspects of what is probably a very unpleasant future world. For earlier pessimistic prognoses, see the books by Kaplan (1997, 2000, 2003).

[522]Hardin (1968), Schofield (1977), Gore (2006), Sachs (2008).

the chaotic polities of Africa, will permit a resolution. The change that the Democratic voters of the United States demanded when they chose Barack Obama as their presidential candidate was that they should be able to express their political beliefs against the dictates of the market place and the imbroglios wrought by imperial hubris. It may well be impossible to deal with the changes that we can foresee in our future.

References and Further Reading

Acemoglu, D., and J. Robinson. 2005. *Economic Origins of Dictatorship and Democracy.* New York and Cambridge: Cambridge University Press.

Acevado, M., and J. I. Krueger. 2004. "Two Egocentric Sources of the Decision to Vote: The Voter's Illusion and the Belief in Personal Relevance." *Political Psychology* 25:11–134.

Adams, J. 1999a. "Multiparty Spatial Competition with Probabilistic Voting." *Public Choice* 99:259–274.

Adams, J. 1999b. "Policy Divergence in Multicandidate Probabilistic Spatial Voting." *Public Choice* 100:103–122.

Adams, J. 2001. *Party Competition and Responsible Party Government.* Ann Arbor: University of Michigan Press.

Adams, J., J. Dow, and S. Merrill III. 2007. "The Political Consequences of Alienation-Based and Indifference-Based Voter Abstention: Applications to Presidential Elections." *Political Behavior* 28:65–86.

Adams, J., M. Clark, L. Ezrow, G. Glasgow. 2006. "Are Niche Parties Fundamentally Different from Mainstream Parties? The Causes and the Electoral Consequences of Western European Parties' Policy Shifts, 1976-1998." *American Journal of Political Science* 50:513–529.

Adams, J., and S. Merrill III. 1999a. "Modelling Party Strategies and Policy Representation in Multiparty Elections: Why are Strategies so Extreme?" *American Journal of Political Science* 43:765–781.

Adams, J., and S. Merrill III. 1999b. "Party Policy Equilibrium for Alternative Spatial Voting Models: An Application to the Norwegian Storting." *European Journal of Political Research* 36:235–255.

Adams, J., and S. Merrill III. 2005. "Candidates' Policy Platforms and Election Outcomes: The Three Faces of Policy Representation." *European Journal of Political Research* 44:899–918.

Adams, J., and S. Merrill III. 2006. "Why Small, Centrist Third Parties Motivate Policy Divergence by Major Parties." *American Political Science Review* 100:403–417.

Adams, J., S. Merrill III., and B. Grofman. 2005. *A Unified Theory of Party Competition.* New York and Cambridge: Cambridge University Press.

Aldrich, J. H. 1983a. "A Spatial Model with Party Activists: Implications for Electoral Dynamics." *Public Choice* 41:63–100.

Aldrich, J. H. 1983b. "A Downsian Spatial Model with Party Activists." *American Political Science Review* 77:974–990.

Aldrich, J. H. 1995. *Why Parties?* Chicago: Chicago University Press.

Aldrich, J. H., and M. McGinnis. 1989. "A Model of Party Constraints on Optimal Candidate Positions." *Mathematical and Computer Modelling* 12:437–450.

Aldrich, J. H., G. J. Miller, C. W. Ostrom Jr., and D. Rohde. 1986. *American Government.* Boston, MA: Houghton Mifflin.

Aldous, R. 2006. *The Lion and the Unicorn.* New York: Norton.

Allen, R. 1988. "The Price of Freehold Land and the Interest Rate in the Seventeenth and Eighteenth Centuries." *The Economic History Review* 41:33–50.

Allport, G. 1954. *The Nature of Prejudice.* Reading, MA: Addison-Wesley.

Almao V. P. 204. "Movimiento Quinta República: Vocación de Masas y Atadura Personalista." In J. E. Molina and A. E. Díaz [Eds.]. *Los Partidos Políticos Venezolanos en el Siglo XXI.* Caracas: Vadell Hermanos Editores.

Alonso, J. F., and A. M. Lago. 1994. *The Foreign Assistance Requirements of a Democratic Cuba: A First Approximation.* London: La Sociedad Económica.

Alt, J. 1984. "Dealignment and the Dynamics of Partisanship in Britain." In P. Beck, R. Dalton and S. Flanagan [Eds.]. *Electoral Change in Advanced Industrial Societies.* Princeton, NJ: Princeton University Press.

Alvarez, R. M., and J. Nagler. 1995. "Economics, Issues and the Perot Candidacy: Voter Choice in the 1992 Presidential Election." *American Journal of Political Science* 39:714-744.

Alvarez, R. M., and J. Nagler. 1998. "When Politics and Models Collide: Estimating Models of Multi-Candidate Elections." *American Journal of Political Science* 42:55–96.

Alvarez, R. M., and J. Nagler. 2000. "A New Approach for Modeling Strategic Voting in Multiparty Elections." *British Journal of Political Science* 30:57–75.

Alvarez, R. M., J. Nagler, and S. Bowler. 2000. "Issues, Economics, and the Dynamics of Multiparty Elections: The British 1987 General Election." *American Political Science Review* 94:131–150.

Ames B 1987. *Political Survival: Politicians and Public Policy in Latin America.* Berkeley: University of California Press.

An, T. S. 1983. *North Korea: A Political Handbook.* Wilmington, DE: Scholarly Resources.

Ansolabehere, S., and J. Snyder. 2000. "Valence Politics and Equilibrium in Spatial Election Models." *Public Choice* 103:327–336.

Anthony, D. W. 2007. *The Horse, the Wheel, and Language: How Bronze-Age Riders from the Eurasian Steppes Shaped the Modern World.* Princeton, NJ: Princeton University Press.

Aradau, C. 2007. "Forget Equality? Security, Liberty, and the 'War on Terror'" Presented at the SGIR Sixth Pan-European International Relations Conference, Turin.

Aragones, E., and T. Palfrey. 2002. "Mixed Equilibrium in a Downsian Model with a Favored Candidate." *Journal of Economic Theory* 103:131–161.

Aragones, E., and T. Palfrey. 2005. "Spatial Competition Between Two Candidates of Different Quality: The Effects of Candidate Ideology and Private Information." In D. Austen-Smith and J. Duggan [Eds.]. *Social Choice and Strategic Decisions.* Heidelberg: Springer.

Arian, A., and M. Shamir. 1990. *The Election in Israel: 1988.* Albany: SUNY Press.

Arian, A., and M. Shamir. 1995. *The Election in Israel: 1992.* Albany: SUNY Press.

Arian, A., and M. Shamir. 1999. *The Election in Israel: 1996.* Albany: SUNY Press.

Aron, L. 2007. *Russia's Revolution.* Washington DC: AEI Press.

Arrow, K. J. 1950. "A Difficulty in the Concept of Social Welfare." *Journal of Political Economy* 58:328–46.

Arrow, K. J. 1951. *Social Choice and Individual Values*. New Haven, CT: Yale University Press.

Arrow, K. J. 1959. "Rational Choice Functions and Orderings." *Economica* 26:121–127.

Arrow, K. J. 1969. "Tullock and an Existence Theorem." *Public Choice* 6:105–111.

Arrow, K. J. 1986. "Rationality of Self and of Others in an Economic System." *Journal of Business* S59: S385–90.

Arrow, K. J. 1988. "Workshop on the Economy as an Evolving Complex System: Summary." In P. Anderson, K. Arrow and D. Pines [Eds.]. *The Economy as an Evolving Complex System*. Reading, MA: Addison-Wesley.

Arrow, K., and G. Debreu. 1954. "Existence of an Equilibrium for a Competitive Economy." *Econometrica* 22:265–90.

Asch, S. E. 1956. "Studies of Independence and Conformity: A minority of One Against a Unanimous Majority." *Psychological Monographs* 70:1–70.

Arthur, B. 1997. "Beyond Rational Expectations: Indeterminacy in Economic and Financial Markets." In J. N. Drobak and J. V. Nye [Eds.]. *Frontiers of the New Institutional Economics*. San Diego, CA: Academic Press.

Aumann, R. 1976. "Agreeing to Disagree." *Annals of Statistics* 4:1236–39.

Austen-Smith, D., and J. S. Banks. 1988. "Elections, Coalitions and Legislative Outcomes." *American Political Science Review* 82:405–422.

Austen-Smith, D., and J. S. Banks. 1990. "Stable Portfolio Allocations." *American Political Science Review* 84:891–906.

Austen-Smith, D., and J. S. Banks. 1999. *Positive Political Theory I: Collective Preferences*. Ann Arbor: University of Michigan Press.

Austen-Smith, D., and J. S. Banks. 2005. *Positive Political Theory II: Strategy and Structure*. Ann Arbor: University of Michigan Press.

Austen-Smith, D., and J. R. Wright. 1992. "Competitive Lobbying for a Legislator's Vote." *Social Choice and Welfare* 19:229–257.

Axelrod, R. 1970. *Conflict of Interest*. Chicago, IL: Markham.

Axelrod, R. 1984. *The Evolution of Cooperation*. New York: Basic Books.

Bacon, R., and W. Eltis. 1976. *Britain's Economic Problem: Too Few Products*. London: Macmillan.

Badinter, E., and R. Badinter. 1988. *Condorcet: Un Intellectuel en Politique*. Paris: Fayard.

Baker, K. M. 1975. *Condorcet: From Natural Philosophy to Social Mathematics*. Chicago, IL: University of Chicago Press.

Baker, K. M. 2004. "On Condorcet's Sketch for a Historical Picture of the Progress of the Human Mind." *Daedalus* 133:56–82.

Banks, J. S. 1990. "A Model of Electoral Competition with Incomplete Information." *Journal of Economic Theory* 50:309–325.

Banks, J. S., and J. Duggan. 2000. "A Bargaining Model of Collective Choice." *American Political Science Review* 94:73–88.

Banks, J. S., and J. Duggan. 2005. "The Theory of Probabilistic Voting in the Spatial Model of Elections." In D. Austen-Smith and J. Duggan [Eds.]. *Social Choice and Strategic Decisions*. Heidelberg: Springer.

Banks, J., G. Bordes, and M. Le Breton. 1991. "Covering Relations, Closest Orderings and Hamiltonian Bypaths in Tournaments." *Social Choice and Welfare* 8:355–363.

Banks, J., J. Duggan, and M. Le Breton. 2002. "Bounds for Mixed Strategy Equilibria and the Spatial Model of Elections." *Journal of Economic Theory* 103:88–105.

Banks, J., J. Duggan, and M. Le Breton. 2006. "Social Choice and Electoral Competition in the General Spatial Model." *Journal of Economic Theory* 126:194–234.

Banzhaf, J. F. 1968. "One Man, 3.312 Votes: A Mathematical Analysis of the Electoral College." *Villanova Law Review* 12:303–332.

Barnett, W., M. Hinich, and N. Schofield [Eds.]. 1993. *Political Economy: Institutions, Competition and Representation*. New York and Cambridge: Cambridge University Press.

Baron, D. P., and J. A. Ferejohn. 1989. "Bargaining in Legislatures." *American Political Science Review* 83:1181–1206.

Barry, B. 1973. "John Rawls and the Priority of Liberty." *Philosophy and Public Affairs* 2:274–290.

Barry, B. 1973. *The Liberal Theory of Justice: A Critical Examination of the Principle Doctrines in A Theory of Justice by John Rawls*. Oxford: Oxford University Press.

Bartels, L. M. 2006. "What's the Matter with *What's the Matter with Kansas*." *Quarterly Journal of Political Science* 1:201–226.

Bartels, L. A. 2008. *Unequal Democracy: The Political Economy of the New Gilded Age*. Princeton, NJ: Princeton University Press.

Basinger, S. J., and T. Hartman. 2006. "Candidate Perception in a Presidential Election."Typescript: Stony Brook University.

Bass, J., and M. W. Thompson. 1998. *Ol' Strom: An Unauthorized Biography*. Atlanta, GA: Longstreet Press.

Bates, R., R. De Figueiredo, and B. Weingast. 1998. "The Politics of Interpretation, Rationality, Culture and Transition." *Politics and Society* 26:603–642.

Bates, R. H. *et al.* 2003. *Political Instability Task Force Report (Phase IV Findings)*. McLean, VA: Science Applications International Corporation.

Baumol, W. J. 1965. *Welfare Economics and the Theory of the State*. Cambridge, MA: Harvard University Press.

Beard, C. 1913. *An Economic Interpretation of the Constitution of the United States*. New York: Macmillan.

Beck, N. 1982. "Does There Exist a Political Business Cycle: A Box-Tiao Analysis?" *Public Choice* 38:205–209.

Becker, J. 2005. Rogue Regime: *Kim Jong-il and the Looming Threat of North Korea*. Oxford: Oxford University Press.

Becker, W.1984. *Die Freiheit, die wir meinen*. Munich: Piper.

Beer, S. H. 1982. *Britain Against Itself*. London: Faber and Faber.

Beer, S. H. 1993. *To Make a Nation*. Cambridge, MA: Harvard University Press.

Bengelsdorf, C. 1994. *The Problem of Democracy in Cuba: Between Vision and Reality*. Oxford: Oxford University Press.

Benoit, K., and M. Laver. 2006. *Party Policy in Modern Democracies*. London: Routledge.

Bentham, J. 1931. *The Theory of Legislation*. C. K. Ogden [Ed.]. London: Routledge & Kegan Paul.

Benton, T. 1856. *Thirty Years View*. New York: Appleton.

Berelson, B. R., P. R. Lazarfield, and W. N. McPhee. 1954. *Voting: A Study of Opinion Formation in a Presidential Campaign*. Chicago, IL: Chicago University Press.

Bergson, A. 1954. "On the Concept of Social Welfare." *Quartely Journal of Economics* 68:233–253.

Berlin, I. 1997. "Two Concepts of Liberty." In H. Hardy and R. Hausheer [Eds.]. *The Proper Study of Mankind*. New York: Farrar, Straus and Giroux.

Berlin, I. 2000. *The Power of Ideas*. Princeton, NJ: Princeton University Press.

Berlin, I. 2002. *Freedom and Its Betrayal: Six Enemies of Human Liberty*. Princeton, NJ: Princeton University Press.

Bianco, W. T., I. Jeliazkov, and I. Sened. 2004. "The Uncovered Set and the Limits of Legislative Action." *Political Analysis* 12:256–276.

Bianco, W. T, and I. Sened. 2003. "Uncovering Evidence of Conditional Party Government: Reassessing Majority Party Influence in Congress and State Legislatures." *American Political Science Review* 99:361–371.

Bianco, W. T., M. S. Lynch, G. Miller, and I. Sened. 2006. "A Theory Waiting to be Rediscovered." *Journal of Politics* 68:838–851.

Bicchieri, C. 1993. *Rationality and Coordination*. New York and Cambridge: Cambridge University Press.

Bikchandani, S., D. Hirschleifer, and I. Welsh. 1992. "Theory of Fads, Fashion, Custom and Cultural Change as Informational Cascade." *Journal of Political Economy* 100:992–1026.

Binmore, K. 1993. "De -Bayesing Game Theory." In K. Binmore, A. Kirman and P. Toni [Eds.]. Cambridge, MA: MIT Press.

Binmore, K. 1994 .*Game Theory and the Social Contract: Playing Fair*. Cambridge, MA: MIT Press.

Black, D. 1948a. "On the Rationale of Group Decision Making." *Journal of Political Economy* 56:23–34.

Black, D. 1948b. "The Decisions of a Committee Using Special Majority." *Econometrica* 16:245–261.

Black, D. 1958. *The Theory of Committees and Elections*. New York and Cambridge: Cambridge University Press.

Blackaby, F. [Ed.]. 1979. *De-Industrialization*. London: Heinemann.

Blais, A., P. Fournier, E. Gidengil, N. Nevitte, and J. Everitt. 2006. "Election 2006: How Big Were the Changes... Really?" Typescript: Université de Montréal.

Block, F. L. 1975. *The Origins of International Economic Disorder*. Berkeley, CA: University of California Press.

Bobbitt, P. 2008. *Terror and Consent*. New York: Alfred Knopf.

Boix,C. 2006. "The Roots of Democracy: Equality, Inequality, and the Choice of Political Institutions." *Policy Review* 135:3–15.

Boix,C. 2003. *Democracy and Redistribution*. New York and Cambridge: Cambridge University Press.

Boix,C., and S. Stokes. 2003. "Endogenous Democratization." *World Politics* 55: 517-549.

Bowles, S. 2006. "Group Competition, Reproductive Leveling and the Evolution of Human Altruism." *Science* 314:1569–1572.

Bowles, S., and J. Gintis. 1982. "The Crisis of Liberal Democratic Capitalism: The Case of the United States." *Politics and Society* 11: 51–1193.

Brady, D. 1988. *Critical Elections and Congressional Policy Making*. Stanford, CA: Stanford University Press.

Branch, T. 1988. *Parting the Waters*. New York: Simon & Schuster.

Branch, T. 1998. *Pillar of Fire*. New York: Simon and Schuster.

Branch, T. 2006. *At Canaan's Edge*. New York: Simon and Schuster.

Brewer, J. 1976. *Party Ideology and Popular Politics at the Accession of George III*. New York and Cambridge: Cambridge University Press.

Brewer, J. 1988. *The Sinews of Power*. Cambridge, MA: Harvard University Press.

British Election Study. 1992. *National Cross-Section Survey Dataset*. University of Essex: ESRC Data Archive.

British Election Study. 1997. *National Cross-Section Survey Dataset*. University of Essex: ESRC Data Archive.

Brittan, S. 1978. "Inflation and Democracy." In F. Hirsch and J. H. Goldthorpe [Eds.]. *The Political Economy of Inflation*. London: Martin Robertson.

Brader, T. A., and J. A. Tucker. 2001. "The Emergence of Mass Partisanship in Russia, 1993-1996." *American Journal of Political Science* 45: 69-83.

Brader, T. A., and J. A. Tucker. 2007. "Reflective and Unreflective Partisans? Experimental Evidence on the Links between Information, Opinion, and Party Identification." Typescript: University of Michigan.

Brody, R.A., and P. M. Sniderman. 1977. "From Life Space to Polling Place: The Relevance of Personal Concerns for Voting Behavior." *British Journal of Political Science* 7:337–360.

Browne, E., and M. Franklin. 1973. "Aspects of Coalition Payoffs in European Parliamentary Democracies." *American Political Science Review* 67:453–469.

Buchanan, J. 1960. *The Works*. In J. Moore [Ed.]. New York: Antiquarian Press.

Buchanan, P. 1998. *The Great Betrayal: How American Sovereignty and Social Justice are Being Sacrificed to the Gods of the Global Economy*. Boston, CA: Little, Brown and Co.

Buchanan, P. 1999. *A Republic, Not an Empire.* Washington, DC: Regnery.

Buchanan, P. 2006. *State of Emergency*. New York: St.Martin's Press.

Buchanan, J. M., and R. E. Wagner. 1977. *Democracy in Deficit: The Political Legacy of Lord Keynes*. New York: Academic Press.

Bueno de Mesquita, B., J. D. Morrow, R. Siverson, and A. Smith. 2002. "Political Institutions, Policy Choice and the Survival of Leaders." *British Journal of Political Science* 32:559–590.

Bueno de Mesquita, B., J. D. Morrow, R. Siverson, and A. Smith. 2003. *The Logic of Political Survival*. Cambridge, MA: MIT Press.

Budge, I., H.-D. Klingemann, A. Volkens, J. Bara, and E. Tanenbaum. 2003. *Mapping Policy Preferences: Estimates for Parties, Electors, and Governments 1945-1998*. Oxford University Press.

Burden, B. C. 1997. "Deterministic and Probabilistic Voting Models." *American Journal of Political Science* 41:1150–1169.

Burnham, W. 1970. *Critical Elections and the Mainsprings of American Politics*. New York: Norton.

Burton, J. 1978. "Keynes' Legacy to Great Britain: Folly in a Great Kingdom." In J. M. Buchanan [Ed.]. *The Consequences of Mr. Keynes*. London: Institute of Economic Affairs.

Butler, D., and D. Stokes 1976. "Endogenous Government Behavior: Wagner's Law or Gotteredammerung?" In S. T. Cook and P. M. Jackson [Eds.]. *Current Issues in Fiscal Policy*. Oxford: Oxford University Press.

Calvert, R. L. 1985. "Robustness of the Multidimensional Voting Model: Candidates, Motivations, Uncertainty and Convergence." *American Journal of Political Science* 29:69–85.

Calvin, W. 1991. *The Ascent of Mind*. New York: Bantam.

Calvin, W. 2006. *A Brain for All Seasons: Human Evolution and Abrupt Climate Change*. Chicago, IL: Chicago University Press.

Calvin, W. 2008. *Global Fever: How to Treat Climate Change*. Chicago, IL: Chicago University Press.

Camerer, C. 1999. "Behavioral Economics: Reunifying Psychology and Economics." *Proceedings of the National Academy of Sciences of the United States of America*. 96:10575–10577.

Campbell, A., P. E. Converse, W. E. Miller, and D. E. Stokes. 1960. *The American Voter*. New York: Wiley.

Canache D. 2002. *Venezuela: Public Opinion and Protest in a Fragile Democracy*. Coral Gables FL: North-South Center Press of the University of Miami.

Caplan, B. 2007. *The Myth of the Rational Voter*. Princeton, NJ: Princeton University Press.

Cardoso, E., and A. Helwege. 1992. *Cuba after Communism*. Cambridge, MA: The MIT Press.

Carlson, D. K. 2004a. "Does Freedom Ring in the Homeland Security Age?" www.gallup.poll.com.

Carlson, D. K. 2004b. "Far Enough? Public Wary of Restricted Liberties." www.gallup.poll.com.

Carlson, D. K. 2005. "Liberty vs. Security: Public Mixed on Patriot Act." http://www.gallup.com.

Carmines, E. G. 1991. "The Logic of Party Alignments." *Journal of Theoretical Politics* 3:65–80.

Carmines, E. G., and J. A. Stimson. 1989. *Issue Evolution, Race and the Transformation of American Politics*. Princeton, NJ: Princeton University Press.

Caro, R. A. 2002. *The Years of Lyndon Johnson: Master of the Senate*. New York: Knopf.

Carter, D. T. 2000. *The Politics of Rage: George Wallace and the Origins of the New Conservatism, and the Transformation of American Politics*. 2nd ed. Baton Rouge, LA: Louisiana State University.

Ceaser, J. W., and A. E. Busch. 2005. *Red over Blue: The 2004 Election and American Politics.* New York: Rowman and Littlefield.

Ceaser, J. W., and D. Disalvo. 2004. "A New GOP?" *Public Interest.* 157:3–17.

Charters, D. [Ed.]. 1994. *The Deadly Sin of Terrorism: Its Effect on Democracy and Civil Liberty in Six Countries.* Westport, CT: Greenwood Press.

Chávez F. H. *Understanding the Venezuelan Revolution: Hugo Chávez talks to Marta Harnecker.* New York: Monthly Review Press.

Choi, J.-K., and S. Bowles. 2007 "The Coevolution of Parochial Altruism and War." *Science* 318: 636–640.

Chrystal, A., and J. Alt 1979. "Endogenous Government Behavior: Wagner's Law or Gotter-dammerung?" In S. T. Cook and P. M. Jackson [Eds.]. *Current Issues in Fiscal Policy.* Oxford: Oxford University Press.

Clark, G. 1996. "The Political Foundations of Modern Economic Growth: England, 1540-1800." *Journal of Interdisciplinary History* 26:563–588.

Clark, G. 2005. "The Condition of the Working Class in England, 1209-2004." *Journal of Political Economy* 113:1307-1340.

Clark, G. 2007a. "What made Brittania Great? How much of the Rise of Britain to World Dominance by 1850 does the Industrial Revolution explain? In K.O'Rourke and A.Taylor [Eds.]. *Comparative Economic History: Essays in Honor of Jeffrey Williamson.* Cambridge, MA: MIT Press.

Clark, G. 2007b. *A Farewell to Alms.* Princeton, NJ: Princeton University Press.

Clarke, H. D., and M. C. Stewart. 1998. "The Decline of Parties in the Minds of Citizens." *Annual Review of Political Science* 1:357–378.

Clarke, H., M. Stewart, and P. Whiteley. 1995. "Prime Ministerial Approval and Governing Party Support: Rival Models Reconsidered." *British Journal of Political Science* 25:597–622.

Clarke, H., M. Stewart, and P. Whiteley. 1997. "Tory Trends, Party Identification and the Dynamics of Conservative Support since 1992." *British Journal of Political Science* 26:299–318.

Clarke, H., M. Stewart, and P. Whiteley. 1998. "New Models for New Labour: The Political Economy of Labour Support, January 1992–April 1997." *American Political Science Review* 92:559–575.

Clarke, H., D. Sanders, M. Stewart, and P. Whiteley. 2004. *Political Choice in Britain.* Oxford: Oxford University Press.

Clarke, H., D. Sanders, M. Stewart, and P. Whiteley. 2006. "Taking the Bloom off New Labour's Rose: Party Choice and Voter Turnout in Britain." *Journal of Elections, Public Opinion, and Parties* 16:3–36.

Cline, W. (2007). *Global Warming and Agriculture Impact Estimates by Country.* Washington, DC: Peterson Institute.

Clymer, A. 2002. "U.S. Attitudes Altered Little By Sept. 11, Pollsters Say." *New York Times* (20 May).

Cohen, S. A. (2002). "Liberty and Security—Can We Have Both?" Paper presented at the conference of the International Society for the Reform of the Criminal Law, Charleston, SC.

Collier, P.2007. *The Bottom Billion* Oxford: Oxford University Press.

Colomer, J. M. 1991. "Transitions by Agreement: Modeling the Spanish Way." *American Political Science Review* 85: 1283–1302.

Colomer, J. M., and R. Puglisi. 2005. "Cleavages, Issues and Parties: A Critical Overview of the Literature." *European Political Science* 4:502–520.

Colton, Timothy J., and H. H. Hale. 2008. "The Putin Vote: The Demand Side of Hybrid Regime Politics." Typescript: Harvard University.

Commager, H. S. 1977. *The Empire of Reason: How Europe Imagined and America Realized the Enlightenment.* Garden City, NJ: Doubleday.

Condillac, E. B. de. 2001 [1746]. *Essay on the Origin of Human Knowledge.* New York and Cambridge: Cambridge University Press.

Condorcet, N. 1994 [1785]. *Essai sur l'application de l'analyse à la probabilité des décisions rendues à la pluralité des voix.* Paris: Imprimerie Royale. Translated in part in I. McLean and F. Hewitt, *Condorcet: Foundations of Social Choice and Political Theory.* Aldershot, UK: Edward Elgar.

Condorcet, N. 1955 [1795]. *Esquisse d'un tableau historique des progrès de l'esprit humain: Sketch for an Historical Picture of the Progress of the Human Mind.* London: Weidenfeld.

Constant, B.1988. *Political Writings.* New York and Cambridge: Cambridge University Press.

Coser, L. 1956. *The Functions of Social Conflict.* Glencoe, IL: Free Press.

Coughlin, P. 1992. *Probabilistic Voting Theory.* New York and Cambridge: Cambridge University Press.

Cox, G. 1987. *The Efficient Secret.* New York and Cambridge: Cambridge University Press.

Cox, G. 1997. *Making Votes Count.* New York and Cambridge: Cambridge University Press.

Crewe, I., B. Sarlvik, and J. Alt. 1977. "Partisan Dealignment in Britain 1964-1974." *British Journal of Political Science* 7:135-168.

Crouch, C. 1985. "The Conditions for Trade Union Wage Restraint." In L. N. Lindbergh and C. S. Maier [Eds.]. *The Politics and Sociology of Global Inflation.* Washington, DC: Brookings Institution.

Crozier, B. 1967. *Franco.* Boston, MA: Little, Brown and Company.

Critchlow, D. T. 2007. *The Conservative Conspiracy.* Cambridge, MA: Harvard University Press.

Cuzán, A. G. 2003. "Franco's Spain and Castro's Cuba: Parallels and Contrasts," Presented at the 5th Annual Meeting of Cuban and Cuban-American Studies at the Cuba Research Institute, Florida International University.

Daalder, H. 1984. "In Search of the Center of European Party Systems." *American Political Science Review* 78:92–109.

Dakhlia, S., and J. Nye. 2004. "Tax Britannica: Nineteenth Century Tariffs and British National Income." *Public Choice* 121: 309-333.

Danforth, J. 2005. "In the Name of Politics." *New York Times*, March 30.

Davies, R. W. 1998. *Soviet Economic Development from Lenin to Khrushchev.* New York and Cambridge: Cambridge University Press.

Davis, D., and B. Silver. 2004. "Civil Liberties vs. Security: Public Opinion in the Context of the Terrorist Attacks on America." *American Journal of Political Science* 48:28–46.

De Swaan, A. 1973. *Coalition Theories and Cabinet Formation*. Amsterdam: Elsevier.

De Vries, M. 1999. *Governing with your Closest Neighbor*. Nijmegen: Ipskamp.

den Uyl, D. 2003. "Inherent Value of Liberty." International Society for Individual Liberty. www.isil.org.

Denzau, A., and D. C. North. 1994. "Shared Mental Models: Ideologies and Institutions." *Kyklos* 47:3–31.

Department of the Air Force. 2002. "America's Challenges in an Unstable World: Balancing Security with Liberty." Special Bibliography Series, No. 100 October.

Dershowitz, A. 2002. *Shouting Fire: Civil Liberties in a Turbulent Age*. Boston, MA: Little, Brown, & Co.

Deutscher, I. 1967. *The Unfinished Revolution: Russia 1917-1967*. Oxford: Oxford University Press.

Diamond, J. 2005. *Collapse: How Societies Choose to Fail or Succeed*. London: Penguin.

Diermeier, D., and R. T. Stevenson. 1999. "Cabinet Survival and Competing Risks." *American Journal of Political Science* 43:1051–1068.

Dixon, K., and N. Schofield. 2001. "The Election of Lincoln in 1860." *Homo Oeconomicus* 16: 49–67.

Dodd, L. C. 1974. "Party Coalitions in Multiparty Parliaments: A Game Theoretic Analysis." *American Political Science Review* 68:1093–1117.

Dodd, L. C. 1976. *Coalitions in Parliamentary Governments*. Princeton, NJ: Princeton University Press.

Domínguez, J. I. 2007. "Cuba's Civil-Military Relations in Comparative Perspective." In M. Pérez-Stable [Ed.]. *Looking Forward: Comparative Perspectives on Cuba's Transition*. Notre Dame, IN: University of Notre Dame Press.

Donald, D. 1995. *Lincoln*. London: Cape.

Douthat, R., and R. Salam. 2008. *Grand New Party*. New York: Doubleday.

Dow, J. K. 2001. "A Comparative Spatial Analysis of Majoritarian and Proportional Elections." *Electoral Studies* 20:109–125.

Dow, J. K., and J. Endersby. 2004. "Multinomial Probit and Multinomial Logit: A Comparison of Choice Models for Voting Research." *Electoral Studies* 23:107–122.

Dowlah, A. F., and J. E. Elliot. 1997. *The Life and Times of Soviet Socialism*. Westport, CT: Praeger.

Downs, A. 1957. *An Economic Theory of Democracy*. New York: Harper and Row.

Duverger, M. 1954. *Political Parties: Their Organization and Activity in the Modern State*. New York: Wiley.

Duverger, M. 1984. "Which is the Best Electoral System?" In A. Lijphart and B. Grofman [Eds.]. *Choosing an Electoral System*. New York: Praeger.

Edsall, T. B., with M. Edsall. 1991. *Chain Reaction: The Impact of Race, Rights, and Taxes on American Politics*. New York: Norton.

Ehrlich, W. 1979. *They Have No Rights: Dred Scott's Struggle for Freedom*. Westport, CT: Greenwood Press.

Ellner S.2000. "Polarized Politics in Chavez's Venezuela." *NACLA Report on the Americas: Report on Venezuela.* Washington, DC: North American Congress on Latin America. 33(6).

Ellner S. 2007. "Trade Union Autonomy and the Emergence of a New Labor Movement in Venezuela." In S. Ellner and T. Miguel [Eds.]. *Venezuela: Hugo Chávez and the Decline of an "Exceptional Democracy."* Lanham, MD: Rowman & Littlefield Publishers.

Ellwood, S. M. 1987. *Spanish Fascism in the Franco Era: Falange Española de las JONS, 1936-76.* New York: St. Martin's Press.

Enelow, J., and M. J. Hinich. 1982. "Ideology, Issues, and the Spatial Theory of Elections." *American Political Science Review* 76:493–501.

Enelow, J., and M. J. Hinich. 1984. *The Spatial Theory of Voting.* New York and Cambridge: Cambridge University Press.

Enelow, J., and M. J. Hinich. 1989. "The Location of American Presidential Candidates." *Mathematical and Computer Modelling* 12:461–470.

Enelow, J., and M. J. Hinich [Eds.]. 1990. *Advances in the Spatial Theory of Voting.* New York and Cambridge: Cambridge University Press.

Fagan, B. 1999. *Floods, Famines, and Emperors: El Nino and the Fate of Civilizations.* New York: Perseus.

Fagan, B. 2001. *The Little Ice Age: How Climate Made History, 1300-1850.* New York: Perseus.

Fagan, B. 2004. *The Long Summer: How Climate Changed Civilization.* New York: Perseus.

Fagan, B. 2008. *The Great Warming: Climate Change and the Rise and Fall of Civilizations.* New York: Bloomsbury Press.

Fainsod, M. 1954. *How Russia is Ruled.* Cambridge MA: Harvard University Press.

Feddersen, T. 1992. "A Voting Model Implying Duverger's Law and Positive Turnout." *American Journal of Political Science* 36: 938-962.

Feddersen, T. 2004. "Rational Choice Theory and the Paradox of Not Voting." *Journal of Economic Perspectives* 18: 99-112.

Feddersen, T., and A.Sandroni.2006. "A Theory of Participation in Elections." *American Economic Review* 96: 1271-1282.

Fehrenbacher, D. E. 1981. *Slavery, Law and Politics: The Dred Scott Case in Historical Perspective.* New York: Oxford University Press.

Fehrenbacher, D. E. [Ed.]. 1989a. *Lincoln: Speeches and Writings 1832-1858, Vol. 1.* New York: Library of America.

Fehrenbacher, D. E. [Ed.]. 1989b. *Lincoln: Speeches and Writings 1859-1865, Vol. 2.* New York: Library of America.

Fehrenbacher, D. E. 2001. *The Slaveholding Republic.* New York: Oxford University Press.

Fidrmuc, J. 2000a. "Economics of Voting in Post-Communist Countries." *Electoral Studies* 19:199–217.

Fidrmuc, J. 2000b. "Political Support for Reforms: Economics of Voting in Transition Countries." *European Economic Review* 44:1491–1513.

Filippov, M., P. Ordeshook, and O. Shvetsova. 2004. *Designing Federalism.* New York and Cambridge: Cambridge University Press.

Filler, L. 1986. *Crusade Against Slavery: Friends, Foes and Reforms 1820-1860*. Algonac, MI: Reference Publications, Inc.

Filtzer, D. A. 1989. "The Soviet Wage Reform of 1956-1962." *Soviet Studies* 41:88–110.

Finer, S. E., R. C. Macridis, K. W. Deutsch, E. A. Nordlinger, and V.Aspaturian. 1968. *Modern Political Systems: Europe. 2nd ed.* Englewood Cliffs, NJ: Prentice-Hall.

Finkelman, P. [Ed.]. 1997. *Dred Scott v. Sandford: A Brief History with Documents*. Boston, MA: Bedford Books.

Fiorina, M. 1981. "Short and Long-Term Effects of Economic Conditions in Individual Voting Decisions." In D. A. Hibbs and H. Fassbender [Eds.]. *Contemporary Political Economy*. Amsterdam: North-Holland.

Fiorina, M. 2005. *Culture War?* New York: Longman.

Fishbein, M, and I. Ajzen. 1975. *Belief, Attitude, Intention, and Behavior: An Introduction to Theory and Research*. Reading, MA: Addison-Wesley.

Floud, R., and D. McCloskey, [Eds]. 1994. *The Economic History of Britain since 1700, Volume 1: 1700-1860*. New York and Cambridge: Cambridge University Press.

Fogel, J.-F. 2003. "Le Dernier Carré Du Pouvoi Castriste." *Le Monde*, 26 Oct. 2003.

Foster, D. P, and Young, H. P. 2001. "On the Impossibility of Predicting the Behavior of Rational Agents." *Proceedings of the National Academy of Sciences of the USA*: 12848-12853.

Fowler, J. H. 2005. "Altruism and Political Participation." Paper presented at the Annual Meeting of The Midwest Political Science Association, Chicago, IL.

Frank, T. 2004. *What's the Matter with Kansas? How Conservatives Won the Heart of America*. New York: Henry Holt.

Frank Leslie's Illustrated Newspaper. 1857. Front page. June 27.

Free Internet Press. 2006. "Senate Immigration Deal Faltering." April 7.

Freedman, J. I., and S. C. Fraser. 1966. "Compliance without Pressure: The Foot-in-the-door Technique." *Journal of Personality and Social Psychology* 4:196–202.

Freeman, C. 1979. "Technical Innovation and British Trade Performance." In F. Blackaby [Ed.]. *De-Industrialization*. London: Heinemann.

French, P. 2007. *North Korea: The Paranoid Peninsula: A Modern History.* London: Zed Books.

Frey, B. S. 1978. *Modern Political Economy*. New York: Halstead Press.

Frum, D. 1994. *Dead Right*. New York: Basic Books.

Fukuyama, F. 1992. *The End of History and the Last Man*. New York: The Free Press.

Fuller, T.1987. "Jeremy Bentham and James Mill." In L.Strauss and J. Cropsey [Eds.]. *History of Political Philosophy*. Chicago, IL: University of Chicago Press.

Gallego, M. 1996. "Interest Groups, Government Turnover and Political Regimes: An Econometric Analysis." *Canadian Journal of Economics* 29:S633–S638.

Gallego, M. 1998. "Economic Performance and Leadership Accountability: An Econometric Analysis." *Economics and Politics* 10:249–287.

Gallego, M., and C. Pitchik. 2004. "An Economic Theory of Leadership Turnover." *Journal of Public Economics* 88:2361–2382.

Gauthier, D. 1986. *Morals by Agreement*. Oxford: Clarendon Press.

Gerber, A. S., D. P. Green, and R. Shachar. 2003. "Voting may be Habit Forming: Evidence from a Randomized Field Experiment." *American Journal of Political Science*. 47:540-550.

Giannetti, D., and M. Laver. 2001. "Party Systems Dynamics and the Making and Breaking of Italian Governments." *Electoral Studies* 20:529–553.

Giannetti, D., and I. Sened. 2004. "Party Competition and Coalition Formation: Italy 1994–1996." *Journal of Theoretical Politics* 16:483–515.

Gödel, Kurt. 1931. "Uber formal unentscheidbare Sätze der Principia Mathematica und verwandter Systeme." *Monatschefte fur Mathematik und Physik* 38: 173–98. Translated as "On Formally Undecidable Propositions of *Principia Mathematica* and Related Systems." In J. van Heijenoort. *Frege and Gödel: Two Fundamental Texts in Mathematical Logic.* Cambridge MA: Harvard University Press.

Goldin, C., and L. Katz. 2008. *The Race Between Education and Technology.* Cambridge, MA: Harvard University Press.

Goldstone, L. 2005. *Dark Bargain.* New York: Walker.

Gonzalez, E., and K. F. McCarthy. 2004. *Cuba After Castro: Legacies, Challenges and Impediments.* Santa Monica, CA: RAND Corporation.

Goodhart, C. A. E., and R. J. Bhansali. 1970. "Political Economy." *Political Studies.* 18:43–106.

Gore, A. 2006. *An Inconvenient Truth.* New York: Rodale.
Gore, A. 2007. *The Assault on Reason.* London: Bloomsbury.

Gray, J. 2007. *Black Mass.* London: Penguin.

Green, D., and I. Shapiro. 1994. *Pathologies of Rational Choice Theory.* New Haven CT: Yale University Press.

Gregory, P. R. 2003. *The Political Economy of Stalinism: Evidence from the Soviet Secret Archives.* New York and Cambridge: Cambridge University Press.

Groseclose, T. 2001. "A Model of Candidate Location When One Candidate has Valence Advantage." *American Journal of Political Science* 45:862–886.

Grugel, J., and T. Rees. 1997. *Franco's Spain.* London: Arnold, 1997.

Gunther, R. 1992. "Spain: The Very Model of the Modern Elite Settlement." In J. Higley et al. [Eds.]. *Elites and Democratic Consolidation in Latin America and Southern Europe.* New York and Cambridge: Cambridge University Press.

Haggard, S., and R. R. Kaufman. 1995 *The Political Economy of Democratic Transitions.* Princeton, NJ: Princeton University Press.

Hahn, J. W. 1978. "Stability and Change in the Soviet Union: A Developmental Perspective." *Polity* 10:542–67.

Hahn, G. 1980. "General Equilibrium Theory." *The Public Interest: Special Issues on the Crisis in Economic Theory.* 123-128.

Hamdi v. Rumsfeld, 542 U.S. 507 (2004).

Hammond, T. H., and G. Miller. 1987. "The Core of the Constitution." *American Political Science Review* 81:1155–1174.

Hardin, G. 1968. "The Tragedy of the Commons." *Science.* 162: 1243-1248. Reprinted in H.E. Daly [Ed.]. *Toward a Steady State Economy.* San Francisco, CA: Freeman.

Hardin, R. 1982. *Collective Action*. Baltimore, MD: Johns Hopkins University Press.

Harkins, S. G., and B. Latane. 1998. "Population and Political Participation: A Social Impact Analysis of Voter Responsibility." *Group Dynamics: Theory Research and Practice* 2:192-207.

Harper, M. 2003 *Adventurers and Exiles*. London: Profile Books.

Harrington, J. 1992 [1656]. *The Commonwealth of Oceana*. New York and Cambridge: Cambridge University Press.

Harrison, M. 2002. "Coercion, Compliance, and the Collapse of the Soviet Command Economy." *Economic History Review* 55:97–433.

Harsanyi, J. C. 1977. *Rational Behavior and Bargaining Equilibrium in Games and Social Situations*. New York and Cambridge: Cambridge University Press.

Hart, H. L .A. 1973. "Rawls on Liberty and Its Priority." *The University of Chicago Law Review* 40:534–555.

Hellwig, T. 2008. "Explaining the Salience of Left-Right Ideology in Post-Industrialist Democracies: The Role of Structural Economic Change." *European Journal of Political Research*: in press.

Hesli, V. L., and E. Bashkirova. 2001. "The Impact of Time and Economic Circumstances on Popular Evaluations of Russia's President. "*International Political Science Review* 22:379–389.

Hewett, E. A.1988. *Reforming the Soviet Economy: Equality vs. Efficiency*. Washington DC: The Brookings Institution.

Hinich, M. J. 1977. "Equilibrium in Spatial Voting: The Median Voter Theorem is an Artifact." *Journal of Economic Theory* 16:208–219.

Hinich, M., J. Ledyard, and P. C. Ordeshook. 1972. "Nonvoting and the Existence of Equilibrium Under Majority Rule. "*Journal of Economic Theory* 4:144–153

Hinich, M. J., and M. Munger. 1994. *Ideology and the Theory of Political Choice*. Ann Arbor: University of Michigan Press.

Hobbes, T. 1960 [1651]. *Leviathan; or the Matter, Forme, and Power of a Common-wealth, Ecclesiastical and Civil*. C. MacPhersonee [Ed.]. Harmondsworth, UK: Penguin,.

Hobbes, T. 2001. [1651]. *Leviathan*. In M. Morgan [Ed.]. *Classics of Moral and Political Theory*. Indianapolis: Hackett.

Hobbes, T. 1998. [1651]. *On the Citizen*, R. Tuck and M. Silverthorne [Eds.]. New York and Cambridge: Cambridge University Press.

Hobbes, T. 1999. [1651]. *Human Nature and De Corpore Politico*. Oxford: Oxford University of Press.

Hollifield, J. F., and C. Jillson. 2000. [Eds.]. *Pathways to Democracy: The Political Economy of Democratic Transitions*. New York: Routledge.

Hoover, H. 1934. *The Challenge to Liberty*. New York: Charles Scribner.

Hopkins, V. C. 1951. *Dred Scott's Case*. New York: Fordham University.

Hotelling, H. 1929. "Stability in Competition." *Economic Journal* 39:41–57.

Hough, J. F., and M. Fainsod. 1979. *How the Soviet Union is Governed*. Cambridge, MA: Harvard University Press.

Howard, R. D., and R. L. Sawyer [Eds.]. 2005. *Terrorism and Counterterrorism: Understanding the New Security Environment, Readings and Interpretations*. New York: McGraw-Hill.

Huckfeldt, R., and C. Kohfeld. 1989. *Race and the Decline of Class in American Politics.* Urbana-Champaign, IL: University of Illinois Press.

Hume, D. 1985 [1752]. *A Treatise of Human Nature.* London: Collins.

Hume, D. 1987 [1742, 1748]. *Essays: Moral, Political and Literary.* E. Miller [Ed.]. Indianapolis, IN: Liberty Fund.

Humphreys, J. 2004. "What Price Security?" *Policy* 20:2–35.

Hunter, A. and J. Sexton. 1999. *Contemporary China.* London: Macmillan.

Hunter, H.-L. 1999. Kim Il-song's North Korea. Westport, CT: Praeger.

Ignatieff, M. 2004. *The Lesser Evil: Political Ethics in an Age of Terror.* Princeton, NJ: Princeton University Press.

Jaffa, H. 2000. *A New Birth of Freedom.* Lanham, MD: Rowman and Littlefield.

Jay, W. 1835. *Inquiry into the Character and Tendency of the American Colonization and American Anti-Slavery Societies.* New York: Leavitt, Lord and Company.

Kahneman, D, and A. Tversky 1984. "Choices, Values and Frames." *American Psychologist.* 39:341–350.

Kallenbach, J. 1960. "Our Electoral College Gerrymander." *Midwest Journal of Political Science* 4:162–191.

Kamien, M. I., and N. L. Schwartz 1981. *Market Structure and Innovation.* New York and Cambridge: Cambridge University Press.

Kanazawa, S. 2000. "A New Solution to the Collective Action Problem: The Paradox of Voter Turnout." *American Sociological Review* 65:433-442.

Kant, I. 1996. *Metaphysics of Morals*, M.Gregor and R. Sullivan [Eds.]. New York and Cambridge: Cambridge University Press.

Kant, I. 2006. *Anthropology from a Pragmatic Point of View*, R.Louden and M. Kuehn [Eds.]. New York and Cambridge: Cambridge University Press

Kaplan, R. D. 1997. *Ends of the Earth.* New York: Viking.

Kaplan, R. D. 2000. *The Coming Anarchy.* New York: Viking.

Kaplan, R. D. 2003. *Surrender or Starve: Travels in Ethiopia, Sudan, Somalia, and Eritrea.* New York: Viking.

Karklins, R., and R. Petersen. 1993. "Decision Calculus of Protestors and Regime Change: Eastern Europe 1989." *Journal of Politics* 55:588–614.

Karol, D. 1999. "Realignment Without Replacement: Issue Evolution and Ideological Change among Members of Congress." Presented at the Annual Meeting of the Midwest Political Science Association. Chicago, IL.

Karol, D. 2001. *How and Why Parties Change Position on Issues: Party Policy Change as Coalition Management in American Politics.* Presented at the Annual Meeting of the American Political Science Association Meeting, San Francisco, CA.

Kass, R., and A. Raftery. 1995. "Bayes Factors." *Journal of the American Statistical Association* 91:773–795.

Katosh, J.P, and M. W. Traugott. 1982. "Costs and Values in the Calculuses of Voting." ,*American Journal of Political Science.* 26:361-376.

Kazin, M. 2006. *A Godly Hero*. New York: Knopf.

Keddie, N. R. 2006. *Modern Iran: Roots and Results of Revolution*. New Haven CT:Yale University Press.

Kenneally, C. 2007. *The First Word*. New York: Viking.

Kennedy, P. 1987. *The Rise and Fall of the Great Powers*. New York: Random House.

Kershaw, I. 2007. *Fateful Choices*. New York: Penguin.

Key, V. O. 1955. "A Theory of Critical Elections." *Journal of Politics* 17:3–18.

Keynes, J. M. 1921. *A Treatise on Probability, Vol. 8 of Collected Writings*. London: Macmillan.

Keynes, J. M. 1933. "National Self-Sufficiency." *Yale Review* 26: 755–69.

Keynes, J. M. 1936. *The General Theory of Employment, Interest and Money*. London: Macmillan.

Keynes, J. M. 1937. "The General Theory of Employment." *Quarterly Journal of Economics* 51: 209–223.

Khanna, P. 2008. *The Second World: Empires and Influence in the New Global Order*. New York: Random House.

Kiewiet, D. R. 1983. *Macroeconomics and Micro Politics*. Chicago, IL: Chicago University Press.

Kim, M.-S. 1973. "North Korean Agriculture, Forestry, and Fishing." In *North Korean Economy*. Seoul: Ilbo Press.

King, A. [Ed.]. 2002. *Leaders' Personalities and the Outcomes of Democratic Elections*. Oxford: Oxford University Press.

King, G., J. Alt., N. Burns, and M. Laver. 1990. "A Unified Model of Cabinet Dissolution in Parliamentary Democracies." *American Journal of Political Science* 34: 846-871.

Kirkpatrick, D. D. 2006. "Demonstrations on Immigration Harden a Divide." *New York Times* (April 17).

Klein, N. 2007. *The Shock Doctrine*. London: Penguin.

Kotz, D. M., and F. Weir. 1997. *Revolution from Above: The Demise of the Soviet System*. London: Routledge.

Kramer, G. H. 1978. "Existence of Electoral Equilibrium." In P. Ordeshook [Ed.]. *Game Theory and Political Science*. New York: New York University Press.

Kreps, D., P. Milgrom, J. Roberts, and R. Wilson. 1982. "Rational Cooperation in the Finitely Repeated Prisoner's Dilemma." *Journal of Economic Theory* 27:245–52.

Krishnaswamy, K. S. 1987. "Economic Change in China: Some Impressions." *Social Scientist*. 15:62–86.

Kristof, N. D. 2002. "Security and Freedom." *New York Times*. 10 September.

Krosnick, J. A. 1988. "The Role of Attitude Importance in Social Evaluation: A Study of Policy Preferences, Presidential Candidate Evaluations, and Voting Behavior." *Journal of Personality and Social Psychology*. 55:196-210.

Laakso, M., and R. Taagepera. 1979. "Effective Number of Parties: A Measure with Applications to West Europe." *Comparative Political Science* 12:3–27.

Ladha, K. 1992. "Condorcet's Jury Theorem, Free Speech and Correlated Votes." *American Journal of Political Science* 36: 617–74.

Ladha, K. 1993. "Condorcet's Jury Theorem in the Light of de Finetti's Theorem: Majority Rule with Correlated Votes." *Social Choice and Welfare* 10: 69–86.

Ladha, K., and G. Miller. 1996. "Political Discourse, Factions and the General Will: Correlated Voting and Condorcet's Jury Theorem." In N. Schofield [Ed.]. *Collective Decision Making.* Boston, MA: Kluwer.

Lange, O. 1938. "On the Economic Theory of the State." In O. Lange and F. Taylor [Eds.]. *The Economic Theory of Socialism.* Minneapolis, MN: University of Minnesota Press.

Lankov, A. 2006. "The Natural Death of North Korean Stalinism." *Asia Policy* 1:95–121.

Lansford, T., and Pauly, J. C. 2006. *To Protect and Defend: U.S. Homeland Security Policy.* London: Ashgate.

Laplace, P. S. 1951 [1814]. *Essai philosophique sur les probabilités.* Paris: Gauthiers-Villars. *A Philosophical Essay on Probabilities.* Translated by F. Truscott and F. Emory. Introduction by E. Bell. New York: Dover.

Lasch, C. 1991. *The True and Only Heaven: Progress and Its Critics.* New York: Norton.

Laver, M. 1998. "Models of Government Formation." *Annual Review of Political Science* 1:1–25.

Laver, M., and N. Schofield. 1990. *Multiparty Government: The Politics of Coalition in Europe.* Oxford: Oxford University Press. Reprinted 1998. Ann Arbor: University of Michigan Press.

Laver, M., and M. Taylor. 1973. "Government Coalitions in Western Europe." *European Journal of Political Research* 1:205–248.

Ledyard, J. O. 1984. "The Pure Theory of Large Two-Candidate Elections." *Public Choice.* 44:7-41.

Lee, K. H. 2007. "Main Policy Directions and Goals for 2007." *Vantage Point* 30:2–7.

Lehmbruch, G. 1980. "Consociational Democracy, Class Conflict and the New Corporation." In P. C. Schmitter and G. Lehmbruch [Eds.]. *Trends Towards Corporatist Intermediation.* London and Beverly Hills: Sage.

Leone, R. C., and G. Anrig Jr. [Eds.]. 2007. *Liberty Under Attack: Reclaiming Our Freedoms in an Age of Terror.* New York: PublicAffairs.

Lewis, C. 2005. "The Clash between Security and Liberty in the U.S. Response to Terror." *Public Administration Review* 65:18–30.

Lewis., P.H. 2002. *Latin Fascist Elites: The Mussolini, Franco, and Salazar Regimes.* Westport: Praeger.

Lijphart, A. 1976. *The Politics of Consociational Democracies.* Berkeley, CA: University of California Press.

Lin, T., M. J. Enelow, and H. Dorussen. 1999. "Equilibrium in Multicandidate Probabilistic Spatial Voting." *Public Choice* 98:59–82.

Linz, J., and A. Stepan. 1996. *Problems of Democratic Transition and Consolidation: Southern Europe, South America, and Post-Communist Europe.* Baltimore, MD: The Johns Hopkins University Press.

Lipset, S. M. 1963. *Political Man: The Social Bases of Politics.* New York: Anchor Books.

Listhaug, O., S. E. Macdonald, and G. Rabinowitz. 1994, "Ideology and Party Support in Comparative Perspective." *European Journal of Political Research* 25:111–149.

Lizzeri, A., and N. Persico. 2004. "Why Did the Elites Extend the Suffrage? Democracy and the Scope of Government, With an Application to Britain's Age of Reform." *The Quarterly Journal of Economics*. 119:705–763.

Locke, J. 2001. *Second Treatise of Government*. In M. Morgan [Ed.]. *Classics of Moral and Political Theory*. Indianapolis,IN: Hackett.

Lohmann, S. 1994. "The dynamics of Informational Cascades: The Monday Demonstrations in Leipzig, East Germany 1989-1991." *World Politics* 47: 42-101.

Lomborg, B. 2001. *The Skeptical Environmentalist: Measuring the Real State of the World*. New York and Cambridge: Cambridge University Press.

Löwenhardt, J., J. R. Ozinga, and E. van Ree. 1992. *The Rise and Fall of the Soviet Politburo*. New York: St. Martin's Press.

Machiavelli, N. 1965. *The Chief Works and Others*. Edited and translated by A. Gilbert. 3 volumes. Durham, NC: Duke University Press.

Mackie, G. 2003. *Democracy Defended*. Cambridge: Cambridge Unversity Press.

MacRae, C. D. 1976. "A Political Model of the Business Cycle." *Journal of Political Economy*. 85:239–263.

Madison, J. [1787]. 1999. *Federalist X*. In J. Rakove [Ed.]. *Madison: Writings*. New York: Library Classics.

Magid, H. M. 1987. "John Stuart Mill." In L. Strauss and J. Cropsey [Eds.]. *History of Political Philosophy*. Chicago, IL: University of Chicago Press.

Malthus, T. [1798], [1830], 1970. *An Essay on the Principle of Population and a Summary View of the Principle of Population*. Harmondsworth, UK: Penguin, edited and with an introduction by Anthony Flew.

Mandelbaum, M. 2002. *The Ideas that Conquered the World*. New York: Public Affairs.

Mann, R. 1996. *The Walls of Jericho*. New York: Harcourt Brace.

Margolis, H. 1983. "The Banzhaf Fallacy." *The American Journal of Political Science* 27:321–326.

Margolis, H. 1987. *Patterns, Thinking and Cognition: A Theory of Judgement*. Chicago, IL: University of Chicago Press.

Margolis, H. 1993. *Paradigms and Barriers: How Habits of Mind Govern Scientific Beliefs*. Chicago, IL: University of Chicago Press.

Marshall, A. 1890. *Principles of Economics*. London: Macmillan.

Martin, S. P, and C. A. Shieh. 2003. "No Evidence for Stochastic Learning in Voter Turnout." *American Sociological Review* 68:153-159.

Marx, K. [1867], 1930. *Capital*. Translated by E. and C. Paul. London: Dent.

Mawdsley, E, and S. White, W. 2000. *The Soviet Elite From Lenin to Gorbachev: The Central Committee and its Members, 1917-1991*. Oxford: Oxford University Press.

Mayhew, D. 2000. "Electoral Realignments." *Annual Review of Political Science* 3:449–474.

Mayhew, D. 2002. *Electoral Realignments*. New Haven CT: Yale University Press.

McCarty, N., K. Poole, and H. Rosenthal. 2006. *Polarized America.* Cambridge, MA: MIT Press.

McCracken, P. 1977. [Ed.]. *Towards Full Employment and Price Stability.* Paris: OECD.

McGann, A. 2006. *The Logic of Democracy.* Ann Arbor: University of Michigan Press.

McKelvey, R. D. 1976. "Intransitivities in Multidimensional Voting Models and Some Implications for Agenda Control." *Journal of Economic Theory* 12:472–482.

McKelvey, R. D. 1979. "General Conditions for Global Intransitivities in Formal Voting Models." *Econometrica* 47:1085–1112.

McKelvey, R. D. 1986. "Covering, Dominance and Institution Free Properties of Social Choice." *American Journal of Political Science* 30:283–314.

McKelvey, R. D, and T. Palfrey. 1995. "Quantal Response Equilibria for Normal Form Games." *Games and Economic Behavior* 10:6–38.

McKelvey, R. D., and J. W. Patty. 2006. "A Theory of Voting in Large Elections." *Games and Economic Behavior.* 57:155–180.

McKelvey, R. D., and T. Page. 1986. "Common Knowledge, Consensus, and Aggregate Information." *Econometrica* 54:109–127.

McKelvey, R. D., and N. Schofield. 1986. "Structural Instability of the Core." *Journal of Mathematical Economics* 15:179–198.

McKelvey, R. D., and N. Schofield. 1987. "Generalized Symmetry Conditions at a Core Point." *Econometrica.* 55:923–933.

McKenzie, L. 1959. "On the Existence of a General Equilibrium for a Competitive Economy." *Econometrica* 27:54–71.

McLean, I. 2002. "W. H. Riker and the Invention of Heresthetic(s)." *British Journal of Political Science* 32: 298–310.

McLean, I. 2004. 'Thomas Jefferson, John Adams, and the Déclaration des Droits de l'Homme et du Citoyen' In R. Fatton Jr. and R. K. Ramazani [Eds.]. *The Future of Liberal Democracy: Thomas Jefferson and the Contemporary World.* New York: Palgrave Macmillan.

McLean, I. 2006a. *Adam Smith, Radical and Egalitarian: An Interpretation for the 21st Century.* Edinburgh: Edinburgh University Press.

McLean, I. 2006b. "The Eighteenth Century Revolution in Social Science and the Dawn of Political Science in America." *European Political Science* 5: 112-123.

McLean, I. 2008. "In Riker's Footsteps: Review Article."*British Journal of Political Science*: in press.

McLean, I., and A. B. Urken. 1992. "Did Jefferson or Madison Understand Condorcet's Theory of Social Choice?" *Public Choice* 73: 445–457.

Mead, W. R. 2007. *God and Gold.* New York. Knopf.

Merrill III, S., and J. Adams. 2001. "Computing Nash Equilibria in Probabilistic, Multiparty Spatial Models with Nonpolicy Components." *Political Analysis* 9:347–361.

Merrill III, S., and B. Grofman. 1999. *A Unified Theory of Voting.* New York and Cambridge: Cambridge University Press.

Merrill III, S., B. Grofman, and J. Adams. 2001. "Assimilation and Contrast Effects in Voter Projections of Party Locations: Evidence from Norway, France, and the USA." *European Journal of Political Research* 40:199–221.

Merrill III, S., B. Grofman, and S. Feld. 1999. "Nash Equilibrium Strategies in Directional Models of Two-Candidate Spatial Competition." *Public Choice* 98:369–383.

Merrill III, S. B. Grofman, and T.L. Brunell. 2008. " Cycles in American National Electoral Politics." *American Political Science Review* 102:1–17.

Merrit, E. 1982. *World Out of Work.* London: Collins.

Micklethwait, J., and A. Wooldridge. 2004. *The Right Nation: Conservative Power in America.* New York: Penguin.

Miguel, E., S. Satyanath, and E. Sergenti. 2004. "Economic Shocks and Civil Conflict: An Instrumental Variables Approach." *Journal of Political Economy* 112: 725–753.

Milburn, J. 2006. "Former GOP Chairman Parkinson Switches Affiliation to Democrat." *Kansas City Star.* (May 30).

Miles, W. F. S. 1995. "Tragic Tradeoffs: Democracy and Security in Chad." *The Journal of Modern African Studies* 33:53–65.

Mill, J. S. 1910. *Utilitarianism, Liberty and Representative Government.* New York: Dutton.

Miller, G., and N. Schofield. 2003. "Activists and Partisan Realignment in the U.S." *American Political Science Review* 97:245–260.

Miller, G., and N. Schofield, N. 2008. "The Transformation of the Republican and Democratic Party Coalitions in the United States." *Perspectives on Politics* 6: 433-450.

Miller, N. 1980. "A New Solution Set for Tournaments and Majority Voting." *American Journal of Political Science* 24:68–96.

Mishel, L., J. Bernstein, and J. Schmitt. 2007. *The State of Working America: 2000-01.* Washington DC: EPI Press.

Mishler, W., and J. P. Willerton. 2003. "The Dynamics of Presidential Popularity in Post-Communist Russia: Cultural Imperative versus Neo-Institutional Choice?"*Journal of Politics* 65: 111–141.

Molina J. E. 2004. "Partidos y sistemas de partidos en la evolución política venezolana: la des-institucionalización y sus consecuencias." In J. E. Molina and Á E. Álvarez [Eds.]. *Los Partidos Políticos Venezolanos en el Siglo XXI.* Caracas: Vadell Hermanos Editores.

Morgan J. 2007. "Partisanship During the Collapse of Venezuela's Party System." *Latin American Research Review* 42:79–98.

Morris, C. 2008. *The Trillion Dollar Meltdown.* New York: Viking.

Moslem, M. 2002. *Factional Politics in Post-Khomeini Iran.* New York: Syracuse University Press.

Mueller, D. C. 1982. "Redistribution, Growth and Political Stability." *The American Economic Review: Papers and Proceedings.* 72:155–159.

Munck, R. 1985. "The Modern Military Dictatorship in Latin America: The Case of Argentina (1976-82)."*Latin American Perspectives* 12:41-74.

Mueller, D. 2003. *Public Choice III.* New York and Cambridge: Cambridge University Press.

Myagkov, M., P.C. Ordeshook, and D. Shakin. 2005. "Fraud or Fairytales? Russian and Ukrainian Electoral Experience." *Post-Soviet Affairs* 21:91–131.

Nachbar, J. 1997. "Prediction, Optimization, and Learning in Repeated Games." *Econometrica* 65: 275–309.

Nachbar, J. 2001. "Bayesian Learning in Repeated Games of Incomplete Information." *Social Choice and Welfare* 18: 303–326.

Nachbar, J. 2005. "Beliefs in Repeated Games." *Econometrica* 73: 459-480.

Nardulli, P. F.1995. "The Concept of a Critical Realignment, Electoral Behavior and Political Change." *American Political Science Review* 89:10–22.

Nash, J. 1950a. "The Bargaining Problem." *Econometrica* 18:155–162.

Nash, J. 1950b. "Equilibrium Points in n-Person Games." *Proceedings of the National Academy of Science, USA*. 36:48–49.

Nash, J. 1951. "Non-Cooperative Games." *Annals of Mathematics* 54:286–295.

Nash, J. 1953. "Two Person Cooperative Games." *Econometrica* 21:128–140.

Nemtzov, B., and V. Milov. 2008. *Putin: The Results*. Moscow: Novaya Gazeta.

New York Times. 2006. "Stem Cell Proposal Splits Missouri GOP." (12 March).

Newton, I., 1984 [1672]. "New Theory about Light and Colours." In A. Shapiro [Ed.]. *The Optical Papers of Isaac Newton*. New York and Cambridge: Cambridge University Press.

Newton, I. 1995 [1687]. *Philosophiae Naturalis Principia Mathematica*. Amherst, NY: Prometheus Books, translated, edited, and with an introduction by A. Motte.

Newton, I. 1704. *Opticks: Or, a Treatise of the Reflexions, Refractions, Inflexions and Colours of Light*. London: Smith and Walford.

Nichols, D. 2007. *A Matter of Justice*. New York: Simon and Schuster.

Norden, D. L. 1996. *Military Rebellion in Argentina: Between Coups and Consolidation*. Lincoln, NE: University of Nebraska Press.

Nordhaus, W. D. 1957. "The Political Business Cycle." *Review of Economic Studies*. 42:167-190.

Nordhaus, W. D. 2008. *A Question of Balance: Weighing the Options on Global Warming Policies*. New Haven CT: Yale University Press.

North, D. C. 1961. *The Economic Growth of the United States*. New York: Norton.

North, D. C. 1981. *Structure and Change in Economic History*. New York: Norton.

North, D. C. 1990. *Institutions, Institutional Change and Economic Performance*. New York and Cambridge: Cambridge University Press.

North, D. C. 1993. "Institutions and Credible Commitment." *Journal of Institutional Theoretical Economics* 149: 11–23.

North, D. C. 1994. "Economic Performance through Time." *American Economic Review* 84: 359–68.

North, D. C. 2005. *Understanding the Process of Economic Change*. Princeton, NJ: Princeton University Press.

North, D. C., and A. Rutten. 1987. "The Northwest Ordinance in Historical Perspective." In D. Klingamen and R. Vedder [Eds.]. *Essays on the Economy of the Old Northwest*. Athens, OH: Ohio University Press.

North, D. C., and R. Thomas. 1970. "An Economic Theory of Growth of the Western World." *Economic History Review* 23:1–17.

North, D. C., and R. Thomas. 1973. *The Rise of the Western World: A New Economic History*. New York and Cambridge: Cambridge University Press.

North, D. C., and R. Thomas. 1977. "The First Economic Revolution." *Economic History Review* 30: 229–41.

North, D. C., and B. R. Weingast. 1989. "Constitutions and Commitment: The Evolution of Institutions Governing Public Choice in Seventeenth Century England" *Journal of Economic History* 49: 803–32.

North, D. C., B. R. Wallis, and B. R. Weingast. 2008. *A Conceptual Framework for Interpreting Recorded Human History.* New York and Cambridge: Cambridge University Press.

Nozick, R. 1974. *Anarchy, State and Utopia.* Oxford: Basil Blackwell.

Nyarko, Y. "Convergence in Economic Models with Bayesian Hierachies of Beliefs." *Journal of Economic Theory* 74: 266–296.

Nye, J. V. C. 1992. "Guerre, Commerce, Guerre Commercial: L'économie politiques des échanges franco-anglais." *Annales: Economics, Societes, Civilisations* 3:613–32.

Nye, J. V. C. 2007. *War, Wine and Taxes.* Princeton, NJ: Princeton University Press.

O'Brien, P. K. 1988. "The Political Economy of British Taxation, 1660-1815." *The Economic History Review.* 41:1–32.

O'Donnell, G. 1973. *Modernization and Bureaucratic Authoritarianism: Studies in South American Politics.* Berkeley, CA: Institute of International Studies, University of California.

O'Donnell, G. 1978. "Reflections on the Patterns of Change in the Bureaucratic-Authoritarian State." *Latin American Research Review* 13: 3-38.

O'Donnell, G and P. Schmitter 1986. *Transitions from Authoritarian Rule: Tentative Conclusions about Uncertain Democracies.* Baltimore, MD: The Johns Hopkins University Press.

Olson, M. 1965. *The Logic of Collective Action.* Cambridge, MA: Harvard University Press.

Olson, M. 1982a. "The Political Economy of Comparative Growth Rates." In D. C. Mueller [Ed.]. *The Political Economy of Growth.* New Haven, CT: Yale University Press.

Olson, M. 1982b. *The Rise and Decline of Nations.* New Haven, CT: Yale University Press.

Olson, M. 1982c. "Stagflation and the Political Economy of the Decline in Productivity." *The American Economic Review: Papers and Proceedings.* 72:143–148.

Olson, M. 2000. *Power and Prosperity: Outgrowing Communist and Capitalist Dictatorships.* New York: Basic.

Ordeshook, P. C., and K. Shepsle [Eds.].1982. *Political Equilibrium.* Boston, MA: Kluwer.

Ostroy, J. 1980. "The No-Surplus Condition as a Characteristic of Perfectly Competitive Equilibrium." *Journal of Economic Theory.* 22:183-207.

Owen, A. and J. A. Tucker. 2008. "Conventional vs. Transitional Economic Voting in Poland, 1997-2005." Typescript: Princeton University.

Paldam, M. 1979. "Is There an Electoral Cycle? A Comparative Study of National Accounts." *Scandinavian Journal of Economics.* 81:323-342.

Paldam, M. 1981a. "An Essay on the Rationality of Economic Policy: The Test Case of the Electional Cycle." *Public Choice.* 37:287- 305.

Paldam, M. 1981b. "A Preliminary Survey of the Theories and Findings on Vote and Popularity Functions." *European Journal of Political Research* 9:181–199.

Palfrey, T. R., and H. Rosenthal. 1985. "Voter participation and strategic uncertainty." *The American Political Science Review.* 79:62–78.

Panah, M. 2007. *The Islamic Republic and the World: Global Dimensions of the Iranian Revolution*. Ann Arbor, MI: Pluto Press.

Paterson, J. 1877. *Commentaries on the Liberty of the Subject and the Laws of England Relating to the Security of the Person*. 2 vols. London: Macmillan.

Pattie, C., P. Seyd, and P. Whiteley. 2004. *Citizenship in Britain: Values, Participation and Democracy*. New York and Cambridge: Cambridge University Press.

Payne, S. G. 1987. *The Franco Regime, 1936-1975*. Madison, WI: The University of Wisconsin Press.

Peacock, A. T., and J. Wiseman 1961. *The Growth of Public Expenditure in the United Kingdom*. Oxford: Oxford University Press.

Penn, E. 2009. "A Model of Far-Sighted Voting." *American Journal of Political Science:* in press.

Perlstein, R. 2008. *Nixonland*. New York: Scribner.

Pérez-López, J. F. [Ed.]. 1994. *Cuba at a Crossroads: Politics and Economics after the Fourth Party Congress*. Gainesville, FL: University Press of Florida.

Pérez-Stable, M. 2007. "Looking Forward: Democracy in Cuba?" In M. Pérez-Stable [Ed.]*Looking Forward: Comparative Perspectives on Cuba's Transition*. Notre Dame, IN: University of Notre Dame Press.

Peterson, P. G. 1982. "Social Security: The Coming Crash." *New York Review of Books* 29:34–38.

Pettit, P. 1997. *Republicanism*. New York: Oxford University Press.

Pettit, P. 2005. "Liberty and Leviathan." *Philosophy, Politics, and Economics* 4:131–151.

Phillips, K. 1969. *The Emerging Republican Majority*. New Rochelle, NY: Arlington House.

Phillips, K. 2006. *American Theocracy*. London: Penguin.

Phillips, K. 2008. *Bad Money*. New York: Viking.

Pinker, S., and P. Bloom. 1990. "Natural Language and Natural Selection." *Behavioral and Brain Sciences* 13: 707–784.

Plott, C. R. 1967. "A Notion of Equilibrium and its Possibility Under Majority Rule." *American Economic Review* 57:787–806.

Polsby, N. 2005. *How Congress Evolves*. Oxford: Oxford University Press.

Poole, K., and H. Rosenthal. 1984. "U.S. Presidential Elections 1968–1980: A Spatial Analysis." *American Journal of Political Science*. 28:283–312.

Poole, K., and H. Rosenthal. 1997. *Congress: A Political Economic History of Roll Call Voting*. New York: Oxford University Press.

Popper, K. 1945. *The Open Society and its Enemies*. London: Routledge and Kegan Paul.

Popper, K. 1959. *The Poverty of Historicism*. London: Routledge and Kegan Paul.

Popper, K. 1972. *Objective Knowledge: An Evolutionary Approach*. Oxford: Oxford University Press.

Popper, K. 1988. "The Open Society and its Enemies Revisited." *The Economist* 307:19–22.

Popper, K. 1992 1934. *The Logic of Scientific Discovery*. London: Routledge and Kegan Paul.

Posner, R. A. 2006. *Not a Suicide Pact: The Constitution in a Time of National Emergency*. Oxford: Oxford University Press.

Posner, R. A. 2007. *Countering Terrorism: Blurred Focus, Halting Steps*. Lanham, MD: Rowman & Littlefield.

Powers, D. V., and J. H. Cox. 1997. "Echoes from the Past: The Relationship between Satisfaction with Economic Reforms and Voting Behavior in Poland." *American Political Science Review* 91:617–633.

Preston, P. 1994. *Franco: A Biography*. New York: Basic Books.

Przeworski, A. 1986. "Some Problems in the Study of the Transition to Democracy," In G. O'Donnell, P C. Schmitter and L. Whitehead [Eds.]. *Transitions from Authoritarian Rule: Comparative Perspectives*. Baltimore, MD: Johns Hopkins University Press.

Przeworski, A. 1991. *Democracy and the Market: Political and Economic Reforms in Eastern Europe and Latin America*.New York and Cambridge: Cambridge University Press.

Przeworski, A. 1992. "The Games of Transition," In S. Mainwaring, G. O'Donnell and A. Valenzuela [Eds]. *Issues in Democratic Consolidation*. Notre Dame, IN: Notre Dame Press.

Przeworski, A. 2006. "Democracy and Economic Development." In E. Mansfield and R. Sisson [Eds.]. *Political Science and the Public Interest*. Columbus, OH: Ohio State University Press.

Przeworski, A., M. E. Alvarez, J. A. Cheibub, and F. Limongi. 2000. *Democracy and Development: Political Institutions and Well-Being in the World, 1950–1990*. New York and Cambridge: Cambridge University Press.

Quattrone, G. A., and A. Tversky. 1984. "Casual Versus Diagnostic Contingencies On Self-deception and on the Voter's Illusion." *Journal of Personality and Social Psychology*. 46:237–248.

Quattrone, G. A., and A. Tversky. 1988. "Contrasting Rational and Psychological Analyses of Political Choice." *American Political Science Review*. 82:719–36.

Quinn, S. 2001. "The Glorious Revolution's Effect on English Private Finance: A Microhistory, 1680-1705." *The Journal of Economic History*. 61:593–615.

Quinn, K., and A. Martin. 2002. "An Integrated Computational Model of Multiparty Electoral Competition." *Statistical Science* 17:405–419.

Quinn, K., A. Martin, and A. Whitford. 1999. "Voter Choice in Multiparty Democracies." *American Journal of Political Science* 43:1231–1247.

Rabinowitz, G., and MacDonald, S. E. 1986. "The Power of the States in U.S. Presidential Elections." *The American Political Science Review* 80:65–87.

Rae, D. 1967. *The Political Consequences of Electoral Laws*. New Haven, CT: Yale University Press.

Rae, D. 1969. "Decision Rules and Individual Values in Constitutional Choice." *American Political Science Review* 63: 40–56.

Rae, D. W, and M. Taylor. 1970. *The Analysis of Political Cleavages*. New Haven, CT: Yale University Press.

Rakove, J. [Ed.]. 1999. *James Madison: Writings*. New York: Library of America.

Rakove, J., A. Rutten, and B. Weingast. 1999. "Ideas, Interests and Credible Commitments in the American Revolution." Typescript: Stanford University.

Ransom, R. 1989. *Conflict and Compromise*. New York and Cambridge: Cambridge University Press.

Raphael, D. D. 1970. *Problems of Political Philosophy.* New York: Praeger Publishers.

Raphael, D. D. 1983. "Individual Liberty." In Griffiths, A. P. [Ed.]. *On Liberty.* New York and Cambridge: Cambridge University Press.

Rashid, A. 2008. *Descent into Chaos.* New York: Viking.

Rawls, J. 1970. *A Theory of Justice.* Cambridge, MA: Harvard University Press.

Rawls, J. 2001. *A Theory of Justice. (Revised Edition).* Cambridge MA: Harvard University Press.

Reich, R. B. 2007 *Supercapitalism.* New York: Knopf.

Reinganum, J. F. 1981. "Dynamic Games of Innovation." *Journal of Economic Theory* 25:21–41.

Richards, D. 1990. "Is Strategic Decision Making Chaotic?" *Behavioral Science* 35: 219–32.

Riker, W. H. 1953. *Democracy in the United States.* New York: Macmillan.

Riker, W. H. 1962. *The Theory of Political Coalitions.* New Haven, CT: Yale University Press.

Riker, W. H. 1964. *Federalism: Origin, Operation, Maintenance.* Boston,. MA: Little Brown.

Riker, W. H. 1965. "Theory and Science in the Study of Politics." *Journal of Conflict Resolution* 56:375–379.

Riker, W. H. 1980. "Implications from the Disequilibrium of Majority Rule for the Study of Institutions." *American Political Science Review* 74:432–446.

Riker, W. H. 1982a. *Liberalism against Populism: A Confrontation Between the Theory of Democracy and the Theory of Social Choice.* San Francisco: Freeman.

Riker, W. H. 1982b. "The Two Party System and Duverger's Law: An Essay on the History of Political Science." *American Political Science Review* 76:753–766.

Riker, W. H. 1986. *The Art of Political Manipulation.* New Haven, CT: Yale University Press.

Riker, W. H. 1987. *The Development of American Federalism.* Boston, MA: Kluwer.

Riker, W. H., and P. C. Ordeshook. 1973. *An Introduction to Positive Political Theory.* Englewood Cliffs, NJ: Prentice-Hall.

Robbins, L. 1932. *An Essay on the Nature and Significance of Economic Science.* London: Macmillan.

Rock, D.1985. *Argentina, 1516-1982: From Spanish Colonization to the Falklands War.* Berkeley, CA: University of California Press.

Rogowski, R. 1989. *Commerce and Coalitions.* Princeton, NJ: Princeton University Press.

Rokkan, S. 1970. *Citizens, Elections, Parties: Approaches to the Comparative Study of the Processes of Development.* Oslo: Universitetsforlaget.

Romero A. 1997. "Rearranging the Deck Chairs on the Titanic: The Agony of Democracy in Venezuela." *Latin American Research Review.*32:7–36.

Rosen, W. 2007. *Justinian's Flea.* New York: Viking.

Rosenthal, H., and E. Voeten. 2004. "Analyzing Roll Calls with Perfect Spatial Voting." *American Journal of Political Science* 48:620–632.

Rothschild, E. 2001. *Economic Sentiments: Adam Smith, Condorcet and the Enlightenment.* Cambridge, MA: Harvard University Press.

Rousseau, J.-J. 1993. *The Social Contract and Discourses.* London: Everyman.

Rousseau, J.-J. 2001. "On the Social Contract." In Michael Morgan [Ed.]. *Classics of Moral and Political Theory*. Indianapolis, IN: Hackett.

Saari, D. 1997. "The Generic Existence of a Core for *q*-Rules." *Economic Theory* 9:219–260.

Sachs, J. 2008. *Commonwealth: Economics for a Crowded Planet*. New York: Penguin.

Sammon, W. 2007. *The Evangelical President*. Washington, DC:Regnery.

Samuelson, P. A. 1954. "The Pure Theory of Public Expenditure." *Review of Economics and Statistics*. 36:387–389.

Sanders, E. 1980. "On the Costs, Utilities, and Simple Joys of Voting." *The Journal of Politics*. 42:854–863.

Sartori, G. 1976. *Parties and Party Systems: A Framework of Analysis*. New York and Cambridge: Cambridge University Press.

Savage, L. 1954. *The Foundations of Statistics*. New York: Dover.

Schaller, T. 2006. *Whistling Past Dixie*. New York: Simon and Schuster.

Schattschneider, E. E. 1960. *The Semi-Sovereign People*. New York: Holt, Rinehart and Winston.

Schlesinger, Sr. A. M. 1939. "Tides of American Politics." *Yale Review*. 29: 220.

Schlesinger, Jr. A. M. 1957. *The Crisis of the Old Order*. New York: Houghton Mifflin.

Schlesinger, Jr. A. M. 1958. *The Coming of the New Deal*. New York: Houghton Mifflin.

Schlesinger, Jr. A. M. 1960. *The Politics of Upheaval*. New York: Houghton Mifflin.

Schlesinger, Jr. A. M. 1973. *The Imperial Presidency*. New York: Houghton Mifflin.

Schlesinger, Jr. A. M. 1986. *The Cycles of American History*. New York: Houghton Mifflin.

Schlesinger, J. A. 1994. *Political Parties and the Winning of Office*. Ann Arbor, MI: University of Michigan Press.

Schmitter, P. C. 1981. "Interest Intermediation and Regime Governability in Contemporary Western Europe and North America." In S. Berger [Ed.]. *Organizing Interest in Western Europe*. New York and Cambridge: Cambridge University Press.

Schnidman, E. A. 2008. "Spatial Modeling of the U.S. Presidential Primary Candidates." Unpublished M.A. thesis: Washington University in Saint Louis.

Schofield, N., 1972. "Ethical Decision Rules for Uncertain Voters." *British Journal of Political Science* 2: 193–207.

Schofield, N. 1975. "A Game Theoretic Analysis of Olson's Game of Collective Action." *Journal of Conflict Resolution*. 19:441–461.

Schofield, N. 1977. ""The Logic of Catastrophe." *Human Ecology* 5: 261-271.

Schofield, N. 1978. "Instability of Simple Dynamic Games." *Review of Economic Studies*. 45:575–594.

Schofield, N. 1980. "Generic Properties of Simple Bergson–Samuelson Welfare Functions." *Journal of Mathematical Economics* 7:175–192.

Schofield, N. 1981. "The Relationship between Voting and Party Strength in an Electoral System." In M. J. Holler. *Power, Voting and Voting Power*. Wurzburg: Physcia Verlag.

Schofield, N. 1983. "Generic Instability of Majority Rule." *Review of Economic Studies*. 50:695–705.

Schofield, N. 1984. "Political Fragmentation and the Stability of Coalition Governments in Western Europe." In M. J. Holler. *Coalitions and Collective Action*. Wurzburg: Physica Verlag.

Schofield, N. 1985a. *Social Choice and Democracy*. Heidelberg: Springer.

Schofield, N. 1985b. "Anarchy, Altruism and Cooperation." *Social Choice and Welfare* 2: 207–19.

Schofield, N. 1987. "The Stability of Coalition Governments in Western Europe: 1945-1986." *European Journal of Political Economy* 3:555–591.

Schofield, N. 1992. "Democratic Stability." In J. Knight, and I. Sened [Eds.]. *Explaining Institutions*. New York and Cambridge: Cambridge University Press.

Schofield, N. 1993a. "Party Competition in a Spatial Model of Coalition Formation." In W. Barnett, M. Hinich and N. Schofield. *Political Economy: Institutions, Competition and Representation*. New York and Cambridge: Cambridge University Press.

Schofield, N. 1993b. "Political Competition and Multiparty Coalition Governments." *European Journal of Political Research*. 23:1–33.

Schofield, N. 1995a. "Rational Choice and Political Economy," *Critical Review* 9:189–211.

Schofield, N. 1995b. "Coalition Politics: A Formal Model and Empirical Analysis." *Journal of Theoretical Politics* 7:245–281.

Schofield, N. 1997. "Multiparty Electoral Politics." In D. Mueller [Ed.]. *Perspectives on Public Choice*. New York and Cambridge: Cambridge University Press.

Schofield, N. 1999a. "The Heart of the Atlantic Constitution: International Economic Stability, 1919-1998." *Politics and Society* 27:173–215.

Schofield, N. 1999b. "Equilibrium or Chaos in Preference and Belief Aggregation." In J. Alt, M. Levi, and E. Ostrom [Eds.]. *Competition and Cooperation*. New York: Russell Sage Foundation.

Schofield, N. 1999c. "The Heart and the Uncovered Set." *Journal of Economics* Suppl 8:79–113.

Schofield, N. 2000. "Core Beliefs and the Founding of the American Republic." *Homo Oeconomicus* 16:433–462.

Schofield, N. 2001. "Constitutions, Voting and Democracy." *Social Choice and Welfare* 18:571-600.

Schofield, N. 2002. "Evolution of the Constitution." *The British Journal of Political Science* 32:1–20.

Schofield, N. 2003a. "The Founding of the American Agrarian Empire and the Conflict of Land and Capital." *Homo Oeconomicus* 19:471–505.

Schofield, N. 2003b. "Power, Prosperity and Social Choice: A Review." *Social Choice and Welfare* 20:85–118.

Schofield, N. 2003c. "Constitutional Quandaries and Critical Elections."*Politics, Philosophy and Economics* 2:5–36.

Schofield, N. 2003d. *Mathematical Methods in Economics and Social Choice*. Heidelberg: Springer.

Schofield, N. 2003e. "Valence Competition in the Spatial Stochastic Model." *Journal of Theoretical Politics* 15:371–383.

Schofield, N. 2004. "Equilibrium in the Spatial Valence Model of Politics." *Journal of Theoretical Politics* 16:447–481.

Schofield, N. 2005. "A Valence Model of Political Competition in Britain: 1992–1997." *Electoral Studies* 24:347–370.

Schofield, N. 2006a. *Architects of Political Change: Constitutional Quandaries and Social Choice Theory.* New York and Cambridge: Cambridge University Press.

Schofield, N. 2006b. "Equilibria in the Spatial Stochastic Model with Party Activists." *Review of Economic Design* 10:183–203.

Schofield, N. 2007. "The Mean Voter Theorem: Necessary and Sufficient Conditions for Convergent Equilibrium." *Review of Economic Studies* 74:965–980.

Schofield, N. 2008a. "Modelling Political Economy." *Homo Oeconomicus:* in press.

Schofield, N. 2008b. *The Spatial Model of Politics.* London: Routledge.

Schofield, N. 2008c "Divergence in the Spatial Stochastic Model of Voting." In M. Braham and F. Steffen [Eds.]. *Power, Freedom and Voting.* Heidelberg: Springer.

Schofield, N. 2009. "An Activist Model of Democracy." In E. Aragones, C. Bevia, H. Llavador and N. Schofield. [Eds.].*The Political Economy of Democracy.* Barcelona: BBVA Foundation.

Schofield, N., and M. Levinson. 2008. "Modeling Authoritarian Regimes." *Politics, Philosphy and Economics* 7:243–283.

Schofield, N., A. Martin, K. Quinn, and A. Whitford. 1998. "Multiparty Electoral Competition in the Netherlands and Germany: A Model based on Multinomial Probit." *Public Choice* 97:257–293.

Schofield, N., and G. Miller. 2007. "Elections and Activist Coalitions in the United States." *American Journal of Political Science* 51:518–531.

Schofield, N., G. Miller, and A. Martin. 2003. "Critical Elections and Political Realignment in the U.S.: 1860–2000." *Political Studies* 51:217–240.

Schofield, N., U. Ozdemir, and E. A. Schnidman. 2008. "A Spatial Model of Party Positioning under Proportional Representation and Plurality Rule." Typescript: Washington University in Saint Louis.

Schofield, N., and I. Sened. 2002. "Local Nash Equilibrium in Multiparty Politics." *Annals of Operations Research* 109:193–210.

Schofield, N., and I. Sened. 2006. *Multiparty Democracy: Elections and Legislative Politics.* New York and Cambridge: Cambridge University Press.

Schonhardt-Bailey, C. 2006. *From the Corn Laws to Free Trade: Interests, Ideas, and Institutions in Historical Perspective.* Cambridge, MA: The MIT Press.

Schumpeter, J. 1942. *Capitalism, Socialism, and Democracy.* New York: Harper.

Seabrooke L. 2006. *The Social Sources of Financial Power.* Ithaca, NY: Cornell University Press.

Seligson, A. L. 2003. "Disentangling the Roles of Ideology and Issue Positions in the Rise of Third Parties." *Political Research Quarterly* 56:465–475.

Seton-Watson, H. 1954. *From Lenin to Malenkov: The History of World Communism.* London: Praeger.

Seyd, P., and P. Whiteley. 1992. *Labour's Grassroots.* Oxford: Clarendon Press.

Seyd, P., and P. Whiteley. 2002. *New Labour's Grassroots.* Basingstoke, UK: Macmillan.

Shapiro, M. J. 1969. "Rational Political Man: A Synthesis of Economic and Social-Psychological Perspectives." *The American Political Science Review.* 63:1106–1119.

Shaw-Taylor, L. 2001. "Parliamentary Enclosure and the Emergence of an English Agricultural Proletariat." *The Journal of Economic History*. 61:640–662.

Shepsle, K. A. 1989. "Studying Institutions: Some Lessons from the Rational Choice Approach," *Journal of Theoretical Politics* 1:131–148.

Shepsle, K. A. 1991. *Models of Multiparty Electoral Competition.* Chur: Harwood Academic Press.

Shepsle, K. A., and B. R. Weingast 1981. "Political Preferences for the Pork Barrel: A Generalization." *American Journal of Political Science*. 25:96–111.

Shikano, S, and E. Linhart. 2007. "Government Formation after the Dutch General Election." Typescript: University of Mannheim.

Sigelman, L., and W. D. Berry. 1982. "Cost and the Calculus of Voting." *Political Behavior* 4:419–428.

Simon, B. 1998. "Individuals, Group and Social Change: On the Relationship Between Individual and Collective Self- Interpretations and Collective Action." In C. Sedikdes, J. Schopler and C. Insko [Eds.]. *Intergroup Cognition and Intergroup Behavior.* Hillsdale, NJ: Lawrence Eribaum.

Simon, H. A. 1959. "Theories of Decision-making in Economics and Behavioral Science." *The American Economic Review* 49:253–283.

Skidmore, T. E., and P. H. Smith. 1997. *Modern Latin America.* 4th ed. New York: Oxford University Press.

Skinner, B. F. 1948. "Superstition in the Pigeon." *Journal of Experimental Psychology*. 38:168–172.

Skinner, Q. 1990. "Thomas Hobbes on the Proper Signification of Liberty: The Prothero Lecture." *Transactions of the Royal Historical Society* 40: 121–151.

Smith, A. 1984 [1759]. *The Theory of Moral Sentiments.* Indianapolis, IN: Liberty Fund.

Smith, A. 1981 [1776]. *An Inquiry into the Nature and Causes of the Wealth of Nations.* Indianapolis, IN: Liberty Fund.

Smith, J. M. [Ed]. 1995. *The Republic of Letters* (3 volumes). New York: Norton.

Smith, J. 2005. *Trading Places. The Two Parties in the Electorate from 1975-2004.* Unpublished Ph.D. Dissertation,Washington University in St. Louis.

Smith, P. H. 2005. *Democracy in Latin America: Political Change in Comparative Perspective.* New York: Oxford University Press.

Southwood, N. 2004. "Preserving Liberty." *Policy* 20:29–32.

Stasavage, D. 2003. *Public Debt and the Birth of the Democratic State.* New York and Cambridge: Cambridge University Press.

Stokes, D. 1963. "Spatial Models and Party Competition." *American Political Science Review* 57:368–377.

Stokes, D. 1992. "Valence Politics." In D. Kavanagh [Ed.]. *Electoral Politics.* Oxford: Clarendon Press.

Strauss, L. 1936. *The Political Philosophy of Hobbes: Its Basis and Its Genesis.* Translated by E. M. Sinclair. Chicago, IL: The University of Chicago Press.

Strauss, L, and J. Cropsey. 1987. *History of Political Philosophy.* Chicago: The University of Chicago Press.

Strom, G. S. 1975. "On the Apparent Paradox of Participation: A New Proposal." *The American Political Science Review*. 26:908–913.

Subcommittee on National Security, Emerging Threats, and International Relations. 2006. "9/11 Commission Recommendations: Balancing Civil Liberties and Security."(6 June)

Sugden, R. 1980. *The Economics of Rights, Cooperation and Welfare*. Oxford: Blackwell.

Suh, D. S. and C.-J. Lee. 1998. *North Korea after Kim Il Sung*. Boulder, CO: Lynne Rienner.

Sundquist, J. L. 1973. *Dynamics of the Party System: Alignment and Realignment of Political Parties in the United States*. Washington, DC: Brookings Institution.

Taagepera, R., and M. S. Shugart. 1989. *Seats and Voters: The Effects and Determinants of Electoral Systems*. New Haven, CT: Yale University Press.

Takeyh, R. 2006. *Hidden Iran: Paradox and Power in the Islamic Republic*. New York:Times Books.

Taylor, M. 1976. *Anarchy and Cooperation*. London: Wiley.

Taylor, M. 1982. *Community, Anarchy, and Liberty*. New York and Cambridge: Cambridge University Press.

Tinker S. M. 2007. "US Oil Companies in Venezuela: An Enduring Alliance." In S. Ellner and S. M. Tinker [Eds.]. *Venezuela: Hugo Chávez and the Decline of an "Exceptional Democracy."* Lanham, MD: Rowman & Littlefield.

Train, K. 2003. *Discrete Choice Methods for Simulation*. New York and Cambridge: Cambridge University Press.

Thurder, P. W., and Eymann, A. 2000. "Policy-Specific Alienation and Indifference in the Calculus of Voting: A Simultaneous Model of Party Choice and Abstention". *Public Choice* 102:ll51–77.

Thurow, L. C. 1980. *The Zero-Sum Society*. New York: Basic Books

Treisman, D. 2008. "The Popularity of Russian presidents." Typescript: UCLA.

Tufte, E. R. 1978. *Political Control of the Economy*. Princeton, NJ: Princeton University Press.

Turing, A. 1937. "On Computable Numbers with an Application to the Entscheidungs Problem." *Proceedings of the London Mathematical Society* 42: 230–265. Reprinted in J. Copeland [Ed.]. *The Essential Turing*. Oxford: The Clarendon Press.

Turing, A. 1950. "Computing Machinery and Intelligence." *Mind* 59: 422–60. Reprinted in J. Copeland [Ed.]. *The Essential Turing*. Oxford: The Clarendon Press.

Tullock, G. 1967. "The General Irrelevance of the General Impossibility Theorem." *Quarterly Journal of Economics* 81:256–270

Tullock, G. 1981. "Why So Much Stability?" *Public Choice* 37:189–205.

Turgot, Ann-Robert-Jacques. 1973 [1766]. "Reflections on the Formation and Distribution of Wealth." In R. Meek [Ed.]. *Turgot on Progress, Sociology and Economics,* New York and Cambridge: Cambridge University Press.

Turner, J. C. 1987. *Rediscovering the Social Group: A Self-categorization Theory*. Oxford: Basil Blackwell.

Ullmann, R. H. 1983. "Redefining Security." *International Security* 8: 129–153.

U.S. Department of State. 2005. "Free Societies Must Balance Security, Civil Liberties, Says Bush." http://www.usinfo.state.gov/special/Archive (8 May).

Urken, A. 1991. "The Condorcet-Jefferson Connection and the Origins of Social Theory." *Public Choice* 72:213–36.

Usher, D. 1981. *The Economic Prerequisite to Democracy.* New York: Columbia University Press.

Voltaire, F. [1738]. *The Elements of Sir Isaac Newton's Philosophy.* (Translated from the French by J. Hanna).London: Stephen Austen.

von Hayek, F. 1976 [1948]. *Individualism and Economic Order.* Chicago, IL: Chicago University Press.

von Hayek, F. 1944. *The Road to Serfdom.* London: Routledge & Kegan Paul.

von Mises, L. 1935 [1920]. "Economic Calculation in the Socialist Commonwealth" In F. von Hayek [Ed.]. *Collectivist Economic Planning.* London: Routledge & Kegan Paul.

veon Laue, T. H. 1993. *Why Lenin? Why Stalin? Why Gorbachev?* New York:Harper Collins.

von Mises, L. 1944. *Omnipotent Government.* New Haven, CT: Yale University Press.

von Neumann, J. 1945 [1932]. "A Model of General Economic Equilibrium." *Review of Economic Studies* 13:1–9.

von Neumann, J., and O. Morgenstern. 1944. *Theory of Games and Economic Behavior.* Princeton, NJ: Princeton University Press.

Waldron, J. 2003. "Security and Liberty: The Image of Balance." *The Journal of Political Philosophy* 11:191–210.

Waldron, J. 2006. "Safety and Security." *Nebraska Law Review* 85, 301–353.

Waldron, J. 2007. "Is This Torture Necessary?" *The New York Review of Books* 54 (16): 40-44 (25 October).

Wallis, J. 2005. *God's Politics: Why the Right Gets It Wrong and the Left Doesn't Get It.* New York: Harper.

Wang, H. 1987. *Reflections on Kurt Gödel.* Cambridge, MA: MIT Press.

Wantchekon, L. 2004. "The Paradox of Warlord Democracy: A Theoretical Investigation" *American Political Science Review* 98:17–33.

Warwick, P. 1979. "The Durability of Coalition Governments in Parliamentary Democracies." *Comparative Political Studies* 11:464–498.

Wegren, S. K., and A. Konitzer. 2006. "The 2003 Russian Duma Election and the Decline in Rural Support for the Communist Party." *Electoral Studies* 25:677–695.

Weingast, B. R. 1979. "A Rational Choice Perspective on Congressional Norms." *American Journal of Political Science.* 23:345-363.

Weingast, B. 1997a. "The Political Foundations of Democracy and the Rule of Law." *American Political Science Review* 2:245–263.

Weingast, B. 1997b. "The Political Foundations of Limited Government: Parliament and Sovereign Debt in 17th and 18th Century England." In J. Drobak and J. Nye [Eds.]. *The Frontiers of the New Institutional Economics.* New York: Academic Press.

Weingast, B. 1998. "Political Stability and Civil War." In R. Bates, A. Grief, M. Levi, J.-L. Rosenthal, and B. Weingast [Eds.]. *Analytical Narratives.* Princeton, NJ: Princeton University Press.

Weingast, B. R., K. A. Shepsle, and C. Johnsen. 1981. "The Political Economy of Benefits and Costs: A Neoclassical Approach to Distributive Politics." *Journal of Political Economy*. 89:642–664.

Westen, D. 2007. *The Political Brain*. New York: Perseus Books.

White, S., S. Oates and I. MacAllister. 2001. "Media Effects and Russian Elections, 1999-2000." *British Journal of Political Science* 35:191–208.

Whiteley, P. 1979. "Electoral Forecasting from Poll Data: The British Case." *British Journal of Political Science* 9:219–236.

Whiteley, P. 1980. "Politico-Econometric Estimation in Britain: An Alternative Interpretation." In P. Whiteley [Ed.]. *Models of Political Economy*. London and Beverly Hills, CA: Sage.

Whiteley, P. 1983. *The Labour Party in Crisis*. New York: Methuen.

Whiteley, P. 1984. "Inflation, Unemployment and Government Popularity." *Electoral Studies* 3:3-24.

Whiteley, P., and P. Seyd, 2002. *High Intensity Participation*. Ann Arbor: University of Michigan Press.

Whiteley, P., P. Seyd, and A. Billinghurst. 2006. *Third Force Politics*. Oxford: Oxford University Press.

Wilder, D., and A. F. Simon. 1998. "Categorical and Dynamic Groups: Implications for Social Perception and Intergroup Behavior." In C. Sedikdes, J. Schopler and C. Insko [Eds.]. *Intergroup Cognition and Intergroup Behavior*. Hillsdale, NJ: Lawrence Eribaum.

Williams, D. 2007. *Condorcet and Modernity*. New York and Cambridge: Cambridge University Press.

Williams, H. 2007. *The Sun Kings*. London: Quercus.

Winik, J. 2007. *The Great Upheaval*. New York: Harper.

Wittman, D. 1977. "Candidates with Policy Preferences: A Dynamic Model." *Journal of Economic Theory* 14:180-189.

Wittman, D. 1995. *The Myth of Democratic Failure*. Chicago, IL: University of Chicago Press.

Wood, G. S. 1991. *The Radicalism of the American Revolution*. New York: Knopf.

Wright, D. C. 2001. *The History of China*. Westport, CT: Greenwood Press.

Wynia, G. W. 1986. *Argentina: Illusions and Realities*. New York: Holmes & Meier.

Yang, M.-S. 2007. "Evaluation and Prospects for North Korea's Economic Durability." *Vantage Point* 30:48–59.

Young, P. 1998. *Individual Strategy and Social Structure: An Evolutionary Theory of Institutions* Princeton, NJ: Princeton University Press.

Zakaria, F. 2008. *The Post-American World*. New York: Norton.

Zakharov, A. V. 2008a. "Candidate Location and Endogenous Valence." *Pubic Choice*: in press.

Zakharov, A. V. 2008b. "A Model of Electoral Competition with Abstaining Voters." *Mathematical and Computer Modelling*: in press.

Zakharov, A. V. 2008c."Voting in 2007 Russian Legislative Elections: The Role of Putin's Approval and Ideology." Typescript: Moscow School of Economics.

Zakharov, A. V., and D. Fantazzini. 2008. "Idiosyncratic Issue Salience in Probabilistic Voting Models: The Cases of Netherlands, UK , and Israel." Typescript: Moscow School of Economics.

Umfassend. Aktuell. Fundiert.

Axel Noack
Business Essentials:
Fachwörterbuch Deutsch-Englisch Englisch-Deutsch
2007. VII, 811 Seiten, gebunden
€ 59,80
ISBN 978-3-486-58261-1

Das Wörterbuch gibt dem Nutzer das Fachvokabular des modernen, internationalen Geschäftslebens in einer besonders anwenderfreundlichen Weise an die Hand.

Der englisch-deutsche Teil umfasst die 11.000 wichtigsten Wörter und Begriffe des angloamerikanischen Sprachgebrauchs.

Der deutsch-englische Teil enthält entsprechend 14.000 aktuelle Fachbegriffe mit ihren Übersetzungen.

Im dritten Teil werden 3.000 Abkürzungen aus dem internationalen Wirtschaftsgeschehen mit ihren verschiedenen Bedeutungen aufgeführt.

Das Lexikon richtet sich an Studierende der Wirtschaftswissenschaften sowie alle Fach- und Führungskräfte, die Wirtschaftsenglisch für Ihren Beruf benötigen. Für ausländische Studenten bietet es einen Einstieg in das hiesige Wirtschaftsleben.

Prof. Dr. Axel Noack lehrt an der Fachhochschule Stralsund BWL, insbes. International Marketing.

Oldenbourg

Durchblick im Dschungel der Kennzahlen

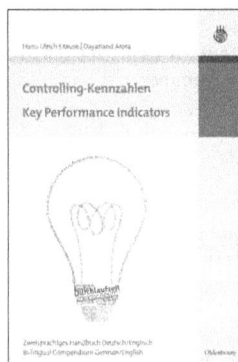

Hans-Ulrich Krause, Dayanand Arora
Controlling-Kennzahlen –
Key Performance Indicators
Zweisprachiges Handbuch Deutsch/Englisch –
Bi-lingual Compendium German/English

2008 | 666 S. | gebunden
€ 49,80 | ISBN 978-3-486-58207-9

Es gibt eine Vielzahl von Controlling-Kennzahlen. Was sie genau bedeuten und welchen betriebswirtschaftlichen Aussagegehalt sie haben, ist allerdings sowohl für Studierende als auch für Praktiker nicht immer auf den ersten Blick erkennbar.

Dieses Buch hilft dabei, im Dschungel der Controllling-Kennzahlen den Durchblick zu behalten – und dies nicht nur auf Deutsch, sondern auch auf Englisch.

Dieses Buch ist der ideale Begleiter durch ein betriebswirtschaftliches Studium und gibt auch Praktikern nützliche Tipps bei der Verwendung und Interpretation von Controlling-Kennzahlen.

Über die Autoren:
Professor Dr. Hans-Ulrich Krause ist Inhaber einer Professur für Betriebswirtschaftslehre mit Schwerpunkt »Controlling/Rechnungswesen« an der Fachhochschule für Technik und Wirtschaft Berlin.

Professor Dr. Dayanand Arora ist Inhaber einer Professur für Betriebswirtschaftslehre mit Schwerpunkt »Finanz- und Rechnungswesen« an der Fachhochschule für Technik und Wirtschaft Berlin.

Oldenbourg

150 Jahre
Wissen für die Zukunft
Oldenbourg Verlag

Bestellen Sie in Ihrer Fachbuchhandlung oder direkt bei uns: Tel: 089/45051-248, Fax: 089/45051-333
verkauf@oldenbourg.de